INNER PEACE— GLOBAL IMPACT

Tibetan Buddhism, Leadership, and Work

A Volume in
Advances in Workplace Spirituality:
Theory, Research, and Application

Series Editor
Louis W. (Jody) Fry, *Texas A&M University-Central Texas*

Advances in Workplace Spirituality:
Theory, Research, and Application

Louis W. (Jody) Fry, Series Editor

Psychology of Religion and Workplace Spirituality (2012)
edited by Peter C. Hill and Bryan J. Dik

Inner Peace—Global Impact:
Tibetan Buddhism, Leadership, and Work (2012)
edited by Kathryn Goldman Schuyler

INNER PEACE— GLOBAL IMPACT

Tibetan Buddhism, Leadership, and Work

Kathryn Goldman Schuyler

Information Age Publishing, Inc.
Charlotte, North Carolina • www.infoagepub.com

Library of Congress Cataloging-in-Publication Data

Inner peace, global impact : Tibetan Buddhism, leadership, and work/edited
by Kathryn Goldman Schuyler.
p. cm.—(Advances in workplace spirituality)
Includes bibliographical references.
ISBN 978-1-61735-918-7 (paperback.)—ISBN 978-1-61735-919-4 (hardcover)—
ISBN 978-1-61735-920-0 (ebook) 1. Leadership—Religious aspects—Buddhism.
2. Work—Religious aspects—Buddhism. 3. Buddhism—Doctrines. I. Schuyler,
Kathryn Goldman.
HD57.7.I56 2012
294.3'36658--dc23

                                                              2012020710

Cover design and photography by Kathryn Goldman Schuyler

Printed in the United States of America

for all of my teachers....

Praise for *Inner Peace—Global Impact*

At this critical time in our world history when the very survival of our planet is at stake, a deeper understanding of practical ways to provide authentic leadership is needed. Kathryn Goldman Schuyler's carefully selected collection of essays weaves together provocative ideas on leadership from a rich variety of perspectives that if taken to heart can begin a much needed transformation. She has connected the wisdom teachings of Tibetan Buddhism and their relevance to the perils and promises of the modern world in a way that is timely and comes as a blessing to us all.

> **—Tsoknyi Rinpoche,** author of *Open Heart, Open Mind*; *Carefree Dignity*, and *Fearless Simplicity*; globally-respected teacher of Tibetan Buddhism, whose projects include the preservation of sacred Tibetan texts and the spiritual care, education, and welfare for over 3,000 nuns in Nepal and Tibet

I have long been interested and amazed at how the influence of the Tibetan People, which is a tiny population from literally the end of the earth, has become so great in modern society. Kathryn Goldman Schuyler's *Inner Peace—Global Impact* helps us understand this phenomenon which continues to ripple through our modern culture in many ways. A fascinating read!

> **—R. Adam Engle, JD, MBA,** Cofounder and former President, *Mind and Life Institute*

This is not leadership as usual. This is leadership as genuinely needed for the challenges of today. The stellar and impeccably credentialed writers Kathryn Goldman Schuyler brings to her volume are well chosen. Together, under her leadership, they powerfully make the vital connections between inner and outer peace. We can't go on without it.

> **—Anne Carolyn Klein, PhD, Rigzin Drolma Rice,** University & Dawn Mountain, author of *Heart Essence of the Vast Expanse* and *Meeting the Great Bliss Queen*

Inner Peace—Global Impact brings a great deal of new information to those interested in Tibetan Buddhism, including scientists. The authors present a thorough and rich view of this tradition that is so fundamental to a person I love and respect deeply—the Dalai Lama. I learned a lot from this!

> **—Paul Ekman, PhD,** author of over 100 articles and 11 books, including *Emotional Awareness*, Coauthored with the Dalai Lama

Inner Peace—Global Impact is a gift to the world at a time when the wisdom of Tibetan Buddhism is more relevant to humanity than ever. We are at a critical turning point in human development, and if we can grasp and put into practice the teachings shared in this book, we will be able to collectively move ourselves to a higher level of development. Our leadership and our organizations need to be more compassionate, just, and selfless, and this book provides both the inspiration and the examples that can guide us to our greater potential as a global human family.

> **—Judi Neal, PhD,** Director, Tyson Center for Faith and Spirituality in the Workplace, Sam M. Walton College of Business, University of Arkansas

In this ground-breaking collection of essays, scholars, Buddhist teachers, psychologists, business leaders, coaches, philosophers, and artists come together for the first time to examine the contributions of Tibetan Buddhism to leadership from their own field of expertise and from their own lengthy meditation experience. This fascinating volume is an essential reading for anyone who wants to know about this emerging paradigm.

> **—Antoine Lutz, PhD,** Senior Scientist, Waisman Lab for Brain Imaging & Behavior, Center for Investigating Healthy Minds, Univ. Wisconsin-Madison, author of 3 book chapters and over 24 peer-reviewed neuroscientific studies of the brain and consciousness.

Like all great wisdom traditions, Tibetan Buddhism is a "Mansion" with many doors, often intimidating to an inquirer. Kathryn Goldman Schuyler has provided rich access through a door that connects to central concerns of work and leadership. In doing so, she gifts all who wish to deepen their exploration of Tibetan Buddhism's important contribution to contemporary organizational concerns.

> —**Andre L. Delbecq, PhD,** J. Thomas and Kathleen L. McCarthy University Professor, Director, Institute for Spirituality of Organization Leadership, Leavey School of Business, Santa Clara University

Considering that we have so much "inner discontent—global conflict" in the world, what *Inner Peace—Global Impact* and its eminent authors present is wise and very relevant. A high quality of themes, authors, and messages for leaders.

> —**Prasad Kaipa, PhD,** CEO Advisor and Coach, Kaipa Group, Sr. Fellow, Center for Leadership, Innovation, and Change, Indian School of Business, Hyderabad, India

CONTENTS

SECTION II.   INDIVIDUALS: HOW TIBETAN BUDDHIST PRACTICE IMPACTS PEOPLE AT WORK

SECTION III.   ORGANIZATIONS: ORGANIZING FOR THE FUTURE

SECTION IV.   RESEARCH: TIBETAN BUDDHISM IN WESTERN SITUATIONS

SERIES PREFACE

Louis (Jody) W. Fry

A major change is taking place in the personal and professional lives of many organizational leaders and their employees as they aspire to integrate their spirituality and religion with their work. Many argue that the reason behind this change is that society is seeking spiritual solutions to better respond to tumultuous social, business, and geopolitical changes. The result has been a remarkable explosion of scholarship that provides the opportunity for more specialized interest areas, including the role of spirituality and religion in shaping organizations: structures, decision making, management style, mission and strategy, organizational culture, human resource management, finance and accounting, marketing, and sales—in short: all aspects of leading, managing, and organizing resources and people. As evidenced in the recent formation of the *Journal of Management, Spirituality and Religion* and the success of the Management, Spirituality, and Religion Special Interest Group of the *Academy of Management*, an emerging field with a broad focus on workplace spirituality is gathering momentum.

This book series, *Advances in Workplace Spirituality: Theory, Research, and Application*, focuses on the study of the relationship and relevance of spirituality and/or religion to organizational life. Its vision is to draw from a diverse range of scholarly areas to become a pivotal source for integrative theory, research, and application on workplace spirituality. The purpose of the series is to (1) provide scholars with a meaningful collection of books in key areas and create a forum for the field, (2) support a growing trend toward paradigm integration and assimilation through the interdis-

Inner Peace—Global Impact: Tibetan Buddhism on Leadership and Work, pp. xiii–xiv
Copyright © 2012 by Information Age Publishing
All rights of reproduction in any form reserved.

ciplinary nature of this series, and (3) draw from a wide variety of disciplines for integrative thinking on workplace spirituality with the broad goal of adding to the value of workplace spirituality theory, research, and its application. The series aims to serve as a meeting forum and help cross-fertilization in these communities. Our sole criterion is academic rigor and scientific merit.

The second book of this series, *Inner Peace—Global Impact: Tibetan Buddhism, Leadership, and Work,* is a groundbreaking collection of first-person narratives, scholarly research, and commentaries by noted social scientists focused on the underlying principles of the Tibetan wisdom traditions relevant for successful leadership in the workplace. The uniqueness of this book lies in the breadth and depth of its contributors. In an endeavor of this type, the quality and depth of knowledge of the editor is of the utmost importance. Kathryn Goldman Schuyler has significant understanding of the subtleties of the various worlds of Tibetan Buddhism, so knew whom to invite into her ambitious exploration of its implications for leadership and work. Dr. Goldman Schuyler invited people to be authors only if they possessed a personal understanding of the subject in addition to having professional qualifications. For example, to portray the leadership contributions of the Dalai Lama, we have his 25-year primary English translator, who is also a noted international scholar. Similarly, Dr. Judith Simmer-Brown is one of very few scholars of the feminine principle in Tibetan traditions. This unique volume breaks new ground, as all of the contributors have the highest professional qualifications and have also sustained a contemplative practice for years. They convey a thoughtful yet vibrant picture of the contents and contributions of Tibetan Buddhism in its 50-year life outside of Tibet.

Louis (Jody) Fry
Series Editor

ACKNOWLEDGMENTS

Writing this book has been a labor of love, supported and encouraged by so many people! If I have neglected to mention you personally, please forgive! First, I offer deep thanks and appreciation to each of the authors, whose contributions are the most immediately tangible: all are busy people who made time to write for this book because they saw its importance. Thupten Jinpa encouraged me at a very early stage, taking time to help think about how it could take shape. Susan Skjei's support encouraged others to join in, as they knew and trusted her. Louis (Jody) Fry, editor of the series, immediately grasped my vision for this book, wanted it in his series, and cheered me on throughout the entire process. George Johnson, President of Information Age Publishing, has repeatedly been flexible and helpful.

Huge assistance came from those who read and provided input on early drafts. Among these Doug Ditto read the whole book, commenting on what was effective and what he found less so. Gabriella Piccioni also helped assess the first draft. Later assistance came from John Baugher, Maureen Berndt, and Frances Nance. Members of the Alliant International University faculty helped in various ways. Sharon Foster gave feedback and encouragement on early chapter drafts at a short writing retreat sponsored by the university. Jay Finkelman and Ira Levin's support were invaluable for completing the book while carrying out a full-time faculty role. Sheila Henderson suggested that I connect with Danny Wedding, who then provided valuable mentoring as I was completing the book. I would like to thank as well the participants in my pilot research project: Bob Cayton, John "Karuna" Cayton, Carol Corradi, Tony Hoeber, Elaine Jackson, Scott Snibbe, and Tom Thorning.

Finally, I cannot possibly express in words my how grateful I am to the Tibetan teachers (and their translators) who have made it possible for people outside of Tibet to connect with this wisdom tradition, since such an opportunity has never before existed. I honor His Holiness the 14th Dalai Lama who has created a huge space for all of us to think, reflect, and grow. Other teachers who have contributed to me and the book in important ways are too many to list, but include (in alphabetical order) Lama Kunga Ngor Thartse Rinpoche, Venerable Lhundrup Nyingje (Paula Chichester), Mingyur Rinpoche, Losang Monlam (Blase Hents), Sogyal Rinpoche, Lama Sonam Tsering Rinpoche, Tashi Lama, Lama Tharchin Rinpoche, Venerable Kirti Tsenshab Rinpoche, Tsoknyi Rinpoche, Lama Dechen Yeshe Wangmo, and Lama Thubten Zopa Rinpoche.

The ground of my capacity to envision and complete this book lies in the contributions of my parents, Jeanne Gordon Goldman and George S. Goldman, who taught me about leadership, usually without my knowing it or them intending to. From them, I received the courage to imagine the seemingly impossible, the willingness to travel paths that others do not see, the persistence to carry ideas through to completion, and the ability to love. My father's sister Berenice Finkelstone showed me the importance of patience, laughter, and long friendships. My husband Jim Schuyler has listened so often as I developed thoughts, helped me hone them, and always encouraged me; his love and emotional support are unlimited. And my loving, creative sister Amber Gordon helps me always to lighten up, yet persist.

PREFACE

Kathryn Goldman Schuyler

Peace starts within each one of us.
When we have inner peace,
we can be at peace with those around us.
When our community is in a state of peace,
it can share that peace with neighboring communities.[1]

—His Holiness the 14th Dalai Lama

This is not a book of wisdom teachings, nor is it purely a book of scholarly research. It is intended for the broad audience of people who are intrigued by Tibet, its teachers and teachings, and the process of global change brought forth by their diaspora. It is also designed for leaders, professors, and consultants in search of new ideas and perhaps even an entirely new paradigm for how leaders could be educated and what may be expected of them. This book was written for you if you:

- Are intrigued by Buddhism or the wisdom traditions of Tibet and are curious about how they may be relevant to leadership and daily work,
- Wonder how these traditions have grown from very little presence in the West 50 years ago to becoming a highly visible global force,
- Feel that leadership theory and practice is missing something important, and "you don't know what it is" (to quote Bob Dylan's song about major societal change),[2]

Inner Peace—Global Impact: Tibetan Buddhism, Leadership, and Work, pp. xvii–xxiv
Copyright © 2012 by Information Age Publishing

- Have been thinking about the need for new paradigms for leadership, whether in the domains of business, politics, or education,
- Are interested in the contribution of spirituality and human development to leadership development.

THE GENESIS OF THIS BOOK

I do not read or speak Tibetan, nor is my expertise in Asian studies or history. I am a sociologist by training, with ongoing interest in the sociology of knowledge, as well as decades of experience consulting to leaders and organizations on strategic change and organizational health. As a person interested in global change, leadership, and the role of organizations in creating healthy societies, I grew interested in this growing presence of Tibetan Buddhism.

Looking back, I see that my background helped me to notice and value these ideas and questions. As long as I can remember, I had been interested in the relationships among societal change, individual human suffering, and awareness or consciousness. I vividly recall sitting on my bed as a young child, looking out the window at the stars and wondering why human beings seemed always to be fighting, always at war. If we were alone in this huge cold universe, I pondered, why did not we experience one another as kin, rather than as enemy? Nothing answered this question for me. Growing up in New York City made me very aware of the great differences and inequities that exist among people.

In college I studied foreign languages and traveled extensively, seeking to see life through many lenses. I became a professional sociologist, viewing sociology as a foundation for effective action on large societal issues, and also a Feldenkrais practitioner, helping people at an individual level to relieve pain and improve performance of all types through embodied learning. In addition, I became an organizational consultant, focusing on coaching executives and their teams, using this as a base to support these leaders' desire to create healthy organizational cultures.[3] After working as a consultant and coach for about 15 years, I shifted my focus to educating the next generation of consultants, becoming a professor in the fields of organizational psychology and organization development. All of these types of work share the common intention of relieving suffering as permanently as possible through learning. All are powerful tools, yet none seemed sufficient for the job at hand.

About 10 years ago, while working as director of a graduate program in organizational studies, I received a large postcard inviting me to a series of talks by Western women who had been practicing Tibetan Buddhist nuns for over 20 years, and who had received their vows from the Dalai

Lama. I was intrigued, as I had never imagined that such a category existed: women, born and educated in the West, who were such devoted practitioners of Tibetan Buddhism that they lived for over 20 years as nuns in a tradition that seemed to me, at the time, completely unconnected with daily life in today's Western cultures. The postcard invited me into a world that I hadn't known existed. Although I "knew of" Tibet and Buddhism, had heard records of Tibetan chanting years earlier, and had noticed a book by the Dalai Lama in airport bookstores in my frequent travels as an organizational consultant, neither Tibet nor Buddhism were part of my daily awareness. Gradually, over the years since I received that invitation, this changed, leading me to practice in these traditions and to the fundamental notion for this book.

The evening of the first of these lectures by Western Tibetan nuns, I learned that a book had been written in the eighth century that provided guidelines to living as a *bodhisattva*—a being of great compassion who is entirely committed to helping others be happy. Since from this perspective, most suffering comes from the way we experience things rather than from the things themselves, a bodhisattva helps people to appreciate the nature of life.[4] I had heard of this concept in a popular rock song, but never dreamed that a book had been written centuries earlier that taught one how to live like this. I jumped into the course and the book in the middle, with a kind warning from a friendly Western monk that I did not have to stay and could leave at any time if it was not what I wanted. This book, which I later learned was at the core of what the Dalai Lama valued in his own learning, turned out to be the door to a cultural tradition that had moved from distant mountaintops in Tibet to my backyard in San Francisco—and everyone's, around the world, thanks (unintentionally) to the unwanted invasion by the Chinese. I do not see their culture as a panacea, but it does provide glimpses of possibilities for human development that are not visible from within the Western social science mindset.

The Tibetan wisdom traditions or Vajrayana Buddhism have been the heart or foundation of the culture of Tibet since the eighth century, when King Trisong Detsen invited the tantric mystic Padmasambhava and others from India. (Note that the main Buddhist terms, such as "Vajrayana," are described briefly in the glossary, for those unfamiliar with them.) These traditions were taught only by people who had personally mastered the practices and were passed on only to those ready to learn them; the more advanced practices were kept private and were passed on from one teacher to the most skilled students. Because they were taught only by those with personal mastery of these practices, it is a living tradition—a set of understandings about life and ways of training one's mind that are not merely intellectual, but alive. For many centuries in Tibet, these wisdom traditions have been a guide to life, a process of analysis and reason, a lifelong training of the mind/heart, a way of aligning people towards compassionate action, and a ground for profoundly valuing the opportunities presented by human life.

THE CONTRIBUTORS AND
STRUCTURE OF *INNER PEACE—GLOBAL IMPACT*

This volume focuses in particular on the contributions that the Tibetan wisdom traditions can make to leadership and the workplace. The topic is approached in varied ways by the authors, who have deep personal knowledge of the particular subjects they address. It is hard to wrap one's mind around a question as large as the contribution of Tibetan Buddhism and the Tibetan diaspora to contemporary leadership and work, since a true understanding of Tibetan culture and what its survival (or loss) may mean to the world requires deep appreciation of the various Tibetan Buddhist traditions, an understanding of societal change processes, and also perspectives on the changing nature of Western society and culture. One person can provide only a limited picture when the topic is so broad, so I invited people to write who brought great diversity of expertise. My goal was to create a book that would provide knowledge from differing perspectives, thereby catalyzing new questions and creating a collage of meaningful perspectives on this aspect of global human change. Because of the complexity and richness of the subject and the goal of fostering an understanding of Buddhism as a practice and not simply as a set of intellectual concepts, I opted to include only contributors with lengthy meditation practices. Some make connections between Tibetan Buddhist theory and leadership theory and practice. Others depict how a few entrepreneurial Tibetan leaders nourished the development of organizations that were critical to the process of transplanting Tibetan teachings and institutions to new soil. Still others have done research related to Tibetan Buddhism and leadership or organizations, while some describe how Tibetan Buddhist practice has influenced their own work.

The book includes people's stories, in the spirit of valuing first-person research, in addition to more widely-recognized approaches to practicing social science. My intention is that this combination will enrich scholarly discourse and also provide information for those who are interested in the phenomenon, yet are not scholars. The blend of voices and perspectives creates a rich picture of how Tibetan Buddhism is becoming an influence on leadership and work. Some were previously published in scholarly journals, others could be, and some are first person narratives or stories. Intentionally, the voices differ. They were not intended to be alike, but to convey the range of what is happening, how it is discussed, and how people have experienced its impact.

Inner Peace—Global Impact has been structured for easy access and modular reading. Each section opens with a brief introduction to its varied contributions, just as this preface conveys a sense of the whole and how the parts fit together.

The first section focuses on the importance of **leadership** in the survival and spread of Tibetan Buddhism in the West. Here, I selected contributors who could cast light on the uniqueness of His Holiness the Fourteenth Dalai Lama as he evolved over time: he went from being largely unknown to becoming a global thought leader. The section also addresses the crucial contribution of the feminine principle as an element in leadership and enlightenment—something largely unseen by most people—and brings out the importance of compassion and ethics in leadership development. The second section shifts its focus to **individuals** in the West, looking at how Tibetan Buddhism has impacted people's lives at work. These contributors are intentionally quite varied, ranging from an anthropologist of dance who was so drawn to the inner meanings of Tibetan Buddhist dance that she focused her entire life towards it, to an airline flight attendant, an artist, and a university professor. This section represents first person research: individuals telling their own stories of transformation. The third section is about the importance of **organizing and organizations**: it describes three of the largest global Tibetan Buddhist organizations, suggesting how it has been important to create new organizations that met the needs and mindset of Westerners. The authors of the chapters in this section have been deeply involved personally in these organizations. Dr. Nick Ribush was one of the founding directors of the organization that he describes, while Susan Skjei was a student of the founder, became a teacher within that tradition, was a corporate education executive, and developed programs to bring these perspectives to managers. Sogyal Rinpoche is a wisdom teacher who created and leads one of the largest global Tibetan Buddhist organizations—Rigpa.[5] The fourth section brings in **research** on the impact of Tibetan Buddhist practices in the West, and the final section concludes the book with **reflections** by teachers who have been deeply involved in contemplative practice for decades: a tenth generation Tibetan yogi (Lama Tharchin Rinpoche), a Western CEO and management professor (Bill George), the consultant/ thought leader who catalyzed global interest in learning organizations (Peter Senge), and a widely-respected Western organizational consultant and Tibetan Buddhist practitioner (Margaret Wheatley) who introduced Western behavioral scientists to the implications of chaos theory and the "new" physics for leadership—implications that are quite similar to those of Tibetan Buddhism's description of the world. Additional background information on each author can be found at the start of each section and in their bios. In their own ways, all are wise and passionate, bringing a great variety of perspectives and experience to the book. Every contributor has sustained a practice of contemplation or meditation for many years and brings this perspective to their writing and their work in the world.

The book was developed to fit the interests of varied groups of people, ranging from those generally interested in Tibetan Buddhism or leadership to scholars in these areas. It has a modular design that lets you, as reader, adapt it to your interests. For example, there are extensive notes at the end of many chapters so that scholars can identify source materials and pursue them, if they wish. At the same time, readers interested in the topic but not the underlying scholarship can focus on the stories and thinking that interest them and skip the notes, or use them to locate other readings in their personal area of interest. *Leadership and organization development practitioners* may choose to begin by reading the chapters about leadership or by picking among those about people's work experiences. *Leaders* looking for ideas they can use to hone their leadership skills might begin with the first section on leadership, the section on organizing, and the final section of reflections by noted leadership educators and consultants. *Scholars and management professors* will be able to access the underlying research by reading the extensive notes, and may choose to begin with the introductory chapter and the chapters based on empirical research, plus the more conceptual contributions from Western thought leaders in the final section. They may also be intrigued by the first person stories by a sociologist and a research psychologist of the personal impact of Tibetan practice. *Students of Buddhism* might read in a different sequence. They are likely to be interested in specific contributors whose work they know, as well as in the ways that Buddhism has been impacting people's lives. They may read about how it evolved in the West from the perspective of Tibetan masters (Sogyal Rinpoche and Lama Tharchin Rinpoche), an eminent scholar and translator (Thupten Jinpa), or people actively involved in developing such organizations for 30-plus years (Susan Skjei, Nick Ribush, and Philip Philippou). They may be most intrigued by the chapters by Tibetan thought leaders, the section on *individuals* with stories about the personal impact of practice, the section on *organizations* (which recounts stories of organizations they may care about), and the chapters by scholars who are serious Buddhist practitioners.

These possible approaches are simply suggestions, as the sequence in which the chapters are read is flexible. Fundamentally, the book is conceptualized like a banquet: an array of tasteful dishes, thoughtfully prepared, blending together well, while differing considerably among themselves in "taste." The presence of these diverse perspectives and the organization of the book come from my deep love of richness and diversity in thought. Perhaps even more important, the scale of the topic required bringing together many knowledgeable minds. I invite you to taste all that whet your appetite, in whatever sequence you like! May you find yourself in deep dialogue with some or many of the contributors—so that this reading itself changes your sense of what questions to ask and what is possible. If it helps you to "connect new dots," raise new questions, and see things in new ways, it will be doing its job.

I would like this book to help change history. It invites you think about how these ancient wisdom teachings can contribute to a major paradigm shift that keeps life sustainable on Planet Earth. Even if we can find ways to grapple with the full meaning of such teachings and incorporate them in the development of leaders, we are still left with questions regarding how to link wisdom, action, and the practical knowledge and skills needed in the worlds of business, government, public service, and education. Such challenges generate work that is feasible, intriguing, and worth doing. This book is appearing after Tibetan Buddhism has lived and grown for 50 years in the West. May it and others that follow contribute to people's creative development of ventures over the next 50 years in the evolution of Tibetan Buddhism, and may our collective efforts bring the taste of these wisdom teachings into our work, organizations, and daily lives.

NOTES

1. Acceptance speech for the *Nobel Peace Prize*, 1989.
2. From Bob Dylan's, "Ballad of a Thin Man," a song recorded on the album *Highway 61 Revisited*, 1965.
3. See "The Possibility of Healthy Organizations: Thoughts Toward a New Framework for Organizational Theory and Practice," *Journal of Applied Sociology* 21, No. 2 (2004): 57-79 and "Practitioner—Heal Thyself: Challenges in Enabling Organizational Health," *Organization Management Journal* 1, No. 1(2004): 28-37. doi:10.1057/omj.2004.9 Also see Kathryn Goldman Schuyler and Linda Branagan, "The Power Line: A Model for Generating a Systemic Focus on Organizational Health," *Sociological Practice* 5, No. 2 (2003): 77-88.
4. Shantideva's *Bodhisattvacharyavatara (A Guide to the Bodhisattva's Way of Life*, also known as the *Bodhicharyavatara)* was written in the eighth century. There are several good translations and commentaries available in English. His Holiness the Dalai Lama used Alexander Berzin's translation for an 8-day course that he taught in Zurich in 2005. It can be downloaded in its entirety from the Berzin Archives, where it is translated as *Engaging in Bodhisattva Behavior* http://www.berzinarchives.com/web/x/nav/eb_toc.html_1487505749.html Other good (and quite different) translations are Stephen Batchelor's *A Guide to the Bodhisattva's Way*

of Life (Dharamsala: Library of Tibetan Works and Archives, 1979/1998) and the Padmakara Translation Group's *The Way of the Bodhisattva* (Boston: Shambhala, 1997). Contemporary commentaries include those by His Holiness the Dalai Lama, *A Flash of Lightning in the Dark of Night: A Guide to the Bodhisattva's Way of Life* (Boston: Shambhala, 1994), Dzigar Kongtrül Rinpoche, *Uncommon Happiness, The Path of the Compassionate Warrior* (Boudhanath: Rangjung Yeshe Publications, 2009), Pema Chödrön, *No Time to Lose: A Timely Guide to the Way of the Bodhisattva* (Boston: Shambhala, 2005), and Geshe Yeshe Tobden, *The Way of Awakening* (Somerville, MA: Wisdom, 2005).

5.   Note that in *Dzogchen* teachings, *rigpa* means "the essential nature of the mind." Being able to sustain awareness of the essential nature of mind in a stable way is one way to describe what may be meant by enlightenment.

CHAPTER 1

A SENSE OF THE POSSIBLE: CAN TIBETAN BUDDHISM REVITALIZE LEADERSHIP AND WORK?

An Exploration in the Sociology of Knowledge

Kathryn Goldman Schuyler

Inner Peace—Global Impact: Tibetan Buddhism, Leadership, and Work, pp. 1–28
Copyright © 2012 by Information Age Publishing
All rights of reproduction in any form reserved.

1

This book addresses the meeting of individuals and cultures across what had been a huge cultural divide—the gap between an isolated, spiritually developed country in the East and the most scientifically advanced, industrially developed countries of the West. Through this meeting of cultures, Westerners have been absorbing core teachings of Buddhism about the interconnectedness of life, the possibility of taming the "wild" human mind, and the fundamental importance of generating compassion for all beings. During a period when many in the West have been seeking greater meaning in life, Tibetan Buddhism has brought rich and subtle explanations that resonated with many, so that its organizations took root throughout Europe, the United States, Australia, and South America (the "West," as used in this book).

After China "liberated" Tibet in 1959, many of the teachers of Tibetan Buddhism (the core of Tibet's culture) literally walked out of their huge, snow-covered, mountainous country. A great many died en route and most had to perform menial work like road-building when they arrived in the hot climates of India and Nepal. Some survived the journey but died of illness in refugee camps. But as a people, they survived and began figuring out how to live and thrive in their new conditions as refugees. Tens of thousands took up residence in India, Nepal, Bhutan, and Sikkim. Some reached Europe or the Americas. The Tibetan wisdom traditions at the heart of their culture had been sourced mainly by classical Indian Buddhist texts and were influenced as well by the local Bon religion. These teachings now impact the thinking and actions of huge numbers of people throughout the world. (While there are many Tibetan texts, these practices were often passed personally from teacher to student in the oral tradition, so the term "teachings" is used throughout this book.) Until the last 30 years, Westerners had no direct access to Tibetan teachings, as they did not exist in print in Western languages. Translator Ngawang Zangpo (Hugh Thompson) has studied and written about the extent to which original Tibetan Buddhist sources were available from the 1950s to the present.[1] Between the early 1950s and the 1960s, only one book presented a genuine Tibetan Buddhist teaching—*The Tibetan Book of the Dead*—and it was in a translation that did not accurately render the meaning or intentions of the underlying text.[2] Only slowly over the decades has this changed, and now hundreds of such texts are available in English and other languages.[3]

These Buddhist traditions can be regarded as a social science developed over a thousand years ago—a set of practices for using the mind to understand and live in accordance with reality. They do not have to be seen as a "religion" (meaning a set of beliefs that one must adhere to, with a belief in a deity foremost among them). Becoming aware of the latent potential innate of the human mind and how it can lead to freedom (what noted scholar and former Buddhist monk Robert Thurman calls *inner modernity)* is foundational to what Buddhism can potentially contribute in the West.[4] The distinction that he makes between regarding modernity as solely related to material development and considering it an attitude or orientation provides a useful frame of reference for thinking about the impact of Tibetan Buddhism in the West.

It is clear that Tibet as a culture and society invested in people's spiritual development, while in general Western societies are materialistic, fast-paced, depend upon consumption and entertainment, and encourage investing in whatever produces the largest profits. In Tibet, from the time of the introduction of Buddhism in the eighth century until the middle of the twentieth century, societal resources were mainly invested in providing opportunities for people to understand wisdom teachings that address what it means to be a human being. Not only is it rare in human history to have an entire culture focused on developing wisdom, but it is also rare for any culture rich in knowledge to be isolated from the rest of the world and then suddenly have most of its sages compelled to disperse around the world and find ways to keep the culture and its perspective on wisdom alive beyond its original boundaries.

Buddhism survived in Tibet, the "land of the snows," for over a thousand years, almost entirely isolated and protected from the rest of the world by choice and by geography. The teachings at the heart of this isolated culture were unavailable in other languages and other countries until the last 50 years. Texts that had been written in Sanskrit and taught in the second century in India were lost in India, but they were translated into Tibetan in the eighth century and survived into the present as a living tradition, influencing what people value and how they make important life choices.

These documents are based on oral teachings given by the Buddha Shakyamuni over 2,500 years ago, intended to help people "wake up" or become enlightened. Enlightenment could be defined as meaning that you do not have to experience yourself solely as the separate person you have believed yourself to be, but that you actually experience the nature of your mind to be pure spacious knowing.[5] In this context, human life is best understood as providing an opportunity to live from a *wisdom perspective* and help others to do the same.[6] Before 1959, aside from having read about them in novels or seen a movie like *Lost Horizon*, perhaps only a few hundred people in the West had any contact with these teachings.[7] Now hundreds of thousands of Westerners know about these traditions and use them for guidance in life.[8]

While a great many books have been written about Tibetan Buddhism or were influenced by Tibetan Buddhism, few address how this cultural move of the Tibetan wisdom traditions to the West is taking place. This can be looked at from an organizational perspective (what organizations have been formed and how they are evolving to enable such considerable change) and from the perspective of the sociology of knowledge (the study of change in what is assumed to be "normal" at different times in history and in different cultures or countries).[9] The thousands of books containing biographies of His Holiness the 14th Dalai Lama and other Tibetan teachers, stories of the experiences of serious Western students, translations of key texts and Tibetan commentaries on them, and scholarly treatises written in the context of Tibetan studies rarely focus on the phenomenon itself: the process by which these teachings are taking root worldwide.[10]

Two books explicitly discuss this large process of culture change. Robert Thurman's *Inner Revolution: Life, Liberty, and the Pursuit of Real Happiness* presents the potential impact of Tibetan Buddhism on American democracy, and Jeffery Paine's *Re-Enchantment: Tibetan Buddhism Comes to the West* tells many stories about Tibetan Buddhist teachers in the West, contextualizing the spread of Tibetan Buddhism in the West in relation to German sociologist Max Weber's perspectives on the role of religion in society and the impact of industrialization.[11] Others discuss the history in detail, but do not explore the sociological implications.[12] There are several relatively recent scholarly collections of chapters on Buddhism in America from differing perspectives, but these authors did not focus on the process of change and the relevance to leadership, which are the main topics addressed here.[13] These books contain excellent scholarly studies of subjects ranging from Buddhism in American prisons, to gay men and women in the American Buddhist community, and to the academic study of Buddhism in America.[14] As Robert Hughes Seager wrote when describing his efforts to develop a book on Buddhism in America, there is little solid scholarship on this topic, let alone on the global process of change that I am addressing here with regard to leadership.[15] A historian, he concluded when discussing "Tibetan Buddhism and the Vajrayana Milieu,"

> Developing a discussion on growth and change within the Tibetan Buddhist religious communities over the past 30 years is much trickier. Despite its rich publishing record in the last 2 decades and its apparent flourishing in the United States, Tibetan Buddhism has little literature that charts, much less interprets, the often baffling relations among the many Tibetan Buddhist teachers, institutions, and lineages.[16]

What makes the recent history of events in Tibet and the spread of Tibetan Buddhism to the West important? There are many fascinating stories, each of which could be the focus of epic movies (such as those already made: *Kundun, Seven Years in Tibet,* and the fictional *Little Buddha*), but a major question is the infamous "so what?" Does it matter for the world if a nation like Tibet is swallowed up by its large neighbor? Nations have invaded one another throughout history. Boundaries change as countries disappear or are merged into others. Entire peoples' identities are relabeled by history. What had been France becomes Germany, or parts of Mexico become the United States, or those living in Estonia become Soviets and then become Estonian again. Is this simply another story of conquest? Or is it more? Tibet's culture, based in wisdom traditions passed on both in writing and "ear-whispered" from one teacher to his (or her) best students for over a thousand years, offers a blend of oral and written knowledge about transforming the mind that is unique on the planet. It is not only a body of literature: it is a living tradition, embodied and carried forward by teachers who have experienced what they teach about the mind, meditation, and happiness—teachers who often seem to radiate the qualities many people yearn for.

The following brief overview of Tibetan Buddhism will make it easier for readers to appreciate the various portions of this book, whether or not they have a background in Buddhism. If you are already familiar with Tibetan Buddhism, you may prefer to skip to the next section *The Sociology of Knowledge: Studying Societal Paradigms.*

BUDDHIST PERSPECTIVES—SOME OF THE BASICS

From the perspective of Tibetan Buddhism, one way of looking at the vast body of the Buddha's teachings (called the *Dharma*), is to see these teachings in terms of three *yanas*: different ways of moving along the spiritual path towards ultimate realization of the nature of one's being.[17] Readers may find this notion helpful if they are already somewhat familiar with Buddhism, but not with Tibetan Buddhism. Organizing the teachings of Buddhism as three yanas developed in India during the seventh century, when Buddhism was beginning to spread to Tibet. The yanas are in part associated with the three *turnings of the wheel*, which are teachings that were given by the Buddha at different points in time in different parts of India. It is said that each turning represents a complete, comprehensive view and set of practices, and that different paths exist because of the wide range of cultures and capabilities of people. Many people in the West are more familiar with the *Hinayana* aspects of Buddhism, which focus on attaining enlightenment or *nirvana* and escaping suffering, than they are with the other two yanas. The *Hinayana* approach regards the Buddha (one who is awake) as the historical Buddha whom most people picture when the term *Buddha* is mentioned. These teachings, given by the historical Buddha Shakyamuni at Deer Park (Sarnath) in about the sixth century B.C.E., focus on obtaining peace through the *Four Noble Truths* and are mainly concerned with abandoning negative actions of the body, speech, and mind to minimize suffering. They took root in Southeast Asia and spread widely there.

The *Mahayana* teachings, given on Vulture Peak Mountain near Rajagriha, focus on developing "great compassion" toward all beings, rather than simply on attaining enlightenment for oneself, and are the form of Buddhism that lives in China, Korea, and Japan. Recognizing that everyone wants to be happy and not suffer, Mahayana Buddhism teaches that one gains peace of mind by caring more for others' well-being than for one's own. The ground is provided by the *Prajanaparamita* sutras (meaning *Perfection of Wisdom* sutras), which present high teachings on *emptiness* or *suchness*. This is defined by Sogyal Rinpoche using a Tibetan phrase *tak ché dang dralwa*, which translates as: "free from permanence and non-existence."[18] *Emptiness* does not mean that nothing exists, but rather that nothing exists forever—and that the notion of having a personal self with any fixity is an illusion. The sutras teach of abandoning attachment to the notion of an individual self or to a belief in the real existence of material phenomena. Most Westerners regard as "mind" what exists only at a relative level: a material mind, embodied in a brain dependent on material causes and conditions. Within the Mahayana view, in an ultimate sense mind is empty of specific materiality and is the source of all there is. In this perspective, life can be understood through two truths: seeing everything as empty is known as the ultimate level of truth; thinking that phenomena are "real" is considered to be relative truth.[19] The Mahayana view was completed in the third turning of the wheel of dharma, given at Shravasti, which focused on developing wisdom: the recognition that all beings have Buddha-nature or basic goodness, building on the foundation developed by the two previous turnings of the wheel. This nature is known to be the same in all beings, from ants and snails to dogs, humans—and buddhas, of which (from this perspective) there are a great many throughout the vast expanse of history. The nature of mind is known to be luminous and clear, but, for all except buddhas, it is covered over with "adventitious stains." In other words, it is like a diamond or other precious jewel that has fallen in the mud. It has tremendous value if one knows what it is and polishes it. Otherwise, it appears to be nothing but a dirty rock. Buddhas recognize the jewel … and most beings have no idea that they possess such a jewel at all, or that it even exists—let alone realize that they "are" the jewel! As a tool for life, the Dharma provides a path out of the confusion that most people have regarding what is real and what is not. It describes how to stop unintentionally causing oneself to suffer. That is its purpose.

Both the Hinayana and Mahayana perspectives are said to require many lifetimes to become enlightened, even eons of time, because they focus on slowly developing the causes for becoming enlightened. The *Vajrayana*, which appeared in India in the seventh century C.E., involves practices that enable the practitioner to connect directly with *Buddha nature* or *the nature of mind*. These practices are designed to allow one to attain enlightenment rapidly, in one lifetime, by bringing into awareness that part of us which is already enlightened (the result), rather than on slowly accumulating causes for becoming enlightened. Such practices cannot be learned from books and reading, as they do not involved conceptual mastery, but *practical* mastery. Vajrayana practices have been passed down for centuries from one person who mastered them to another. They require transmission from someone who has realized this view, rather than just understanding it conceptually. As these thrived in India at the time in history when Buddhism went to Tibet, Tibet became a Vajrayana culture.

Buddhism is nontheistic and does not require believing in a god, but instead asks that one question all assumptions. Instead of being considered a *philosophy*, which implies a solely cognitive approach, those who follow the Dharma as a path call Buddhism a *view* that all life is precious because all beings are interconnected. Human life is considered particularly precious, as human beings are considered to be best positioned among all forms of life to understand the nature or purpose of life, which is the process of becoming enlightened. Tibetan literature even has a form of biography known as *namtar*: spiritual biographies of enlightened beings (some of which have now been translated into English).[20] The culture of Tibet focused people's attention on this process of transformational learning and assumed that such learning was grounded in helping others. The core notion was to place others' well-being and happiness higher than one's own. Such a cultural intent is not often found on our planet and can be seen as essential for human survival. Several Himalayan countries were Vajrayana Buddhist in culture, but Tibet was by far the largest, with the largest body of texts and teachers. The only remaining one is very small Bhutan, with a population under one million.

Viewed in this way, all of Buddhism is a profound learning process within a paradigm of spirituality. As the Buddha said,

Buddhas do not wash away sins with water,
Nor do they remove the sufferings of beings with their hands,
Neither do they transplant their own realization into others.
Teaching the truth of suchness (emptiness) they liberate (others).

The Buddha was a teacher, not a healer or miracle worker. But he was a teacher within a different paradigm for learning and study from that of Western higher education—one that did not see learning as entirely a cognitive process. This fundamental distinction regarding the nature of learning in Tibetan Buddhism and in Western thought leads directly to the sociology of knowledge.

THE SOCIOLOGY OF KNOWLEDGE: STUDYING SOCIETAL PARADIGMS

This book explores the global process by which Tibetan Vajrayana Buddhist teachers and teachings are moving around the world, considering it within the larger context of the sociology of knowledge, and approaching it through the eyes, experiences, and thinking of a diverse group of people who have been deeply involved in Tibetan Buddhism.[21] The sociology of knowledge focuses on how the different worldviews in which people are "innocently" immersed influence what they consider to be normal or ordinary in life. As Peter Berger and Thomas Luckmann wrote in their influential book *The Social Construction of Reality*, the world is not simply a fixed set of things that are "real": people actively construct the patterns that they then regard as a typical or normal life in a given social context. *Reality* does not exist in itself, but is socially formed. Buddhism too sees what most humans consider to be *reality* as a construction, but offers a different type of description and analysis of the way that it is constructed. Where sociology, going back to the writings of Charles Horton Cooley in the early 1900s on the *looking glass self* and later George Herbert Mead's *social behaviorism*, considers the self to be grounded in how we interact with others, Buddhism grounds the construction of reality in quasi-universal patterns of behavior in humans reacting to being in a material human body.[22] Through study and the varied practices of the three yanas (which might be described as first "cleaning up one's act" in the Hinanaya; then having deep compassion for oneself and all beings as one loosens grasping for things in competition with others—and understanding that in "reality" all are interdependent and connected; and finally being able to maintain *pure vision* of the nature of all beings) one "wakes up" from a subject-object trance. Viewed in this way, human life is an opportunity to train our minds, which includes our hearts, to deconstruct what appears to be true, through understanding the underlying, omnipresent nature of cause-and-effect. While Buddhist teachers may appreciate anthropological or sociological insights, the important learnings are fundamentally acultural and universal, although the practices and teachings are seen to vary with individual, cultural, and historical differences.

On the other hand, in sociology we often focus on individuals as being caught up in broad processes of social change. Historically, as sociologists we have incorporated into our field the study of the evolution of what Karl Mannheim described as *Weltanschauungen* (societal mindsets).[23] As I became interested in the Dalai Lama as a leader, I found myself increasingly immersed in something unique and fascinating: the translation of a cultural mindset from one society where it was at home to another that was extremely different from it in many significant ways. If the reality that I, my neighbors, my professional colleagues, or our leaders had been accepting was not generating the kind of world we hoped to live in (as so many people seemed to feel)—Tibetan Buddhism offered an alternative approach to human development and societal change. Tibetan culture had persisted in relative isolation from the influence of other cultures from roughly the eighth century through the middle of the twentieth century, when the Chinese took over and the 14th Dalai Lama went into exile in India. Rarely in the course of human history has a culture so conceptually rich been so isolated and then had to cope with being abruptly launched into the midst of other cultures with significantly different norms and values. Many cultures have been invaded and destroyed, but what I realized, as I began to investigate, was that here was a particularly literate and highly developed culture that could be observed in the middle of a significant process of change. In addition, it happened to have a leader in this particular Dalai Lama who had, from the start, reached out globally for assistance (which he did not get) and who had, by the time I began this research, become an acknowledged master of global communication. It was evident that the Tibetan diaspora was already influencing the thinking and values of many thousands of people across the planet, but to what extent and in what ways?

Although Robert Thurman has urged that Tibet be considered an outstanding example of "inner modernity," as mentioned previously, people tend to think of modernity solely in terms of what he called "outer or secular modernity."[24] Peter Berger, Brigitte Berger, and Hansfried Kellner pointed out in their 1973 study of the "modern" mind that one of the unique things about modernity is that its intellectual leaders generally consider it superior to everything else.[25] Their book, *The Homeless Mind*, is an important study of modernization and development from the perspective of the sociology of knowledge. They define *modernization* as equivalent to "the institutional concomitants of technologically induced economic growth" which "consists of the growth and diffusion of a set of institutions rooted in the transformation of the economy by means of technology."[26] As discussed more fully in the conclusions of my study on entrepreneurship (Chapter 17), it is possible to draw intriguing parallels between the way that Tibet invested in technologies for internal transformation (inner reality) while the West invested in technologies for developing the external world (material reality).

Berger, Berger, and Kellner's description of the "modern mind" is dramatically different from the Tibetan Buddhist view of life. Berger, Berger, and Kellner's *modern mind* is characterized by *"mechanisticity," "reproducibility," "participation in a large organization," "measurability," "componentiality,"* "the *separability of means and ends,"* "the *segregation of work from private life,"* "*emotional management,"* and most important "*anonymous social relations.*"[27] The Tibetan Vajrayana view involves seeing oneself as being intimately a part of all there is, with everything alive and interdependent, and no separation at all between one's work and life. While organic, community-type cultures may often have more unified "life-worlds" than do cultures that are highly industrialized, Buddhist Tibet was unique in the complexity and richness of its spiritual culture and the vast number of texts upon which it was based. The extent to which the Tibetan Buddhist and materialist Western mindsets differ make it all the more intriguing that Tibetan Buddhism has developed such roots in the West, as the underlying assumptions, values, and lifestyles are so much in contrast. Is it possible that "homeless" modernized minds may seek the kind of home that was natural in the Tibetan context? A great many people who grew up with Western, "modern" lifestyles and values are training themselves in the view of Mahayana and Vajrayana Buddhism. Can the deeper meanings take root and develop Western forms without losing their coherence, integrity, and richness?

BRIEF BACKGROUND: TIBET

Vast numbers of people world-wide have heard of the Dalai Lama today, but only 50 years ago few people outside of Tibet knew of his existence or, if they did, accorded much importance to him or to his native land. He and Tibet were regarded by most Westerners as something akin to an exotic orchid: a rare species whose existence could be appreciated by some but required special conditions to exist. Where many varieties of orchids require hothouses in order to survive, Tibetans and their leader, the *Dalai* (foremost) *Lama* (teacher) seemed to require ice—the snowy mountain lands of Tibet, sometimes called the roof of the world. Since the time of the Chinese invasion and takeover of Tibet in 1959, the 14th Dalai Lama and those who could leave have lived as refugees, forming a government in exile in Dharamsala, India. As mentioned, Tibetans who had been accustomed to being scholars, doctors, and monks or nuns in a cold climate had to learn to support themselves through the harsh manual labor of building roads in extreme heat. Many died during the first decade in refugee camps in India, unable to survive the shocking contrast in life-style, climate, and culture. But more survived, and the Dalai Lama has become a major global thought leader. Many Tibetan teachers transcended the initial shock of having to survive without their country and began to travel and teach in Europe, the Americas, Australia, and New Zealand.

Tibet was a large country geographically, of roughly 965,000 square miles (the size of western Europe) but small in numbers, with a population of about 6 million.[28] It was composed of three provinces: U-Tsang, Kham, and Amdo. Today, there are probably about 2.7 million Tibetans remaining in the parts of China that are officially called the Tibet Autonomous Region (TAR). Many ethnic Tibetans live in Kham and Amdo, which were incorporated into the Chinese provinces of Qinghai and Sichuan. (What the Chinese government identifies as Tibet is actually only 40% of the historical country.) Approximately 140,000 Tibetans live in exile outside of China. They have been able to sustain a cultural identity, although this may be growing more difficult with the passage of time. Regarded by the Chinese as being backward and simple because their culture valued inner development over modernization, those remaining within the land of historical Tibet have had little opportunity for education or influential jobs unless they do their studies in the Chinese language and repudiate traditional Tibetan values. Instead of improving in recent years, the situation has grown worse with regard to cultural autonomy, although a few noted wisdom teachers within Tibet have gathered thousands of students at times over the last few decades.[29]

Despite the efforts of the Chinese government to eradicate the influence of the Dalai Lama and Tibetan Buddhism, the impact of this small Buddhist country and its spiritual values has grown worldwide, so that there are now probably over a thousand Tibetan Buddhist meditation centers located on all continents, with large concentrations in India, the United States, Australia, and Europe. Most of the main Tibetan teachers have physical centers that people visit periodically for teachings, and these teachers also travel a great deal and teach world-wide. The Dalai Lama has taught one of the main teachings, known as the Kalachakra, at least 32 times to over 1.6 million people.[30] Whereas before the Chinese invasion, virtually no Tibetan Buddhist texts had reliable translations into other languages, now hundreds (if not thousands) of sutras, tantras, and Tibetan commentaries on the original texts written since the eighth century are widely available online in many languages, with comparable numbers of books in print. I have heard Tibetan teachers comment many times on the irony of the situation: although they do not want to be living in exile with their country occupied, the impact of their culture and teachings has been vastly amplified by the actions of the Chinese.

This has become a unique instance: a rare and complex culture has to survive outside its home, on alien soil, in order to survive at all. This is fascinating anthropologically, and also an important story from the perspective of leadership development. Since the 1930s, there has been a fascination in the West with the notion of *Shangri La*—a country of enlightenment and peace hidden away within lands of constant ice storms, as described in James Hilton's *Lost Horizon*, which was initially a best-selling novel and then was made into an Oscar-winning movie. This presented an alternative type of leader not seen in the West—one who combined personal depth based on extensive spiritual training with practical leadership skills. Yet only a handful could visit or experience the real teachers firsthand, with extreme difficulty.

Now, all who wish can study with their choice of Tibetan teachers throughout the West. It is easy to obtain translations of texts over the Internet that for centuries were not available except in Tibetan, were never seen outside of Tibet, and were only made available to small numbers of people within Tibet. Tens of thousands of Westerners have completed retreats in the Tibetan style, ranging in time from a few weeks to 12 years. (A *retreat* is a period of time that one does contemplation, meditation, or other awareness practices, either alone or with others, most often away from one's home. Tibetan masters carry out lengthy retreats of many years.) Buddhism is growing in some countries as a major religion. As Robert Thurman described the situation in his book *Why the Dalai Lama Matters*, when Chairman Mao heard that they had captured Lhasa but the Dalai Lama had escaped, he is reported to have said, "Ah, then we have won the battle for Lhasa, but lost the war for Tibet!"[31]

Tibet is not being presented in this book as a perfect society or way of life to be copied mindlessly. It had problems, as does any society, but that is not the focus of this book, which is to explore the impact of practices developed within the culture of Tibet over the centuries to foster wisdom as they begin to spread in the West. The practices described in this book both require and develop mindful attention to all of one's actions and how one is doing them—it is not an approach that asks one to copy anything.

TIBETAN BUDDHISM AND WESTERN PERSPECTIVES ON SPIRITUALITY AND LEADERSHIP

At the start of the research for this book, I interviewed Tibetan teachers who had matured and taught in Tibet before the Chinese takeover. I wondered whether teachings that were meaningful within Tibet's closed, spiritual culture could also be relevant in secular applications in the materialistic, open, driven culture of the West. Looking at this question from the perspective of Western social scientific explanations, these interviews and my participant observation at Buddhist teaching centers suggested that the survival of the teachings seemed to be based on the combination of several factors, with leadership and organizing as two of the main ones. I was not originally seeking to study the leadership or organizing of Tibetans who had relocated in the West. However, as I conducted interviews with teachers and their senior Western students, leadership seemed to be a significant factor, worth exploring further. For example, I saw that two key early teachers, Chögyam Trungpa and Lama Yeshe, could easily be viewed as entrepreneurial leaders, as could the 14th Dalai Lama, who crafted a global role never before imagined for a Dalai Lama.[32] The leadership of these three people (and the development of their organizations) suggested critical success factors for the growth of Tibetan Buddhism in the West.[33] I began to see the foundation blocks for the survival of the Tibetan wisdom traditions in the West as being the combined presence and interaction of a few core elements.

These seemed to be (1) entrepreneurial leadership and creative organizing by a number of Tibetan masters and their students, supported by the receptivity of Western students, (2) the creation of many less publicly visible teaching centers that teach and preserve the essential teachings of the multiple Tibetan lineages, and (3) the development of translators (which is outside the scope of this book). Noticing this made me want to learn more with regard to the leadership and organizing of the main global organizations. It led me to seek people to write chapters who had deep personal knowledge of these global schools and their leaders, so that the book would be based on "insider knowledge." Such *emic perspectives* are very important for understanding a culture, particularly one that is different from one's own in fundamental ways.

I hoped to see how the types of leadership that have emerged since the takeover in 1959 have made a difference in the survival of the teachings and their spread in the West, which is a little-researched topic. The only books I have found about the Dalai Lama as a leader and the implications of Tibetan Buddhism for leadership or work did not take into account the Vajrayana elements in Tibetan culture and have not attempted to address the questions raised here.[34] Until now, the experiences and perspectives of Tibetan Buddhism have scarcely been included in discourse about leadership, outside of Robert Thurman's books. (For example, he has argued that it was the institution of the Dalai Lamas in the fifteenth century that enabled Tibet to last as one entity as long as it did, thereby facilitating the preservation of the underlying wisdom traditions.)[35] However, instead of addressing the political history of Tibet, I and the other authors have drawn on the Buddhist view and recent organizational developments to discuss how Tibetan Buddhism is surviving in the West and the implications of these wisdom traditions for developing leaders in the world outside of Tibet. We have explored how organizing and organizations contributed to the survival of these traditions and considered how they are expressed in the daily work life of a variety of Westerners.

Reflecting on leadership theory, scholars have long debated whether leaders are born (trait theory) or made (developmental theory).[36] Some scholars have explored the stages of development of leaders in ways that enable a deep appreciation for the complexity of the components of leadership excellence. In particular, both Robert Kegan's work on adult developmental stages and William Torbert's work applying adult development theory directly to leaders are useful for conveying the rich complexity of the issues surrounding leadership development.[37] In addition, Peter Senge has impacted leadership scholars and executives across the business world with his work on systemic approaches to leadership development (*The Fifth Discipline*) and its holistic nature (*Presence: Human Purpose and the Field of the Future*).[38] However, as Bill George said in his interview (Chapter 19), few leaders learn leadership from scholars or their research, despite ongoing attempts to teach it in business school programs and leadership training around the world.

As a culture, Tibet opted not to make the choice between "born" or "made," instead working actively with both. From the Vajrayana Buddhist perspective, highly realized beings are able to choose where and how they are reborn, whereas most beings die, are terrified for some period of time, not knowing where they are or what is happening to them, and are then reborn somewhere, depending upon what they did in their life. The Tibetan word for such a highly realized being is *tulku*. Whether one believes in rebirth or not can be bracketed for the moment, in order to better appreciate what Tibetans believe and how the culture functions. Tulkus are believed to be able to take rebirth by choice and do so both in wealthy families and peasant families. The 14th Dalai Lama "took rebirth" in a peasant family; others, like Sogyal Rinpoche, were born into families full of teachers, and one of the major teachers in post-invasion Tibet, Khenpo Jigme Phuntsok, was born in a family of nomads. After being recognized as a reincarnation of a wise teacher, the young child receives a thorough and rich education, with a consistent focus on developing his or her compassion for all sentient beings and innate wisdom. If one looks at such a system from the perspective of Western psychology, with its knowledge of the importance of teachers' beliefs about children's potential, whether or not one believes in tulkus and reincarnation one can see how this system would tend to produce wise and compassionate beings.[39] (In other words, all of the teachers surrounding the young tulku have deep confidence in the continuity of mind and the potential of the young child.) For centuries in Tibet, considerable societal resources were invested in developing spiritual leaders. The recognition of tulkus continues today, but without the resources of a whole society behind it.

The most evident foundation for any book on leadership in relation to Tibetan Buddhism and the Tibetan diaspora is the person of its current leader, the 14th Dalai Lama, who has become one of the most well-known leaders on the planet. He has provided thought leadership to scientists and ordinary people world-wide, in addition to guiding the people of Tibet for half a century of exile. He seems to be equally at ease dialoguing on a public stage with noted physicists and neuroscientists in ways that extend their research in new directions as he is engaging with national leaders like German Chancellor Angela Merkel and former President George W. Bush of the United States. His writings, teachings, and his very being suggest that more human development is possible than many scientists believe. He is unique in many ways as a leader and human being, as discussed in depth in the chapter by Geshe Thupten Jinpa and also in the selection by Huston Smith about their first meeting in 1964 (when the Dalai Lama was still largely unknown in the West). He has personally reached millions of people world-wide, influenced a great many national leaders, and contributed substantially to the survival of Tibetan culture.

The 14th Dalai Lama himself does not claim to be an expert on leadership, science, or politics—only to be a "simple Buddhist monk." Others gave him the title of high lama—he does not use it to be placed higher than others. In my own experience of him, his importance lies in how he combines what we can call *the power of presence* with deep compassion for all living beings. Tenzin Gyatso, known as the 14th Dalai Lama, talks with crowds of thousands as if he were chatting in his living room. He is warm, funny, completely at ease, and able to talk extemporaneously in a highly coherent, well-organized way that touches what vast numbers of people find important. In public talks, he is like the grandfather one always wished for, yet he can switch modes and deliver an erudite scholarly talk about a Tibetan text later the same day, without needing any notes. For the latter, he is equally present and organized, but his style changes, and the exceptionally well-trained scholar in him allows him to talk for hours on complex philosophical points. He is always very present and at ease, with his structure of thought fed by the underlying stream of classical Buddhist thought.

It seems reasonable to attribute at least in part the wisdom of the Tibetan leaders and teachers to the training they receive. Traditional Tibetan Buddhist education aimed for a holistic development process that transcended the division we have as Western educators between "heart" and "mind" and taught that reality is ultimately not solely material. Its core concepts present a non-Western alternative perspective on leadership and what it requires.

Core Concepts Relevant to Leadership and Work

It can be difficult to distinguish between those things that are part of Tibetan culture in a historical sense (so that they are not relevant for Americans or Europeans or Australians) and things that are part of Tibetan culture and are *missing* from Western culture—and so should be retained and even cultivated. Given this caution, I see several interconnected themes that offer potentially important contributions to Western perspectives on leadership and leadership development:

- seeing the heart and mind as one, not separate;
- viewing compassion (inseparable from wisdom) as the foundation for excellent leadership and ethics;
- being convinced that one can only understand who one is and what is important through contemplation;
- recognizing that a broader view of life is needed than materialism;
- understanding the crucial role of the feminine principle in both leadership and life.

As Geshe Jinpa mentions in his interview (Chapter 3), whereas Western education views intellectual learning as being in many ways superior to developing the heart, no such distinction exists in Tibetan classical education. From the Tibetan perspective, when one gestures and says "my mind," one should touch the heart. Locating the mind in the heart does not indicate lesser value for the skills of making intellectual distinctions, as there are centuries-long scholarly traditions in all of the branches of Tibetan learning. It is simply a different foundation. Having the mind and heart as one eradicates centuries of debate over the relative importance of the head and heart in decision-making. The fear of being "soft" as a leader evaporates. It is assumed that a leader should be compassionate, as that is the foundation for both the Mahayana and Vajrayana perspectives described earlier in this chapter. One cannot be considered a good or excellent leader unless one has a deep sense of compassion for all beings, not only for human beings. This is a distinctly different perspective from the Western conviction that Darwin's theories implied that life is a struggle for survival in which the toughest win. The notion of life as a constant battle where only the fittest survive may not be a fair representation of what Darwin actually thought, but it is how he is remembered, and it is the shadow he now casts over leadership thinking.[40]

Taking this to the next logical step, people from many parts of the globe typically assume that it is natural for one to seek leadership in service to oneself—to seek fame, power, or wealth. The Tibetan wisdom traditions teach that this will only lead to problems. Robert Greenleaf's *servant leadership* is based on similar foundations and has become influential over the last few decades.[41] The Tibetan wisdom perspective provides well-reasoned arguments for the importance of serving others, which leads to the importance of ethics as a living part of one's learning, rather than as a philosophical field of study.

The Dalai Lama chose to title a book *Ethics for the New Millennium* when he wanted to reach a broad general public and clarify what his traditions could bring to the world.[42] The way that he outlined the main concepts made them testable, as one would expect of a social science book. When one looks at the first chapter on "Modern Society and the Quest for Human Happiness" in this light, it is evident that sentence after sentence was written so that the assumptions could be tested if data were gathered. The entire first chapter can be read as a series of interrelated cause and effect statements that describe how people's assumptions relate to their ethics, their level of happiness or anxiety, and the nature of modern life. Most historical critiques of modern or postmodern life come out of Western assumptions about people; they go back to the eighteenth century dialogues between Hobbes and Rousseau about "natural man" being good or basically selfish. Here, the underlying *view* (philosophy) is different, which is what opens new possibilities. Western "natural man" may seem hopelessly naïve if one looks back at Rousseau's writings, but Tibetan Yogis who teach or live from profound simplicity are not. The cultural roots are sufficiently different from ours in the West that they open a path where the door has been shut for centuries in the West. *Natural* or *ordinary* is not a hypothetical "noble savage," but a wise yogi (man) or yogini (woman) who has realized the purity of his or her ultimate inner nature and lived either in retreat—or in almost any occupation in "normal" life. The belief, as previously mentioned, is that all of us human beings have an innate inner lucidity and clarity. If we recognize this, we are yogis—or buddhas. Very few of us do. The whole paradigm is different, from its foundation.

Because of the innately clear mind (that we do not know is there), the foundation for learning and understanding in this tradition is contemplation, but not only contemplation—contemplation grounded in a view of human nature as being potentially a Buddha. The traditions emphasize the role of the teacher or master, believing that only one who has seen such a possibility can open it up for others. Everything that exists materially functions at what is called a "relative level." No one claims that there is no floor to stand on or that cars will not damage you if they hit you. All of that is the relative level, which is where human life takes place. Sociology, psychology, and other sciences study the relative level, and journalism describes it. People get caught up in their suffering at the relative level. The feelings of hurt and suffering are very real at this level, but from the perspectives being introduced in Western society from Tibet, as well as from other wisdom traditions, the question is whether there is a path out of such suffering. In the Tibetan wisdom traditions, that path is the Dharma.

From this point of view, we are not primarily material beings. What is fundamental is the nature of mind—which is to be able to generate and create out of emptiness. Such generativity without specific contents is hard for many of us to conceptualize or even imagine, yet it is of fundamental importance and underlies the epistemology and ethics of Tibetan Buddhism. Their culture was grounded in understanding that every living being is interconnected and shares a common "core": the nature of mind, which has been described by those who understand as being like light or the sky, yet cognizant. In most of us, this sky-like nature of mind (*rigpa*) is completely obscured by the fear-based habits we have developed to protect ourselves from perceived threats. It gets obscured or covered over as we (people, animals, all) experience fear and separation from one another and then react to our own fear. Gradually the fears and projections become strong enough to completely cover any recollection or awareness of who or what we really are.[43] Of course, Tibetan history includes power struggles, wars, and the material issues that all cultures face, but in Tibet, the essential view of life and its nature contrasted significantly with the assumptions that underlie the main lines of thought within the West: the conflict between Social Darwinism or Hobbes' "struggle of all against all" and the naïve hopefulness of Romanticism.[44]

Why does this difference in mindsets matter for leadership development and planetary sustainability? Vajrayana Buddhism implies a vast and challenging role for leaders in such a world: they need to master both themselves and the process of governing. They need the equivalent of what we've humorously come to regard as the training of a Jedi knight (one popular image of such a role, as seen in the movie *Star Wars*) infused into all facets of their education. An MBA strong in both business analysis and cultural competence is not sufficient. Most people are cast in waters that are far too rough for their ability to swim—or govern. As the popular phrase would have it, they are clueless. From the perspective of applied behavioral science, using a model known to many as the *Johari Window*, they are living their lives in a box where they do not even know what they don't know. And we—humanity—need them to lead and solve problems relating to planetary sustainability. It is simply not feasible with the current set of assumptions.

What these traditions suggest is needed isn't "book knowledge," it is experiential learning at the most profound level. The "highest" teachings are in some ways simple and straightforward when one is open for them and ready for them. If one is seeking to find fault or criticize, it is easy to do so, as these teachings can seem not to make sense when viewed from the commonsense view of life as it is lived in "modern" society. From the perspective of adult development theory (e.g., Kegan, Torbert), we might suspect that many people accept the more concrete teachings readily because these match their personal level of development, whereas the "higher" teachings, known as *Dzogchen* or *Mahamudra*, historically were secret teachings, accessible to very few students. Now, there are excellent teachers alive in the West and translated texts that discuss how the ultimate nature of mind and reality are one and are not material.[45] It is essential to study personally with a living teacher to absorb these perspectives, as without contact with a person who understands the real meaning, the words on the page in the texts are unlikely to convey the deeper intentions inherent in them. They hold the encoded tacit knowledge of Tibetan Buddhism. *Tacit knowledge* refers to those practices that are so subtle and complex that they cannot be fully described in words, and so can only be mastered through apprenticeship, rather than from reading and solitary study.[46] Since one cannot master opera singing, downhill skiing, or the correct pronunciation of a foreign language simply by reading, how could people expect to understand or develop mastery of Tibetan Buddhist practice solely through reading? Buddhist practice invites more significant shifts in a person and far deeper processes of individual transformation than learning sports or languages, so how could reading be sufficient?

Other concepts are fundamental for appreciating how the Vajrayana or Dzogchen teachings can contribute to an understanding of the nature of leadership. Margaret Wheatley's book *Leadership and the New Science* and Peter Senge's work have articulately presented the importance of looking at leadership development within the context of *complex living systems*.[47] Joanna Macy's extensive contributions to societal change, grounded in deep ecology, are based on her extensive study of both the Dharma and general systems theory[48] The ancient Tibetan wisdom traditions offer a view that in many ways is very similar to such a systems approach. From the Tibetan perspective, life is a highly complex system functioning entirely interdependently. This is known as *interdependent origination*: everything impacts everything else; one cannot isolate single causes or effects, and nothing occurs that is not caused in this complex systemic way. Solutions to today's global problems would demand complex and subtle solutions that take such interdependence into account.

Another useful concept to bring into executive development is that of the *bodhisattva*, as discussed in two chapters (Chapters 5 and 17). Briefly, a bodhisattva is a being who aims to become enlightened so as to be able to help others. From this perspective, the most meaningful aid one can provide to another is not material aid, but assistance in understanding the nature of life, so that one isn't repeatedly caught in a process quite akin to swimming upstream against the current. From this perspective, leading others can be compared to shining a light ahead so others can see the way. Using this analogy, the leader needs to have light and to know a path. Without both of these, a person isn't able to be very helpful, no matter how much one wishes to be. One is more or less encouraging people to keep moving despite being lost in the dark and bumping into things like walls or falling off metaphorical cliffs. One aims for enlightenment, because otherwise one is still in the dark (so to speak) and one does so not for oneself, or to cease involvement in the activities of life, but entirely to aid others. This is an intriguing way to conceptualize servant leadership: intelligently, one masters the skills and ways of being that one seeks to have others learn.

Finally, *active training in ethics* is inseparable from *training in meditation*. In Western thought, these would be perceived as quite distinct, but they are highly interdependent in Tibetan Buddhist teaching. While many Westerners understand meditation to be simply calming the mind, in Tibetan teaching such a calm mind is only the foundation for what one must learn, which involves refining one's capacity to be present, awake, and attentive. *Mind training* refers to noticing and immediately dropping one's fear, dislike, or envy of others. The training teaches one to work at all times in daily life to notice moments of blame and self-pity and replace them with valuing others more than oneself. It is an active, vigorous process of watching one's thoughts and reactions, while recognizing the complex, systemic interdependence of all life and appreciating the powerful nature of the mind to create one's environment. One cannot become wise without seeing and respecting the complex mutual causation that leads so many beings to be trapped in experiencing life as they do with "no exit": seeing this, one develops compassion—and compassion is foundational to ethics. As mentioned, the Dalai Lama wrote *Ethics for the New Millennium* to generate global awareness of the importance of ethics in daily life and for the survival of the planet.[49] The focus on the mind is not simply a way to diminish stress or increase happiness, as Western scientific studies often suggest in describing the uses of Eastern meditation practices. More fundamentally, meditation generates a deep shift in attitude towards the value of all beings. It leads to respecting others and their needs and involves being attentive and awake. If leaders were trained in this way, international politics might become quite different from what we accept today.

CONCLUSIONS

Perhaps we can learn from this formerly isolated, humanly rich, and different culture so grounded in the belief that we have it in us to become enlightened beings. Tibetan texts affirm that there have already been many enlightened beings, suggesting this is a reasonable goal. Being compassionate and wise requires commitment and action over the whole of one's lifetime—but so does getting rich or powerful, and it has far more beneficial impact and no likelihood of harm. Tibet's misfortune and diaspora provide an opportunity for Western social scientists to learn from these ancient teachings in ways that can enhance the development of globally-oriented business and political leaders who could actually work collaboratively to produce a sustainable planet.

My hope for this book is that it will contribute to the growing social science dialogue on the potential contributions of the Tibetan wisdom traditions and contemplative education. It is important that they be recognized and discussed in their full complexity. Rather than being incorporated into leadership training in ways that use them only for managing stress or improving health (which trivializes them), these practices and the wisdom behind them can be sources for changing the way leaders think and act. Some Tibetan masters have expressed concern about how Westerners teach based on Tibetan traditions. For example, Sogyal Rinpoche asked, in a keynote address that he gave at a conference on *Buddhism in America* in 1998,

> ... where will the popularity of Buddhism lead? Are we witnessing the conversion of Buddhism into a product, something which is quick and easy to master and which ignores the patient discipline and application that is really needed on the Buddhist path, as on any other spiritual path? In trying to make Buddhism palatable to American tastes and fashions, are we subtly editing and rewriting the teachings of Buddha? Is there a risk of Buddhism being "sold" too hard and being too pushy, even evangelical? Commercial-style grasping seems foreign to Buddhism, where the emphasis has always been on examining ourselves.[50]

Much has changed since 1998 when he raised these questions, with regard to both the numbers of people involved and the seriousness of their intentions, yet the questions remain real today. The chapters in this book will provide context for readers to reach their own conclusions on these points.

I look forward to further research and discussions of the implications of these teachings for the development of executives, organizational consultants, politicians, engineers, and professors. Only if there is first, second, and third person research can we discover the full potential of the wisdom traditions for our very different Western world. Such serious study has begun in psychology, researching one of the traditions (mindfulness meditation), and in neuroscience (studies that compare the brains of long-time meditators with novices and nonmeditators). There has been little scholarly attention from the perspective of leadership studies, organizational behavior, or the sociology of knowledge.[51] Moreover, almost all of the clinical psychology research on meditation and mindfulness has been based on only one approach to meditation, and research remains to be designed that will incorporate the full view of these wisdom teachings. Such research may offer paths to access the higher levels of development that Kegan and Torbert posit.[52] Of course leadership development for accessing such higher levels is simply a possibility, but teachings that have been used for centuries helping human beings to develop should not simply be cast aside, forgotten, or ignored as we create new ones that have no grounding in either what the Tibetans call "lineage" or what those who study knowledge organizations call "tacit knowledge."

Can the fusion of ancient wisdom teachings and Western education develop wise leaders? Only future sages will be able to answer, looking back at what happens during the rest of the twenty-first century. However, adding the pure, accurate transmission of these formerly secret "ear-whispered" Tibetan teachings to the clamorous mixture of elements in Western culture opens the possibility for a shift in the underlying Western paradigms. The contribution of the meanings and the practices could make a significant difference in leadership in the world.

NOTES

1.   Ngawang Zangpo, *Guru Rinpoche: His Life and Times* (Ithaca, NY: Snow Lion, 2002), "Guru Rinpoche Now—In Print," 89-98.

2.   For an excellent translation and explanation, see Robert Thurman, *The Tibetan Book of the Dead: The Great Book of Natural Liberation Through Understanding in the Between* (New York: Bantam Books, 1993).

3.   The main publishers of books containing Tibetan Buddhist texts and commentaries are Shambhala Publications, Wisdom Publications, Snow Lion Publications, and Rangjung Yeshe Publications, all of which have websites that recount their history and contain current lists of books. Snow Lion's website has a list of books published by others as well.

4.   See Robert Thurman, *Inner Revolution: Life, Liberty, and the Pursuit of Real Happiness* (New York: Riverhead, 1998), especially pp 34 - 36.

5.   According to His Holiness the Dalai Lama, "The Tibetan word for enlightenment is *byang chub*, which etymologically carries a sense of two different aspects. One is the purification aspect where the state represents a total elimination of all the impurities. The second aspect is the realization

of full wisdom…. The dimension of purification represents a state of total elimination of all impurity and fault, afflictions of the mind. The second aspect refers to the realization that represents the totality of the full awareness of knowledge or wisdom." http://www.lamayeshe.com/ index.php?sect=article&id=253&chid=509

6. There are a great many introductions to Tibetan Buddhist thought—perhaps hundreds. A few excellent starting places are *The Buddhism of Tibet* by H.H. the Dalai Lama, translated and edited by Jeffrey Hopkins, with Anne Klein (Ithaca, NY: Snow Lion, 1975 / 1987), *The Tibetan Book of Living and Dying* by Sogyal Rinpoche (New York: HarperCollins, 1992 / 2002) and *Joyful Wisdom: Embracing Change and Finding Freedom*, by Mingyur Rinpoche (New York: Three Rivers Press, 2009). A somewhat more thorough, yet entirely readable, overview for novices is presented in *The World of Tibetan Buddhism*, Vols 1 and 2 by Reginald Ray (Boston: Shambhala, 2000, 2001). Patrul Rinpoche's *The Words of My Perfect Teacher* (Boston: Shambhala, 1998) is a highly readable book, given that it was written in the nineteenth century, and is recommended by many Tibetan teachers. Readers interested in the relationship of Tibetan Buddhist thought with contemporary science may find H.H. the Dalai Lama's *The Universe in a Single Atom: The Convergence of Science and Spirituality* (New York: Morgan Road Books (Random House), 2005) quite helpful, along with Mingyur Rinpoche's *The Joy of Living: Unlocking the Secret and Science of Happiness* (New York: Harmony Books, 2007).

7. *Lost Horizon* by James Hilton was first published in 1933 and released in 1939 as one of the first paperbacks (New York: Pocket Books). It was made into an Oscar-winning movie in 1937, also called *Lost Horizon*.

8. Statistics on Westerners practicing Tibetan Buddhism don't seem to exist. I have estimated numbers by investigating how many people have attended major teaching given by the Dalai Lama, combined with gathering data from some of the larger international organizations. These organizations don't have global statistics either, so all totals can only be estimates.

9. Peter L. Berger and Thomas Luckmann, *The Social Construction of Reality: A Treatise in the Sociology of Knowledge* (New York: Anchor Books, 1966). Karl Mannheim, *Essays on the Sociology of Knowledge* (New York: Oxford University Press, 1923/1952). Alfred Schutz, *Collected Papers I: The Problem of Social Reality*, ed. Maurice Natanson (The Hague: Martinus Nijhoff, 1962).

10. In addition to searching on the web for specific relevant topics, a good site to develop a sense of the large number of books is http:// www.snowlionpub.com/ which has an online catalogue that includes not only their own books, but those published by many other publishers as well. Another good overview can be found at http://www.buddhanet.net/ l_books.htm, which lists and describes many websites that list Buddhist books. This same site also has a page devoted to listing a wide range of Tibetan sites: http://www.buddhanet.net/l_tibet.htm

11. See Thurman, *Inner Revolution* (Note #4) and Jeffery Paine's *Re-Enchantment: Tibetan Buddhism Comes to the West* (New York: W.W. Norton, 2004). For Max Weber's discussions of enchantment, religion, and industrialization,

see Max Weber, *The Protestant Ethic and the Spirit of Capitalism* (New York: Charles Scribner's Sons, 1958).

12. Notable among these are Rick Fields' *How the Swans Came to the Lake: A Narrative History of Buddhism in America* (Boston: Shambhala, 1981/1986/1992), Stephen Batchelor's *The Awakening of the West: The Encounter of Buddhism and Western Culture* (Berkeley, CA: Parallax Press, 1994), and Richard Hughes Seager's *Buddhism in America* (New York: Columbia University Press, 1999). Both Fields and Batchelor begin the story in ancient times, going back to the Greeks, Gnostics, early Western explorers, and continuing up to the early years of the twenty-first century. Fields devotes considerable attention to the contribution of Zen Buddhism in the twentieth century, as it was Zen that reached America in the decades before Tibetan Buddhist teachers could begin to travel. The story of Tibetan Buddhism is presented with considerable detail in the last portion of Fields' book. Batchelor quotes the 14th Dalai Lama and refers to Tibet throughout his book, which is organized by the main figures that influenced the history of Buddhism in interaction with the West. Looking specifically at Tibet, Batchelor has chapters on the key figure in the history of the four schools of Tibetan Buddhism, but anyone seeking a complete overview should use a different source, as this book focuses on selected historical figures and does not aim to provide a comprehensive history. Seager described his book and the process of writing it in a chapter titled "Buddhist Worlds in the USA: A Survey of the Territory," in Duncan Ryuken Williams and Christopher S. Queen (eds.), *American Buddhism: Methods and Findings in Recent Scholarship* (Surrey, England: Curzon Press, 1999).

13. See in particular the edited volumes of scholarly articles of Nalini Bhushan, Jay L. Garfield, and Abraham Zablocki (eds.), *TransBuddhism: Transmission, Translation, Transformation* (Amherst, MA: University of Massachusetts Press, 2009); Charles S. Prebish and Kenneth K. Tanaka (eds.), *The Faces of Buddhism in America* (Berkeley, CA: University of California Press, 1998); and Williams and Queen (eds.), *American Buddhism*.

14. For Buddhism in the prisons, see chapter by Constance Kassor, in *TransBuddhism*. For perspectives on women, see Rita M. Gross, "Helping the Iron Bird Fly: Western Buddhist Women and Issues of Authority in the Late 1990s." For perspectives on gay Buddhists, see Roger Corless, "Coming out in the *Sangha*: Queer Community in Buddhist America," in *Faces of Buddhism*. For Buddhism in academia, see Charles S. Prebish, "The Academic Study of Buddhism in America: A Silent *Sangha*," Robert E. Goss, "Buddhist Studies at Naropa: Sectarian or Academic?" and Seager, "Buddhist Worlds in the USA" and the Appendxes which list dissertations and theses on American Buddhism and on topics related to Buddhism, in Williams and Queen (eds.), *American Buddhism*.

15. Seager, "Buddhist Worlds in the USA".

16. Ibid., 248.

17. There are various different ways of understanding how Buddhism describes the paths through life towards wisdom; readers interested in the history of Buddhism and in understanding its various schools should

not rely on this brief approximation. Even within the Tibetan Vajrayana perspective there are numerous overviews that will differ, depending upon the specific tradition and practices that the author follows. What I present in this introduction is based on the descriptions of Reginald Ray, in his two-volume work, *The World of Tibetan Buddhism, I. Indestructible Truth: The Living Spirituality of Tibetan Buddhism* (Boston: Shambhala, 2000) and *II. Secret of the Vajra World—The Tantric Buddhism of Tibet* (Boston: Shambhala, 2001). See especially pp. 66-68 of the latter for an overview of the Tibetan perspective on the three yanas. Ray also addresses this topics through the words of Tibetan major teachers in his book *In the Presence of Masters: Wisdom from 30 Contemporary Tibetan Buddhist Teachers* (Boston: Shambhala Publications, 2004), pp. 14-21. Other useful sources on the web include the Berzin Archive http://www.berzinarchives.com, Rigpa Wiki http://www.rigpawiki.org, and http://www.kagyuoffice.org/buddhism.3vehicles.html which are reliable online resources for three particular teaching traditions within Tibetan Buddhism.

18. http://www.rigpawiki.org/index.php?title=Emptiness

19. See Ray, *Secret of the Vajra World*, 98-101.

20. See Janice D. Willis, *Enlightened Beings: Life Stories from the Ganden Oral Tradition* (Boston: Wisdom Publications, 1995).

21. See Note #4.

22. Charles Horton Cooley, *Human Nature and the Social Order* (New York: Scribner's, 1902), George Herbert Mead, *Mind, Self, and Society* (Chicago: University of Chicago Press, 1934).

23. *Social Construction of Reality*; Mannheim, *Essays on the Sociology of Knowledge*; Schutz, *Collected Papers I: The Problem of Social Reality.*

24. Thurman, *Inner Revolution.*

25. Peter Berger, Brigitte Berger, and Hansfried Kellner, *The Homeless Mind: Modernization and Consciousness* (New York: Vintage Books, 1973).

26. Ibid., 9.

27. Ibid., 26-35. The phrases are in italics here because they are in italics in the original source.

28. Several good source of information about Tibet can be found on the Internet. Among the most comprehensive are http://www.tibetnetwork.org/tibet-at-a-glance/ and http://www.tibet.net/en/index.php

29. See *Buddhism in Contemporary Tibet*, edited by Melvyn Goldstein and Matthew Kapstein (Berkeley: University of California Press, 1998) and for current news, websites like www.tibetcustom.com, http://dalailama.com/, and http://www.highpeakspureearth.com/, which "provides insightful commentary on Tibet related news and issues and provides translations from writings in Tibetan and Chinese posted on blogs from Tibet and the People's Republic of China." One such teacher was Khenpo Jigme Phuntsok (1933 - 2004).

30. The source of this information is the website of the Office of the Dalai Lama   http://www.dalailama.com/teachings/kalachakra-initiations   which

lists the dates, locations, and number of people that attended each Kalachakra ceremony.

31.   Robert Thurman, *Why the Dalai Lama Matters* (New York: Atria Books, 2008), 60.

32.   Jeffery Paine's *Re-Enchantment* (Note #11) is a key source for appreciating the contributions of these two early leaders.

33.   This is not intended to diminish the importance of many others who are not addressed in this book, like Tharthang Tulku, Gyatrul Rinpoche, or scholars who found positions in U.S. universities. They too can be seen as entrepreneurial leaders, but I was not able to include all whom I would have liked to include.

34.   See The Dalai Lama and Laurens van den Muyzenberg's, *The Leader's Way* (London: Nicholas Brealey Publishing Ltd, 2008) for one book that focuses on leadership and Tibetan Buddhism. However, it does not address the Dalai Lama himself *as a leader*, nor does it encompass the third turning teachings. Other recent books on Buddhism and business or work, are Lloyd Field's *Business and the Buddha: Doing Well by Doing Good* (Boston: Wisdom Publications, 2007), Michael Carroll's *Awake at Work: 35 Practical Buddhist Principles for Discovering Clarity and Balance in the Midst of Work's Chaos* (Boston: Shambhala Publications, 2004/2011) and *The Mindful Leader* (Boston: Shambhala Publication, 2007); and Michael Chaskalson's, *The Mindful Workplace: Developing Resilient Individuals and Resonant Organizations with MBSR* (Malden, MA: Wiley-Blackwell, 2011).

Readers interested in the broader implications of leadership for spirituality and vice versa can read a number of recent publications in this area. A classic is Ian Mitroff and Elizabeth Denton's *A Spiritual Audit of Corporate America: A Hard Look at Spirituality, Religion, and Values in the Workplace* (San Francisco: Jossey Bass, 1999). Western scholarly perspectives on spirituality and the workplace were discussed by a variety of scholars in Jerry Biberman and Len Tischler's (eds.) book *Spirituality in Business: Theory, Practice, and Future Directions* (New York: Palgrave Macmillan, 2008). Viewed collectively, the authors in their book made a strong case for growing interest in the West in spirituality, both in general and in the workplace. In the context of scholarly studies of spirituality in the workplace, researchers have generally been focused on what happens at the individual level (not on groups or organizations as a whole) and on ways that individuals have experienced transcendence and interdependence in life within or because of what they did at work. With regard to leadership and spirituality, scholars have focused on the ways by which leaders "create vision and value congruence across the strategic, empowered team, and individual levels and, ultimately ... foster higher levels of organizational commitment and productivity." (See Louis W. Fry, "Toward a Theory of Spiritual Leadership," *The Leadership Quarterly*, 14 (2003): 693.)

35.   See Thurman, *Inner Revolution*.

36.   There is a vast amount of scholarship about leadership theory, as well as about the practical aspects of leadership development, so it would be impossible to address it fully in an endnote. For readers who are interested

but who are not familiar with the key authors, a good summary of the current status of leadership theory is *The Bass Handbook of Leadership: Theory, Research, and Managerial Applications* by Bernard M. Bass and Ruth Bass, based on Stogdill's original work in the 1970s (New York: Free Press, 2008).

37. See Robert Kegan, *In Over Our Heads: The Mental Demands of Modern Life.* (Cambridge, MA: Harvard University Press, 1994) and Susan Cook-Greuter, "Making the Case for a Developmental Perspective," *Industrial and Commercial Training* 36, no. 7 (2004): 1-10. William Torbert has made major contributions in this area, and most of his books can be downloaded in their entirety from the web at http://escholarship.bc.edu/william_torbert/ including his 1987 book *Managing the Corporate Dream: Restructuring for Long-Term Success* Homewood, IL: Dow-Jones Irwin), which outlined a full series of developmental stages for managers.

38. See Peter Senge, *The Fifth Discipline: The Art and Practice of the Learning Organization* (New York: Doubleday, 1990/1994); Peter Senge, C. Otto Scharmer, Joseph Jaworkski, and Betty Sue Flowers, *Presence: Human Purpose and the Field of the Future* (Cambridge, MA: Society for Organizational Learning, 2004).

39. Robert Rosenthal and Lenore Jacobson, *Pygmalion in the Classroom: Teacher Expectation and Pupils' Intellectual Development* (New York: Holt, Rinehart & Winston, 1968).

40. As Paul Ekman has pointed out in his article "Darwin's Compassionate View of Human Nature" (*JAMA.* 2010;303(6):557-558 (doi:10.1001/jama.2010.101)), there is another side of Darwin from the one generally known. He wrote that "Darwin proposed that natural selection would favor the occurrence of compassion" in his book *The Descent of Man, and Selection in Relation to Sex.* Not only this, but Darwin referred to people gradually developing sympathy for "all sentient beings"—the same phrase used in Tibetan Buddhism, which is not a phrase known to have been used elsewhere by other spiritual traditions.

41. See http://www.greenleaf.org/ which lists Greenleaf's articles and books, as well as those written about this approach and its influence in the various domains of leadership. See also Robert K Greenleaf, *On Becoming a Servant-Leader* (San Francisco: Jossey-Bass Publishers, 1996).

42. The Dalai Lama, *Ethics for the New Millennium* (NY: Penguin Putnam, 1999).

43. See Prayer of Kuntuzangpo: http://www.dharmamedia.org/media/kagyu/drigung/general/prayer_of_kuntuzangpo/Prayer_of_Kuntuzangpo.pdf

44. For a fascinating account of Tibetan history, see Thomas Laird, *The Story of Tibet: Conversations with the Dalai Lama* (New York: Grove / Atlantic, 2006).

45. For example, see anything by Longchen Rabjam (written in the 14th century), and, in particular, *The Precious Treasury of the Basic Space of Phenomena* (Junction City, CA: Padma Publishing, 2003). An explanation by the Dalai Lama of one of Longchen Rabjam's texts is in The Dalai Lama, *Mind in Comfort and Ease: The Vision of Enlightenment in the Great Perfection* (Boston: Wisdom Publications, 2007).

46. See particularly Ikujiru Nonaka and Hirotaka Takeuchi's groundbreaking book *The Knowledge Creating Company* (New York: Oxford University Press, 1995).

47. Margaret Wheatley, *Leadership and the New Science: Discovering Order in a Chaotic World* (San Francisco, CA: Berrett-Koehler Publishers, 1999/2006); Senge, *Fifth Discipline.*

48. Joanna Macy, *Mutual Causality in Buddhism and General Systems Theory* (Albany, NY: SUNY, 1991).

49. Ibid.

50. Sogyal Rinpoche, *The Future of Buddhism* (London: Rider, An Imprint of Random House, 2002), 8.

51. Kenneth Liberman, *Dialectical Practice In Tibetan Philosophical Culture* (New York: Rowan and Littlefield, 2004).

52. Kegan, *In Over Our Heads*; Torbert, *Managing the Corporate Dream* (see note #37).

SECTION I

LEADERSHIP: TIBETAN BUDDHISM AS A SOURCE FOR NEW PERSPECTIVES

> *… benevolent and skillful social action can be a path toward enlightenment. It is important that we do not become discouraged and that we shoulder our responsibility for this world and its future generations with great determination and foresight[1]*
>
> —HH the 14th Dalai Lama

This section explores the unique contributions of His Holiness the 14th Dalai Lama as a leader, the concept of a *bodhisattva* (what it means and what it brings to leadership theory) and the central importance of the feminine principle in Tibetan Buddhism, as represented by the *dakini*, focused on its implications for leadership in today's world. While there are many books on the Dalai Lama, very few consider his development and contributions as a leader, and none, to my knowledge, have examined the role of the feminine principle in the context of leadership.

The section opens with a short vignette by **Huston Smith**, incomparable story-teller of the essence of all religions, who was one of the first Western scholars to meet the Dalai Lama, in 1964. He is one of the most respected scholars of religion alive today and is the author of 14 books, including his best-selling first book *The World's Religions*, which has sold over 2½ million copies.[2] This short chapter is included as important history in the shaping of the Dalai Lama's perspectives: we now know how significant meetings with scientists and scholars have been in the develop-

Inner Peace—Global Impact: Tibetan Buddhism, Leadership, and Work, pp. 29–31
Copyright © 2012 by Information Age Publishing
29

ment of his thinking and in the way he has chosen to influence public thought worldwide. Readers who wish to learn more about the Dalai Lama's initiatives in this arena can read his book *The Universe in a Single Atom: The Convergence of Science and Spirituality*.[3] Most of his contact with Western scientists has been arranged through an organization that was developed entirely for this purpose, known as *Mind and Life*.[4] Through Dr. Smith's story, readers can see the importance he accords to the Dalai Lama's humility and his freedom of mind.

For a more detailed discussion of the 14th Dalai Lama as a leader, I interviewed **Thupten Jinpa**, the Dalai Lama's long-time English translator. This chapter addresses the uniqueness of the way that His Holiness has developed his role as both a secular and spiritual leader on a global scale. Dr. Jinpa is highly qualified for presenting this topic, as he has had a close relationship with His Holiness for over 25 years and is a noted scholar with a PhD from Cambridge University, as well as an advanced Tibetan monastic degree called the *geshe lharampa*, which takes 20 years of study, concluded by a rigorous examination process. Dr. Jinpa's analysis shows the importance of four main themes in the Dalai Lama's presence as a leader: (1) how he embodies compassion, (2) his understanding of the interdependence of all things as central to both Buddhist thought and practical leadership, (3) his long-time commitment to secular ethics as being critical for the West, and (4) his humility (as Dr. Smith also pointed out) and his focus on "self-examination" by leaders—something many leaders omit. The chapter offers a personal commentary on the Dalai Lama as a leader from one who has been present at the vast majority of his important speeches and teachings in the West, and grounds this in Dr. Jinpa's analysis of the differences between traditional Tibetan Buddhist education and Western education.

To introduce the pivotal role of the feminine principle in Tibetan Buddhism and its implications for Western leaders, I invited **Judith Simmer-Brown**, who is a professor in the religious studies department at Naropa University and the author of the foremost book on the *dakini* principle that is available in English.[5] This book is a thorough scholarly presentation grounded in decades of personal experience, as Dr. Simmer-Brown is an *acharya*—a designated senior teacher of Tibetan Buddhism. She brings both spiritual authority and scholarship to her topic. Few Westerners are familiar with the importance of the feminine (the dakini) in Vajrayana Buddhist thought and practice. While one sees men dominating leadership historically in Tibet, the dakini is essential for enlightenment, and a woman (Yeshe Tsogyal) was a central figure in conveying the ancient teachings in a way that can be accessed in today's world. The chapter presents a concept not widely known in Western scholarship—that of *nonconceptual* *wisdom*—as being central to the potential contribution of the feminine principle to leadership.

The section closes with a chapter that I wrote about the possibility of integrating mind training and embodied learning into leadership development, using case studies of management development nourished by Buddhist practice and embodied learning. In contrast with Western notions that meditation involves "emptying" or "quieting" the mind, the traditions of mind training bring the practitioner into lively contact with whatever is actually happening, incorporating ethical training as well. This chapter is a scholarly exploration of the implications of the principles and practices of *lojong* (mind training) for the development of leaders, both Buddhist and non-Buddhist.

NOTES

1. His Holiness The 14th Dalai Lama, foreword to Robert Thurman, *Inner Revolution: Life, Liberty, and the Pursuit of Real Happiness* (New York: Riverhead Books, 1998), xiv.
2. See the following books, among others, for which I have listed earlier editions. Most have been reissued many times. Huston Smith: *The Religions of Man* (New York: Harper & Row, 1958), *Beyond the Post-Modern Mind* (New York: Crossroad, 1982), *Forgotten Truth: The Common Vision of the World's Religions* (New York: Harper & Row, 1985, 1976; HarperSanFrancisco, 1992); *Why Religion Matters: The Fate of the Human Spirit in an Age of Disbelief* (New York: HarperCollins, 2001), *The Way Things Are: Conversations with Huston Smith on the Spiritual Life* (Berkeley: University of California Press, 2003), *Buddhism: A Concise Introduction* (New York: HarperSanFrancisco, 2004) and Huston Smith / Jeffery Paine, *Tales of Wonder: Adventures Chasing the Divine, An Autobiography* (New York: HarperOne/HarperCollins Publishers, 2009).
3. His Holiness The 14th Dalai Lama, *The Universe in a Single Atom: The Convergence of Science and Spirituality* (New York: Morgan Road Books, 2005).
4. The history of the Mind and Life organizations and descriptions of its many conferences are described thoroughly on the web at www.mindandlife.org
5. *Dakini's Warm Breath: The Feminine Principle in Tibetan Buddhism* (Boston: Shambala, 2001).

CHAPTER 2

THE DALAI LAMA AND THE DEVELOPMENT OF BUDDHISM IN THE WEST[1]

Huston Smith

Excerpted with permission from *Tales of Wonder, Adventures Chasing the Divine, an Autobiography* (Harper). Copyright © 2009 by Huston Smith.

Inner Peace—Global Impact:Tibetan Buddhism, Leadership, and Work, pp. 33–36
Copyright © 2012 by Information Age Publishing

INTRODUCTION

Huston Smith, noted scholar of philosophy and religious studies, was one of the first Westerners to meet the 14th Dalai Lama, in 1964, only 5 years after he left Tibet. Here he reflects on this first meeting and their long friendship. I chose to open the book with this brief piece as it conveys an important perspective on both the Dalai Lama himself and the early moments of its spread to the West.

I experienced His Holiness the Dalai Lama as the most complete human being I have known. Venerated in Tibet as practically a god, the Dalai Lama shows me rather what a fully developed human being can be. He is wise and well-informed about what is going on in the world, but what makes him unique in my experience is that, loaded as he is with these virtues, when we conversed he came across as just another human being that I was talking with. No airs, no flares—just another down-to-earth human being I happen to be hanging out with.

His humility makes me humble, and I will add one other human trait. He was (and is) a superb diplomat and statesman. He has offered to give his country, Tibet, to the Chinese with only one condition attached: that its people be allowed to retain their language, their religion, and their customs. I find these terms astoundingly generous, but the Chinese will not accede to them. They are demanding not only that the land of Tibet be theirs; they are demanding that the Tibetan *people* become Chinese. What self-respecting human being would agree to that? It would amount to giving up one's identity—the person that one is.

When I met him in 1964 in Dharamsala, I expressed my sympathy for the Tibetan people and proposed that he visit America. He said that I was the first person to make that suggestion. I could not but be impressed: here was someone raised like a king and venerated like a god, yet he exhibited not the faintest trace of egotism.

We conversed through a translator, but after ten minutes as I rose to leave, he mumbled to himself in English, "I must decide what is important. Decide now." Then he said to me, "Please, would I sit down again, and could I stay longer?" It was due to a misunderstanding. On my calling card was Massachusetts Institute of Technology, and since I taught at MIT, the Dalai Lama assumed I must be a scientist. Since his arrival in the modern world only a few short years before, the new scientific theories he was hearing about, from DNA to the big bang, had intrigued him. Did they disprove Buddhism, or did they validate it? Surely a professor from MIT could answer his questions. Fortunately I had recently heard the Harvard astrophysicist Harlow Shapley lecture on the big bang, on how the universe expands and contracts—which suggests there may have been more than one big bang. The Dalai Lama concurred: "It's bang bang bang."

From my explanation of DNA, he concluded that DNA was compatible with Buddhist reincarnation. "But if the words of the Buddha and the findings of modern science contradict each other," the Dalai Lama added, "the former has to go." He was not setting science above religion, but expressing his conviction that the two are allies, different roads to one reality. In *The Universe in a Single Atom: The Convergence of Science and Spirituality*[2] he would later write: "When I count my teachers of science, I include Huston Smith among them." I wish that he had had that day a better, a more MIT-ish, MIT teacher.

That quiet afternoon in Dharamsala began a lifelong friendship. Among many cherished memories I particularly remember the time I arranged for him to speak at Syracuse. Someone in the audience asked him, "What should I do with my uncontrollable anger?" and the Dalai Lama sang out in English, "Control it." Another questioner kept goading him to assert Buddhism's superiority over Christianity. The Dalai Lama finally stopped the pest: "If I say anything against the Lord Jesus, the Buddha will scold me." Later, in Bodh Gaya, my student Phil Novak (later my coauthor of *Buddhism: A Concise Introduction*) asked the Dalai Lama to explain how rebirth works. Phil knew the usual metaphors of one candle flame lit from another or the apple seed that grows into a new apple tree, but he was still perplexed, saying, "We're not candles or trees, we're human beings." After reflecting a moment, the Dalai Lama answered, "Yes, something that might be called a self does continue from lifetime to lifetime, but it is so different from what we usually mean by self that it is better not to speak of it."

As I listened, I was reminded of the story of the man who asked the Buddha, "Is there no self?" When the Buddha gave no answer, the man exclaimed, "So there is a self!" to which again the Buddha made no reply. Later the Buddha's attendant asked him, "You always say there is no self. Why did you not answer the man?" The Buddha explained that the man had not wanted to heal himself or to help anyone but merely to form a theory. Helping and healing—not hypothesis and beliefs—were the Buddha's concerns as they have been the Dalai Lama's. Listening to him in Bodh Gaya, I felt I was not only at the place of the Buddha, but almost in his presence as well.

Back then my academic colleagues considered my interest in Buddhism odd and obsolete, as if I had taken up, say, blacksmithing. Today every other person I know is, if not a Buddhist himself, someone whose sister or first cousin is. Why has Buddhism become so popular in America? The short answer: because it appeals to one's own experience, not dogma, and because it offers practical help. I used to wonder why Buddhism had no key poetic text the way Hinduism has the Bhagavad Gita and Taoism the Tao Te Ching. Then I realized that Buddhism deals less in poetic metaphors than in practical methods. And the starting point of those methods (as well as their end point) is your own mind.

When I think of freedom, or of the mind and its power, I think of the Dalai Lama at the precise moment he left Tibet. Behind him were the mountains of his homeland and everything he knew, now forever closed to him; before him lay the unknown horizon, where everything would be unaccustomed and unfamiliar. In his perilous escape he could bring with him nothing but his thoughts; he had nothing to offer the unknown world except his thoughts. Thoughts are intangible, ephemeral—as delicate as the flower the Buddha held out to his disciple. Yet from that flower, or rather from the Dalai Lama's thoughts, almost inconceivably, has arisen a whole new world of Buddhism in the West. As Daisetsu Suzuki said to me, "Is that fragile?"

NOTES

1. This chapter is based largely on selections from Huston Smith's autobiography, reprinted with his permission. Huston Smith/Jeffery Paine, *Tales of Wonder: Adventures Chasing the Divine, An Autobiography* (New York: Harper-One/HarperCollins Publishers, 2009).

2. His Holiness The Dalai Lama, *The Universe in a Single Atom: The Convergence of Science and Spirituality* (New York: Morgan Road Books, 2005).

CHAPTER 3

THE FUNDAMENTAL EQUALITY
OF ALL OF US:
THE FOURTEENTH DALAI LAMA
AS A GLOBAL LEADER

An Interview With Geshe Thupten Jinpa

Kathryn Goldman Schuyler

Inner Peace—Global Impact: Tibetan Buddhism, Leadership, and Work, pp. 37–46
Copyright © 2012 by Information Age Publishing

Thupten Jinpa: There is no doubt that His Holiness the Dalai Lama of Tibet is one of the most well-known global figures of our time. With his characteristic red robe, shaven head, and bespectacled smiling face, the image of the Dalai Lama is familiar to all who have taken interest in the world beyond their own immediate circle.

Now, for many, the Dalai Lama is the leader of the Tibetan people, a revered figure of the Buddhist world; for many others, he is a champion of peace and human rights; for millions perhaps, the Dalai Lama simply represents the best of human conscience. Yet, not many see the nitty-gritty side of this person's everyday struggle—his work in leading the Tibetan people to rise to the existential threat they continue to face, exerting leadership within his own monastic community, leading the movement to modernize the classical education system of the monasteries, especially by bringing in modern science, being an example to the younger generation of his people, and bearing the standard for the value that his Tibetan culture cherishes. In addition to all this are the global missions that he has set for himself in two specific areas: the promotion of fundamental human values through what he calls a "secular approach to ethics" and promotion of greater harmony and understanding among the world's great religions. Together with his dedication to the cause of safeguarding the welfare of the Tibetan people and their ancient civilization, the Dalai Lama calls these "the three commitments" of his life.

It is understandable that many people see only the joyful and truly happy face of the Dalai Lama, so loved by millions across the world. But the real human side of him, the one where he gets up early in the morning, spends his entire life working, talking, writing, thinking, traveling, contemplating the fate of our world, this is the part not many have the chance to see and appreciate. I have had the honor to serve the Dalai Lama as his principal translator now for over twenty-five years, accompanying him on countless travels across the world, joining him in his numerous ongoing conversations with scientists and thinkers from various academic disciplines as well as professions, and assisting him on many of his major writing projects. The profile of the person that has come to emerge is that of a truly remarkable man by any known standards.

One of the central themes that have come to occupy the Dalai Lama's view of the world is the deepening of his recognition of the principle of interdependence, which is being made increasingly stark as our world becomes more and more intertwined. So this understanding of the interconnectedness of everything is, if you will, the philosophical cornerstone of the Dalai Lama's worldview. This concept underpins his understanding of the importance of the natural environment, the workings of today's global economy, as well as the social and political issues of our time, including even the reforms that are required on the part of his own

Tibetan tradition to survive and thrive in today's increasingly global world. Bringing this understanding of deep interdependence to every area is a key aspect of the way in which the Dalai Lama approaches everything in life and the world, at all levels. Because of this philosophical outlook, the Dalai Lama came to recognize the critical importance of ecology at a very early stage. Right from his first visit to the West in 1973, he began speaking forcefully on the issue.

I think the Dalai Lama has made a very significant contribution to the world in raising awareness of the principle of interdependence as an integral part of one's worldview. Primarily through his travels and his writings, the Dalai Lama has succeeded in bringing this concept of interdependence to the forefront of people's thinking. Over and over again, he has been pointing to the truth of this, how something happens here and the repercussions are felt thousands and thousands of miles away.

Another key thing that the Dalai Lama has brought to the global stage is the demonstration of the power of human compassion. Today if compassion as a principle is increasingly being accepted as a social norm and value that must not only be cherished, but also be a necessary part of our method of dealing with conflicts, this is thanks largely to the Dalai Lama's constant advocacy of the principle. An obvious consequence of this principle of compassion is a way of dealing with problems in which one never loses sight of the humanity of the person one is dealing with. This is something that he has done primarily through his own personal example. This can be seen particularly in his interactions with the Chinese Communist authorities, regarding the resolution of the Tibetan situation. He always distinguishes between what people do and the people themselves; he never negatively judges the person, but just the action. He may disapprove of an action, yet maintain compassion for the individual. This perspective always leaves room for some possibility of correction on the part of the person— be they criminal or whatever—you allow yourself to see the perspective of that person *as a human being* while maintaining a strong moral stand on the action that has been done. It's very difficult. He brings this out in *Ethics for the New Millennium*, when he says that we do bad things and then we regret it, but we're not going to kill ourselves because of that.[1] We're able somehow to forgive ourselves, and there we're able to distinguish between "you as a person" and "the wrong thing that you have done." It is this ability to distinguish between you as a person and the actions that you have done that makes it possible for you to forgive yourself.

Kathryn Goldman Schuyler: and many people don't ...

Thupten Jinpa: ... yes, but this is what is needed when you relate to others. In a sense what this principle of compassion states is that one should: "always treat human beings as ends in themselves and not as means to an end." This is somewhat similar to the Kantian idea, but in His Holiness' language, it is compassion. You recognize the humanity of the person. You disapprove of the action, and you make judgments upon the action. That's a core aspect of who he is as a leader.

The other key quality that he brings is a significant degree of self-examination. This is what is lacking in many modern leaders. Many modern leaders are entirely focused on others and outside forces, and when you don't have this self-examining kind of critical perspective, then you open yourself to grand delusions, whereas if you have this self-critical kind of appraisal, then in a sense it protects you from being deluded.

The idea is that you need to be able to guard your speech when you are talking in public, and you should also be able to guard your thoughts. So a self-critical perspective becomes very important. This is why, if you look at His Holiness, despite this tremendous adoration from the Buddhist world, particularly the Tibetans, and also despite admiration from millions of people, on a personal level he is very humble. There is no inflated ego problem there. What makes that possible?

Kathryn Goldman Schuyler: That's so important. In the leadership literature on ethics, we see that so many leaders have become corrupted who had been viewed as excellent and then do things because they act as though they felt entitled.

Thupten Jinpa: That's why among the various world leaders, His Holiness was very impressed by Havel and Carter.[2] The reason is very simple. I asked him once "what is so wonderful about these leaders?" He said that despite being world leaders, on a personal level they are very humble. When he first visited Havel's place he saw that the president was making his own tea. There were no servants running around. President Carter was the same. He was doing carpentry, and his wife and he were making their own tea in the cup, and that really impressed His Holiness. Human beings are in some senses quite weak. Power and adoration can lead to addiction to power. In actual fact, power is not real; power is acquired when people accord you a certain respect, and so you need leaders who are at least more self-aware thank others. I think this is another very important aspect of the Dalai Lama as a leader.

Along with it comes a sense of humility. One of the key things that His Holiness brings up in his general public talks is that at a fundamental level we are all equal. This is very important for him, so that he knows that all differences among people are contingent. They are all due to circumstances. At the fundamental level, when everything is stripped down, everybody's the same. We all want to be happy, we all wish to overcome suffering, and however that may translate, essentially "we are all same." This belief in the absolute equality of beings when it comes to our fundamental human nature is a very important part of his leadership and who he is.

One of the things that people find amazing about the Dalai Lama is that when they meet him, he makes them feel valued and that they matter. I've worked for His Holiness for almost a quarter of a century now, and one thing that is amazing is that how he engages with a person really depends upon the level of engagement on the part of the other, not on who they are or what they do.

One of the problems is that often people in a position of power and leadership end up believing that somehow they are intrinsically superior. The Dalai Lama's emphasis on the notion of the fundamental equality is grounded in his recognition that if you are in a leadership position, you need to accept this position with a sense of gratitude—not a sense of entitlement, and once you've taken it with a sense of gratitude then you are much more likely to use power more responsibly. If you take it as an entitlement, then you don't really feel that you are accountable to others. You then might use your position in any way that satisfies your need and gratification. So these differing attitudes have very different consequences. So these are the things that we can see about the Dalai Lama's approach to leadership, from the way in which he himself acts as a leader and the kind of ideas that he brings to the table.

Kathryn Goldman Schuyler: His Holiness the 14th Dalai Lama has developed a thoroughly unique role in the world as a secular and spiritual leader on a global scale. I'd be very interested in how he's developed this.

Thupten Jinpa: I don't think that he developed it consciously. In many ways, it's been an organic process, coming from his dedication to the causes he has been championing. There's a consistency in his message, and he has been doing it since the 1970s, you know, when he first started traveling internationally. In addition to the basic sameness of human beings and the importance of recognizing our interdependence with our environment, he has also focused on promoting basic human values and a spirituality that is not tied to religion.

In the initial days he didn't call it "secular ethics," but in essence, that is what it is, and over time the Dalai Lama has come to use to refer to this task as the promotion of fundamental human values through a secular approach to ethics. Through this the Dalai Lama was looking for a way to promote and discourse on these values in a language that is universal and inclusive, but at the same that does not presuppose any kind of religious basis or dogma. That is one of the consistent messages that he has been propagating wherever he went. Also, right from the beginning he was very quick to realize that promoting understanding across the different traditions is an important and urgent task, so he took a very active role in this through personal friendships with the previous Pope, His Holiness John

Paul II. In different parts of the world, he was always trying to participate in a local interfaith gathering, so that on the local level the public would come to value forums where people from different faiths sit together and pray together.

He has been very consistent from the beginning throughout all of his travels. On top of that, he has been connecting his promotion of secular ethics to his dialog with scientists, so that one could use scientific findings as a way of promoting the benefits of human values. So although dialog with scientists has an intellectual dimension, there is also a very strong practical ethical dimension, which is to seek ways in which basic fundamental human values can be promoted in a secular manner. Often when scientists (who in many cases are not even spiritual people) sit down with him, they feel at a visceral level how he truly cares. They feel how he's thinking long term and that for him the ultimate imperative is to do good —and always bring compassion as the core of one's motivation.

Over time the words *peace* and *compassion* have become very closely identified with His Holiness, so he's really seen as someone who represents compassion in his life. When we look at the way in which he talks about the oppression the Tibetan people have faced under the Chinese, the way in which he tries to seek a solution through negotiation, and the way in which even he uses the language, like "Chinese brothers and sisters," I think he has come to be personally associated with compassion not only as someone who talks about it, but someone who actually embodies it and lives it. Whatever their personal attitude toward a particular religion, or toward religion in general, most educated people aspire for peace, are quite fed up with the war and conflict, and would like to believe in humanity—the goodness of humanity—so I think that when they see someone like His Holiness, it makes them encouraged and empowered.

I remember several years ago His Holiness was in Vancouver, and Archbishop Desmond Tutu introduced him at a very large public talk.[3] Archbishop Tutu said something very moving as part of his introduction; he said "You know, one of the reasons people love the Dalai Lama so much is because he makes them feel proud because he's one of us— another human being." That, I think, captures what a lot of people feel. They see in His Holiness a kind of embodiment of something that is good in humanity—and looking at his example and listening to him makes people keep their faith in humanity. People would like to keep their faith in humanity! These are probably the factors that over time made His Holiness come to assume this position globally.

Kathryn Goldman Schuyler: What do you think causes people to feel that he is truly "His Holiness"—that you are happy that he is part of this same humanity—as you were saying? What is it that people pick up or sense about him?

Thupten Jinpa: I think there are several things. One is that despite all his international fame and stature, when people have a chance to interact with him, they see that he's quite humble on a personal level. He's very approachable and down to earth; he doesn't have an attitude of being "holier than thou." Also he has a sense of humor: he's a genuinely happy person, despite all the things that have happened to his people, in his own personal life as a refugee, and having to constantly deal with problems of the Tibetan people. At a fundamental level, anyone who has a chance to interact with him comes out feeling that "here is a happy person." I think that is probably an important factor.

Also, His Holiness is genuinely compassionate. You feel that. There is hardly any trace of bitterness in him. At the same time he can be firm when he needs to be. You don't see this combination often in people, because generally if you find someone who is quite disciplined, along with that comes a sense of purity and a certain intolerance toward people who they see as falling beneath their standards. What seem to be for many people contradictory characteristics, you see in the Dalai Lama without any conflict. He's also very warm. You feel in his presence warmth and genuineness that people find very attractive. He doesn't pretend. So there's an authenticity, and the level of integrity of His Holiness is quite impressive. You don't often see well-known people on the international stage who have that level of integrity. So there's all of this, and then when you have a chance to interact with him, you don't feel there's the tension of a person who's trying to juggle all of these factors to try to impress people and make himself look good. He's just himself. That kind of sense of ease and freedom, integrity, joy, compassion, warmth, and genuineness is what makes people very drawn to him— because most of us would like to be like this.

Kathryn Goldman Schuyler: Many of us practice for many decades without feeling like we're like that! How do you see who he is and his values being rooted in Tibetan thought or practice?

Thupten Jinpa: There is no doubt that a lot of what we see in him comes from his Tibetan cultural upbringing. He attributes a lot of this to his good fortune in having a very compassionate mother, who not only took good care of her children but whenever the opportunity arose, never failed to show compassion for others, strangers, and especially beggars and the more unfortunate people. He attributes a lot of that to her, but I think that his optimism and general compassionate stance vis-a-vis the world and others come from his traditional Buddhist upbringing and a deep engagement with his classical Buddhist philosophical heritage.

We shouldn't forget that his educational upbringing is that of classical Buddhist training, part of which involves not only intellectually studying and understanding, but integrating them and embodying them in one's very person. Many of the philosophies that he has engaged with include a deep recognition of the interdependent nature of reality and the transient nature of things. In the cause-and-effect chain, if we do not want certain types of consequences, then the stage to intervene is when things are at their stage of initial causation- that is when the conditions are beginning to come together. Once all the conditions have come together and the events have moved to a point of explosion, there is then not much one can do to prevent the outcome. These are all typically classical Buddhist philosophical orientations. From a very young age he was trained in this, and these must exert a very powerful influence on his character and the whole world-view with which he deals with the world.

Kathryn Goldman Schuyler: Since you have experienced both Western and Tibetan Buddhist higher education, how would you describe the difference for people who don't know those traditions? ... the way that it becomes so much part of the person?[4]

Thupten Jinpa: If you compare someone who's brought up in a conventional contemporary system, versus someone like the Dalai Lama, who was brought up in a classical monastic education, the main difference is that in the contemporary education system the whole emphasis is on the development of the rational part of the human brain and acquisition of knowledge and information, much of which is technical. Very little attention is paid to what one would call the development of the character of the individual on the basis of being exposed to the more ethical part of the training.

Another important difference is that in the contemporary modern educational system, there is no concept of contemplative practice as being part of one's educational upbringing, so even when something like ethics is taught, it's taught purely as an academic subject. "How do we understand such-and-such is a good act, or such-and-such is a wrong act? How do we differentiate between the two?" Whereas in the classical monastic education system, alongside an intellectual discourse on ethics, there are contemplative practices aimed specifically at the development of the character of the individual: cultivating greater compassion, awareness, and mindfulness in one's everyday life. Contemplation is used to deepen one's appreciation of the dynamics of cause and effect, in addition to intellectually mastering the concepts. In the classical monastic education there are contemplative practices, sometimes referred to as meditation, which allow the individual over a long period of time to integrate the knowledge, so that it becomes part of the nature of that individual. I think these are the main differences that we find between a typical contemporary education versus the kind of education the Dalai Lama has received.

Kathryn Goldman Schuyler: As a leader in the world and doing practice, what might be the range of time that His Holiness devotes to such contemplative practice?

Thupten Jinpa: He spends on average about 4 to 5 hours a day: about 3 to 4 hours in the morning when he gets up at 3:30 a.m. and then another hour in the evening before he goes to bed. These are formal sitting silent meditations. It depends from individual to individual, but most Tibetan Buddhist practitioners—the serious ones—will have somewhere in the range of half an hour to 2 hours a day.

Kathryn Goldman Schuyler: In closing, let's return to his belief in the fundamental equality of beings, and how it is the ground for his focus on ethics and the environment....

Thupten Jinpa: If you look at the way that he articulates his approach to secular ethics, there is just no difference between one's self and others. He recognizes the fundamental equality of one's self and others at the most fundamental level, which is the aspiration for happiness and the wish to overcome suffering. He sees that recognition at a very gut level, not just at the intellectual level, as a very important part of the development of what he calls "the sense of oneness of humanity": that somehow we're all part of the same family, and we're interconnected. This idea of fundamental equality is a very important premise for him. It's also the premise upon which he would argue that our natural capacity for empathy or compassion is based and by further developing and embracing this recognition of our fundamental equality, one will be able to strengthen and further develop our own natural capacity for empathy so that we can connect even with strangers and learn to care for their well-being. So you can see that not only is this concept very important in his own Buddhist thought, but more importantly, this concept plays a key role in the formulation of a system of ethics and talking about ethics—a discourse on ethics that doesn't require resorting to any religious concepts and beliefs.

Kathryn Goldman Schuyler: What do you think we haven't yet touched upon that's important for understanding who His Holiness is?

Thupten Jinpa: One of the main things about His Holiness the Dalai Lama, despite all the hardships that he and his people have faced, is his belief in the power of the individual and inner resources of human beings. That's what makes him inspiring as a leader. He is very much grounded in the belief that within ourselves we have all the spiritual resources and he lives that in all he does with people, in every interaction. It's a simple idea but it's a very powerful concept.

NOTES

1.   His Holiness the Dalai Lama, *Ethics for the New Millennium* (NY: Riverhead Books, 1999).

2. Vaclav Havel, a well-known playwright, was the last President of Czechslo-vakia and the first President of the Czech Republic. Jimmy Carter was the 39th President of the United States from 1977 to 1981.
3. Archbishop Desmond Tutu was the first Black South African Archbishop. He received the Nobel Peace Prize in 1984 and the Mahatma Gandhi Peace Prize in 2005.
4. For additional information on classical Buddhist training in Tibet, see two articles published by Geshe Thupten Jinpa: "The Dalai Lama: Dimensions of Spirituality" in Clive Erricker and Jane Erricker (eds.), *Contemporary Spiritualities: Social and Religious Contexts*. (London: Continuum, 2001) and "The Dalai Lama and Tibetan Monastic Academia" in Rajiv Mehrotra (ed.), *Understanding the Dalai Lama*. (New Delhi: Penguin Books, 2004) and available as a Kindle edition.

CHAPTER 4

LEADING FOR CHANGE, DIALOGUE FOR OPENNESS

Feminine Principle Teachings For Leaders

Judith Simmer-Brown

According to Tibetan legends, the great Indian spiritual adept Padma-sambhava (considered to be the master who brought Buddhism to Tibet in the eighth century) underwent enormous hardships while seeking the teachings that would complete his spiritual realization. Upon hearing of the renowned female guru called Secret Wisdom, the Queen of Dakinis, he traveled to the gates of her palace. With tremendous urgency, he

Inner Peace—Global Impact: Tibetan Buddhism, Leadership, and Work, pp. 47–66

attempted to send a request to the queen through her beautiful young maidservant, Kumari. The girl ignored him and continued to carry enormous brass jugs of water suspended from a heavy yoke across her shoulders. When he pressed his request, Kumari continued her labors, remaining silent. The great master became impatient, and through his yogic powers magically nailed the heavy jugs to the floor. No matter how hard Kumari struggled, she could not lift them.

Removing the yoke and ropes from her shoulders, she stepped before Padmasambhava, exclaiming, "I see that you have developed great yogic powers. What of my powers, great one?" Her sparkling smile revealed shining fangs, and she drew a crystal knife from the girdle at her waist. Her three eyes flashed, and she sliced open her heart center, revealing the vivid and vast interior space of her body. There was displayed the entire sacred *mandala* of the universe, a beautiful symbolic representation in brilliant colors. Abashed that he had not realized with whom he was dealing, Padmasambhava bowed before her and humbly renewed his request for teachings. In response, she offered him her respect as well, adding, "I am only a maidservant," and ushered him in to meet the Queen Secret Wisdom.[1]

This simple maidservant is a messenger of her genre, the *dakini* in Tibetan Buddhism. As can be seen from her name Kumari, "beautiful young girl, the crown princess," she may be humble in demeanor but she is regal and commanding in her understanding of the nature of reality. Her fangs show that her beauty is not merely conventional, but terrifying, and her three eyes stare into limitless space. Like many dakinis, she teaches directly not through words but through actions. Specifically, she teaches with her body, cutting open her very heart to reveal her wisdom. In her heart is revealed the ultimate nature of reality, empty and vast. And within its vastness are all phenomena, all sense perceptions, emotions, thoughts, and cognitions as a sacred diagram of the entire world, the mandala.[2]

One of the most distinctive and remarkable bodies of Tibetan Buddhist teachings to consider when contemplating contributions to leadership and organizations is that known as the feminine principle, or dakini, teachings. These are teachings that developed in the yogic traditions of Tibet and India, applying less to the monastery and government and more to lay and yogic practice communities associated with the oral Nyingma and Kagyü lineages, especially in East Tibet. These teachings relate especially to leadership for change.

The dakini is a female goddess figure who represents the wisdom cultivated in Tibetan Buddhist meditation and yoga. The lore of the oral tradition reveals dakinis as magical, visionary beings who appear in legends, visions, and dreams, demonstrating the true nature of reality through various skillful means. Practices that enact this view are central to Tibetan Buddhist meditation. The renowned Tibetan Buddhist master, Chögyam Trungpa,[3] relied on these teachings in the founding of his North American organizations, and he structured their leadership and governance on this principle.[4] As a longtime Shambhala practitioner and professor of Buddhism from one of his organizations, Naropa University, I initially learned aspects of this tradition from him. This motif of Tibetan tantric Buddhism became the subject of my practice and scholarly work, and serves as the basis for the material in this chapter.

The dakini teachings have been influential in the esoteric yogic traditions of Tibet and India since the eighth century, and are still powerful influences in especially the Kagyü and Nyingma practice traditions of Buddhism. The word *dakini* is a Sanskrit word with ambiguous etymology; the Tibetan equivalent, *khandro* means "she who flies," referring to the female deity who lives in limitless vastness.[5] Dakinis may appear to practitioners as embodiments of core truths of the tradition, the impermanent, nonsubstantial, and dynamic nature of reality. Their powers are revered, for they particularly have the ability to evoke profound wisdom in the practitioner. Over the centuries, oral Tibetan traditions developed a more nuanced, multileveled understanding of the dakini, becoming a central symbol of yogic practice.

A disclaimer is necessary. I am not an expert in or scholar of leadership training; I am a religious studies professor specializing in Indo-Tibetan Buddhism. This chapter does not relate to Tibetan organizations, such as the Tibetan government or monastic institutions, that have their own organizing principles and traditions, both inside and outside of Tibet.[6] It is not based on a scholarly study of the lives of Tibetan women, or of their role in organizational life either in Tibet or in exile.[7] The chapter is not a particularly feminist read of the dakini lore and often violates the tenets of feminism, as it is not intended to make statements about the female gender, but about the feminine as an organizing principle in life, which is something quite distinct from the gender.[8] My challenge here is to accurately present the Tibetan tradition on these teachings as I have received them and to suggest resonances for the field of leadership.

Still, when I look back at my 35 years as a professor at Naropa University, I realize that I have been a leader who has played many different roles in the life of a fledgling, and then fully accredited University. I have been a dean, for decades a department chair, and I have served on multiple committees, task forces, and governance groups. I have been at turns an innovator and a reactionary, an advocate and entrenched conservative. Most leadership skills I have learned the hard way, by trying to lead from a position of arrogance, personal vision, and ambition—and these methods have understandably backfired. Only in the last decade or so have I realized that I must lead from a different stance, one shaped by my decades of contemplative training and practice. I learn more about this every day.

When Chögyam Trungpa, Rinpoche, a senior incarnation and treasure-discoverer[9] of the Kagyü and Nyingma schools, came to the West, he felt that acknowledgement of and respect for the "feminine principle" teachings were woefully lacking in Western culture. In our patriarchal environment, leadership roles have been consistently occupied by men, or by women who are culturally rewarded for embodying stereotypic masculine styles. Rinpoche saw that this created issues in communities and organizations, producing an imbalance that accentuated certain kinds of knowledge, skills, and communication styles associated with the masculine, at the expense of the feminine. Recovering the lost feminine was very much a priority in his work, but as we discovered, Tibetan notions of feminine were not like Western ones. Drawing from his own tradition, he taught that the feminine was especially associated with nonconceptual wisdom of the nature of reality, especially the impermanent and insubstantial qualities we experience. During his first decade of teaching in the United States (1971-1981), he emphasized these teachings to rebalance the cultural deficiencies he discovered here. Those of us who studied with him and worked in his organizations benefited enormously from these unconventional teachings, as they gave a refreshing perspective on chaos, unpredictability, relationships between women and men, and leadership styles. Selected themes from those teachings are explicated in this chapter.

OVERCOMING IMMUNITY TO CHANGE: THE GREAT MOTHER

> We all know that change is hard, but we don't know enough about why it is so hard and what we can do about it.... [T]he change challenges today's leaders and their subordinates face are not, for the most part, a problem of will. The problem is the inability to close the gap between what we genuinely, even passionately, want and what we are actually able to do. Closing this gap is a central learning problem of the twenty-first century.[10]

The Harvard University Change Leadership Group has identified strengthening organizations' capacities for change as one of the most pressing contemporary issues in leadership training.[11] Most leadership training has focused on management skills that remain "inside the box" of previous paradigms. Typically, it has not addressed organizations' and individuals' "immunity to change"[12] that has made it difficult for leaders to develop the necessary flexibility, vision, and collaboration to succeed in challenging times like these. Everyone feels anxious about change, not just leaders or organizations, and yet change is probably the only reliable thing in our lives. It is important to develop literature that prepares leaders and their organizations to adapt to the inevitable changes they will always face. Collaborators on leadership for change, such as Robert Kegan, Lisa Laskow Lahey, and Ronald A. Heifetz and his colleagues, are producing work that helps individuals and organizations train for change in a variety of refreshing new ways. As Heifetz and his colleagues affirm, adaptive models of "leadership for change demand inspiration and perspiration."[13]

Immunity to change refers to hidden internal maps that we develop in ourselves and in our organizations in order to succeed, and these maps are essentially stress-management systems. This immunity resides not in rational thought but in emotions, especially in the form of attempting to manage anxiety.[14] Anxiety about change is not the episodic kind, but pervades all of our experience and is common to all humans. Effective leaders often develop immunity to change in order to remain highly functioning, focused, and effective in their activities, but this kind of immunity operates at a tremendous personal cost.

> Inevitably, they create blind spots, prevent new learning, and constantly constrain action in some aspects of our living. These costs show up when we are unable to deliver on some genuinely desired change, the realization of which would bring us to a new, higher level of functioning in ways we truly want to attain.[15]

We can replace the immunity to change that is currently constricting us with a more expansive way of seeing our world, enabling us to become more responsive, creative, and effective in leadership, in organizations, and in our lives in general.

The writings coming out of this conversation provide a compelling view of change, but the real challenge is not developing the view (itself radical and revolutionary), but the presence or absence of methods for how to overcome immunity to change and how to enact flexibility, adaptability, and skill. As Kegan and Lahey write, "for most people greater insight, however exhilarating, is insufficient to bring about lasting change."[16] How does a leader prepare herself, her organization, and her colleagues and employees for genuine change? How can leadership become a practice, to use Heifetz's term, "as a verb, not a job. Authority, power, and influence are critical tools, but they do not define leadership."[17]

This perspective about change has ancient roots. Tibetan Buddhism has long relied on a profound understanding of change as the true wisdom of the way things really are. Buddha Shakyamuni in the sixth century B.C.E. taught about impermanence as one of the foundational discoveries of enlightenment. "Whatever arises also ceases," he taught in one of the earliest texts,[18] and he reminded his first students in innumerable ways that nothing lasts. Later in his career, he taught that nothing has substantial, permanent existence, and that misunderstanding this is what leads to all human suffering. These teachings formed the foundational view of Buddhism throughout the world. However, as we saw above, having insights is not enough. How can these insights influence how we actually conduct ourselves in our lives and in the workplace?

Tibetan Buddhism is known especially for its many skillful methods of accelerating the necessary transformations about which the Buddha spoke. Drawing from the Indian tradition, ingenious methods of meditation practice were developed that demonstrated something more than a merely intellectual understanding of the profundity of the Buddha's realization. The teachings and practices that cultivate understanding and manifest the capacity to change are especially embodied in teachings known as the "feminine principle," otherwise known as the dakini wisdom teachings.

In Tibetan Buddhism, wisdom (*prajna*, or *sherap*) refers to the special intuitive knowing cultivated in meditation, a kind of wisdom that transcends concept, limit, or boundary of any kind. The teaching is subtle. Humans are conventionally ensnared by a conceptual approach, and these concepts blind us to the unfettered, brilliant qualities of our actual experience. It is unimaginable to move beyond these concepts, for they condition every moment of our lives and shape our sense of identity, our relationships, our emotions, our sense perceptions, our very dreams. Most attempts to point out the binding nature of our conceptual landscape merely intensify our concepts as we grope to fit even spiritual teachings into our previously devised categories. It is our concepts that make us resistant to or immune to change.

Organizations, like people, fall into habits about how things work, about who is in charge, what the mission is, what procedures are, how decision-making should take place, and what the products should be. In these economic times, however, the old ways of doing business are not working any more, and the companies that are ready to "morph" into fresh thinking, new products, streamlined management, and so forth, are the ones that will succeed. This means that learning how to adapt quickly and drop habitual ways of thinking and doing is essential to survival. And this means changing the mind of the leader first.

The Buddhist tradition speaks of the qualities of an adaptable and open mind: the clearest description is a mind that is not trapped in concepts and ideas. Concepts are our most damaging blinders; while they are useful for awhile, they quickly expire. They have a limited shelf life. As leaders, we need to cultivate awareness, freshness, flexibility of mind in ourselves and the members of our organization; ideas are useful tools, but they are not the end we seek. We seek the creative, unbounded, embodied space of our experience—what is called the *Great Mother* (*yum chenmo*) in Tibetan Buddhism.

While it is difficult to break free from conceptuality, Tibetan meditation provides various skillful methods to aid practitioners in opening themelves. Mindfulness-awareness meditation relaxes the mind and reveals the contrast between thoughts and the nature of mind itself. Devotional practices submerge concepts in love and longing for the unconditioned, thereby allowing a glimpse of vastness. Analytic meditation points out the limitations of logic that may demonstrate validity but can never find the truth. Visualization practices show that all our experience is dreamlike, devoid of permanence and solidity. All of these methods fall under the purview of the personalized form of the Great Mother, the nonexistent queen of all impermanence, emptiness, and space, the compassionate midwife of the practitioners' awakening. Above all, the feminine principle is about the dawn of nonconceptuality in personal experience, supported by one of these practices.

The Great Mother tradition is one of the oldest in Buddhism, and it became a strong theme in Tibet. It developed from the renowned *Prajnaparamita* (literally, "wisdom-gone-beyond") tradition of India, in which nonconceptual wisdom was personified as feminine, though in "her" essence, nothing whatever can be represented. Eventually the Great Mother was portrayed as a dancing goddess figure with unsettling appearance, like that of Kumari described above. Visions of a powerful dakini would appear to the practitioner as a reminder of the certainty of change, insubstantiality, and vastness at key points in spiritual development. The dakini reigns over a world that is luminous, brilliant and insubstantial, available to us more through observation via our sense perceptions than through our concepts. What is required is that we open to this vast brilliance with the support of practices of presence, mindfulness and awareness, and wonder. This requires the discipline of opening to vastness in some daily way. That is what the myriad practices of Tibetan Buddhism present to us.

Such insight is very helpful in our organizational life. The "leadership for change" literature seems full of suggestions for how leaders can be "change agents," rather than spokespersons for the change that is already afoot in our world. There are wonderful suggestions in this literature about how to prepare our employees, colleagues, and organizations for change, but how do we prepare ourselves for change? Leaders are subject to the realm of the Mother as much as anyone else, perhaps more.

Leaders often labor under the delusion that they are (or should be) in control of all factors in the workplace. We feel that order and predictability are our friends, and chaos is our enemy—in short, we are "immune to change."[19] When things do not work out as we had envisioned, we become frustrated and more controlling, or we deflate into hopelessness and a sense of failure. From a Tibetan perspective, this is hubris for a leader, for it breeds brittleness and frustrates effectiveness and success. Clarity about the true nature of reality means that we see the wisdom in chaos, and impermanence permeates all aspects of the workplace. The effective leader overcomes her immunity to change.

Reliance on the Great Mother supports this. From the larger perspective of how things really work, our attempts to control and order the world are delusional if we think that we are ultimately in charge. Trungpa Rinpoche described our attempts to regulate and control as a kind of futile administration that is an "overground," while the genuine nature of reality is functioning at a more "black-market" level. The overground level is the artificial structure that we use to organize the world; the underlayer is the way things really are. The underlayer is the level of the Great Mother.

> The overlay of the reality is unable to detect the underlayer of the reality anymore. The surface may go quite nonchalantly, it usually does, but the undercurrent is extraordinarily powerful, that it begins to manufacture a world of its own, in the feminine principle of potentiality, and embryonic, and resourceful, and glamorous at the same time.[20]

From this perspective, we as leaders do not need to be change agents as much as we need to acknowledge the certainty of change, no matter what, and prepare ourselves to facilitate a more realistic and flexible relationship with change in ourselves, our organizations, and the individuals within those organizations.

In some of my more difficult years at Naropa University, this perspective has been meaningful to me. Over 10 years ago, I playfully founded a small secret society of longtime employees, both staff and faculty, that I called "Black Market of the Mother," referring to the "underlayer" described above. The society has no meetings, no secret handshakes, no membership cards, and no manifesto. It is merely a loose association of members who are ready to embrace the vital, powerful, dynamic, and "glamorous" qualities of change that constantly sweep our small university. I electronically send to its members, as a kind of induction, a brief quote by Naropa's founder on the certainty of change, including the quote above. We affirm that whatever new managers or executives we may have, whatever department chairs or deans, whatever academic plan or accreditation requirement, the underlying genuineness of inspiration at our contemplative university relies on impermanence, nonsubstantiality, and chaos. We are all subject to it, and openness to this protects the heritage of the university from long-term effects of manipulation and control from any quarter, including our own.

CONTAINER AND DIALOGUE: THE MANDALA PRINCIPLE

It is certainly not enough just to embrace change, nonsubstantiality, and chaos in an organization. How is one to understand the dynamics of an ever-changing world? How does one lead, participating effectively in the reality of how things work this way? The servant girl Kumari gave clues to how to understand change. Beneath the reality of impermanence, there are predictable dynamics for how things work, in the Tibetan view. This dynamic is described as a mandala, a representation of the complete functioning of the universe as it is, physically, psychologically, and spiritually. This manifestation is naturally sacred and brilliant in its wholeness, even within the dynamics of impermanence. As a symbol, the mandala also expresses a method transforming a confused, conceptual understanding into a view that is based on impermanence, emptiness, and luminosity. Such a view, according to Tibetan tantra, is completely clear because it is based upon understanding things as they are, ultimately empty of inherent existence and full of the qualities of wholeness and wakefulness.[21]

In the narrative above, the dakini Kumari revealed the sacred mandala in the limitless vastness of the interior of her body by cutting open her heart center. Dakinis have the power to awaken this vision, if we can embrace the realm of impermanence and luminosity; we then have the ability to see our world as inherently whole and sacred. Traditionally speaking, mandalas are iconographically represented as two-dimensional diagrams or three-dimensional reproductions of a prescribed universe, represented by a palace, throne, or pedestal in the midst of an environment of dramatic beauty.

The features of the mandala (in Tibetan, *kyil-khor*) are based on a central focal point (*kyil*) surrounded by (*khor*) boundary walls, perimeters, or realms. The center and perimeter are seen as interdependent, and that is the key to the power of the form. In the sacred mandala, the dynamic between center and fringe is not based on struggle or competition. The central deity of the Tibetan tantric mandala is not a supreme being or an existent being of any kind, for that matter. The perimeter boundaries are as important and powerful as the center, and they are not existent either. Instead, the mandala is an expression of the dynamics of the world, once the profound understanding of space, of emptiness, is realized. With no supreme being or god of any kind, everything in the world is a transparent emanation, a play of empty space. From this perspective, the haunting qualities of the unseen lend a kind of magic to experience.

In a broader context, the mandala is a paradigm through which we can understand the natural functioning of any occurrence. Mandalas are like Tibetan "systems theory"[22] and from this view every situation operates on the dynamic of the mandala principle. If we look at examples like cities, we see that an individual city like Washington, DC has developed its own way of working like a living organism, with a center of power and activity and support systems. Geographically, we can see that Washington has a central business district and suburbs, linked with expressways and beltways. This systems approach can be found in many instances in our everyday world. The atom has a nucleus and revolving electrons that emit energy that holds the whole configuration together. Communication networks have a common vision and organizing principles. Swarms of bees decide collectively about the suitability of new sites for hives. The workplace has intricate patterns of activity and communication, with interconnecting roles. When one understands the dynamic relationships in these naturally existing mandalas, it is possible to glimpse the view of sacredness as presented in Tibetan Buddhism.

When we embrace change, we begin to discover a more inherent, lively way that systems work, patterned as mandalas. Within organizations, power may not be held by the boss, but by other figures within the leadership, and power is found in many different styles in different corners of the organization. The effective leader can begin to read how the naturally existing mandala is at work in an organization, and through this insight can bring into harmony and communication these pockets of power, so that an organization can move forward and adapt to new circumstances. This requires identifying the mandala at work, and cultivating the underlying way that power works in that mandala, bringing it to the surface.

The conventional way in which naturally existing mandalas work is that they cannot acknowledge that they are mandalas or systems with their own dynamics and parameters. It is especially difficult for mandalas to acknowledge the natural power radiated between the center and the perimeter boundary. The center would like to manipulate its boundary, or the perimeter would like to overthrow the center. From a conventional point of view, the mandala may be a dictatorship in which the central figure does not acknowledge or respect the perimeter, and so it imposes its tyranny. Or, conversely, the perimeter does not acknowledge or respect the central power, and so it undermines, conspires, and overthrows the center, creating rebellion, chaos, or anarchy. When this happens, everything is reduced to the lowest common denominator, and sacred world is impossible to discover. Pain, paranoia, and self-serving preoccupation overtake the power dynamic, and it is impossible for anyone to thrive. We see this dynamic at work in organizations, flowing between the extreme of too much power centralized in one or two people who serve as the leaders, to the extreme of no centralized leadership, in which the organization languishes or experiences outbreaks of power struggles between factions.

When we do not see the mandala principle at work, we constantly reject, grasp, or attempt to manipulate the world around us to make it into something other than what it is. It is difficult to feel ourselves empowered to be in our own environment and to experience its richness. When this happens, we cannot experience our jobs or communities in a sacred way. It feels as though everyone at work acts independently. Since power and survival are the only issues, we are able to act only from power and survival instincts. We indulge in hope that perhaps in a different time, like next year, everything will be going more smoothly—the dean will be less demanding, the office more efficient and peaceful, our faculty colleagues less preoccupied and overwhelmed. Then we will be able to experience career fulfillment! When we relate to things in this way, there is no empowered center or perimeter in our world. We feel we are dispensable parts of the workplace and have no power to affect the environment there. Or we feel completely in control in the workplace, but no one else is helping and supporting us, and we feel overwhelmed. This brings an experience of constant pain, and when we reject even this pain, we make our personal situations hopeless.

The only transformative choice that remains, according to Tibetan Buddhism, is to take our seats in whatever world we find ourselves in, and acknowledge it as a sacred mandala, as the completely perfect environment in which to live and work. This means settling in to our jobs, our marriages, our communities, and committing to all of the difficult parts of them. Our lives can only be seen in this way if we include everything, all the positive qualities as well as all that we would like to ignore, reject, or distance ourselves from, everything in ourselves and everything in situations around us.[23]

While Tibetan Buddhism has developed skillful practices for revealing the structure of the mandala, there are current practices in leadership that are also tremendously effective for realizing the mandala. The best example can be found in the leadership literature on dialogue, or the "art of thinking together," a method by which the "architecture of the invisible" can be surfaced in our organizations.[24] Dialogue, derived from *dialogos*, refers to the "flow of meaning" in conversation that developed in civil society from the time of the Greeks. Physicist David Bohm revitalized this practice, extrapolating from his discoveries in physics that there is an underlying "implicate order" in organisms that has more to do with the whole than with particles. Bohm considered all the conventionally-perceived phenomena to be momentary abstractions of a more fundamental flow of wholeness that underlies them.

On this stream, one may see an ever-changing pattern of vortices, ripples, waves, splashes, etc., which evidently have no independent existence as such. Rather, they are abstracted from the flowing movement, arising and vanishing in the total process of the flow. Such transitory subsistence as may be possessed by these abstracted forms implies only a relative independence or autonomy of behavior, rather than absolutely independent existence as ultimate substances.[25]

His views challenged the fundamentals of physics and became part of the entire movement of quantum physics. At a key point in his career, Bohm's friendship with the iconoclastic Hindu philosopher, Jiddu Krishnamurti, opened his eyes to the dynamics of the human mind beyond thought that revolutionized his view.[26] Later in life, he began to experiment with organizations and groups, launching a practice of communication that has less to do with individual insights and more to do with the wisdom that is found in the communications of the whole group.[27]

Bohm's protégés, such as William Isaacs, Chris Harris, and Peter Senge, along with other social scientists like Margaret Wheatley and Juanita Brown, have developed practices of dialogue in organizations as ways to foster and strengthen the implicate order, a notion that parallels the Tibetan mandala principle in contemporary settings.[28] This practice highlights the importance of communication "beyond thought," in which members of a group are able to transcend the habit of individual thought and to think with others.[29] The training methods of William Isaacs, Bohm's most direct protégé and member of the MIT Dialogue Project, build skills that reverse our customary approaches. Usually, we think alone and then adhere unreasonably to our conclusions, defending them, promoting them, and adhering to them in spite of any evidence to the contrary. This leads us to a stance of debate in our relationships with others. Isaacs suggests that such approaches reinforce the four experiences of fragmentation, idolatry, certainty and violence that cause organizations and groups to be dysfunctional.[30] The implicate order is submerged and invisible when this happens, and we are held hostage to the limited nature of individual intelligence.

The practice of dialogue directly counteracts this tendency, and builds the ability of groups to discover their own natural dynamics and intelligence. Practicing the four skills of listening, respecting, suspending, and voicing counteract the four experiences of fragmentation, idolatry, certainty, and violence.[31] Deep listening acknowledges our connection with others, and overcomes the fragmentizing tendency to see ourselves as isolated beings. Respecting counteracts the idolatry of considering our own ideas as superior to others and opens us to genuinely considering issues anew. Suspending is the opposite of defending, which is the habit driven by the hubris of certainty when we think alone. Voicing allows us to express our resonance to the wisdom of others, quite different from the violence we express when we defend our own ideas to the end.[32] Altogether, these are the core practices associated with changing our habits of relying excessively on thoughts, especially our own, a reliance that cripples the potential of our organizations, communities, and societies.

None of this can work, however, unless these practices take place within a safe space, what has been called a *container*.[33] A container is an environment with definite boundaries in which human energy can be held so that "it can be transformative rather than destructive."[34] Isaacs speaks of the container as holding human intensity, like a cauldron that has energy, possibility, and safety. In such a defined field, dialogue can take place.[35] These are key practices for uncovering the natural system of intelligence and wholeness at the heart of our communities—understood in Tibetan Buddhism as the mandala.

It is fascinating to me that luminaries within the MIT organizational development world use this term "container." When Trungpa Rinpoche first came to America in 1971, he found ingenious ways of articulating the core teachings of Tibetan Buddhism. His colloquial, everyday word for mandala principle was "container." Whenever we did practice programs or whenever he gave teachings, he paid special attention to the container, and asked that we guard the boundaries around it, follow the disciplines within it, and treasure the special opportunities we had to be within it. His use of the word seems identical to that of Senge, Scharmer, Isaacs, and others. It is likely that this terminology came into their work from students of Rinpoche's such as Francisco Varela and Eleanor Rosch who were themselves involved in dialogue with colleagues at MIT.[36] The very evolution of the dialogue movement has part of its impetus from Indian philosophy in Krishnamurti's work, and from Tibetan Buddhism in the work of Chögyam Trungpa.

Containers or mandalas are sacred realms in which nonconceptual wisdom can be accessed and understood. We could speak of this wisdom as magical, for it blooms between individuals, and it dawns in the wholeness of the environment. Once we open to our situations, step into them, and accept them as they are, inescapably, we take our seats in the center of our mandalas and establish boundaries. To establish boundaries, we identify the natural limits for this particular system and create a container, both physical and mental, in which this system can operate. Then it is possible to work with the situation, and a sense of totality begins to emerge. The mandala view—or the container—allows us to experience the natural goodness and inherent workability. It is this view that is called in Tibetan Buddhism sacred outlook (*daknang*). From this view, the world is seen as sacred in a self-existing way.

In groups that have developed dialogue relationships, people develop a sense of community that is radically different. After one of David Bohm's dialogue experiments in 1984, he reflected on what happened:

> In the beginning, people were expressing fixed positions, which they were tending to defend, but later it became clear that to maintain the feeling of friendship in the group was much more important than to hold any position.... A new kind of mind thus begins to come into being which is based on the development of an common meaning that is constantly transforming in the process of the dialogue. People are no longer primarily in opposition, nor can they be said to be interacting; rather, they are participating in this pool of common meaning which is capable of constant development and change.[37]

Dialogue creates an environment that is fluid and responsive to change while inviting its members to yield their personal territory to the benefit of the whole. In this way, the mandala principle, or the implicate order, provides dynamic structure that lends itself to the certainty of change that pervades our organizations. It also builds confidence in the organization without tying it to the ideas or plans of a specific leader or manager.

How does the leader manifest in an impermanent, brilliant world? For this perspective, we return to the dakini, the anthropomorphic representation of the Great Mother. Dakinis relate to mandalas in several important ways. First, dakinis are important inhabitants of mandalas in classical Tibetan iconography. Sometimes a dakini may inhabit the central seat as a meditational deity, either alone or with her consort, and sometimes she appears in a retinue representing aspects of her complete, enlightened wisdom. Second, dakinis are also the protectors of the boundaries of the mandala, fiercely guarding the sacredness that is discovered there. In this manifestation, dakinis are wrathful and threatening. Third, dakinis are emblems or symbols of the nonconceptual wisdom that can be discovered within the mandala. This is the most important way dakinis are tied to the mandala.

For the leader, this means that leaders need to see themselves as inhabitants of the mandala or container as well, part of the implicate order of how the organization, community, or group works. Setting ourselves apart limits our effectiveness, but to lead, we must become skillful as conveners or facilitators to ensure that the implicate order is expressed. Secondly, in order to effectively lead, the leader must also have skill in protecting the boundaries of the container. Isaacs describes this as a "way to sustain and deepen the sense of safety that people feel."[38] This is done by attending to the physical environment, the group agreements, and protocols for communication. Most of all, the leader must hold a view of sacredness of what occurs within the mandala, willing to accommodate even that which she would normally reject. That includes painful, chaotic, or threatening dimensions that would unseat a leader interested only in control. Nonconceptual wisdom can come sometimes in painful or threatening guises.

Iconography of the wisdom-dakini is very specific and diverges from forms in Western religious traditions, in that it often uses cemetery symbols of impermanence, death, and destruction, consistent with the Mother aspect described above. She is depicted as naked like the true nature of reality, wearing jewelry fashioned of bone fragments, ornamented with skulls and jewels, constantly juxtaposing motifs of impermanence and splendor. Sometimes she wears necklaces of symbolic severed heads and carries a drinking cup made from a human skull, representing the Mother aspects of the dakini. She is always a messenger of impermanence, the certainty of death, the lack of solid existence, and the pervasiveness of chaos throughout our lives.[39] She represents seemingly irreconcilable paradoxes of our experience and demonstrates that genuine wisdom is found within those paradoxes.

As leaders, we must be willing to celebrate impermanence in this way and to appreciate the constantly-changing dynamic of our organizations. From this perspective, we could see ourselves dancing nakedly, as the dakini dances. She dances freely, hair flying, and with a graceful sweep of her limbs, she exudes a captivating but very direct presence, symbolizing the mind resting in the true nature of reality. Her dance displays the vast and dynamic quality of the space of the mandala. While the dakini dances within the themes of life and death, there is no tragedy or sadness in her dance. The naked and dancing dakini represents the wisdom, joy and freedom from attachment, if self-cherishing has been abandoned. Rather than arousing only revulsion and disgust in others, she joins the quality of the sensuous and vibrant womanliness with the reminders of impermanence and death. She sees all the realities of life and death, youth and ageing, attraction and revulsion, without being seduced into duality.

In the face of the dakini, we see guidance for how to regard her. She gazes into unfathomable space, and her body itself is luminous, empty of solidity. At the same time, her face is not blank; she smiles with passion and intensity, fully engaged in the extremes of life. This seeming contradiction between engagement and vast vision captures her contradictions. She refuses to accept the logic of life versus death, gain versus loss, and pain versus pleasure. This is the power and joy of the dancing dakini.

BRINGING THE DAKINI INTO OUR ORGANIZATIONS

While lessons for leadership and organizations from the dakini lore are very much in accord with recent literature on leadership, it is not enough to theoretically understand the importance of adaptability to change. We are not really psychologically or physically ready to change—or even conceptually, for that matter. Change is difficult and threatening, and it is challenging to really prepare ourselves for the groundlessness and fear that change brings. We need the constant reminders that change affects us all, and it is helpful to have a meditation practice that introduces this awareness and gives us the skills to "lean into" change. The dakini practices of Tibetan Buddhism are all about this.

These practices include contemplation of what are called "the four reminders," four simple statements that bring certainty about impermanence into our daily lives. They are reminders that (1) we have a very precious life and a special opportunity to awaken to the truth of existence; (2) everything in our life is pervaded by impermanence; (3) it is certain that we will all die at some point; and finally, (4) worldly concerns are trivial in the face of these reminders.[40] All Tibetan Buddhist practice is grounded in these reminders, and symbols of them are prominent in all the dakini practices. They are recited aloud daily at the beginning of one's meditation practice session.

When we practice these contemplations, we experience heartbreak that our ideas about how things work are not really true. It is difficult to let go of our fantasies of long-term, durable success. We cannot accept that growth is not an endless upward progression, and that the market or the success of our organization is not guaranteed. For this reason, contemplating the four reminders is difficult and painful. The Tibetan Buddhist tradition tells us that, over time, these contemplations bring certainty about change that is accompanied by joy and freedom. As the great yogi, Padampa Sangye, taught,

> At first, to be fully convinced of impermanence makes you take up [the path of meditation]; in the middle it whips up your diligence; and in the end it brings you to the radiant dharmakaya (wisdom of the Buddha).[41]

This is the journey symbolized by the dakini. The heartbreak of the realization of impermanence blossoms into a heartfelt diligence. This second stage involves the recognition that we and others have perpetuated our own suffering by indulging in unrealistic expectations, and that effective leadership is a compassionate path of cultivating awareness of how things really are. Only then can we dance with the dakini in the fields of impermanence, tapping into the freedom and joy of awakening.

While saying this, I have observed that many Buddhists began their practice because of personal experiences of impermanence that changed the trajectories of their lives. These losses opened them, softened them, and made them wise. After many years of practice, however, these same practitioners develop conviction that everything will change except their Buddhist teachers or organizations, demonstrating that they have merely transferred their expectations of permanence to a new object. When our teacher, Chögyam Trunpga, Rinpoche, died in 1987, our organizations went into tailspins that still continue for some practitioners after all these years. The journey of relating to impermanence is lifelong, challenging, and deeply personal, and no one of us has completed that journey.

Once we develop more flexible minds, greater abilities to adapt, and stronger commitments to work with the whole of our lives and our organizations, we can begin to enhance the dynamic energies of the mandala principle wherever we are. Beginning this journey is frightening, because we do not know where it will lead; however, trusting the implicate order of our organizations and engaging in dialogue practice together, we find fresh directions and confidence that we could never have conceived. This requires a greater understanding of differing styles of power and wisdom, and appreciation for the basic goodness within the organization and its members, yearning to express their gifts. An effective leader for change commits to highlighting the inherent wisdom that is already present within the organization and endeavors to harmonize that wisdom through dialogue, communication, and empathy.

Leadership for change is a tremendously challenging field for organizations, and the Tibetan Buddhism tradition has unique perspectives that can shape our journeys as leaders. Especially, the ancient yogic wisdom of the dakini tradition has definite lessons for the leader, helping her to understand the perilous, fresh, and always transformative path of dancing within change.

NOTES

1. Adapted from Kenneth Douglas and Gwendolyn Bays, tr., *The Life and Liberation of Padmasambhava*, *Padma bKa'i Thang*, as recorded by Yeshe Tsogyal, *Le Dict de Padma*, translated into French by Gustave-Charles Toussaint (Berkeley: Dharma Publishing, 1978), 218-220.

2. The material for this chapter derives from a sustained study of the dakini that can be found in my book, *Dakini's Warm Breath: The Feminine Principle in Tibetan Buddhism* (Boston: Shambhala Publications, 2001). Some sections have been adapted directly from my book. Here, 1-2. (Hereafter cited as *Dakini's Warm Breath*.)

3. Chögyam Trungpa (1939-1987) was a major teacher of the Kagyü lineage who was supreme abbot of Surmang Monastery and governor of Surmang District from a young age. Under Chinese oppression, he fled Tibet in 1959 along with hundreds of other tulkus and their followers, both monastic and lay. In 1963, he began academic study at Oxford University, and founded a retreat center in Scotland. In 1971, he and his British wife emigrated to the United States, one of the first Tibetan Buddhist teachers in America. His is the author of numerous books on Tibetan Buddhism and

meditation. He is best known for his secular teachings in *Shambhala: The Sacred Path of the Warrior* (Boston: Shambhala Publications, 1985). For more information, see Fabrice Midal, *Trungpa: His Life and Times*; Fabrice Midal, *Recalling Chögyam Trungpa*; Jeremy Hayward, *Warrior-King of Shambhala: Remembering Chögyam Trungpa*.

4. Trungpa Rinpoche founded an international network of meditation centers, now known as Shambhala, located throughout North America, Europe, Latin and South America, and Asia. This network has its headquarters in Halifax, Nova Scotia. He also founded the Nalanda Translation Committee, Gampo Abbey, *The Shambhala Sun* and its derivative *Buddhadharma Magazine*. In 1974, he founded the fully accredited college and graduate school, Naropa University, in Boulder, Colorado.

5. Simmer-Brown, *Dakini's Warm Breath*, 45-53.

6. Rebecca Redwood French, *The Golden Yoke: The Legal Cosmology of Buddhist Tibet* (Ithaca, NY: Snow Lion Publication, 2002); Helen Boyd, *The Future of Tibet: The Government-in-Exile Meets the Challenge of Democratization* (Peter Lang, 2005).

7. Janet Gyatso and Hanna Havnevik, eds., *Women in Tibet, Past and Present* (New York: Columbia University Press, 2005); Janice D. Willis, *Feminine Ground: Essays on Women and Tibet* (Ithaca: Snow Lion, 1987); Hannah Havnevik, *Tibetan Buddhist Nuns: Cultural Norms and Social Reality* (Oslo: Norwegian University Press, 1990).

8. Hermann-Pfandt, *Dakinis: Zur Stellung und Sybolik des Weiblichen in tantrischen Buddhismus* (Bonn: Inica et Tibetaica Verlag, 1990).

9. Rinpoche was a *tulku*, or incarnate lama, who became enlightened in a previous life centuries ago, and who chose rebirth in a lineage of teachers, carrying on the compassionate and beneficial activities of his realization. This is also spoken of sociologically as a way of holding continuity of power over time, an effective way of structuring Buddhist institutions in Tibet. He was also a *terton*, a visionary revealer of fresh new texts and teachings (called *terma*, or treasures), an innovation that continually refreshes tulku lineages in Tibet. See Geoffrey Samuels, *Civilized Shamans: Buddhism in Tibetan Societies* (Washington: Smithsonian Institution, 1993) and Franz Michael, *Rule by Incarnation: Tibetan Buddhism and the Role of Society and State* (Boulder: Westview Press, 1982).

10. Robert Kegan and Lisa Laskow Lahey, *Immunity to Change: How to Overcome It and Unlock the Potential in Yourself and Your Organization* (Boston: Harvard Business Press, 2009), 1-2.

11. Tony Wagner, "Leading for Change," *Education Week*, August 15, 2007, www.edweek.org/login.html?source=http://www.edweek.org/ew/articles/2007/08/15/45wagner.h26.html&destination=http://www.edweek.org/ew/articles/2007/08/15/45wagner.h26.html&levelId=2100

12. Kegan and Lahey, *Immunity to Change*.

13. Ronald A. Heifetz, Marty Linsky, and Alexander Grashow, *The Practice of Adaptive Leadership: Tools and Tactics for Changing Your Organization and World* (Cambridge: Harvard Business Press, 2009).

14. Kegan and Lahey, *Immunity to Change*, 48-49.

15. Ibid., 48.

16. Ibid., xii.

17. Heifetz et. al., *The Practice of Adaptive Leadership*.

18. Buddha Gotama, *Majjhima Nikaya: The Middle Length Discourses of the Buddha* (USA: Theravada Tipitaka Press, 2010), 56.

19. Kegan and Lahey, *Immunity to Change*.

20. Chögyam Trungpa, *Glimpses of Space* (Halifax: Vajradhatu Publications, 1999).

21. This section of the chapter is adapted from Simmer-Brown, *Dakini's Warm Breath* (see chap. 4).

22. Here I refer to systems theory from the scientific world of cybernetics that involved a paradigm shift in many related fields. The word in popular use is also applied to the fields of family therapy, organizational development, and business and industry. Altogether, this work began in science and was pioneered by Von Bertalanffy in the 1950s.

23. This is not to say, of course, that there is no room for change or political action. From a Tibetan tantric perspective, change can only be facilitated from a perspective of commitment to the mandala. Then the strategies and skillful actions are suitable to the totality of the situation, rather than being based on impulsiveness or rejection of what we do not like. This kind of engaged activity requires taking the long view and a contemplative perspective.

24. William Isaacs, *Dialogue and The Art of Thinking Together* (New York: Doubleday, 1999), 30-31. (Hereafter cited as *Thinking Together*.)

25. David Bohm, *Wholeness and the Implicate Order* (Boston: Routledge, 1980), 48.

26. Ibid., 25-33.

27. David Bohm, *On Dialogue* (Abingdon, Oxon: Routledge, 2004), 1-54.

28. Ibid.; Chris Harris, *Hyperinnovation: Multidimensional Enterprise in the Connected Economy* (New York: Palgrave Macmillan, 2002); Peter Senge, *The Fifth Discipline: The Art and Practice of the Learning Organization* (New York: Doubleday, 1990); Margaret Wheatley, *Turning to One Another: Simple Conversations to Restore Hope to the Future* (San Francisco: Berrett Koehler Publishers, 2002/2009), Foreword for *Dialogue Education at Work: A Casebook*, by Jane Vella and Associates (San Francisco: Jossey Bass, 2003) and portions of *Leadership and the New Science: Discovering Order in a Chaotic World* (San Francisco: Berrett-Koehler Publishers, 1992 / Third Edition 2006); Juanita Brown and David Isaacs, *The World Café: Shaping Our Futures through Conversations that Matter* (San Francisco: Berrett-Koehler Publishers, 2005).

29. Isaacs, *Thinking Together*, 92-93.

30. Ibid., 49-69.

31. Ibid., 79-81.

32. Isaacs, *Thinking Together*, 83-176.

33. Peter Senge, C. Otto Scharmer, Joseph Jaworski, and Betty Sue Flowers, *Presence: Human Purpose and the Field of the Future* (New York: Doubleday, 2004), 34-36. (Hereafter cited as *Presence*.)

34. Ibid., 35.

35.   Isaacs, *Thinking Together*, 242-244.
36.   *Presence*; see also Francisco Varela, Evan Thompson, and Eleanor Rosch, *The Embodied Mind: Cognitive Mind and the Human Experience* (Cambridge: MIT Press, 1992).
37.   Quoted in Isaacs, *Thinking Together*, 40.
38.   Isaacs, *Thinking Together*, 250.
39.   *Dakini's Warm Breath*, 127-144.
40.   Patrul Rinpoche, *Words of My Perfect Teacher* (Boston: Shambhala Publications, Revised Edition, 1998), Part One; Khandro Rinpoche, *This Precious Life: Tibetan Buddhist Teachings on the Path to Enlightenment* (Boston: Shambhala Publications, 2003).
41.   Patrul, *Words of My Perfect Teacher*, 57.

CHAPTER 5

INCREASING LEADERSHIP INTEGRITY THROUGH MIND TRAINING AND EMBODIED LEARNING[1]

Kathryn Goldman Schuyler

Adapted with permission from Goldman Schuyler, K. (2010). Increasing leadership integrity through mind training and embodied learning. *Consulting Psychology Journal: Practice and Research, 62,* 21–38. Copyright © 2010 by the American Psychological Association.

As a scholar and consultant, I have been strongly influenced by Chris Argyris' repeated demonstrations that very few people live by the values they espouse.[2] This has made me accord less importance to the values that my clients espouse and more to methods that might enhance their capacity to live with less of a gap between what is espoused and what is actual. After years of practice as both an internal and external organizational consultant, coaching 200-plus executives at the VP level and higher, and supporting roughly 50 projects of organizational change, I began to feel that the work we did together was helpful, but did not go as deeply as needed. Executives became better leaders in their colleagues' eyes, and many attained significant promotions. Nonetheless, something was missing. I sought to develop this missing element.

In recent years, consultants have gone beyond methods commonly used in organizational psychology, supporting the development of leaders and their organizations in a variety of ways, including drawing on ancient wisdom, incorporating mind-body research, learning from contact with horses, and building on stages of adult development.[3] Nonetheless, as Richard Boyatzis pointed out "there are few models or theories of how individuals change and develop in sustainable ways, and most programs and the research on them focus on single characteristics, rather than on transformational shifts in a leader's way of being and leading."[4]

Noted scholars Ikujiro Nonaka and Hirotaka Takeuchi asserted in their seminal book on knowledge management that "the most powerful learning comes from bodily experience."[5] Regardless of this, only a relatively small percentage of organizational and leadership consultants incorporate what is known about the contribution of embodied knowing in support of leaders' ability to live with high levels of stress, understand systems change personally, and explore the physical foundations of integrity.[6] One meaning of *integrity*, as will be discussed later in this chapter, is the engineering notion of structural solidity—the capacity to hold together and resist the pressure of external forces. This context has not often been used in looking at leadership integrity and will be developed here.

As research studies show, such bodily-experience-based learning is grounded in the increasingly-understood domain of brain plasticity. Some neuroscientists are interested in the implications of Eastern ways of training the mind, as studies have shown that those with such training appear to develop a higher level of control over brain functioning than many psychologists thought possible.[7] Within the field of organizational studies, Weick has been one of the most well-known scholars to address the relevance of Buddhist mind training.[8] There are empirical studies of its use in management development, as well as considerable discussion of the term mindfulness in the behavioral science literature.[9] Embodied learning and mind training are grounded in similar perceptions of the importance of attention and awareness in developing effective, powerful action in the world.

This chapter proposes an integrated approach to leadership development consultation incorporating somatic awareness and intentional mind training as a foundation for acting with integrity. It draws on what is known from over fifty years of refinement of transformational somatic learning practices and many centuries of Buddhist practice in training the mind, called *lojong* in Tibetan Buddhism. A *somatic* approach to personal development means one that involves awareness of oneself physically, from the Greek word *soma* or sensed body, used by Paul in the New Testament to distinguish "the luminous body transformed by faith," from *sarx*, which designates the body as "a hunk of meat."[10] As described by Hanna, somatics is an evolving field, which "holds that first-person human experience must be considered of equal scientific and medical importance as outside, third-person observation."[11] Within the array of existing somatic practices, this chapter addresses solely the *Feldenkrais Method*, because this approach is more oriented toward learning and the role of the brain than other somatic practices, and it is one with which I am deeply familiar.

Somatic learning methods and Tibetan mind training will be described in more depth later in the chapter, but a quick overview may be useful now. The Feldenkrais Method is respected internationally for producing dramatic change in people ranging from children with severe neuromotor disorders to top athletes and musicians. Although relatively small as a profession (roughly 5,000 certified practitioners working in North America, Europe, Australia, New Zealand, Israel, and Asia), research has been carried out on many continents. Most of it is from medical, physical therapy, or psychotherapeutic perspectives. This research shows that use of the method leads to decreased pain and improved function, improved functioning after strokes, improved functioning after spinal injury, improved balance among the elderly, reduced perceived stress, improved balance and quality of life among people with multiple sclerosis, reduced state anxiety, and increased self-confidence and improved body image among people with eating disorders.[12] Although Moshe Feldenkrais himself was most interested in developing flexible minds, not bodies, as he said at a course that I attended at the Mann Ranch in 1979, Feldenkrais research has mainly focused on pain reduction and other bodily issues. Having reviewed the most recent lists of research on the method, I am not aware of empirical studies of its use in organizational consulting or coaching, other then my published case study.[13]

Feldenkrais was a world-renowned physicist and engineer who developed his method for enhancing learning and performance and taught it around the world from the 1950s until 2 years before his death in 1984.

Described by thought leaders including Karl Pribram, Margaret Mead, and Jean Houston as a genius, Feldenkrais used touch and *nonhabitual* movement patterns to help his students to change the way they moved and learned. His method is grounded in distributing movement throughout the body and particularly the spine and ribs, so that no one part of the structure has to bear the burden for the rest. Combining such core insights with in-depth knowledge of the human nervous system and the function of the brain in movement, he recognized that the physical bases of learning happen only in intimate interdependence with all other aspects of a person, such as how they feel, what they sense and notice, and what they want to accomplish in life.[14]

The Feldenkrais Method uses nonhabitual movements, sometimes facilitated by gentle touch, to enable learners to sense how to move more easily and powerfully in order to enable both physical and broader change.[15] Learners are encouraged to experiment and be attentive to the *way* that they move, rather than to focus on attaining an outcome at all costs. In the process, learners notice how they approach the given task and where they hold on and use force unnecessarily. Such holding on reduces the fluidity and power of all actions that involve movement—and what actions do not? Practitioners guide the learners through increasingly complex and varied movement patterns, which, in ways comparable to the learning of young children, tap into the inherent plasticity of the brain. Although existing research has shown the effectiveness of these methods with respect to the reduction of pain and improved physical performance, anecdotal evidence shows that by learning to move more easily, people experience surprising outcomes with regard to learning—which was Feldenkrais' main interest and my own. I studied with him from 1979-81, was internationally certified to practice in 1983, and was authorized to assist internationally in training new practitioners in 2003, so have extensive experience with the method.

I have incorporated these somatic approaches alongside more traditional organizational development and clinical sociological methods in my coaching and graduate teaching.[16] I have been intrigued by the potential offered by combining these methods for awareness training with experiential approaches to training the mind developed centuries ago in India and Tibet, in order to enable clients to more completely and deeply shift their habitual responses to the many difficult situations faced constantly by leaders. Some readers, accustomed to regarding Buddhism as a religion, may assume it is primarily a set of beliefs and institutions. I am writing instead from the perspective of spirituality as an array of change practices, using Reggie Ray's definition: "By spirituality, I mean those kinds of activities that directly serve the inspiration for maturation, transformation, and ultimately, realization."[17] Note that even by referring to these practices as *Buddhism* (which is an etic, not emic term), one overlays an outsider's assumptions on these practices. In fact, they are viewed by their "users" as practical, effective tools, tested over centuries for understanding and changing the way people unintentionally cause problems for themselves and one another in the course of daily life and work. The *dharma* (Buddhism) might actually be considered to be a historically early Asian approach to applied social science. Insiders refer to this set of practices as *the dharma*, so I will use I will use this term in place of *Buddhism*, since the latter elicits connotations, based on people's beliefs about religion, which are not relevant to this chapter. My focus is not on religion, but on the transfer of methods from one arena to another—a process that is applicable to bringing somatic learning and Tibetan mind training into use among Western corporate leaders.

The tradition of mind training (*lojong*) is at the core of the Tibetan approach to life. Two classical texts, both written during the eleventh century, provide the foundations for the widely used practice. The simplest is the following short set of statements entitled the *Eight Verses for Training the Mind* (*Eight Verses*) written by Geshe Langri Tangpa (1054-1093). These methods enable a student to notice and shift his or her relationship to the thoughts that emerge spontaneously as he or she moves through daily life. They are intended to overcome selfishness: the belief that one's own desires and concerns are more important than those of others. According to a study of the impact of lojong in Tibet over the centuries, the *Eight Verses* are the most widely practiced version of mind training.[18]

EIGHT VERSES FOR TRAINING THE MIND
BY GESHE LANGRI TANGPA

1. With a determination to accomplish the highest welfare for all sentient beings, who surpass even a wish-granting jewel, I will learn to hold them supremely dear.

2. Whenever I am with others, I will practice seeing myself as the lowest of all, and from the depths of my heart, I will respectfully hold others as supreme.

3. In all actions I will learn to search into my mind, and as soon as a destructive emotion arises, since it endangers myself and others, will firmly face and avert it.

4. I will learn to cherish ill-natured people, overwhelmed by wrong deeds and pain, as if I had found a precious treasure, for they are difficult to find.

5. Whenever others, out of jealousy and envy, treat me in unjust ways, may I accept this defeat myself and offer the victory to them.

6. Even if someone whom I have helped or in whom I have placed my hopes does great wrong by harming me, may I see that one as a sacred friend.

7. In short, may I offer both directly and indirectly all joy and benefit to all beings, my mothers, and may I myself secretly take on all of their hurt and suffering.

8. May they not be defiled by the concepts of the eight mundane concerns and, aware that all things are illusory, may they, ungrasping, be free from bondage.

    (Combination of multiple translations of classical text from The Dalai Lama, "Eight Verses for Training the Mind," in *Kindness, Clarity, and Insight*, trans. Jeffrey Hopkins, (Ithaca, NY: Snow Lion, 1998), 117-134; Thubten Gyeltsen, *Keys to Great Enlightenment: Commentaries on Geshe Langri Tangpa's Eight Verses on Thought Training and Togmey Zangpo's The Thirty-Seven Bodhisattva Practices.* (Long Beach, CA: Thubten Dhargye Ling, 2006) and Geshe Sonam Rinchen and Ruth Sonam, *Eight Verses for Training the Mind* (Ithaca, NY: Snow Lion, 2001).

Recent writings by Boyatzis and McKee presented mindfulness as a source of renewal for burned-out executives on the path toward *resonant leadership* and as a key tool in intentional change.[19] However, they based their practice and research on Kabat-Zinn's extensive work, which is the approach referenced in most Western behavioral science research. There are distinct differences between Kabat-Zinn's approach and the Tibetan mind training described in this chapter. Over the centuries, the Tibetan approach to the dharma came to emphasize the importance of compassion and relieving the suffering of all beings, rather than just one's own, while Kabat-Zinn's mindfulness training, as taught in hospitals throughout the world, focuses more on relieving a person's individual stress.[20] The use of meditation as mind-calming (shamatha practice) along with *mind training in compassion* is referred to as *Mahayana* or the *Great Vehicle*. This chapter identifies how mind training and somatic learning have been discussed in research, clarifies how they work, shows how they have been used in consulting, and describes how they can be used synergistically in processes of leadership development.

These two approaches to learning and life (the *Feldenkrais Method* and *mind training*) differ in their underlying assumptions about reality, yet are compatible with one another as practices. Both are designed to generate deep change in how a person views life and takes action. While dharma practitioners emphasize that everything in what people call "reality" (the world of material objects and action upon and between them) is impermanent and can be expected to change, the Feldenkrais Method grounds all learning in movement—which is also changing and impermanent. "Movement is life," Feldenkrais often said to us during the Amherst Professional Training Program.[21] Tibetan mind training focuses on bringing a person in touch with what is "behind" the changing relative reality to what exists "ultimately," which is often referred to as "the sky-like nature of mind" or the "luminous nature of mind."[22] Feldenkrais did not posit anything other than this life of moving, sensing bodies. Despite these distinctions between them, both methods are skillful ways to train a person to slow down and pay attention to what is actually happening in the moment.

Leadership training tends to be primarily cognitive and conceptual, using language to think about actions. Tibetan Buddhist practice and the Feldenkrais Method both train learners to notice at a microlevel their movement, breathing, and state of mind. The student develops the habit of paying close attention to what is taking place at a given moment, rather than being distracted by expectations based on past experience. Such repeated experiential training causes change at the level of *tacit knowledge*—familiarity with a subject that lets a person act effectively without being able to fully describe how. I believe that this *tacit* part of human "knowing" is the ground for change in values and long-standing habits.[23]

A few organizational practitioners have been incorporating somatic learning combined with spirituality for several decades. Strozzi-Heckler is a well-known practitioner of a martial arts-based approach to embodied learning. He brought his work into corporate venues after projects with the U.S. military.[24] His vivid presentation of his work with the Green Berets addressed the spiritually grounded self-awareness that can be developed through training in aikido and its importance for leadership development. Other scholars and consultants have also incorporated aikido-based somatic awareness and spirituality into their organizational consulting and discussions of management.[25] Among these authors, Phillips explicitly linked his approach with the development of integrity: he opened his book with a quote from a manager:

> I have to wear a lot of faces. And I hate it. I wish I could be the same person at work, at home, and with friends. I want my life to be all one piece, not a lot of fragments working against each other. Isn't that what integrity means?[26]

Thus, there are two differing approaches to somatic awareness development. The more common one, referred to above, is based in the martial arts (most often in aikido). This is useful in leadership development, because successful leaders need to manage power dynamics, and this approach may bring about a comfort with oneself and the uses of power in action. The Feldenkrais Method is different, although it was created by a master of one of the martial arts (judo). It involves learning to observe and sense oneself in action, without acting "against" anyone. There is no overlay of combat—only a focus on learning to observe oneself in action and finding ways to vary the way that one does anything while reducing the effort involved.

WHAT DOES IT TAKE TO "ADHERE TO A CODE OF VALUES"?

It seems to me that when we are in tune with ourselves at many levels, we can move through the world with a higher level of integrity. Lying to others begins with lying to oneself. Across the globe, there has been considerable evidence of lack of integrity among leaders.

Integrity is typically addressed in the leadership literature as "adherence to a code of values."[27] I found the way that Chris Argyris and Donald Schon defined the term quite useful:

> Webster's unabridged dictionary offers as the first meaning of integrity (from the Latin *integritas*, "integer") "the quality or state of being complete; wholeness; entireness; unbroken state." ... In the conventional sense, then, a person of integrity is a whole moral person (like the biblical Job, who is described as *tam v'yashar*, "whole and straight"), and a person who lacks integrity is "broken" or "incomplete."[28]

As mentioned earlier, few leaders act in accord with their espoused values.[29] Argyris' method for shifting this situation has been to ask people to observe themselves in action and write in two columns what they say and what they actually think (which is expected to be at odds with what they espouse). The somatic approach proposed here is quite different. Both require self-observation, but somatic learning and mind training take a less cognitive approach than Argyris does and build more directly on neuroplasticity.

In order to provide a cross-disciplinary theoretical foundation for thinking about integrity, I suggest that transforming the underlying tendencies of the everyday mind may be possible if we integrate Buckminster Fuller's notion of integrity as structure and function, Feldenkrais' use of physical movement as a foundation for all learning, and the principles of Tibetan Mahayana mind training.[30] As suggested above, both of these are complex, subtle systems approaches to change that have been employed with great effectiveness in arenas outside of management. However, they are little known among leadership consultants or executives. Somatic learning has been shown to transform a person's way of moving to such an extent that children and adults with severe neuromuscular and cognitive disabilities have become able to speak, move, and think in ways that their physicians had stated could not happen.[31] Similarly, although methods from mindfulness training have been widely used to enable people to manage stress and improve health, they have only occasionally been applied to improving executive performance.[32] There appear to be no formal research studies that investigate the use of such methods in executive coaching, although they are occasionally used in this arena, as they were in a multiyear program in Genentech's IT Department that provided mindfulness meditation training to over 600 workers during a merger integration process.[33] Leadership development can be enhanced by drawing upon such widely used and tested approaches to human development.

Whereas most definitions of integrity focus on following codes of values, Feldenkrais and Fuller addressed it concretely in relation to structure and function. According to Fuller, integrity meant having the capacity to hold one's shape in the face of external forces:

> What most people don't understand is that most building and other man-made structures do not have true structural integrity because in a structure with true structural integrity, tension and compression are evenly balanced. Most buildings, however, have the majority of the tension component buried deep in the ground with heavy foundations. Thus, when the Earth moves during an earthquake, the tension component of a building shifts often causing the building to shift or collapse. This is not true for the structure that Bucky invented, the geodesic dome.[34]

What is the equivalent in a human being? One might regard it as the capacity to "hold the shape" of our actions, both physical actions and those undertaken with regard to other people or systems. "Adherence to a code" makes it seem that living with integrity is a cognitive or mental act, whereas viewing it from a structural/functional perspective brings in a more corporeal element. What is it, in the way people sense themselves, move, and feel that allows them to retain their values in the face of perhaps unimaginable difficulties? What kinds of training in change would enhance a leader's capacity to have such integrity while still being able to change what needs to change? What would enable a person to feel Fuller's "true structural integrity"?

STRUCTURAL AND FUNCTIONAL INTEGRITY
THROUGH SOMATIC LEARNING

From the Feldenkrais perspective, the structural integrity of a human being is based on being able to rely on the skeleton for support. Typically, this is how a healthy child maintains balance, but by the time a person reaches adulthood, most people use their muscles constantly to maintain a stance that involves leaning somewhat forward or backward with parts of the body.[35] When a person develops such a "skeletal awareness," relatively less work is done by the muscles, and the sense of ease in action increases. Feldenkrais believed, or at least hoped, that such physical transformation was all that was needed for people to live the life they dreamed.[36] My thirty years of practice suggest to me that the method has such a transformative impact on a person's life only when it incorporates values and *being*, as well as movement. Combined with compatible deep training in ethics and being, such as mind training (lojong), it may generate leaders able to live from a physical and spiritual sense of integrity.

The Feldenkrais Method provides an approach to change that is grounded in how humans learn to move. The more aware one is of the feel and details of oneself in movement, the more present one is, the more ready to act appropriately to what is actually happening. Feldenkrais called one facet of the learning process he created *Awareness through Movement*.[37] The student is guided through movement sequences of "nonhabitual" movements in order to pay more attention to the *how* of what one is doing, as compared with our more customary focus on *what* one is doing. Whereas most training and education address learning to do something in what is deemed the *correct* way, this learning process instead asks the student to move slowly with awareness in order to notice the quality of movement. The learner is taught to reduce effort and to experiment with variations of the original movement, until the action feels easy and even effortless.[38] In this way, one discovers a "right way" for oneself, which is a type of learning process that can be extrapolated to many areas of life.

While the Feldenkrais Method is commonly regarded as a tool for improving movement, Feldenkrais himself saw it as a means for crafting a healthy life. As he wrote, in defining what it means to be a healthy person

> If a human being needs no medical services for years and has no complaints of pains or aches, is he or she healthy? If, on the other hand, this same person leads a dull, uninteresting life with marital difficulties that end up with suicide—is that a healthy person? And is a person who never brings his or her work to an end one way or another, and who keeps changing employment only to avoid his duties time and time again—is he in good health? ... A healthy person is one who can live his unavowed dreams fully. There are healthy people among us, but not very many.[39]

I have seen the method be quite effective in teaching people to slow down and pay attention to subtle aspects of how they move, as well as to reflect on implications of such changes for their lives. However, the method does not necessarily impact the way a person thinks about ethics and values. It can influence these areas of life but this is not inherent in the process, whereas it is core to the dharma.[40]

MIND TRAINING AND MINDFULNESS AS FOUNDATIONS FOR LIVING WITH INTEGRITY

Within the dharma, *mind training* refers to a process of "ridding ourselves of negative mental states and fostering and developing constructive ones."[41] It can be distinguished from *meditation*, a practice that typically involves sitting tall and still to focus and clear one's mind. As defined by Sogyal Rinpoche, one of today's foremost teachers of the dharma, meditation is a process intended to bring the mind "home" and allow it to rest in natural peace so one is spacious and at ease.[42] This is distinct from *mindfulness*, although they are closely related, as mindfulness generally refers to learning to pay attention and be aware of what one is sensing and noticing. Mind training does not necessarily involve meditative practices. It is a learning process that can be invoked in the midst of activity, in order to shift one's attitude to compassionate action. Mindfulness, meditation, and mind training all have centuries of teaching and practice associated with them.

Mindfulness in Recent Behavioral Science Research and Interventions

Mindfulness training has been popularized in the United States as a way of reducing stress and enhancing health. Over the last 2 decades, it has come to be used in hospitals throughout the United States and the world for stress relief, cancer care, reducing blood pressure, dealing with auto-immune disorders, controlling eating disorders, and many other pathologies.[43] A review of the literature on its use in psychotherapy concluded "that mindfulness-based approaches will become helpful strategies to offer in the care of patients with a wide range of mental and physical health problems."[44]

Mindfulness has been discussed in the organizational sciences, but not as extensively as it has been with regard to psychotherapy. Interest is growing: for example, a workshop on mindfulness research at the 2009 Academy of Management Annual Meeting filled the room with over 50 participants. Levinthal and Rerup emphasized the difference between mindful behavior and mind-less routines, addressing situations in which mindful action is useful in organizations or presents an added cost.[45] Weick's recent writings suggested the value of incorporating such thinking into the study of organizations. His recent papers on mindfulness distinguished between "the prevailing way to conceptualize mindfulness ... [which] has been to borrow from Langer's ... ideas that are essentially a variant of an information-processing perspective" and a nonconceptual approach, building on Tibetan dharma's epistemology. His writings implicitly support the use of this latter for management development: "... as people become more aware of the workings of the mind and accept those workings as the resources for collective action, they are in a better position to produce wise action."[46]

Mindfulness, the Practice of the Feldenkrais Method, and Management Training

I see common ground between mindfulness training and the practice of the Feldenkrais Method. As I mentioned, both the Feldenkrais Method and mindfulness training produce what Nonaka and Takeuchi discussed at length in the context of organizational learning as *tacit knowledge*: familiarity with a subject that lets a person act effectively without being able to fully describe how.[47] Weick and Sutcliffe contrasted conceptual Western mindfulness with the direct knowing of Eastern mindfulness, suggesting that "when people work in the conceptual mode, they develop knowledge by description rather than acquaintance" which leads to increased categorical knowing, with the unintended consequence of increasing the distance from the phenomena itself. Just as mindfulness training brings one into the present by sitting still and focusing on the subtle flow of the breath, so does Awareness through Movement train one to slow down and sense small, almost imperceptible differences in the way one carries out an action.[48] The latter may translate more readily into the workplace than traditional meditation practice, since it involves observing oneself in action, rather than in stillness. Both bring one into closer, more direct contact with the phenomenon, rather than increasing distance.

Extrapolating from Weick's and his colleagues' insights to the development of ethics and integrity in leadership development, it seems that leaders learn a lot *about* integrity and ethics, but little about how to feel and live by it. This latter would require *embodied knowing*, which Johnson describes as being a particular form of tacit knowledge that instills understanding deep into a person's bones, breathing patterns, and movement. When integrity is addressed through conceptual learning, which is the normal Western mode, it is not surprising that such training has little impact. Carolyn Wiley's empirical study showed the influence of professional codes of conduct to be roughly 11% on human resources professionals, whereas the influence of one's family upbringing (which generates tacit knowing) was roughly 68%.[49] Training may increase the likelihood that people will notice how they feel when making a decision or acting, rather than ignoring such somatic feedback. This may increase the likelihood that people will be aware of the kinesthetic responses that take place when one begins to act in a way that lacks integrity. There is almost always some sign when a person attempts to falsify feelings, either to themselves or to others, as Ekman noticed regarding facial expressions.[50] Ekman's extensive research, now being used for practical applications such as airport screening of travelers, shows that people can learn to distinguish between a genuine smile and one that is artificial. With sufficient training, anyone can perceive the inevitable small differences in the use of the facial muscles.

Because I am concerned with how embodied learning transfers to daily life activities and the extent to which a leader will act with integrity under pressure, I decided to focus on mind training, where the practice takes place *within daily perceptions and actions* rather than on meditation, which takes place primarily in retreat or while sitting on a meditation seat.

MIND TRAINING—TRANSFORMING ORDINARY REACTIONS

Adherents to varied theoretical perspectives on human behavior agree that it is useful for managers to be able to respond to people thoughtfully rather than react automatically, particularly when the reaction is anger. The research on emotional intelligence shows the value of being able to resonate positively with people.[51]

Over the last decade, many research-based conversations have taken place between the Dalai Lama, advanced meditative practitioners, and Western behavioral scientists addressing the societal importance of overcoming those emotions that are defined by the Tibetan meditation traditions as *destructive*: "those that cause harm to ourselves or to others."[52] These discussions and related research have addressed the neurological basis of behavior, introducing scientists to Buddhist understanding and familiarizing eminent Buddhist practitioners and scholars with contemporary research on the brain.[53] Reducing the impact of such emotions is core to the practice of lojong and could help leaders act with integrity.

These traditions have a distinctly different perspective on emotions such as anger from that of Western psychotherapy. From the Tibetan dharmic perspective, destructive emotions are not part of who a person really is. From this perspective, at one's most essential core, a human being and all sentient beings have an ultimate nature of mind that is referred to as *luminous*: it is pure, clear basic awareness, "without any coloration from mental constructs or emotions."[54] Learning to ground one's sense of oneself in identification with one's essential luminosity, rather than in one's personality, could have significant impacts on leaders. As we know from our work as consultants, our leader/clients often take on the responsibility for moving an entire organization from failure to success. This may require hundreds or thousands of people to change their behavior and to respond in new ways in the face of difficulty. Recent organizational writings have addressed what this demands of leaders by describing systems change in terms of leaders' *presence* and *resonance*.[55] In the context of lojong, transformational change requires that people not be controlled by negative emotions. The leader must be free of such emotions, or how can s/he help others? As Shantideva's eighth century text describes a leader's dilemma:

> When I promised to liberate from their disturbing emotions
> Wandering beings in the ten directions
> As far as the ends of space,
> I myself was not freed yet from disturbing emotions,
> And didn't even realize the extent of my (being under their control);
> Wasn't it crazy to have spoken (like that)?
> But, as this is so, I shall never withdraw
> From destroying my disturbing emotions.[56]

The inclusion of such practices in leadership development gives a method for uprooting destructive emotions before they take over and dominate the leader's actions unintentionally. According to the Dalai Lama, "the longer you are accustomed to the afflictions within you, the more prone you become to their re-occurring, and then your propensity will be to give in to them."[57] As scientist-monk Matthieu Ricard has said, "Such emotional states impair one's judgment, the ability to make a correct assessment of the nature of things."[58] It is a serious problem when a leader's judgment and ability to perceive are interfered with, yet this is common and probably a major undiscussed constituent of Chris Argyris's discussions of why "smart people can't learn"[59]—or act with integrity. While the lojong practice is not easy to master, learning to notice negative emotions as they arise and uprooting them immediately, can, with practice, generate an inner calm that is different in nature from what is often called self-discipline: simply controlling the outer expression of anger or other such emotions.

The *Eight Verses* train the practitioner in a sequence of attitudes and actions that over time can profoundly transform one's habitual states of mind. The foundation is what the Dalai Lama and others call a "good heart." Rather than assuming that temperament is innate and lasting, from this perspective the foundation of happiness is learning.[60] One uses the *Eight Verses* as a process of training (or "taming" or disciplining) one's mind, so that the negative emotions described previously do not remain habitual and ultimately will not arise.

Rather than regarding oneself as more important than everyone else, one learns to treat others with respect, whatever their status or role. One commits to watching one's mind attentively during all actions, so as to notice and immediately "face and avert" any negative emotion as soon as it arises "since it endangers myself and others." If removed immediately, the negative emotion becomes easier to remove in the future. From this perspective, emotions are seen as addictive: if one becomes accustomed to them, they become habitual. Going beyond this, one trains oneself to value meeting what popular business training books often call "difficult people": "ill-natured people, overwhelmed by wrong deeds and pain."[61] Meeting such people and not reacting negatively to them helps the practitioner to reduce the tendency to view oneself as better than others and to excuse one's own behavior while judging others and their actions. As one works through the successive verses, the challenges become greater to the "natural" tendency to value oneself over others. At each step, one learns to demand more altruistic attitudes and actions of oneself, reducing what is labeled "self-cherishing." The final verses remind the practitioner of the interdependent nature of all human actions, so that he or she increasingly perceives and acts from a systemic mindset, grounded in compassion.

In an exploratory qualitative study of entrepreneurial leaders, I found that those who used these practices said that the people they managed became more loyal and dedicated, even when wages were low. One leader emphasized how helpful he found these practices in cross-cultural contexts. He described his experience as follows:

> In other countries and cultures they have different ways of communicating, so it's a lot more normal to get angry. I've found that being patient in those situations really pays off. With the angriest people, it usually takes three attempts. They'll get super angry and I'll deflect it.... After three times, that person totally changes. All of a sudden my relationship with that person changes, and we become kind of friends or allies to solve the problem together.... I can't tell you how many times I've seen this![62]

The core notion expressed by the interviewees was that all dharmic practice involved changing one's own state of mind while focusing on cherishing others rather than oneself—which is the heart of lojong practices.

APPLICATIONS IN LEADERSHIP COACHING AND CONSULTING

Given the paucity of research studies about consulting that address these approaches, I opted to present and discuss the experiences of two management consultants in addition to my own, so as to convey a concrete sense of the potential these methods offer for generating deep and lasting change. Based on interviews I conducted with them in March 2009, I will first discuss the work of these consultants, who ground their consulting in over twenty years of study and practice of Tibetan dharma, and will then describe how I brought the principles of the Feldenkrais Method into processes of career development.

Susan Skjei has been consulting in leadership coaching and organizational transformation for over 20 years. Formerly vice-president and chief learning officer of a large technology company, she was responsible for developing its learning and change management strategy and implementing it across 40 countries and 8,500 employees worldwide, as well as for implementing a virtual corporate university to provide education and training throughout the world. She is a senior teacher in a particular Tibetan tradition known as *Shambhala*, which focuses on societal change grounded in personal transformation. She has taught in the United States, Canada, and Europe, and is the founder and director of the Authentic Leadership program at Naropa University in Boulder, Colorado, which has over 300 alumni from organizations such as Sprint, AT&T, Sun Microsystems, state and federal government, and many small businesses and non-profit organization. John "Karuna" Cayton is a business psychologist and psychotherapist who has been counseling leaders, groups, and families since 1989. He worked for over 12 years with Tibetan refugees in Nepal and is a teacher in a Tibetan tradition that is different from Skjei's, emphasizing study and dialog more than meditative practices. One of Cayton's coaching clients was profiled in *Fortune*,[63] generating widespread interest in his approach, which draws on much of what I have described above.

Both address integrity in their individual coaching but tend not to use the term itself and describe their work as fundamentally involving transformative learning. Skjei describes her focus as "developing authentic leaders through self reflection, conscious conversations and embodied action." The core competencies she emphasizes are the ability to be fully present, to engage skillfully and compassionately with others, and to lead systemic change with insight and compassion. Cayton emphasizes training in "how thinking works" in the context of "not just changing the specific behaviors that are resulting in leadership and interpersonal difficulties, but in transforming the mindset, attitudes, and belief systems that underlie the behavior." Both have worked with some clients for many years and with others for a short series of coaching sessions.

Skjei's *Authentic Leadership Training Program* is grounded in Tibetan mind training, but does not explicitly refer to classical texts or use dharmic terms. A basic premise is that all people have significant blind spots with regard to how they shape their world. Students learn to look at how the mind creates assumptions and beliefs that then create their world. One of the most widespread Tibetan practices related to mind training is a breathing and visualization practice called *tonglen*, referred to in the last two lines of the *Eight Verses*, and taught in the Authentic Leadership Program. In the first part of the course, students learn and practice basic mindfulness meditation, which involves watching the breath and the mind in order to be present to whatever is happening. The course then teaches students how to cultivate compassion for themselves and others through the tonglen practice, which involves picturing that one is taking in one's own and others' negative emotions and suffering on the in-breath and sending out openheartedness, confidence, and well-being to others on the out-breath. Although they have not collected data systematically, which could be a further step for the program, Skjei said that the students describe being able to notice when negative emotions color their views and proactively use this method to change their perception of situations in the workplace.

Skjei's experience with one client shows how she incorporates the fundamentals of such Tibetan mind training in a way that yields practical outcomes. The executive director of a not-for-profit organization was a student in the Authentic Leadership Program. As Skjei described her, "she was a highly mission-driven person who approached her work from a fierce sense of fairness and wanting to protect the disadvantaged." However, "she took on others' jobs and responsibilities, not allowing them to fail, which weakened the group." As Skjei described it,

> through coaching that addressed her early experiences of fairness and unfairness, and experience in the tonglen breathing practices, she was able to breathe space and openness into her reactions to her staff in meetings. During one session, she began crying, realizing how exhausted she was, and that she was not developing her people, much as she wished to do so. Later, she reported back that she was increasingly able to wait and not jump in so fast, so that staff members took on more responsibility and worked out their own conflicts. This freed her time for additional projects and was a huge breakthrough.

Cayton's coaching draws explicitly on mind training as well. He believes that

> Mindfulness gets considerable exposure, but it's not enough. It brings awareness, but is not proactive. In mind training, you have a difficult situation arise and then use the difficulty to create higher qualities in yourself, such as compassion, empathy, wisdom, courage. Mindfulness doesn't have this effect: it helps you not be triggered by difficult situations, without going further. A good lojong practitioner even invites the triggers: 'Oh good, this is great!' This means that uncomfortable situations are confronted and

through a particular kind of dialog, people begin to re-evaluate their own understanding of their values, and the relationship between their values and what they are doing. Once you have such a conversation, it never goes away, even many years later.

He sees his greatest value as being his ability to help executives challenge and shift their mindsets, developing their capacity to confront and deconstruct their beliefs about themselves and their values. In describing his work with one executive, he emphasized that the man was not interested in spirituality per se, but realized after a number of coaching sessions that he wanted to be a full human being and bring this into the workplace. After some time, the client began to view any situation that came up as an opportunity to be fully human—fully engaged, passionate, oriented to learning. "He likes intensity, as do most executives in start-ups. Lojong has that intensity." As he described his work with this client, much of the process was educational, challenging him to deconstruct his fixed ideas about the meanings of things like "success," "being compassionate," and "being cut-throat."

Cayton regards the core of this approach as being a process of becoming continually engaged in learning from every experience, inviting all experiences to be viewed as a way for a client to become more fully the person one wants to be. To convey what he believes too often happens in today's business world, in which executives often lack such deep willingness to challenge themselves and each other, Cayton described a start-up that was sold for a high price—despite the fact that the company's only product never worked. As he described the corporate culture, "their key value was 'being an expert.' Their product was 18 months behind schedule and it didn't work. They hid these facts and were bought for huge amount. Everyone was afraid to say that they didn't know."

The following brief case studies show how the Feldenkrais approach to embodied learning and coaching has been used for transformational learning and suggests the potential of this method for use in management development. They describe how I have brought somatic learning into my work with managers and students of consulting.

Jeanne (pseudonym) was a young project manager working in Silicon Valley at the height of the boom years (1997-2001) who had sessions with me over a period of 4 years, incorporating the Feldenkrais Method and career coaching. This learning process helped her to become a person who was quite confident about the choices she was making, instead of having wide-ranging interests and skills but considerable uncertainty about how to use them. A published description is available, so I will not describe what transpired in detail, but instead provide a high-level overview of the case and its implications.[64]

Jeanne had been a project manager in several companies and had been doing quite well, but the work had ceased to be satisfying to her. We blended Feldenkrais and career coaching sessions by conducting them sequentially within the framework of 2-hour sessions that were initially held weekly and then took place as needed. I regarded my role as being to initiate a direction, both in movement or discussion, and also to be open to following where Jeanne's focus and energy at that moment might lead us. From a Feldenkrais perspective, the practitioner needs to be ready to build on whatever the person brings that day—which is how I approached both the somatic learning and Jeanne's exploration of her ideas and feelings about herself and work.

The experience shifted her perspectives on work. She moved from trying to figure out where she fitted in, to becoming aware of how she actually felt and what energized her, and then building her life around that. Our work together progressed through several stages. What brought her to me initially was physical discomfort. This is what draws many people, since the method can help to reduce or eliminate pain. After Jeanne discovered how she could feel at ease, she began thinking about reviewing and perhaps changing her life, and inquired about career coaching. She knew what she was unhappy about, but not what she wanted in life. In the coaching process, I moved back and forth between helping her to sense what she was actually feeling and helping her to articulate her values and interests. Although she had asked initially for career coaching, we discovered that in reality, the traditional Western notions of "career," "goals," and "focus" made her uncomfortable. Over time, as I helped her sense herself as "delicious" and flowing, she began being willing to let herself know and state what she truly loved and disliked.

My original intent was to help her in a more traditional way to set career goals and develop a plan for actualizing them. I had done such work countless times before in business settings. But by adding the Feldenkrais awareness and movement, Jeanne went to deeper levels of self-knowing and honesty. Just as Cayton spoke of helping his clients deconstruct their values in conjunction with the concept of mind training, I found that moving into increasingly deep awareness of her feelings inspired Jeanne to deconstruct her ideas of success and career.

As neuroscientists have shown in recent years, movement with attention is core to the learning of children and can change the brain of adults.[65] However, little or no research has been conducted yet on the extent to which it can impact adults' mindsets and actions in such areas as life choices and leadership. The published case study of coaching Jeanne was an attempt to carefully document such a process.[66]

I have also incorporated somatic learning based on the Feldenkrais method into courses taught to graduate students at two universities studying to become organizational consultants. In describing the learning process, most of the students said that they had experienced far greater change than they had expected. A detailed description of this work is in print and can be downloaded from my website.[67] During the graduate course described in this article, which had been offered as an elective to students in organizational, sports, and clinical psychology programs, students were given a brief experience of the types of movement sequences used in the method and a description of the core principles and were invited to use these to make a change in any area of the work or personal lives that they wished. They applied this in areas ranging from physical activities (e.g., losing weight or exercise) to improving their relationships with their children to reducing stress in the workplace and changing their management style.

Usually people experiencing the Feldenkrais Method only participate in guided movement sequences or in hands-on individual "lessons," without any particular cognitive input, but in these courses students experienced movement (although less of it) and also read about it and were asked to use this as a lens to reflect on their lives. This combination seemed very powerful, as again and again the course had significant impacts on the participants.

IMPLICATIONS

Similarities Across These Methods

I have found that Feldenkrais Method sessions at times evoke a state of mind that is quite similar to what many people experience in mindfulness training. As Allen, Blashki, and Gullone described the psychological mechanisms involved in mindfulness in their survey of published research, mindfulness involves "paying attention in a particular way: on purpose, in the present moment, and nonjudgmentally."[68] This statement could equally well be used to describe what develops in effective practitioners and students of the Feldenkrais Method. Traditional mindfulness develops awareness through stillness, whereas Feldenkrais develops awareness through movement. Both develop awareness. Both are processes of deep learning that foster new approaches almost subliminally, reaching around, beyond, or beneath the discursive, analytical mind. Neither focuses on developing explicit knowledge or information about one's patterns, instead enabling them to change gradually, almost imperceptibly, by eroding their foundations through slowing the person and causing them to pay attention in the present to simple actions. This combination of heightened awareness, attention to detail, and calm can be useful in many leadership situations involving crisis management, as well as in distinguishing among the varied needs of different individuals and groups in an organization.

At the heart of these methods is a focus on enhancing awareness—bringing learners into the present to sense subtle shifts in the body or mind. In doing so, they develop parts of the mind that pay attention, that simultaneously feel and notice differences, and quiet the more discursive mind that runs a seemingly endless commentary on one's actions.

Both Tibetan practices and the Feldenkrais Method focus on and appreciate the body as a way to gain the broadest possible learning. Moshe Feldenkrais was not interested in movement for its own sake: he was interested in it as a way to improve the way people learn. Through the process of varying movements and experimenting with them, a student improves his or her ability to learn from experience. Because the movements are not done in order to get to a specific result, but are carried out in a spirit of exploration to discover what happens, the student uses his or her own movements as the subject of a quasi-scientific experiment.

Both mind training and somatic learning provide tools for moving into greater harmony with oneself and noticing when such a "felt sense" is not present.[69] This sense can be regarded as the somatic foundation for integrity; in its absence, actions lack grounding.

Having a choice of approaches that accomplish similar ends is in the spirit of both methods: both rely on what might be called *the repetition of discovery*. I coined this term to refer to their unique way of working with repetition. Both methods involve repeating processes mindfully. In working with clients, I help them see that learning of new ways of moving cannot be "held onto." Instead, the student is encouraged to rediscover the learning in as many ways as possible. By learning how to find ease of movement over and over again, a student learns multiple things simultaneously. At the tacit learning level, he or she discovers the importance of generating situations that foster discovery, in contrast to learning to seek the "right answer." This is profoundly different from much business training; most students expect there to be "an" answer that they must learn and hold onto. Both the Feldenkrais Method and dharmic practices teach instead that nothing can be "held onto": the effort of holding on changes what was being held into something else that was not wanted. Only by finding out how to recreate over and over again the important discoveries can the learner retain them.

Enabling Transformational Change

Feldenkrais believed that learning directly from the body and movement would be sufficient for deep life change—not just for improvement of movement and relief of pain. I believe that in order to impact arenas of social action such as leadership development, a practitioner needs to incorporate tacit learning of values and self-structuring. This is comparable to the way Tibetan mind training teaches that emptying one's mind is not sufficient, as the mind will always return to its former patterns after one stops meditating, unless one learns about the nature of mind and life. People "… cannot eliminate mental obscurations merely by familiarizing themselves with calm abiding meditation alone. It will only suppress the disturbing emotions and delusions temporarily."[70] The "latent potential of the disturbing emotions" can only be destroyed by wisdom, which means understanding that things always will change (*impermanence*) and that everything takes place only in interdependence on all other things, which is called *dependent origination*.

Ethics and self-discipline teachings about the importance of a good heart and caring for others' happiness are the foundation for all learning in Tibetan Buddhism. From this perspective, mindfulness alone could not be sufficient for fostering integrity in leaders; such development would need support from mind training. I believe that the key is developing awareness and value for other beings. Both can be developed many ways, but this cannot be skipped, if the planet is to have ethical, bold, aware leaders.

Designing Nonconceptual Leadership Learning

How does one learn to put others first, to eradicate negative emotions, and to value difficult people? As a New Yorker, I used to hear the old joke in which someone asked a cab driver "How do I get to Carnegie Hall? I'm in a hurry!" The unexpected answer was "Practice, practice, practice!" A true musician practices not with mindless repetition but through mindful exploration and expression of the structure of the music itself. Neither playing an instrument nor having inner peace and a "mind wishing enlightenment for all" (*bodhicitta*, or *mind of awareness*) are innate nor learned through mindless repetition. This has major implications for the design of executive development. Somatic learning can be incorporated to accelerate the process: it can help a learner sense the difference somatically when he or she is acting with integrity and when not.

A study by Nembhard and Edmondson on psychological safety and leader inclusiveness provides another empirical base for use of such an approach in leadership development. Having defined *leader inclusiveness* as "words and deeds by a leader or leaders that indicate an invitation and appreciation for others' contributions … in discussions and decisions in which their voices and perspectives might otherwise be absent," they described such inclusiveness as a way to create psychological safety and moderate the impact of different levels of status within teams.[71] The impact was particularly noticeable in lower status members of the teams that they studied, who normally did not feel free to speak and were unlikely to participate actively unless the leader was inclusive. This suggests that what is taught in lojong (not placing oneself above others and cultivating genuine respect for them) may have a measurable value with regard to team performance. Aspects of their study could perhaps be replicated with the incorporation of mind training and somatic awareness to see whether the use of these practices shifted non-inclusive leaders toward greater inclusiveness over time.

CONCLUSIONS

Consultants often recognize that leaders need to integrate systems thinking with deep awareness if they are to be effective. Cultivating integrity requires that one be aware of oneself in action and generate attitudes appropriate to the situation, rather than being reactive. The combination of mind training and somatic learning can foster this type of aware, appropriate action.

While most leadership training tends to be primarily cognitive and conceptual, the use of somatic approaches develops a different and important set of skills. Focusing the learner on close observation at a microlevel of movement, breathing, and one's state of mind can yield change at the level of tacit knowledge, an arena where we "know" but usually cannot articulate what we know. Unless leadership development touches the encoded tacit knowledge within, deeper levels of change are unlikely.

The methods described in this chapter can, I believe, be used to develop leaders who can remain calm and aware, who can notice and immediately uproot negative emotions, who can be inclusive of people whatever their status in an organization, and who can truly appreciate all the people they lead. It is unrealistic to expect humans to develop these competencies quickly, but years of experience in these various practices have shown that they do produce the desired effects when used with intention over a sufficiently long period of time. Bringing such methods into the leadership development arena could help leaders face the complex set of challenges presented by this fast-moving time of change.

NOTES

1.   Adapted with permission. The official citation that should be used in referencing this material is [Goldman Schuyler, K. (2010). Increasing leadership integrity through mind training and embodied learning.

Consulting Psychology Journal: Practice and Research, 62, 21–38.]. The use of this information does not imply endorsement by the publisher. Note that some changes will be found between this version and the earlier published article.

2. Chris Argyris, "Skilled Incompetence," *Harvard Business Review* 64, no. 5 (1986), "Teaching Smart People How to Learn," *Harvard Business Review* 69, no. 3 (1991).

3. Greg Holliday, Matt Statler, and Melanie Flanders, "Developing Practically Wise Leaders Through Serious Play," *Consulting Psychology Journal: Practice and Research* 59 (2007): 126–134; Kay Rudisill, "The Effect Of Aikido Training On Computer-Mediated Communication Between Virtual Teams," (PhD diss., The University of Phoenix, 2005); Kathryn Goldman Schuyler and Ellen Kaye Gehrke, "What Your MBA Never Taught You: Your Body, Your Heart and a Horse Can Teach You to Lead Real and Lasting Change!" Paper presented at the Global Forum on Business as an Agent of World Benefit, Case Weatherhead School of Management, Cleveland, 2006; Susanne Cook-Greuter, "Making the Case for a Developmental Perspective," *Industrial and Commercial Training* 36, no. 7 (2004): 1-10; Robert Kegan, *In Over Our Heads: The Mental Demands of Modern Life* (Cambridge: Harvard University Press, 1994).

4. Richard Boyatzis, "An Overview of Intentional Change from a Complexity Perspective," *Journal of Management Development* 25 (2006): 610.

5. Ikujiro Nonaka and Hirotaka Takeuchi, *The Knowledge-Creating Company* (NY: Oxford University Press, 1995): 239.

6. Don Hanlon Johnson (Ed.), *Bone, Breath, and Gesture* (Berkeley: North Atlantic Books, 1995); Don Hanlon Johnson (Ed.), *Groundworks* (Berkeley: North Atlantic Books, 1997); Jenny Hoogstrate Barrett, "A Qualitative Study Exploring the Use of Somatic Awareness as a Guide and Intervention in Organizational Consulting" (Unpublished Masters Thesis, Sonoma State University, 2004); Richard Strozzi-Heckler, (Ed.), *Being Human at Work: Bringing Your Somatic Intelligence Into Your Professional Life* (Berkeley: North Atlantic Books, 2003, hereafter cited as *Being Human at Work*).

7. Sharon Begley, *Train Your Mind, Change Your Brain: How a New Science Reveals Our Extraordinary Potential to Transform Ourselves,* (NY: Ballantine Books, 2007); Norman Doidge, *The Brain that Changes Itself: Stories of Personal Triumphs from the Frontiers of Brain Research,* (New York: Penguin, 2007).

8. Karl E. Weick and Ted Putnam, "Organizing for Mindfulness: Eastern Wisdom and Western Knowledge," *Journal of Management Inquiry* 15 (2006): 275-287; Karl E. Weick and Kathleen M. Sutcliffe, "Mindfulness and the Quality Of Organizational Attention," *Organization Science* 17 (2006): 514–524.

9. M. Cayer, M. and C. Baron, *Développer un Leadership Postconventionnel par une Formation à la Présence Attentive* [Developing Post-Conventional Leadership Through a Mindfulness Training Program]. *Revue Québécoise de Psychologie* 27 (2006): 257-271; Nicholas B. Allen, Grant Bashki, and Eleaonora Gullone, "Mindfulness-Based Psychotherapies: A Review of

Conceptual Foundations, Empirical Evidence and Practical Consider-
ations," *Australian and New Zealand Journal of Psychiatry* 40 (2006): 285-294.

10.   Strozzi-Heckler, *Being Human at Work,* 2; Johnson, *Bone, Breath, and Gesture,*
xiv.

11.   Thomas Hanna, *Somatics*: *Reawakening the Mind's Control Of Movement, Flexibility, and Health* (Reading, MA: Perseus Books, 1988): xiv.

12.   Awareness Through Movement," (Masters Thesis, California State University, 2006); D. Bearman and Stephen Shafarman, "Feldenkrais Method In
The Treatment Of Chronic Pain," *American Journal of Pain Management* 9
(1999): 22-27; Dinesh G. Nair and others, "Assessing Recovery In Middle
Cerebral Artery Stroke Using Functional MRI," *Brain Injury* 19 (2005):
1165-76; Carl Ginsburg, "The Shake-A-Leg Body Awareness Training Pro-
gram: Dealing With Spinal Injury And Recovery In A New Setting," *Somat-
ics* 5, no. 4 (1986): 31-42; S.E. Hall et al., *Study Of The Effects Of Various
Forms Of Exercise On Balance In Older Women* (Unpublished Manuscript.
Healthway Starter Grant, File #7672, Dept of Rehabilitation, Sir Charles
Gardner Hospital, Nedlands, Western Australia, 1999); F. Vrantsidis, K.D.
Hill, K. Moore and R. Webb, "Getting Grounded Gracefully: Effectiveness
And Acceptability Of Feldenkrais In Improving Balance And Related Out-
comes For Older People: A Randomized Trial," *Journal of Aging and Physical
Activity* 17 (2009): 57-76; Susan K. Johnson, S.K, Janet Frederick, Michael
Kaufman, and Brenda Mountjoy, "A Controlled Investigation Of Bodywork
In Multiple Sclerosis," *The Journal of Alternative and Complementary Medicine*
5 (1999): 237-43; Jim Stephens and others, "Awareness Through Move-
ment Improves Quality of Life in People with Multiple Sclerosis," *Journal of
Neurological Physical Therapy* 27 (2003): 170-179; G.A Kerr, F. Kotynia, and
G.S. Kolt, "Feldenkrais Awareness Through Movement And State Anxiety,"
Journal of Bodywork and Movement Therapies 6 (2002): 102-107; U. Laumer
and others, "Therapeutic effects of *Feldenkrais Method Awareness Through
Movement* in patients with eating disorders," *Psychotherapie, Psychosomatik,
medizinische Psychologie* 47 (1997): 170-180.

13.   Kathryn Goldman Schuyler, "Clinical Sociology, Career Coaching, And
Somatic Learning" in S. Dasgupta (Ed.), *The Discourse Of Applied Sociology:
Volume II. Practising Perspectives* (London: Anthem Press, K, 2007b): 33 – 50.

14.   Moshe Feldenkrais, *Body And Mature Behavior: A Study Of Anxiety, Sex, Grav-
itation, And Learning* (New York: Harper and Row, 1949); *Awareness Through
Movement* (New York: Harper and Row, 1972); *Body Awareness As Healing
Therapy: The Case Of Nora* (Berkeley: Somatic Resources, 1977), "On
Health," *Dromenon* 2, no. 2 1979: 25-26; *The Elusive Obvious* (Cupertino,
CA: Meta Publications, 1981).

15.   Feldenkrais, *Body and Mature Behavior; Awareness Through Movement*; *The
Elusive Obvious*.

16.   Kathryn Goldman Schuyler, "Awareness Through Movement Lessons As A
Catalyst For Change," *The Feldenkrais Journal* 15 (2003); Goldman Schuyler,
"Clinical Sociology, Career Coaching, And Somatic Learning."

17.   Reginald Ray, *Secret Of The Vajra World*, (Boston: Shambala, 2002).

18. A. Semilof, *The Lojong: Altruism in Tibetan Culture*. (Unpublished Ph.D. dissertation, Union Institute and University, United States – Ohio, 2006. Retrieved April 28, 2008, from Dissertations & Theses: Full Text database: Publication No. AAT 3242039).

19. Richard Boyatzis, and Annie McKee, *Resonant Leadership* (Cambridge: Harvard Business School Press: 2005).

20. Jon Kabat-Zinn, *Coming to our Senses: Healing Ourselves and the World Through Mindfulness* (New York: Hyperion, 2005).

21. *The Amherst Professional Training Program* was the third and last Professional Training Program taught by Moshe Feldenkrais, which took place in Amherst, MA from 1980-1983. The first was in Tel Aviv, Israel from 1969-1971, and the second was in San Francisco, CA from 1975-1977.

22. Sogyal Rinpoche, *The Tibetan Book Of Living And Dying* (San Francisco: Harper Collins, 1993): 48 – 49; The Dalai Lama, "Eight Verses For Training The Mind" in *Kindness, Clarity, and Insight*, trans. J. Hopkins (Ithaca, NY: Snow Lion, 1998): 117-134.

23. See chapter 18 for another discussion of the role of tacit knowledge in Buddhist practice.

24. Richard Strozzi-Heckler, *In Search of the Warrior Spirit: Teaching Awareness Disciplines to the Green Berets* (Berkeley: North Atlantic Books, 1990/2003).

25. J. G. Clawson, J. G. and J. Doner, "Teaching Leadership Through Aikido," *Journal of Management Education* 20 (1996): 182-205; Fred Phillips, *The Conscious Manager* (Online download: Lulu.com 2002/2008); Kay Rudisill, "The Effect of Aikido Training on Computer-Mediated Communication Between Virtual Teams."

26. Fred Phillips, *The Conscious Manager*, 1.

27. Craig E. Johnson, *Meeting the Ethical Challenges of Leadership: Casting Light on Shadow* (Los Angeles: Sage, 2009).

28. Chris Argyris, and Donald Schön, "Reciprocal Integrity: Creating Conditions that Encourage Personal and Organizational Integrity" in *Executive Integrity: The Search for High Human Values in Organizational Life*, ed. S. Srivastva, 197 (San Francisco: Jossey-Bass, 1988).

29. Chris Argyris, "Skilled Incompetence," "Teaching Smart People How to Learn."

30. R. Buckminster Fuller, *Critical Path* (New York: St. Martin's Press, 1981).

31. Kathryn Goldman Schuyler, "A Systems Approach to Learning and Change: Cindy's Story" *Somatics* 14, no. 3 (December, 2004); Johnson, *Groundworks;* Don Hanlon Johnson and Ian Grand, *The Body in Psychotherapy: Inquiries in Somatic Psychology* (Berkeley: North Atlantic Books, 1998).

32. Kabat-Zinn, *Coming to our Senses* and the extensive documentation of research on mindfulness in psychotherapy in Shauna L. Shapiro and Linda E. Carlson's *The Art and Science of Mindfulness: Integrating Mindfulness Into Psychology and the Helping Professions* (Washington DC: APA, 2009). (Hereafter referred to as *Art and Science of Mindfulness.*)

33. See http://www.appropriateresponse.com/what_we_do/programs.html

34. See http://www.bucky-fuller-synergy.com/integrity.html downloaded on April 26, 2008.

35. Hanna, *Somatics*.
36. Feldenkrais, *Awareness Through Movement*; "On Health," 25-26.
37. Feldenkrais, *Awareness Through Movement*.
38. Kathryn Goldman, "Reflections from the Mountain: Paradigms for Change," *OD Practitioner* 30, no. 1 (1998): 18-26. (Can be downloaded from www.coherentchange.com).
39. Feldenkrais, "On Health," 26-27.
40. Goldman Schuyler, "Awareness Through Movement," Goldman Schuyler, "Cindy's Story" (Can be downloaded from www.coherentchange.com).
41. Geshe Sonam Rinchen and Ruth Sonam, *Eight Verses for Training the Mind* (Ithaca, NY: Snow Lion, 2001): 7.
42. Sogyal Rinpoche, *The Tibetan Book of Living and Dying*.
43. Kabat-Zinn, *Coming to our Senses;* Shapiro and Carlson, *Art and Science of Mindfulness*.
44. Allen, Blashki, and Gullone, "Mindfulness-based Psychotherapies," 292.
45. Daniel Levinthal and Claus Rerup, "Crossing an Apparent Chasm: Bridging Mindful and Less-Mindful Perspectives on Organizational Learning," *Organization Science* 17 (2006): 502–513.
46. Weick and Putnam, "Organizing for Mindfulness," 275-287; Weick and Sutcliffe, "Mindfulness and the Quality of Organizational Attention," 514–524.
47. Nonaka and Takeuchi, *The Knowledge-Creating Company*.
48. Weick and Sutcliffe, "Mindfulness and the Quality of Organizational Attention," 520.
49. "Ethical Standards for Human Resource Professionals: A Comparative Analysis of Five Major Codes," *Journal of Business Ethics* 25 (2000): 93-114.
50. Johnson, *Bone, Breath, & Gesture*; Johnson, *Groundworks*; For Ekman's work, see Daniel Goleman, *Destructive Emotions: How Can We Overcome Them? A Scientific Dialogue with the Dalai Lama* (New York: Bantam, 2003), 128 – 131.
51. Daniel Goleman, Richard Boyatzis, and Annie McKee, *Primal Leadership: Learning to Lead with Emotional Intelligence* (Cambridge: Harvard Business School Press, 2004).
52. Goleman, *Destructive Emotions*.
53. Begley, *Train Your Mind, Change Your Brain*; Goleman, *Destructive Emotions;* The Dalai Lama and Howard C. Cutler, *The Art Of Happiness* (NY: Riverhead Books, 1998).
54. Goleman, *Destructive Emotions*, 80.
55. Peter Senge, C. Otto Scharmer, Joseph Jaworkski, and Betty Sue Flowers, *Presence: Human Purpose and the Field of the Future* (Cambridge, MA.: Society for Organizational Learning, 2004); Boyatzis and McKee, *Resonant Leadership*.
56. Shantideva, Engaging in *Bodhisattva Behavior,* Translated from the Tibetan, as clarified by the Sanskrit, by Alexander Berzin. (Printed from www.berzinarchives.com, 2005) (Several other excellent translations of this 8th century text exist, both from the Sanskrit and from the Tibetan).
57. The Dalai Lama, *Transforming The Mind: Teachings on Generating Compassion*, trans. Geshe T. Jinpa (London: Thorsons, 2000), 120.

58. Ricard as cited in Goleman, *Destructive Emotions*, 76.
59. Argyris, "Teaching Smart People how to Learn."
60. The Dalai Lama, "Eight Verses for Training the Mind"; The Dalai Lama & Cutler, *The Art of Happiness*.
61. The Dalai Lama, "Eight Verses for Training the Mind," 98,101.
62. Kathryn Goldman Schuyler, "Being a Bodhisattva at Work: Perspectives on the Influence of Buddhist Practices in Entrepreneurial Organizations," *Journal of Human Values* 13 (2007): 52. (Re-published as chapter 18 in this book.)
63. Stephanie Mehta, "Confessions of a CEO," *Fortune* 156, no. 10 (2007, November 12).
64. Goldman Schuyler, "Cindy's Story." (Can be downloaded from www.coherentchange.com).
65. Begley, *Train Your Mind, Change Your Brain*; Doidge, *The Brain that Changes Itself*.
66. Goldman Schuyler, "Clinical Sociology, Career Coaching, and Somatic Learning."
67. Goldman Schuyler, "Awareness Through Movement Lessons." (Can be downloaded from www.coherentchange.com).
68. Allen, Blashki, and Gullone, "Mindfulness-Based Psychotherapies," 288.
69. Eugene T. Gendlin, *Focusing*, 2nd ed. (New York: Bantam Books, 1982).
70. The Dalai Lama, " Eight Verses for Training the Mind," 82.
71. Ingrid Nembhard and Amy C. Edmondson, "Making It Safe: The Effects of Leader Inclusiveness and Professional Status on Psychological Safety and Improvement Efforts in Health Care Teams," *Journal of Organizational Behavior* 27 (2006): 941-96.

SECTION II

INDIVIDUALS: HOW TIBETAN BUDDHIST PRACTICE IMPACTS PEOPLE AT WORK

This free and well-favored human form is difficult to obtain.
Now that you have the chance to realize the full human potential,
If you don't make good use of this opportunity,
How could you possibly expect to have such a chance again?[1]

These personal vignettes are first-person accounts by long-time Buddhist practitioners, reflecting on the impact of their practice on their lives and work. For some, this meant developing an entirely new aspect of their work, whereas for others, it deeply influenced that way that they did what they were already doing, on a day-to-day basis. They can be seen as "raw data" for thinking about the varied ways that Buddhist practice is impacting people's work. Most are shorter than the typical scholarly chapter, intentionally, and they have fewer notes and references.

I aimed to have as great a variety of types of work as possible in a small number of selections, so as to convey the range of types of people drawn to such study and practice, as well as how it affects them. Most do not write regularly in their professional lives, so do not look for traditional scholarly writing—although there is some, because one author is a professor of sociology. My goal was to bring in different voices and perspectives, to bring alive Western experiences of Tibetan Buddhism at work. As one author said, "This is really hard to write! It's much easier to write a schol-

Inner Peace—Global Impact: Tibetan Buddhism, Leadership, and Work, pp. 95–97
Copyright © 2012 by Information Age Publishing

95

arly paper or to write an article about a topic outside oneself. Writing about how my own work has been influenced or nurtured by my spiritual practice is quite challenging."

Lin Lerner's piece on "Bringing Lingdro to the West" is located first, because it is as much about the leadership she has had to develop, as it is about herself and her dancing. In this sense, it bridges this section and the preceding one. Dr. Lerner is an anthropologist of dance who was so entranced by a particular form of Tibetan dance that she uprooted her life to move to Nepal and India to study it. I urged her to think about herself as a leader and write about what it takes to transplant and preserve an art form that might well have died otherwise, since its existence depended upon the communities in which it lived—and, for the most part, those communities had been completely disrupted by the Chinese invasion. Although so-called "Tibetan dance" can still be seen in Tibet, it has been thoroughly changed by the Chinese.[2] Where it used to be a communal spiritual activity, it has become a form of entertainment with an entirely different set of "rules" and expectations. People have become "performing artists" following Chinese norms about beauty, singing style, the separation of dancing and singing, and many other things. Bringing this dance form to the West to help it survive, where there was (and for the most part still is) no infrastructure for its support, required courage, adventure, and persistence.

John Eric Baugher is a sociology professor who has become intensely interested in Tibetan Buddhism and, in particular, in research on hospice work with the dying. In "Learning to Rest," he provides a vivid picture of his journey through academic life. As readers, we get a rare glimpse of what it felt like to deal with some of its challenges, and we see how Tibetan Buddhist practice has, over time, been shifting his perspectives on himself and on academia.

Scott Snibbe is an internationally exhibited artist whose art focuses on interaction between the viewer and the object viewed or between the viewer and his or her concepts about ...himself? Art? What an object is? Permanence? His piece explores the twin themes of being an artist and as a result having to be a business person as well, locating both within the frame of reference of Buddhist practice. I encourage readers to look at his art on the web, since what we could include in the book had to be more static that his art actually is. The art can be seen at http://www.snibbe.com/

Carl Mangum has devoted his life to the practice of social work. Wherever he goes, his resonant laugh, warmth, and deep listening bring people to him. Raised a Christian in Louisiana, in the middle of the last century, he found and turned to Tibetan Buddhism as a source of wisdom useful in his personal life and practice. He is, at heart, a very private and modest person. He helps the reader see how Tibetan Buddhist concepts can be helpful for the people with whom he works who are Southerners with no desire to become Buddhist, but a strong desire to be happier than they are!

Dana Browning (pseudonym) has been a flight attendant for close to three decades and a Tibetan Buddhist for almost as long. Her dedication to learning and service are high. Her deceptively simple description of the way she brings Buddhism into her work in the air is a rare opportunity for most of us to see through the eyes of one of the many people whom we meet and talk with, but rarely know personally. The world of a flight attendant is an interesting phenomenon because it is one that touches most readers, yet we do not really see into it from the flight attendant's side.

Paul Ritvo is a clinical psychologist and research scientist. He is a 30-year Tibetan Buddhist practitioner who is currently devoted to scientific research on cancer prevention, AIDS treatment, and mindfulness meditation. He is an associate professor in the School of Kinesiology and Health Science in the Department of Psychology at York University in Toronto, where he focuses on health behavior change via group therapy, telephone, print, and interactive internet programming.

As different as they are, there are common themes across these personal stories—tales that can be approached as "raw data" for qualitative research. Further work could be done in this area, since this section can only be suggestive with such a small number of people. In their own ways, all are adventurous, deeply committed to what they are doing, willing to face themselves and any negative emotions, and are deeply caring people. All are quite observant, which requires being present, and in their own ways, innovative. This is not the kind of innovation that necessarily creates new art, like Scott Snibbe, but the kind of innovation that brings a freshness to one's life and allowed them to find a ground in their meditative practice for reframing their profession in significant ways.

NOTES

1. From the *Bodhicharyavatara*, as selected by Sogyal Rinpoche for inclusion in teachings on the preciousness of human life, in *A Gide to the Practice of Ngondro*, 2nd edition, Trans. Rigpa Translations, (www.rigpa.org, 2007), 50.
2. Anna Morcom, "Modernity, Power, and the Reconstruction of Dance in Post-1950s Tibet,"JIATS, 3 (December 2007), THL #T3129, 42 pp. http://www.thlib.org/collections/texts/jiats/#jiats=/03/morcom/all/

CHAPTER 6

BRINGING LINGDRO TO THE WEST

A Dance of Blessing and Peace

Lin Lerner, Dance Ethnologist and Tibetan Ritual Dancer

There was electricity in the air and heightened expectation. Chattering groups of Tibetan children, parents, and grandparents—sitting on the ground in the dusty courtyard of the monastery—were waiting. A hush came over the crowd when a lama in red monastic robes entered the circle. Chanting, he blessed the ritual ground of the dance area and sanctified the performance. Then, dancers holding long white offering scarves of silk slowly and majestically filed into the arena. With powerful strides, their voices in full song, the men appeared first, followed by the fluidly graceful

Inner Peace—Global Impact: Tibetan Buddhism, Leadership, and Work, pp. 99–112
Copyright © 2012 by Information Age Publishing

women who echoed their notes. Circumambulating the courtyard, they dazzled the viewers with their brilliant silken costumes and infectious melodies. The men began to stamp, hop, and whirl, while the women turned and swayed. The entire courtyard was a vortex of movement and prayer. In a moment of crescendo, the dancers exited.

MY QUEST: ADVENTURE, SCHOLARSHIP, AND DANCE

I have been fortunate to have had the opportunity to be adventurous. I envision myself as an explorer of three realms: the world of movement, the world-at-large, and the world of the mind. Dancing was always an integral part of my childhood: moving beautifully and expressively not only uplifted my emotions, but also my sensibilities and spirit. Continuing into my university years, I pursued modern and ethnic dance, eventually teaching yoga, dance, and movement study at Barnard College. I yearned to understand the unity of mind and body, especially the dance's particular expression of that union.

At Columbia University in the early 1970s, I studied *Laban's* systems of movement analysis and notation and worked on Alan Lomax's Choreometrics Project for the Bureau of Applied Social Research, studying culture in terms of movement. There I observed, catalogued, and sorted numerous films of dances from all parts of the world. One film that profoundly changed my life depicted a Tibetan black hat dancer moving slowly, deliberately, spiraling in space. The image embodied an otherworldly quality. Mesmerized by its continuous hypnotic whirl and the powerful inner experience it projected, I vowed to pursue the dance and understand the mind behind the movement. Because I intuitively felt that I would not be able to comprehend the nature of movement until I understood the nature of stillness, I pursued classes in Zen meditation at a center in New York City. There I found the practice of Buddhism not only calming, but mind expanding and prophetic for the self.

I followed my Zen studies with a course on theater exercises taught by students of Chögyam Trungpa Rinpoche. Since he was the only lama I knew in America, when he visited New York, I asked him to recommend a ritual dance teacher. His choice, a lama in India, near Dharamsala, the seat of the Tibetan government in exile, gave me a focus. In 1974, I cropped my hair and left for India with his letter of introduction and a backpack filled with super-eight film.

DANCE IN THE TIBETAN WISDOM TRADITIONS

Dance has been an integral component of Tibetan Buddhist rituals for centuries. Through song and movement, voice and body, dancers experience connections between the inner world of the spirit and the external phenomenal world. Tibetans think of the shared experience of ritual dance as a "skillful means" to realize the enlightened state.[1] Its survival is important to the preservation of Tibetan culture. Traditions such as the *Lingdro* are crucial artifacts of cultural identity, particularly necessary when a culture has been threatened or uprooted. Since the Chinese take-over in 1959, when Tibetan culture and religious practices were banned, the Tibetan people have been influenced by secular interests. Young Tibetans who were denied access to their religion have gravitated toward disco dance and other popular genres. In the more remote regions, how-ever, traditional folk and even ritual dances are performed in villages and small temples, although some of their folk dance costumes and styles now reflect the Chinese influence. Different styles and traditions of Gesar dance can be found in the Eastern regions of Kham and Golok.

As a dance ethnologist and student of dance, I was fortunate to be introduced to a traditional Tibetan dance early in my studies of Tibetan (*Vajrayana*) Buddhism. It has been my great fortune to learn the Lingdro ritual dance cycle and teach it in the West. *Lingdro Dechen Rolmo* (The Music of Great Bliss which is a Dance of Ling) is an offering prayer in song and movement dedicated to *Ling Gesar*, an active and powerful ema-nation of *Padmasambhava*—a yogi and teacher who established the Bud-dha Dharma in Tibet. *Gesar*, much like King Arthur, is the subject of Tibet's most famous epic. He represents the enlightened, compassionate hero who overcomes all obstacles and is predicted to usher in peace in a time of chaos and disruption. As a holder of this lineage of teaching (I was given the complete transmission of all of the dances by the recognized teacher and holder of this tradition), I have the responsibility to transmit the knowledge I have received as purely as possible.[2]

This essay describes the Lingdro, my history with the dance, and espe-cially the process of working with students in the West. In teaching students in the United States and Europe, I recognize that they learn differently from Tibetan students, who live in close communities in a holistic fashion. The Western dance groups are of necessity fluid; the commitment of stu-dents is shaped by their modern lives and multiple responsibilities. The dance occupies their spare time, wedged between jobs and family life—even if their feeling for the dance and its meaning is deep and resonant. For these reasons, new organizational frameworks are needed to allow the Lingdro to thrive and to survive when I cease teaching.

In Tibetan (Vajrayana) Buddhism, all practices are said to symbolize outer, inner, and secret levels of meaning. On the outer level, this rite vanquishes external obstacles in the world, as we know it; on the inner level it is intended to overcome afflicted emotions and unseen aspects of ourselves; and on the secret level of our mind and heart, it aims to tran-scend the mind's discursive thoughts. These layers reveal progressively deeper levels of experience or knowledge. The practitioners, in search of understanding, ultimately arrive at the center of their own being. The *mandala*, used widely in Tibetan Buddhism, looks like a maze of circles and squares drawn in sand paintings, painted on scrolls, and constructed in three-dimensions. It functions as a map of this process and as a mystic diagram; it reveals the subtleties of the awakened Buddha mind. A mandala can serve as an organizing principle for creating groups. My work is a part of this dynamic process: enabling Lingdro mandalas of positive energy to thrive in different locales.

Tibetans believe that the Lingdro creates a *tendrel*,[3] or auspicious connection. It is a symbolic dance of good luck that connects us to positive energy, and enhances the well-being of those who dance and witness it.[4] The dance is an offering to the teachers and deities who lead us on the path to enlightenment (the *Bodhisattva* path), encouraging generosity, kindness, and the desire to help others. In addition, the Lingdro is a powerful rite of exorcism: an occasion for stamping out negativity and welcoming bliss.

THE SOURCE: INDIA

In the West, a dancer begins his training by drilling on basic exercises. He then works on movement phrases and combinations and finally learns a complete dance. In the traditional method of instruction in much of Asia, a dancer immediately begins learning a standard repertory piece. He imitates the teacher over and over again until the dance is learned and then begins a new piece.[5]

The locales I visited in India were not on the typical tourist route. There were no guidebooks to help me, and there were few books about Tibetan Buddhism available at that time. Because I had previously been to India in 1970, I was not shocked by seeing cows in the roads or abject poverty. I breathed in the mingled smell of dust, curry, night-blooming jasmine, humans, and animals. My eyes feasted on the brilliant *saris*, the red spit of *pan* juice in the dirt, and marigolds and jasmine strung into garlands. Everywhere, people were crammed into doorways, out on the streets, and reaching out their hands for *baksheesh* (alms).

Although the British were no longer the colonial rulers, their legacy was palpable. Educated people spoke English, a network of antiquated trains traversed the country, and sweet milk *chai* tea was available everywhere. In the fall of 1974, I embarked on a tortuous journey by train and bus over precarious mountains in remote regions. When I finally reached Tashijong, I had an audience with Khamtrul Rinpoche (recommended by Trungpa Rinpoche), who refused my request to learn ritual dance. He felt it was not proper for his yogi teachers, with their strict vows of celibacy, to be my tutors. Furthermore, they knew no English.

Dejected, I returned to Dharamsala, where I was introduced to Anzin Rinpoche, a lama representative of the Tibetan government in exile. Fortunately, he knew of a dance performed by both men and women in the Orissa refugee settlement, where his family lived. The dance was particularly important to his brother, His Eminence Namkha Drimed Rinpoche, a reincarnate lama who spontaneously composes practices to Ling Gesar and is considered to be the embodiment of Gesar himself. Since Anzin Rinpoche knew I would be welcome there, he proceeded to arrange for my papers. After 3 months, I received permission from the Indian government to stay in the camp.

I rode the noisy, dusty, cramped trains for days from Dharamsala to Delhi, to Calcutta, and finally to Berhampur, Orissa on the east coast between Calcutta and Madras. When I arrived, I was met by Anzin Rinpoche's sisters who escorted me to the right bus. Our journey entailed a bumpy, five-hour ride followed by a mile-long hike through corn and millet fields to their home in the remote, hilly, desert-like region. The Tibetan refugees in Chandrigiri Settlement lived in mud houses without running water or electricity. Despite their grim situation, they were proud, deeply religious, and devoted to their ritual practices. Most had become farmers; a smaller number worked in a carpet factory. They were connected to one another through communal activities and religious rites, one of which was Lingdro Dechen Rolmo.

The Lingdro was received as a *terma*[6] (hidden text) meditative vision by Mipham Rinpoche, a great nineteenth century yogi, scholar, and visionary. Later, some of Mipham Rinpoche's Lingdro dances were lost. In order to preserve and strengthen this sublime song and dance tradition, Reting Rinpoche (regent and tutor to His Holiness the 14th Dalai Lama) and devotee of Gesar, requested the layperson Norbu Sangpo to compose a number of the Lingdro dances and appointed him teacher of the entire cycle of thirteen dances and holder of this dance lineage.

The members, devoted to their revered dance leader, affectionately called him Pa Norzang, or Pala. As a refugee in Orissa, Pa Norzang organized a volunteer club which danced the Lingdro. They performed on special occasions, especially to entertain distinguished visitors. Some camp members helped the group make properties (props), and individual dancers made and owned their own costumes. Rehearsals were held outdoors or in someone's house or storeroom.

During my first week in Orissa, I was taken to a granary storage building which was cleared away to enable the unimpeded movement of the brilliantly costumed dancers. After that, I went to Pala's house every day, where taking tea and cookies was a prerequisite to my Lingdro tutorial. Pa

Norzang taught Tibetans the Lingdro songs first, so they would understand the text before learning the movements. Since the words were not translated into English, he broke with tradition and taught me the movement, the universal language, first. I began by following behind him, copying each move. We repeated an entire dance again and again until I learned it. For 6 months he, assisted by his daughter Yangzom, transmitted this sacred lineage of thirteen dances to me. Passing through Dharamsala on my way home, I was granted an interview with His Holiness the Dalai Lama, who said he was pleased that I would be bringing this dance to the West.

LAUNCHING THE LINGDRO IN AMERICA: NEW YORK AND CALIFORNIA

Traditionally, Lingdro groups are organically grown. The seed of inspiration is planted by a lama or student, watered by the activity of teaching, fertilized by the devotion of the students, and blossoms into the offering of performance.

After my return to America in 1976, I met His Holiness Dudjom Rinpoche, the spiritual head of the temple in Orissan Camp Number Three. He was the head of the Nyingmapa lineage of Tibetan Buddhism and an acknowledged *dzogchen* master; he was regarded by many as an emissary of Padmasambhava. He heard that I had studied the Lingdro and said he was waiting to meet me. I was moved by his gentle, spacious wisdom and asked to become his student. In 1978, I followed him to Kathmandu, where he gave initiations, which are direct transmissions of energy and insight that enable one to undertake a particular meditation practice or ceremony.

I became a member of Yeshe Nyingpo, the dharma center he established in New York City, yet I did not plan to teach the Lingdro until another student who knew of my ritual dance experience asked me to teach it. As a special offering to our teacher, I began to assemble a group. I announced at his teachings that I would be happy to teach the Lingdro, and a handful of students responded. The board of the center agreed to let us use a modest room in their brownstone for rehearsals. Luckily an excellent dancer who was a psychologist and yoga teacher joined us; he became the lead dancer. Others followed. At this time, the group was comprised of New York men and women who were able to attend my free, weekly, sometimes biweekly classes.

Subsequently, I enlisted the help of some students in creating the elaborate props, costumes, and headdresses that enable the dancers to represent Gesar, his minister-warriors, and their goddess wives. My teacher's

Figure 6.1.   Yangzom and Pa Norzang dance. (Courtesy Lin Lerner)

Figure 6.2.   Jampa Thokmey, Yangzom, and Pala. (Courtesy Lin Lerner)

Figure 6.3.   Lin and Yangzom Dance, Orissa. (Courtesy Lin Lerner)

Figure 6.4.   Bill Blechingberg Dancing the Lingdro. (Courtesy Lin Lerner)

Figure 6.5.   Tara Friedensohn Dancing the Lingdro. (Courtesy Lin Lerner)

wife, a princess with exquisite taste, generously contributed colorful bro-
caded costumes and necklaces that she herself had strung. I supple-
mented these with some *chuba* blouses and dresses that I purchased in
Nepal.

At the outset, I had many roles: teacher, director, scheduler, and costume and properties manager. But I felt confident only in my ability to
teach. When we began, I tried to transmit the movements in the "traditional" Tibetan manner: asking students to copy and repeat them. When
this didn't work well, I broke down the movements into segments, calling
them out as we moved. I labeled each step: left, right, hop, and encouraged the dancers to notate the steps for themselves. Since some of these
sequences were repeated in different dances, students gradually became
confident.

At first, I was tentative about teaching the three songs I had learned in
the settlement. In 1978, I commissioned the translator, John Reynolds,
who worked with Chagdud Tulku (an early Tibetan teacher in the United
States,) to render the Lingdro text into English. I also began to give some
of the transliterated texts to my students to memorize. My singing voice is
adequate, but I lack the range and flexibility necessary for trills. Although
our group tried to sing *a cappella* tunes, we kept returning to our own
Western rhythms, which reminded me of 1950s rock n' roll. In the end,
we decided to dance to taped music of Pa Norzang and his group.

In 1980, Dudjom Rinpoche purchased a resort motel complex in
Greenville, NY to accommodate his students from all over the world who
were attracted to his peerless teachings and charismatic presence. This

permanent upstate retreat center, named Orgyen Chö Dzong (OCD), also served New York's Yeshe Nyingpo community. Dudjom Rinpoche's purchase marked a new era for our Buddhist community and for the Lingdro. We had a larger performance space and overnight accommodations. When Rinpoche's students converged in this area for his teachings, saw our Lingdro group perform, and heard His Holiness endorse the Lingdro as a path to realization, some joined us. In 1983, His Holiness left for France and ultimately passed away there in 1987, leaving his New York centers to his son and heir His Holiness Shenphen Dawa Rinpoche. However, before he left, he personally thanked me for dancing the Lingdro and said that he planned to have dancing at his centers.

The New York Lingdro group is a model for all of the other groups. We dance regularly, and perform at least twice yearly for lamas and meditation practitioners, for His Holiness Shenphen Rinpoche at OCD, and elsewhere when His Excellency Namkha Drimed Rinpoche is visiting New York. We have also been presenting the Lingdro as a dance for peace in public spaces such as art galleries, colleges, and schools, and at community events such as the Walkway Across the Hudson River. The possibility of forming other groups arose when Lama Tharchin Rinpoche, whom I first met in Orissa, paid a visit to OCD in the 1980s. He had moved to Santa Cruz, CA, and he invited me to his new retreat center *Pema Ösel Ling* (POL), where he was initiating a *drupchen,* a week-long cycle of ritual practice. Drupchen is a powerful practice that involves chanting *mantras* and visualizing mandalas. It culminates in a day-long performance of masked dances (*cham*) representing the deities visualized in the practice. Lama Tharchin envisioned a program with several of the Lingdro dances alternating with the cham.

I arrived with my 4-year-old daughter Tara, Lingdro music, an outline of dances, and several large duffle bags filled with costumes. We were also carrying a tent and sleeping bags. As it turned out, the California-based cham teachers, who knew nothing about the Lingdro, had started rehearsals and were using the rehearsal space throughout the day. Adjusting quickly, our newly formed group agreed to practice the Lingdro at breakfast time in a room near the kitchen, and that schedule continues to this day.

Lama Tharchin introduced the Lingdro as a special and sacred dance of sublime origin, yet since it is not a masked dance, most people still regarded it as a folk dance, not important enough to merit our rigorous rehearsal schedule. Over the past 20 years, however, the Lingdro has become honored and appreciated at POL, yet it still does not have a stable group of dancers. I never know who will be returning or who will sign up for other dances that may conflict with our practice and performance time. Still, new students appear each year, and I work extra hard to prepare them for our performance.

All age groups are welcome to participate in the dances at POL. While I have always taught teenagers, in 2009 I agreed to teach children aged 10 to 12 years of age. Their vibrant energy, eagerness, and sincerity invigorated the group. I discovered that the children were more committed and more likely to be prompt than the adults.

Under drupchen conditions, participants must learn four dances in 10 days. I give small bits of information, encourage students to write down the steps, distribute song texts, and enlist older students in teaching newer ones.

New Horizons: The Lingdro in France

In 2005 His Holiness Shenphen Dawa Rinpoche asked to have sixteen Lingdro dancers perform for the 25th anniversary of OCD. I gathered dancers from New York, Boston, California, and France, using class breaks for dance training and rehearsals. Our actor-lead dancer from New York led, and a young and enthusiastic dancer from Paris, well versed in martial arts, assumed the important role of last dancer in line. In subsequent years, other students from Paris and from the south of France have joined my Lingdro teaching sessions when they return to OCD for His Holiness Shenphen Rinpoche's summer retreat seminars.

In 2006, I stopped in Paris en route to Morocco and taught a Lingdro class both to students who had studied in New York and to new people. In a student's rear garden, we sowed the seeds of an official French group. At the urging of a senior student, and with the support of a woman who has studied steadily in the summers at OCD, a Paris group has formed. They rehearse regularly and have been making and ordering their own costumes and properties and plan to officially organize as Lingdro France.

TO SUSTAIN THE TRADITION

Maintaining my commitment to my dance teachers to pass on this wisdom tradition, I have attempted to be focused, pragmatic, and flexible. As needs arose, I created more codified teaching materials including song texts, accompanying meditation practices, reading lists, step charts, mailing lists, and most recently costume and property lists and patterns.

Lingdro groups are loosely organized and continue to evolve. As more participants join and new groups develop, better organization is required. The next stage will require a more professional approach: an information packet composed of the music and visuals including CDs and DVDs, pamphlets providing the background information and explanations of the meaning of the dance cycle, formally organized booklets with sections of the translated text, and detailed, do-it-yourself information on costumes and properties including photographs, patterns, suggestions for construction, and where the materials can be obtained. A Lingdro website is needed, which will require a secretary for internet communications and for organizing archival materials for use on the site.

Since none of the Lingdro dancers has full knowledge of either the Tibetan cultural background or the dance steps, it remains my responsibility to transmit the Lingdro to future generations in the West, but with the increased scale and complexity of tasks, it has grown too large and complex, and requires more formal organization.

CONCLUSION

In college, I focused on the arts. My goal was to be the best choreographer, modern dancer, and teacher in America. I aspired to attain both the expertise as well as the glory on this quest. I was passionate about the dance's physicality, power, expressiveness, and striking beauty. Eager to improve my technique, I spent my spare time in dance classes, observing dance performances in New York City, and performing. Most of my performances were solo. Since my body was my instrument, I was self-consciously concerned about my appearance: about the line of my body and its image. Since studying the Lingdro, my goal has shifted to include an inward focus on realization, and an outward concern for others and their well-being. The dance is not just an end, but the means to an end: the goal being engendering positive circumstances and the enlightened view. I am involved in this communal activity in which the whole is definitely more powerful than the sum of its parts.

Many years ago, when I felt compelled to study Tibetan dance, I found myself embarking on a lifetime mission: to rescue and perpetuate the Lingdro, an authentic ritual dance for peace. This commitment changed my perspective and the course of my life. I began to experience my world in a very different fashion. Through my contact with the Lingdro, I encountered people and a culture where nothing was superficial. Everything had a deeper and richer meaning and led me to my teacher, His Holiness Dudjom Rinpoche, who pointed out to me a world view far more expansive than the two dimensional egoistic and materialistic one we adhere to in the West. I began to feel a connection to all other beings and to see that specialness and beauty in all circumstances. I experienced the possibilities of ritual dance as not just an aesthetically appealing or technically interesting activity, but one that has a purpose: to create peace and happiness in the world and to deepen one's awareness.

With regard to my dance ethnographic work, I initially went to India to study Tibetan ritual dance and analyze it. However, I found that I needed to immerse myself in the Tibetan culture in order to fully learn it, for the analysis and constant inquiry separated me from the experience, and my teacher needed to teach freely without my constant inquiry. I allowed myself to learn in his manner and then sort out my data afterward. For me, the dance's inner experience far outweighed the Western scientific investigation. I realized that it was necessary to study meditation in order to understand the Lingdro, for the dance relies on inner balance as a reference point—a vast and humbling perspective.

The Lingdro is a wisdom dance; a *terma* from a great yogi and mystic. Its goal is to benefit people. At the outer level it averts negativity and engenders positive circumstance. On the inner level, it transforms afflicted emotions, and on the secret level it enables the practitioner to rest in pure awareness. Because the *Dzogchen view* (a sense of a profoundly simple contact with the nature of mind) pervades the performance, the dancers and audience members can experience a very profound level of meditation. Since I always briefly explain the dance to the audience, they are included in the experience. Lingdro performers inform the Lingdro with their Buddhist practice, which transports them beyond thoughts of themselves and the place in which they are performing and transforms ordinary dance into compassionate activity.

I now concentrate on teaching the Lingdro to students interested in performing the dance and give transpersonal workshops on the inner experience and healing qualities of ritual dance to the public. This often presents a totally different experience to people who might not have encountered this way of seeing. Taught this way, they do not remain fixated on studying analytical information or specific steps, and are better able to absorb the larger meaning and intentions of the dance.

I consider the Lingdro to be my offering to the Western students who have asked me to teach them; to my Lingdro teachers, Norbu Sangpo and his daughter Yangzom, who generously transmitted this sublime tradition to me; to the lamas who have guided me to my true nature; and to the world. I dance and teach so it may alleviate all suffering and bring consciousness to all. May its energy ripple out, helping us to confront these challenging, tumultuous times. May it build bridges of peace around the world.

NOTES

1. In Tibetan practices, *skillful means* refers to appropriate compassionate activity which benefits many beings.

2. To be a lineage holder refers to a person who receives teachings and or empowerments and is authorized by a teacher transmit it to others.

3. A *tendrel* in Vajrayana Buddhism is an auspicious connection, coincidence or omen.

4. The dance is considered a method of liberation through sight, depending on the devotion understanding and good karma of the viewer.

5. Carl Wolz, Bugaku, *Japanese Court Dance* (Providence: Asian Music Publications, 1971), 2.

6. A *terma* is a hidden treasure or teaching concealed in order to be discovered at a later, more appropriate time.

CHAPTER 7

LEARNING TO REST

Transforming Habits of Mind in Higher Education

John Eric Baugher, Sociology Professor[1]

"If we try to solve society's problems without overcoming the confusion and aggression in our own state of mind, then our efforts will only contribute to the basic problems, instead of solving them."

—Chögyam Trungpa—*Shambhala*

Inner Peace—Global Impact: Tibetan Buddhism, Leadership, and Work, pp. 113–123
Copyright © 2012 by Information Age Publishing

The discipline of sociology was founded on the Western Enlightenment ideal of seeking knowledge as a means for creating a more humane society. Yet in my 10 years as a professor of sociology I have found the academic world to be plagued by numerous emotional afflictions and related social dynamics that obscure the tremendous potential our work has for transforming our own workplaces, the lives of our students, and the broader social world. My intention in this short reflection is to illustrate how Tibetan Buddhism, first introduced to me through the teachings and writings of meditation master and scholar Chögyam Trungpa Rinpoche and his students, has led to a fundamental turn around in how I approach my work as a professor of sociology.[2]

The dynamics I will discuss in this essay are not recent in origin, but instead relate closely to the critique of American cultural habits made by psychologist William James in "The Gospel of Relaxation," an address first given to the graduating class of the Boston Normal School of Gymnastics in 1895. James explained how the mind can become its own "prison-house," not solely as a matter of individual psychopathology, but as a reflection of a broader cultural condition. The greatest hindrance to the work of students and teachers in the United States, James suggested, could be found not in the nature or quantity of work demanded in academic settings, but "in those absurd feelings of hurry and having no time, in that breathlessness and tension, that anxiety of feature and that solicitude for results, that lack of inner harmony and ease."[3] To illustrate the kind of breathlessness and tension James had in mind, consider the following experience I had as part of my socialization into the profession.

Getting tenure is thought to be the most pivotal moment in a professor's life, a view that was first impressed upon me in my second year of graduate school. It was Easter 1994, and my girlfriend and I took a 3-day canoe trip along the Black Creek in Southern Mississippi to enjoy nature and to take a break from our daily routines split between sitting in front of our computer screens and searching the stacks at the Howard-Tilton library on Tulane's uptown campus. We were both in the middle of writing our Master's theses, and I was having a difficult time paddling down the river without thinking about all the writing I was not getting done. Apparently, I did not make for the most enjoyable camping partner. On the second day of our trip my girlfriend pointed out the obvious: I could keep myself miserable worrying about my thesis during the entire trip or I could allow myself to relax and take in the beauty of the tea-colored river, white sand bars and deep green pines as we meandered through the De Soto National Forest. Either way I would make no progress on my thesis. Perhaps it was her compelling logic, I am not quite sure, but something in me clicked as we sat by the campfire, and without much effort I relaxed into the rest of our trip with very little thought about how refinery workers in Louisiana were coping with the stress of working in the explosively toxic petrochemical industry.

If only it were that easy to learn how to rest. At the time I was working as a research assistant for a professor in the sociology department, and we had an appointment in her office the day after I returned from the canoe trip. She asked me about the weekend, and I eagerly told her about the gentle river and its sandy banks, and before I could recount my campfire epiphany I was shamed into silence with the invective "We academics don't take breaks until we get tenure!" While her methods of professional socialization were the harshest among the faculty I encountered in graduate school, the underlying message of making a virtue out of working compulsively permeated the culture that I was becoming a part of. In the fall of 2009, 15½ years after this encounter, I was granted tenure and promoted to Associate Professor. Fortunately, I did not wait a decade and a half to begin cultivating a way of being beyond all the breathlessness and tension, grasping for results, and lack of inner harmony and ease that so pervades the academic world.

I am thankful for the measure of job security and academic freedom I enjoy as a result of being granted tenure, especially in the current climate of crisis in higher education. Yet such freedom and security, contingent on ever shifting external conditions, pales in importance to the freedom I have begun to experience through practicing *shamatha* or "calm abiding" meditation and *lojong* or "mind training" practices that Chögyam Trungpa and other Tibetan lamas have brought to the West. These practices are not concerned with self-improvement, which would imply some sort of defect in one's basic nature, but of relating directly to one's experience and working *with* rather than *against* that energy. Shamatha is the principle method for getting to know one's own mind and developing the capacity to rest in the natural flow of experience rather than attempting to solidify or suppress that experience with conceptual thoughts regarding, for example, what I perceive others are doing to me or how they or I should be different.[4] There are two main approaches to Lojong: the "Eight Verses" described in Goldman Schuyler's chapter on leadership and the one that I use involving daily contemplation of 59 pith mind training slogans which serve as antidotes to the habitual strategies of self-protection that cause suffering for oneself and others.[5] The intention of both practices is to free the mind from clinging to the worldly preoccupations of gain and loss, fame and obscurity, pain and pleasure, and praise and blame so the heart can naturally open to a direct, compassionate encounter with all that is. Through shamatha and lojong the practitioner loosens the hold of these habitual ways of conceptualizing experience and trains in resting mindfully in the present rather than getting worked up by hopes for the future or fears resulting from ruminations on past experiences.

These practices have profoundly affected my teaching philosophy and strategies for learning; my research agenda, epistemology, and practice of research ethics; and more generally, how I seek to interact with students, colleagues, administrators, and members of the wider community. It is beyond the scope of this vignette to illustrate in detail these many influences, and instead I focus here on how lojong practice has transformed how I work with anger and related "negative" emotions in my capacity as a sociologist.[6] I take this approach for two reasons. First, frustration and anger are common experiences among those working in large bureaucratic organizations such as higher education, and my hope is that the personal experiences I recount below will illuminate how lojong practice could provide powerful antidotes to the suffering many persons face today even in quite different work contexts.[7] Second, in some occupational cultures, such as the military, and some forms of competitive sport (e.g., boxing and ice hockey) aggression is held up as a virtue, a dynamic that also defines the "argument culture" of higher education. As Georgetown University professor of linguistics Deborah Tannen writes, the "ceremonial combat" and "ritualized opposition" that characterizes common ways of teaching, conducting research, and exchanging ideas creates "an atmosphere of animosity that poisons our relations with each other at the same time that it corrupts the integrity of our research."[8]

ADDING KEROSENE TO THE FIRE

The starting point for working towards an enlightened society, or what the Vietnamese Zen master, poet and social activist Thich Nhat Hanh calls "engaged Buddhism," is taming our own mind.[9] As Chögyam Trungpa writes, "If we try to solve society's problems without overcoming the confusion and aggression in our own state of mind, then our efforts will only contribute to the basic problems, instead of solving them."[10]

I got a glimpse of this basic insight in the spring of 2004 while participating in a "peace" march that ran along the border of the campus where I was teaching. I had been bickering with a colleague in the department for some time, and our conflict with each other was beginning to affect some of our graduate students. The situation I found myself in was absurd. Here I was marching through town in protest against U.S. military aggression in the Middle East when a student in the department marching alongside me asked rather pointedly why faculty members in our department could not get over our personality conflicts and focus on issues that really mattered. I certainly saw his point. Why would we let penny-ante workplace squabbles stand in the way of expressing collectively our common outrage against the U.S. war of aggression in Iraq? Yet a more fundamental point was beginning to dawn on me as I went home with a sore throat from hours of screaming the cadence "What do we want? *PEACE!!* When do we want it? *NOW!!!*"

A central delusion in many contemporary academic circles is that anger is a defining virtue of the publicly-engaged intellectual along the lines that "If you're not angry, you're not paying attention." In his recent book, *Therapy Culture*, for example, British sociologist Frank Furedi expresses the view that without enduring states of anger there is virtually no possibility of mobilizing and sustaining social movements aimed at transforming society for the better.[11] Our work as educators and public intellectuals is to help us keep our heads out of the sand, and sometimes we will experience anger as our research brings into focus the many injustices of the world that we frankly would rather not take in. And when something painful is brought to our awareness we often feel quite restless: "We can't just sit by and let this happen, we've got to stand up and do something!" This sentiment is quite understandable, yet I have become curious why doing *something* typically involves a lot of yelling and finger pointing.

There is good reason to believe that peaceful actions of civil disobedience are more morally persuasive and socially healing in the long-term than a sea of angry voices. The same is true with respect to how we respond to more personal "injustices" we experience in and outside the workplace, whereby defensive acts of self-righteousness typically add kerosene to the fire of our suffering. As the eighth-century Buddhist sage Shantideva wrote "should I serve my dark defiled emotions, they will only harm me, drawn me down into grief." Rather than shoring up our self-righteousness through indulging our anger, the practice of shamatha involves remaining steady, allowing one to directly connect with the underlying energy of one's injured innocence rather than remaining ignorant about one's emotions by becoming overwhelmed by them.[12] To turn the conventional view on its head: When I indulge in anger, I lose my capacity to pay attention!

THE GENUINE HEART OF SADNESS

The university, like all bureaucratic organizations, is a system for sorting individuals into hierarchies of status. The tenure system is central to this sorting process, and when I landed a tenure-track position at the State University of New York (SUNY) in New Paltz in my last year of graduate school I sure felt like one of the lucky ones. But my good fortune quickly turned sour. New Paltz is located in the Hudson Valley about an hour and a half north of New York City, and shortly after I moved to New Paltz the planes hit the Twin Towers. The chaos in the broader society was mirrored in my personal life. On October 3, 2001, four days before the first bombs were dropped in the War in Afghanistan, I learned that my spouse had been having an affair with her Tai Chi teacher. Three weeks later one of my dearest friends from graduate school died suddenly from a brain hemorrhage at the age of 44. I felt completely groundless, and at the time, lacked the inner resources to respond to such suffering with compassion and insight. My suffering was intensified by a profound loneliness as the weight of 9/11 overshadowed and rendered invisible to others the many losses I was facing in my life.

I worked in a department where there was little space for recognizing my basic humanity, a situation routinely faced by grieving individuals working in bureaucratic organizations.[13] Shortly after discovering my wife's infidelity, for example, I sought a listening ear in one of my colleagues who offered his perspective that "Well, like I always say, we humans weren't meant to be monogamous." The sociology department had been marked for decades by long-standing animosities among particular members of the department, and as two of the key players were retiring during my first year on the job, another colleague and I quickly rushed in to fill the void of venom in the wake of those retirements. Personality conflicts and power struggles are commonplace in hierarchical organizations, as is the process of dehumanizing the losers in such zero-sum power struggles. But what is essential to the story I tell here is not whether others were able to recognize my humanity, but that *I was unable to do so.*

The suffering I experienced in the workplace resulted from my own lack of inner resources, particularly my inability to hold my own grief with patience and tenderness. One subset of the lojong slogans focuses precisely on how we can transform any circumstance we face through responding with patience, which as Trungpa explains, has "a sense of dignity and forbearance."[14] I felt so deeply alone, yet in my inability to sit with the depth of that pain, my mind oscillated restlessly between self-judgment and self-righteous condemnation of others. It was all the same strategy whether I was condemning myself for being in denial about the affair, my colleague for his ineffectual words of comfort regarding human nature or President Bush for his part in squandering the wide international sympathy towards the U.S. immediately following 9/11. For some time righteous anger shielded me from experiencing the rawness of my sorrow—the sadness, irritation, anger, fear, and broken-heartedness. It also shielded me from seeing how all of the adversity I was facing could help me become a more compassionate and intelligent human being. A central point of the lojong teachings is that "when the world is filled with evil, transform all mishaps into the path of enlightenment."[15]

I came up for my first personnel review at the beginning of the second year of my initial 3-year appointment at SUNY. Mirroring the ignorant assumption I had formerly held that my now ex-wife had cherished our relationship, I entered this review completely unaware of what was in store for me. It was common knowledge that I was enmeshed in a conflict of personalities with a more senior member of the department, but I had naively assumed that my review would focus on my work performance— the quality of my teaching, research, and service to the university – but instead it centered on my "lack of collegiality." The committee recommended a shortening of my next contract so that I would be evaluated again in a year to check on my progress. Instead of helping to defuse the tensions in the department through the skillful means of "absorbing unjustified blame,"[16] I responded defensively fearing that a paper trail was being created for subsequently weeding me out. I was fired the following year.

Karma or the law of causality is central to a Buddhist understanding of reality and the beginning point of lojong practice.[17] According to the Buddha's teachings, all of our actions, whether thoughts, words or deeds, are like seeds that will eventually "bear fruit" in terms of experience in this or future lives.[18] The concept of karma can be easily misinterpreted as a justification of existing inequalities and mistreatment of others. I neither condemn nor justify how I was treated as an employee of the state of New York, but instead turn the story here in a different direction altogether. My suffering at SUNY was driven by my own ignorance, and what I have experienced through meditation and lojong practice is freedom from that ignorance and an increasing capacity to hold feelings of anger, frustration and injured innocence in what Trungpa calls the "genuine heart of sadness," that soft spot of relating courageously and directly to the experience of discomfort. The point is not that sadness is somehow better than anger, but that anger, when not held tenderly, can become a "cocoon" of self-righteousness that inhibits clear seeing and the capacity to skillfully relate to our inner and outer environment.[19] The same can be said of sadness, which when not held with an open heart of acceptance can become a seed for relating quite aggressively towards ourselves and others.

Particularly relevant to the experiences I recount here is the lojong slogan "be grateful to everyone," which invites the practitioner to become curious about his or her habitual reactions when becoming irritated or angry with another. The point of the slogan is not to pretend that you are not really irritated when you are, but to acknowledge the tremendous *value* irritating persons offer for one's own development. As Pema Chödrön writes in her commentary on this slogan: "Others will always show you exactly where you are stuck.... Without others provoking you, you remain ignorant of your painful habits and cannot train in transforming them into the path of awakening."[20] As we train ourselves to pay attention when we become angry, irritating persons can become for us kind teachers who give us the chance to become more compassionate human beings.

I defensively struggled to protect my damaged reputation in reaction to my first personnel review at SUNY, and then through spiritual practice had fortunately gained some capacity to respond differently to the outcome of my second personnel review the following year. I did try to protect my job through means of written appeal (e.g., documenting the numerous violations of university by-laws in my personnel review that had compromised due process and helped create the context for my dismissal), yet simultaneous to this external *social* process was an internal *spiritual* process of increasing disarmament and opening of the heart. This internal spiritual healing was deepened by my increasing awareness of how total my loss of public face truly was. In the course of the appeal process I learned that someone had started a rumor that I, in a fitful rage, had thrown a chair in a classroom full of students. This rumor, assumed to be unequivocal fact, had been taken as a "red flag" solidifying the perception of administrators and many members on the peer committee that I had a "potential for violence" associated with "mental illness." I felt deeply hurt and saddened. But I also understood that in light of this view it made perfect sense that terminating my contract was "in the best interest of the university."

And just as my ex-wife had shown me the fragility of my identity as loving husband and "nice guy," my social death at SUNY graced me with the profound opportunity to see more deeply the *emptiness* or dependent arising of all labels we may put on ourselves or others. With this experiential understanding of *shunyata*, that all things are relational and without any inherent existence unto themselves, has come a deepened commitment to overcoming ignorance and attaining insight for the benefit of all who suffer.

EPILOGUE

During the course of writing this reflection I ran into one of my former colleagues from SUNY. We were speaking on the same panel at the second annual conference of the Association for Contemplative Mind in Higher Education,[21] where he presented a timely and insightful paper on how lojong practice could help professors develop more constructive and respectful relationships with students.[22] One of the gifts of meeting him at this conference was the refreshing feeling that I was seeing who he truly is for the first time despite having had worked in the same department with him for four years. Then, over Thanksgiving I was speaking with my brother-in-law about how I had become reacquainted with an old colleague from SUNY, and remembering all my complaining years ago about the hardships I was going through in the workplace, he asked "Was he one of the good guys or one of the bad guys?" I smiled and felt deep gratitude for the comfort and ease that has come through the on-going practice of freeing the mind from such dualistic constructions that for so much of my life have imprisoned the heart's innate wisdom and obscured my ability to see the basic goodness in all beings.

NOTES

1. I thank Jamie Douglas, Lynn Eldershaw, Peter Kaufman, Patti Knoblauch, Joshua Merrill, Andrea Mortello, and Kathryn Goldman Schuyler for helpful feedback on earlier drafts of this chapter.

2. I have never met Chögyam Trungpa, and instead it has been through his senior students, his writings and the *Shambhala* trainings he created that I have come to practice in the Nyingma and Kagyu lineages of Tibetan Buddhism. I am particularly indebted to Pema Chödrön for her profound and deeply accessible interpretations of the Mahayana path. For an introduction to the Shambhala view and method of meditation see Chögyam Trungpa, *Shambhala: The Sacred Path of the Warrior* (Boston: Shambhala, 1988). Like many Americans, my first encounter with Buddhism was through the writings of the Vietnamese Zen master, poet, and social activist Thich Nhat Hanh. Particularly relevant to this vignette is his profoundly important book *Anger: Wisdom for Cooling the Flames* (New York: Riverhead Books, 2002).

3. William James, *Talks to Teachers on Psychology: And to Students on Some of Life's Ideals* (NY: Henry Holt & Company, 1901), 203, 214.

4. For a concise explanation of shamatha practice see Pema Chödrön *The Wisdom of No Escape* (Boston: Shambhala, 1991), 13-20.

5. For detailed commentaries on the approach based on 59 slogans, see Chögyam Trungpa, *Training the Mind and Cultivating Loving-Kindness* (Boston: Shambhala, 2005); Pema Chödrön, *Start Where You Are: A Guide to Compassionate Living* (Boston: Shambhala, 2003), and Dilgo Khyentse, *Enlightened Courage: An Explanation of Atisha's Seven Point Mind Training* (Ithaca, NY: Snow Lion Publications, 1993). For commentaries based on the eight verses approach, see H.H. The Dalai Lama, *Lighting the Way* (Ithaca, NY: Snow Lion Publications, 2004), 21-51, and Thupten Jinpa, *Mind Training: The Great Collection* (Boston: Wisdom Publications, 2006), 275-289.

6. For an illustration of how Mahayana Buddhism has influenced my pedagogic strategies, see "Contemplating Uncomfortable Emotions: Creating Transformative Spaces for Learning in Higher Education," in *Contemporary Approaches to Learning & Inquiry across Disciplines*, eds. O. Gunnlaugson, H. Bai, and E. Sarath (NY: SUNY, forthcoming).

7. See Eric Fay, "Derision and Management." *Organization* 15, no.6 (2008): 831-850; Likewise, sociologist Robert Jackal points out that anxiety is a central experience in the corporate world where anger and blame are expressed through "socially accepted modes of waging combat," *Moral Mazes: The World of Corporate Managers* (NY: Oxford University Press, 1988): 37.

8. Deborah Tannen, "Agonism in the Academy: Surviving Higher Learning's Argument Culture." *Chronicle of Higher Education* (March 31, 2000), B7; retrieved from http://web.me.com/chrisminnix/English_102 _E-Anthology_and_Resources/Section_Two_CB_1_files/ Tannen,%20Deborah.%20.pdf; see also DeborahTannen, *The Argument Culture: Stopping America's War of Words* (NY: Random House, 1998). For an important commentary on how lojong practice could help counteract the "culture of negativity" in higher education, see Peter Kaufman, "The Zero Sum Game of Denigrating Students," *Encounter: Education for Meaning and Social Justice*, 23, no. 1 (2010): 38-45.

9. Thich Nhat Hanh, *Interbeing: Fourteen Guidelines for Engaged Buddhism* (Berkeley, CA: Parallax Press, 1988).

10. Trungpa, *Shambhala: The Sacred Path of the Warrior*, 126.

11. Furedi, *Therapy Culture: Cultivating Vulnerability in an Uncertain Age* (NY: Routledge, 2004); Drawing inspiration from the work of Thich Nhat Hanh, Michael Schwalbe writes in his recent introductory sociology text that curiosity, care and hope are the three central virtues of the "sociologically mindful" person, yet he too concludes that sociology is "supposed to inspire outrage" as a means to promote social change. *The Sociologically Examined Life: Pieces of the Conversation* (Boston: McGraw-Hill, 2008), 250.

12. See Pema Chödrön, *No Time to Lose: A Timely Guide to the Way of the Bodhisattva* (Boston: Shambhala, 2007), 94-95; on shamatha practice as skillful means for working with experiences of "injured innocence," see Mark Epstein, *Going on Being: Buddhism and the Way of Change* (NY: Broadway Books, 2001), 86-87.

13. Joyce D. Davidman and Kenneth J. Doka (eds.), *Living with Grief: At Work, At School, At Worship* (Washington, D.C.: Hospice Foundation of America, 1999).

14. Trungpa, *Training the Mind*, 61-62.

15. Ibid., 62-65.

16. Ibid., 72.

17. The first lojong slogan is "First, train in the preliminaries" or "four reminders" that turn the mind toward the dharma. These are (1) the preciousness of human birth, (2) the reality of death, (3) the law of karma, and 4) the inevitability of suffering caused by self-centered preoccupations; Ibid., 7-8.

18. Khyentse, *Enlightened Courage*, 116.; H.H. the Dalai Lama, *Kindness, Clarity, and Insight* (Ithaca, NY: Snow Lion, 1984), 26-27.

19. For further description of the "genuine heart of sadness" and "cocoon," see Trungpa, *Shambhala: The Sacred Path of the Warrior*, chapters 3 and 7.

20. Pema Chödrön, *The Compassion Box: Book, CD, and Card Set* (Boston: Shambhala, 2003).
21. For information on upcoming events, see http://www.acmhe.org/
22. See Kaufman, "The Zero Sum Game of Denigrating Students."

CHAPTER 8

THE ART OF NOW

Scott Snibbe, Artist

SLEIGHT OF HAND

As a little boy I performed a series of experiments. In the first, staring at my hand, I commanded it: "move, hand." Yet it did not move. This puzzled me, as language had recently given me power to demand what I desired and reject what I didn't, to please or to hurt, and to otherwise control the world around me. Yet my words had no effect on my most prized possession: my body. *How is it, I wondered, that my mind acts to move me through space and time?*

Inner Peace—Global Impact: Tibetan Buddhism, Leadership, and Work, pp. 125–134

In a second experiment a short while later, I stared at my hand without speaking, and carefully searched for it. For sure I could find my hand dead-center in its palm, and in its digits, bones, skin, and blood; yet as I moved towards my wrist its boundary became fuzzy. *Where does the hand end and the arm begin?* I asked myself. Later, learning more about biology, I discovered with even more certainty that there is no distinguishing between a hand cell and an arm cell, or a hand atom and an arm atom. Upon close examination, the boundary between these parts becomes fuzzy. So I asked myself *if I can't find where it starts or ends, does my hand really exist at all?*

In a final childhood experiment, this time undertaken with an instrument—an Olympus 35mm camera—I took a series of photos of myself using its timer. In each photo I hid my hand and forearm behind an object—the one I recall most vividly was a small statue of Saint Francis. Behind his back, I fluttered my hand furiously as the shutter triggered. Later, when the prints returned, I started at the photo, reflecting on the hand behind the saint's back still moving.

Only in college would I learn the formal terms for these kind of questions: *phenomenology*, exploring direct perception and how we control our bodies; *ontology*, concerning the categorization and boundaries of objects like my hand; and *epistemology*, asking what we can believe in the observed world. And even later still would I come across a deeper inquiry of these questions in the Buddhist exploration of *emptiness*: how things exist (or do not) as a continual exchange and interdependence with all other things, dependent on their parts, on their causes, and, most importantly, on a mind labeling them. But ultimately I didn't want to study these ideas, but to continue playing with them experientially in the same way I had as a boy.

"USELESS PROGRAMS?"

My early conceptual fascination found a concrete outlet 1 day as a 10-year-old when I walked into a classroom filled with Apple II computers and was taught how, using computer languages, I could paint glowing orange, purple, and green shapes upon its screen. I felt I could have lived with those first glowing shapes forever and begged my parents until they bought me a computer of my own to explore this intangible world. From that day forward I knew that was what I wanted to do with my life: to create graphics and interactivity that existed nowhere, and had no purpose but to delight and inspire.

How to turn this interest into a career eluded me as I attended university in the eighties. In a computer graphics research lab, my day job was to research new ways to create three-dimensional animations for movies and education. But at night I continued my personal inquiry into an infinite abstract world, writing programs that created light, color, and form based on a person's movements with the mouse. I could not stop myself from continuing this work because it brought me to a blissful state of pure concentration where I lost all sense of the past or future: not only while using the programs, but also while creating them. I became completely absorbed in an activity where my mind flowed into computer code and moving imagery. Although some of my Buddhist friends might be skeptical of one's ability to meditate in front of a computer, these were my first tastes of prolonged meditative states before knowing what they were.

I had a few fans of my peculiar computer experiments, but for the most part, the work was either ignored—as long as my more productive activities continued—or ridiculed as "useless programs" without an educational or functional purpose. This term is something I gradually came to adopt as the label for a new type of computer-based interactive art, and I affirmed it to myself and gradually to others: *useless programs, yes; as useless as a song, a poem, or a story.*

Without hope of finding a job making useless programs, I joined some friends at Adobe Systems to create useful software for movie special effects. Just as I had in school, I spent my spare time (and some of my work time) refining uselessness into more and more rarefied forms. The result, which I called *Motion Phone* was the first work of interactivity that I displayed publicly, debuting at a computer conference in 1995. The response was overwhelmingly positive, and I was invited to dozens of international art shows to exhibit my experiment in galleries and museums.

My work now had a label, *interactive art*, which I enthusiastically embraced as a hobby, attending about a hundred art shows over the next few years, and expanding the work from the computer screen to the physical world. Seeing my first works in a gallery made me want to get rid of the screen completely, because the table, chair, keyboard, and monitor turned the free space of the museum into an offshoot of the office.

Instead, I wanted to find a way to honor people's bodies as the purest form of interface, and bring them towards the direct experience I had while programming, which was more difficult for them to achieve with a clumsy mouse and keyboard. Thus I became one of the first artists using the body itself as an interface.

I used cameras and projectors for the first time in a work called *Boundary Functions* to draw lines between people as they move about on a large floor. Inspired by my childhood experiments, *Boundary Functions* was an interactive projected floor that made the invisible visible, demarking people's personal space, and showing that this space, though we call it our own, is in fact defined by others and changes without our control. The interface to the artwork became a mere movement through space, as effortless and spontaneous as child's play.

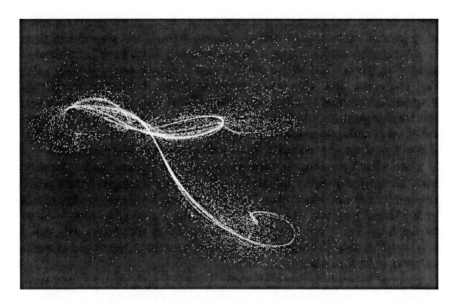

Figure 8.1.   Gravilux, Interactive screen-based artwork, 1998. (Courtesy Scott Snibbe)

Figure 8.2.   Blow Up, Interactive wind wall, Yerba Buena Center for the Arts, 2005. (Courtesy Scott Snibbe)

Figure 8.3.   Outward Mosaic, Interactive wall, Institute for Contemporary Arts, London (2006). (Courtesy Scott Snibbe)

Figure 8.4.   Transit, 58-monitor video installation, Los Angeles International Airport, 2009. (Courtesy Scott Snibbe)

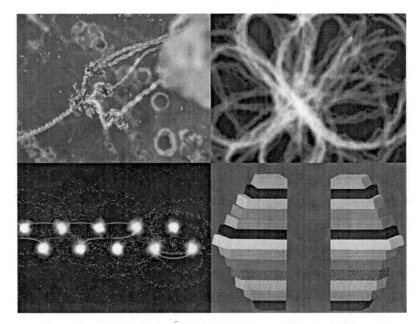

Figure 8.5.   Björk's Biophilia App Album, produced by Scott Snibbe, 2011. (Courtesy Scott Snibbe)

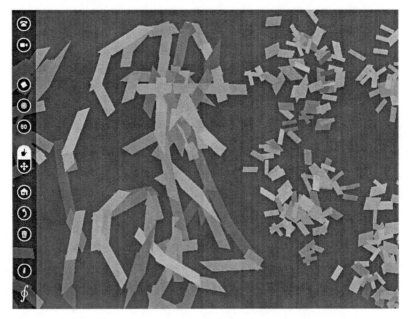

Figure 8.6.   MotionPhone, networked abstract animation program for iPad and iPhone, 2012. (Courtesy Scott Snibbe)

SELLING NOTHING

This artwork became more and more popular, so much so that I was able to stop working for corporations and opened my own studio full-time in San Francisco in 2001. Well-known galleries were approaching me to create saleable work and dealers coached me on how to do so. One gallery owner described success succinctly, as he spread his arms out first as wide as he could; next as tall as they could stretch; and finally, holding two palms near each other to describe a thinner third dimension. These were the ideal dimensions of a work of art: big enough to feel valuable, but small enough for a person to carry out of the gallery in her arms as a proud purchase.

I worked for several years on prototypes of such works, eviscerating laptops, affixing them to walls, and refining a high-art white box aesthetic. But my love of the immaterial prevented me from ever letting one of these out the door. And, via my recent conversion to Buddhism through my brother and the Dalai Lama, I was introduced to the idea that one should avoid producing *desire objects* for one's livelihood, which generally increase the delusion of attachment in those that encounter it. Not to mention that the high price tags of such objects in the five-figures were daunting, and I was certain the screens would break within 5 or so years, causing a maintenance headache or at least a lot of anger. So I sought out a more entrepreneurial way to make a living from an immaterial approach to the medium that would leave people unbothered by acquisitiveness.

I put more attention towards interactive digital projections like *Boundary Functions*, which I loved for their lack of substantiality. In their essence mere moving light, people's minds caught hold of their forms: dancing with lines; laughing at their captured shadows; chasing soft rectangles; or molding malleable light, none of which actually existed in any solidity. I loved watching people chase—or be chased by—virtual shadows as if they were real.

Inspired by nature, movement, and energy, most of my works had a legitimate science story you could tell about each of them: from gravitation to cells; animal behavior to sociology. Science museums began to approach me to purchase these intangible exhibits for their collections, as a new form of educational tool unavailable in a book or school; and also, especially, to engage children, who needed experiences to be predominantly visceral and playful in order to engage them.

This business grew and I found myself becoming a kind of clean-living Warhol, with a growing number of employees in an art factory. With the expanding organization, I tried to embody the principles that had inspired me, allowing my employees to work not just mechanically, but to contribute creatively in all aspects of our projects, and to solve problems in their own ways, working to suit each of their individual minds.

As a recent student of Tibetan Buddhism, I was surprised to find precise terms for these ideas I had been exploring since childhood: *emptiness* and *dependent arising* described the interdependent nature of reality—that nothing exists as an independent, partless object from its own side. And the terms *calm abiding* and *insight* described the concentrated blissful states I experienced while creating and that my audience sometimes fell into while playing.

One of my vows as a Buddhist was not to proselytize, but I often reflected upon how I could promote and embody these Buddhist ideas in the interactive experiences that we more and more referred to as *products*. When I had worked in a research lab during the late 90s, I had proposed a research project called Samadhi, with an unsubstantiated, but intriguing claim, that it could be possible to create a business that promotes concentration and long-term engagement through certain types of interactive experiences. My proposal was rejected, but now on my own, I was hearing reports of such states spontaneously arising in our viewers at museums all over the world.

In France, an exhibit slated for 1 year was extended to 5. Parents, depending on whether they were in a hurry or wanted a break, alternately complained or celebrated that their children could not be removed from states of engaged, concentrated play. The museum staff reported that they themselves would return again and again, sometimes many times a day, to interact during breaks that relaxed, refreshed, and even exercised them. What did this exhibit do? Titled *Shadow Mosaic*, it recorded and played back people's shadows over-and-over in a four-by-four grid. Merely reflecting what otherwise was fleeting, the fascination and engagement brought people into the present, to a state where they stopped regretting the past and anticipating the future and fell into an unselfconscious childlike state of now.

CUT OUT THE MIDDLE MAN

With the success of my new business came many struggles, from economic downturns, to competition, difficulties with employees, technical shortcomings, and also demands from our customers to flatten and literalize otherwise original open-ended, playful experiences. I realized that sometimes the biggest obstacle in creating something magical for audiences were our clients themselves. As a company, we were accustomed to taking huge risks to make open-ended play a new kind of product. Sometimes our customers did not always share our comfort with risk, and the pure joy of an artwork would get diluted and drained by committees and checklists that tried infuse them with pedagogical usefulness. And another force, that of making payroll, would sometimes cause me to give up on the extended efforts that might otherwise have made a better product.

With a decade of such compromises behind me, I was excited by the announcement of the Apple's iPad interactive tablet in 2010 and its online app store. Suddenly, there was a way to cut out the middleman and take the more outlandish ideas I had shelved over the years directly to an audience. I adapted three programs I had written in the 90s (Gravilux, Bubble Harp, and Antograph), to run on the iPad and released them all at once in the App Store. The result was astonishing. Waking up that weekend and reviewing the sales charts, my programs had risen to number one positions in their categories and were receiving tens of thousands of downloads per day. And the reviews in the app store were intriguing:

> "The app may not serve any useful purpose, but it is the most fun I have had in a long time."—Huniper

> "Calmed me down after a bad day" —RobertM

> "I spend hours at my computer. Sometimes I just need a distraction that doesn't demand a lot of thought. This app is perfect. It's mesmerizing. It can be almost meditative and then frenetic; depends on what you want it to be. If you want action, buy a game. This is for your Zen zone." —j. c.

> "I didn't know what to think before I got it, but 30 calming (and lost) minutes later, I'm having to pull myself away! It's definitely a relaxing app, allowing you to simply get lost in your own universe." —R.Porter

At last I had empirical evidence for my claims of, in some small way, inducing a positive, meditative state. A friend who is a the director of a meditation retreat center put it more elegantly: "It is exciting to think that you have created something that those who spend hours 'diddling' with electronics, could actually use to create beauty and perhaps see the limitless nature of mind itself. The opposite seems to be the goal-oriented games that appear to be just an extension of the every day life."

DOES IT MATTER?

As excited as I am now to finally find success in integrating business, art, and spirituality, I think often to the more difficult times I faced. During a magical time when one of my lamas visited me in San Francisco, a time when I was felt fed up a material world that seemed only to bring more problems, we talked and walked all day and night. He taught me a way of looking into my mind, turning down the volume of external stimuli to reveal a luminous, infinitely expansive internal reality more attractive than any physical pleasure. This practice he called *Mahamudra*. The lama also showed me that outside of the meditation room, reality is still filtered through our minds. There's no such thing as objective reality, and by using the techniques of Vajrayana Buddhism we can tune our minds to transform everyday life, even seeing the disgusting and dangerous as reflections of a subtler, beautiful, energetic reality.

I asked my lama about my life choices and showed him some of the work with interactive art. Should I stick with this, I asked? Or would it be better to become a "full-time" Buddhist, working in a center or even becoming a monk. After reviewing the works I'd created, my lama told me that what I was doing was important: it was a tool that could teach and reveal hidden aspects of reality, particularly its dependent origination. It was also a way to direct people towards the less substantial, to awaken people in a modest way to alternate "invisible" realities. And finally, he said, "You make Buddhism cool." Encouraged, I moved forward with the expansion of my art studio into its current corporate form.

I am not sure I made the right decision for my own mind, because with more success comes more attachment to this world. The Eight Worldly Dharmas are those that the Buddha taught bring us no true satisfaction: seeking praise, avoiding blame; seeking fame, avoiding disrepute; seeking pleasure, avoiding pain; and seeking gain, avoiding loss. Really, is there much else but these that concern me?

So I hope that despite my own delusions, my useless toys help people a small bit, in a way that doesn't fall into the self-selecting "lifestyle," "self-help," or "wellness" ghettos, but appeals to everyday people as pure fun, yet tricks them into spending a little one-on-one time with their own minds to get to know the bliss that sits waiting inside, ready to be discovered in every moment.

CHAPTER 9

FLYING HIGH AND SERVING OTHERS ISN'T ALWAYS SMOOTH SAILING

Dana Browning (pseudonym), Flight Attendant

As a flight attendant for a major airline, my job is a fertile ground for my Buddhist practice. It has given me lots of time off to practice meditation, study, and attend retreats. The goal of meditation is "enlightenment"—rather a nebulous term at that. Actually, the whole idea of meditation practice is to overcome one's overly wild, distracted, often emotional mind and develop a more open and compassionate attitude towards oneself and others. It also allows one to develop inner strength and calm, so that one can face the rather chaotic pace of modern life from a place of peace and open heartedness. For me, my practice gives me space with which to deal with the often claustrophobic environment on an airplane. I can touch into my own wisdom and sanity to face whatever situation arises in my job.

My job itself has a certain timeless quality to it. With irregular hours, time zone changes, and day and night flying, time begins to have very little meaning. My practice has helped me learn to let go of beginnings and endings of trips. We will get there when we get there. I sleep and eat when I can and just try to rest in the present moment. That sense of timeless moments also helps me not get caught up in whatever drama is happening.

People are what make my job interesting. This is where I get the most opportunity to integrate my Buddhist practice. Dealing with difficult people is probably the hardest part of my work. The airline company wants us to be all things to all people: the welcoming flight attendant, sexy stewardess, personable waitress, problem solver, psychologist, bartender, team player, policeman, and most important, to show authority and leadership

Inner Peace—Global Impact: Tibetan Buddhism, Leadership, and Work, pp. 135–138

in enforcing regulations and handling emergencies. Since deregulation, management also wants us to do all of this with fewer workers, often having to be in two places at once. Add to this the fact that we work with a different team of people each trip. Always meeting and working with new people that you have never met means you can not have preconceived ideas about who people are or how things are going to work. It is very easy to assume someone knows their job, yet in fact they may not have worked on that particular airplane for years. This can lead to confusion in the timeliness and order of the food and beverage service and makes it harder to deliver good quality service.

Sometimes, for whatever reason, flight attendants aren't good team players. This puts added stress on the other flight attendants, who are already understaffed. For example, one time an attendant named Steve, whom I had never worked with, came into the galley when I was gone and reorganized everything. I was quite taken aback. It was a great breach of respect in the working environment. I was responsible for the galley, yet now I didn't know where anything was, which caused confusion for us all. I was pretty mad and was ready to lay into him. Instead I took a deep breath and tried to connect with my basic goodness, taking in the anger and confusion and letting out patience and kindness. This gave me time to think that it was toward the end of the day with only one more food service to do, and I would probably never see him again. This was his way of working, and he had probably been told many times before—so I didn't even bother. I just said to everyone that service would be delayed while I reorganized everything due to the changes Steve had made. In the future if I ever fly with Steve again I will be on guard for his disruptive behavior and set strict boundaries with him about how I organize my galley. Just knowing you will probably never have to work with a person again helps put space around the situation and motivates you to try to work things out in the moment.

All sorts of drama can develop on an airplane among crew members and with passengers. In the past, we sold a high quality of service, but now standards have sunk to the lowest common denominator. Flying used to be first class, but now it's more like bus service and trash pickup. Passengers get on board with all sorts of unrealistic expectations. Sometimes they are afraid or completely stressed out. They are often disappointed, angry, or even sick. Alcohol contributes significantly to creating difficulties between passengers and crew. My job is to meet passenger needs, solve their problems, pacify their anger, and serve them in a timely, polite, and friendly way. It is easy to fall into anger or impatience or get caught up in the drama.

Being a Buddhist has given me many methods to deal with these difficult interpersonal relationships. Among these practices are the ideas of

Bodhicitta and *Tonglen*. Bodhicitta (open heartedness) is the idea that throughout many lifetimes all sentient beings have at one time been my mothers. Using one's love for the mother gives one the ground to practice patience and loving presence. It is accompanied by a meditation practice called Tonglen or sending and taking. The practice of Tonglen involves taking in the negative, angry, impatient, heavy energy, and sending out kindness, light, and understanding. By connecting with my own suffering and negativity first, I can identify with other people's stress and anger. I then connect with my own Bodhicitta, which allows me to rest in loving presence and creates space around whatever happens. I have been trained in my practice to step back, breathe in, and take in all the negativity, allowing a sense of peace to arrive. Just resting in this sense of loving presence often turns around a difficult situation. For example, a passenger who has had too much to drink becomes very upset and argumentative when he is told no more drinks. At that point I try to rest in loving presence, not getting caught up in his anger, being sympathetic while letting him know he can't have any more to drink. Most of the time, such passengers will give up and eventually fall asleep. If a passenger gets on the airplane irate because he didn't get his expected seat assignment or doesn't like where he is sitting, it can become difficult. I can let this upset me, or I can take a breath, take in his anger, and send back sympathy and understanding. I may point out that the airplane is full, with every seat taken, ask him where he wants to move to and what he wants me to do about it. By creating space around the situation, I allow the passenger to come to his own realization about his seat assignment without having to say "No, you can't change seats." It seems counter intuitive but you don't really have to do anything: just take that breath of dark, heavy emotional energy, and let go with the sense of relaxation and space. That alone can defuse the energy of the situation so that wisdom arises naturally.

The Vajrayana tradition offers many visualization practices that can be used during my work day. These visualization practices are reminders that I always have with me; my main goal is to develop compassion for others and the wisdom to deal with whatever event, positive or negative, that comes my way. To see this with calm equanimity is the goal.

I have to admit I'm not always successful. That is why it is called practice. Some days, when faced by an onslaught of hundreds of tired, weary, stressed out people, I find myself short tempered and not very personable. It is at those times I try to have *maitri* towards myself. Maitri means love and kindness toward oneself and others. It is an innate, human desire for happiness that is free from suffering. The Buddha said "one who loves himself well, never harms another." At these times I try to have compassion and understanding for myself and to face my tiredness and grumpiness. I look to see that is a universal condition, not just me, one that is shared with all others. I can then let go and try to see the transience or impermanence of my own feelings and emotions and treat myself more gently, knowing that at the end of the day it will be over and as much past as any dream. This practice of maitri can also develop into empathy for my fellow passengers and workers. Modern neuroscience is discovering how human beings resonate with other human beings. If I can generate love and kindness toward myself and others, that can be catching and give positive energy to those around me.

I feel very fortunate to have had this job. The more I practice, the more growth opportunities open to me. It seems to take on a life of its own. After 40 years, I still love working with my fellow flight attendants and passengers. I have met some remarkable people through my job. The more I am open to it, the more reward I receive from it. It constantly presents me with a fertile ground to base my Buddhist practice on and greatly enriches my spiritual life.

NOTE

1.   This is a pseudonym, to protect the author's privacy.

CHAPTER 10

RELEASING OUR ATTACHMENT

Carl B. Mangum, Clinical Social Worker

I am a clinical social worker in private practice. A broadly accepted principal in my training is that the more a therapist processes his/her own issues, the more effective he/she can be in helping clients access their own belief systems, feelings, thoughts, memories, and fantasies. In my practice, I have found that the most important tool I can bring to this work is a viewpoint that blends my Christian heritage with the training in Tibetan Buddhist philosophy I have pursued as an adult.

Buddhism, broadly stated, holds that the self has no solid basis. Starting from that premise, I can focus on helping my clients release their ego-driven attachments, so they can start living in the present moment rather

Inner Peace—Global Impact: The Influence of Tibetan Buddhism on Leadership and Work in the West, pp. 139–149

than in segments of the painful past. This is very much in line with my training in psychosocial therapy, where the primary goal is to help clients retrieve all the energy that they have focused in such a way that it keeps them anchored in the past.

ASSEMBLING MY TOOLS

I started with Transactional Analysis as my approach to therapy and then added Tibetan Buddhist principles. More recently, I have added Logosynthesis techniques. My goal is always to find an approach that is most effective for resonating with the client.

My introduction to Tibetan Buddhism occurred in 1975 as part of my psychotherapeutic training. I met and began working with a married couple who operated as a psychiatrist/psychologist team. My new mentors had been influenced by contact with Chögyam Trungpa Rinpoche, a Tibetan Buddhist master.

Early in the training, my mentors gave me a simple mental exercise that they told me had been passed down for centuries. The exercise was to deliberately recall an issue over which I had been angrily obsessing and then, just as deliberately, to let the obsession flow out of my mind with the next outgoing breath. I was to repeat this procedure for at least 5 minutes. At first, I was not impressed and considered the whole thing quite simplistic. But I had made a commitment to do the practice, so I kept at it. Very shortly, I was overcome by how very effective this "simple" exercise actually proved to be. I returned for more, and I have continued now for over 30 years.

Meditation, as I have been taught and as I practice it, basically comes down to sitting, learning to be aware of each outgoing breath, and observing my thoughts and feelings as they arise. I continue to find this discipline of "the mind watching the mind" to be a fascinating challenge. Over the years, as I have learned to be still, I have noticed all kinds of thoughts and repetitive themes that come bubbling up from just below the surface of my usual level of consciousness. Through meditation, I have recognized repetitive patterns in my own life. This includes deeply ingrained and often unnoticed habits, like focusing outside myself for the cause when something unpleasant happens. Focusing outward is generally recognized as blaming, as opposed to recognizing my own role in a chain of events. The importance of this kind of awareness has become central to my life and practice. The art of sitting and not doing, just relaxing and noticing what my mind is doing, continues to motivate me to focus on learning new strategies in my everyday life. The energies that I previously focused outside myself continue to flow back for me to use in the present moment. I recognize this as true empowerment and something I wanted to share with my clients. Realizing that these practices might be challenging for the very conservative, largely Roman Catholic community where I practice, I began by cloaking the strategies as part of the intuitive common sense embedded in the local culture. Working in that way, I have found these practices to be remarkably effective in assisting my clients.

I began traveling to retreat centers for further instruction and supervised practice in Tibetan Buddhist meditation. The training helped me learn to observe my own habitual patterns. I was able to notice and face old habits of mind that were negatively affecting my life and relationships, such as fear of conflict with people important to me and then anger at myself when I didn't speak up. The instruction I received in meditation practice was to let the memories arise, label them discursive thinking, and let them go with the next outgoing breath. Not letting the thoughts be my focus and letting them go just "wore them out" so I no longer felt either attachment or aversion. I had freed the energy that had been previously invested in the thoughts.

USING THE TOOLS IN PRACTICE

Over the years, through practical experience, I have found four themes of Tibetan Buddhism to be most useful in working with my clients. These are the (1) Four Contemplations That Turn the Mind; (2) Awareness Training; (3) Releasing Attachments Arising Out of Ego; and (4) Buddha Nature as Being at the Core of Essence.

To provide a framework for understanding how I use these themes, I have provided below a fictionalized case of mutual complaints from a couple going through a divorce. This is not, it should be stressed, an actual case. Rather this is an example developed by combining what I have noticed with a combination of patterns across multiple professional experiences.

Sample Case

Mary Beth: "Not expecting him to come home is such a relief. I can go to sleep and not worry about his safety. However, thoughts of what he is doing keep appearing. Is he having fun with someone? Going to neat places without getting a sitter? And the marvelous places he gets to go where he can just leave all the responsibilities with me and just go on with his life. I don't get that choice. I have the children, the house, the creditors … all needing care. These thoughts and worries don't just come at night, but all day, every day.

Can you imagine working with me? I've had plenty of complaints. My house has never been so clean. For one thing, his stuff isn't all over the place. But the stress keeps me in a cleaning mode. I've been cleaning things I didn't even know I had. I have no close fiends anymore. My friends are all married. The "meat market" is scary. Where do I fit? Not only do all my children look like him, but one child is acting more and more like him and that just drives me crazy."

Sam: "She's got this lawyer and all I hear is how much more money she needs. When I do try and speak to her, she tells me what the kids need. And my time with the kids is filled with information about what they want. It's like I'm made of money. It's just not right. I don't know what I'm going to be doing with my job. Mary Beth just makes mountains out of mole hills, especially when dealing with picking up the kids for a visit. She needs to know time and place in advance. And, why can't she have the kids ready, just because I forgot to call one time? Now, it's like I'm not expected to show up, ever. Sometimes, I think it would be nice to get back together. It would certainly eliminate some of the things we fight about now and at least my clothes would be washed and food cooked. I just thought everything was OK. I don't know what got into her. She had a nice home, a car, and she could have spending money anytime she asked."

Having set the stage, I will now discuss the four Tibetan Buddhist themes and how I would use them in working with this couple.

Theme 1: Four Contemplations That Turn the Mind

My translation of this concept can be expressed roughly as (1) Life is impermanent; death is certain. (2) Your positive and negative thoughts and behaviors create habits that lead to more of the same; (3) Pain and suffering are just part of ordinary life; (4) This life is precious and we have the potential to free ourselves from our past, so that we may move on to higher levels of consciousness.

Without revealing Buddhism as the source, I often present these concepts as the basic realities of living human life: We are all going to die; all actions create results and consequences; You cannot get away from discomfort and pain; and we do have capacity for creating difference in our lives.

What I would say during a therapeutic encounter with Mary Beth and Sam, either together or individually, might be: "That is life. Why sweat these inevitable realities?" Summing up the basic realities of life helps motivate clients to reframe their thinking, feeling and acting. The message I convey is that "You can stew in your discomfort or you can start creating your life differently." I have found that the act of assimilating these realities creates a powerful motivation for change.

In our fictional example, neither Mary Beth nor Sam exhibit serious motivation to change from a basic blaming orientation in their thinking, feeling, or behavior. Helping the two of them to refocus their energy or attention would give them the opportunity to would support them in changing their direction. I tend to focus on enhancing the clients' existing capacity to change by providing them with small opportunities to experience a broader range of choice. More choice helps galvanize the motivation for change. Thus, the parties in our sample case could, through growing awareness, develop increased willingness to engage in the process of developing new, more effective life skills.

Theme 2: Awareness Training

Awareness training is central to Tibetan Buddhist meditation practice. Awareness is characterized as the capacity to be conscious of immediate experience. Awareness helps clients move out of thinking about changing and connect with real experience to help them go beyond confusion and misunderstanding at the root of negative emotions such as attachment, pride, jealousy, and hatred. Awareness developed through the practice of meditation is similar to awareness created in the psychotherapeutic process. Both act like catalysts in advancing the process of change.

Awareness of habitual responses and modes of thinking is a first step in bringing processes that have operated below the threshold of consciousness into conscious awareness. This awareness is essential to self-directed change. Any habitual structure that remains largely below the conscious level remains inaccessible to systematic conscious restructuring. This means that conscious energy is not readily accessible for intentional directed change.

In our fictional case, neither Mary Beth nor Sam show awareness of themselves as being key players in their ongoing drama, so they have very little choice in being able to use their minds to change the course of events. Both can be seen as living out of their past and as very attached to their own representation of reality and viewpoint. Neither is focused on the "now" of managing their lives by being aware of what they are doing and how they are reacting in the context of the immediate moment. This leads to a vicious circle of creating more of the same. Sam and Mary Beth are each wrapped up in their own pain and suffering, their fears, shame, sadness, grief, anger, and guilt, as well as their thoughts about themselves, others, and life.

These conflicting viewpoints create a habitual and nonfunctional situation in the present moment, with the partners devoid of awareness of what they are actually doing. Being attached to their historical identities, Mary Beth and Sam are stuck in the current situation, with little conscious awareness of the strategies that they developed early in life under conditions that provided inadequate support or compassionate direction. These patterns of thinking, feeling, and behaving use up energy, which is therefore not available for new and more creative strategies for living their lives more effectively. Helping clients to meditate enables them to become more conscious and to notice their own thoughts, feelings, and reactive behavior without attachment. Understanding how they are personally suffering can lead to awareness of the process that creates the suffering and can help open the door to freedom in the moment, right now.

I would point out that to Mary Beth that her complaint about Sam's apparent freedom and her unspoken wish to see him in her place indicates she has focused on her own distress and situational discomfort. I would aim to help her discover how this focus on her distress creates more distress and would work with her to help her begin to think about what it is that she really wants. With Sam, the pervasive complaints center on his idea that "it's all about money." I would acknowledge that reality in his life and then point out that no matter what, life circumstances will change over time. I would then challenge him to enter into a discussion of how he wants to create his life in this moment, right now.

Theme 3: Releasing Attachment

According to Tibetan Buddhist philosophy, the self's lack of solid basis is the core to releasing attachments arising out of ego. From our previous life experiences, we created mental structures and belief systems that gave us a starting point for dealing with and understanding new life experiences. Structure adds predictability to our world. While the strategies may have been useful and necessary at the time we created them, as time goes on, they may cease to be helpful and may even become detrimental. A Model-T Ford, functionally advanced for its time, has limited usefulness in modern life. Some structures that were adaptive and effective for survival for a child growing up in a conflicted and chaotic environment can be extremely limiting for the same person in an adult life under different living conditions. Dysfunctional habits rooted in the past and played out in the present can become significant obstacles to effective functioning in life, relationships, and workplaces. Some examples include holding tightly to a fixed idea or approach to an issue; intensely attempting to control certain outcomes; being unwilling to let go of people, places, things, or ideas; having a limited ability to listen to differing ideas. This kind of limitation can be generally characterized as rigid adherence to rules and extreme inability to think "outside the box."

In therapeutic practice, I have presented clients with the idea of ego as a mental construct they have developed for themselves that is highly vulnerable to the winds of their current life experiences. I have observed that we tend to see others in the light of our own experiences, and how others relate to us influences how we see ourselves. The act of letting go of attachment to our ego (or concept of ourselves) increases our ability to see the many layers of our own selves and others. As I have grown in my capacity to help clients gain awareness of their own habitual patterns, I have become more effective in helping them focus their energy on what is transpiring in the "Now." With this focus, my clients have the opportunity to open themselves to creative imagination and find novel solutions for their own problems. Awareness of awareness can help them shift to a different place.

Our fictional character Mary Beth is saying "it's not fair to me that he gets to do all those things." She has her energy focused on Sam and not on resolving the complexities of her own current life situation. The focus on herself and "it's not fair" gets in the way of using her energies to move through her daily challenges. I might ask her, "How old is that part of you that says it's not fair?" I might also ask, "Do you really want the focus of your energy to be on Sam? Which one of your selves is going to be in charge here? What would you be doing differently if there were no self to protect or no self to be mad at? The selves you are trying to protect and the focus of your frustration are past history. Living takes place in the present. Where do you want to live?"

The same applies to Sam with his focus on "all she wants is money" and "I am a money machine." Since he seems to feel "used," I might ask him, "Do you really think money is your only value? Do you really want your resentment towards Mary Beth to be the focus of your life? Do you want to continue focusing on your resentment over your feeling that what you produce is more important than who you are? What would you be doing differently if there were no self to protect from feeling inadequate if you're not producing." My questions would continue similarly to those I asked Mary Beth about the choice between living life in the present or staying stuck in the past.

Theme 4: Buddha Nature

To understand my connection to Buddhism, it is important to understand my connection to Christianity. I was raised in the Methodist

Church, but as a teenager "crossed over" to the First Christian Church, which was conveniently located across the street. I was drawn to the other church because it offered something I had not found before—a living sense of community and connection and, even more important, something beyond myself. I became very involved in First Christian Church, participating in the youth group and taking part in other services.

My Christian upbringing included the concept that man is created in the image of God. One could rephrase this as meaning that our essence is in the image of God. Tibetan Buddhism, on the other hand, describes this innate nature or essence as being beyond dualistic conception, an original purity, an evenness free from suffering, and a great basic space. This essence is also called an "ultimate sphere of emptiness with its radiance of compassion" and "beyond transition and change."[1]

My experience with Tibetan Buddhist literature, in conjunction with my previous religious background, has immeasurably enriched my concept of mankind as being created in the image of God. Approaching this concept from the perspective of our essence has proven very helpful to me both in life and in my therapeutic practice. The understanding I have gained from practice has opened a pathway for me to go beyond religious dogma. This has allowed me to connect with and affirm the essence of the underlying and fundamental truths that I believe the dogma was intended to represent.

The Buddhist emphasis on Buddha Nature has helped me to focus my attention on the spiritual and its place within the therapeutic process. Psychotherapeutic theory includes a spiritual element, which came to the fore for me when I read Victor Frankel's *Man's Search for Meaning*.[2] Frankel, an Auschwitz survivor, told the story of how he managed to maintain his sense of his own essence despite terrible experiences in the concentration camp. Frankel later became a leader in creating Existential Therapy. In my experience, I recall times when I was ready to let go of a part of my life and was unsure where this new direction would lead me. I felt both excitement and fear. What was most meaningful for me at those times of wavering between choices was connecting with my essence beyond ego. In that way, I discovered what was core for me at that time in my life. In the process, I developed a trust that I would gain important understanding and awareness, however things turned out. This experience helped me be compassionate toward myself at such choice points, as well as willing to learn from the choice I had made. This has been critical in helping me transcend my apprehensions at times of choice and continues to lend meaning to my life.

The concept of Buddha Nature has close parallels to psychological theory and to elements of my psychotherapeutic training, which has been most useful in actual work with clients. Important influences for me in this area have included Carl Rogers' non-directive therapy and Bob and Mary Goulding's *The Power is in the Patient*, with their concept of "hooking the free child."[3] Some of the best sources of insight on the Tibetan Buddhist understanding of Buddha Nature can be found in the writings of Longchen Rabjam.[4]

How does this Buddhist theme apply in practice? In our fictional case, neither Mary Beth nor Sam is able to focus on going beyond the present moment or has access to consciousness of their own essential nature. Both show little awareness within themselves of the essence that flows naturally from a true connection. When people recognize the essence in themselves, they become more compassionate toward others. The first step in connecting with innate essence is to free bound-up energy, which can then be experienced as essence. Mary Beth and Sam are held back by their own issues, which they are not yet open to changing. One of my goals is to help them start to experience their own essence. Helping them free their bound-up energy gives them a clear choice between inherited patterns and operating out of essence.

When Sam says, "I don't know what got into her" he reveals his limited grasp and superficial connectedness with his life and his wife. Lack of connectedness with his own essence is consistent with his limited awareness of his wife's inner essence. The idea of his wife as a person with her own essence seems to be unfathomable to him. By focusing on his experience of not knowing what is going on in Mary Beth's mind, we can begin to open a small crack in the wall of separation. Of course this will be difficult for Sam, as he seems to have learned early in his life that he would not find support for processing issues so close to the heart. Such deeply personal experiences would have to be buried in the back of his mind so he could get by while functioning in an emotional desert, with no support or compassion. Whenever Sam experiences a challenging life situation, he closes up and moves on, just as he probably had to do when he was a young boy.

In therapeutic practice, my goal is to expand a crack in the wall and allow vulnerability to emerge. By exploring Sam's experience of not knowing what is going on with Mary Beth, I acknowledge his pain and affirm that his rigidity was the best tool he had available at the time. This provides a starting point for establishing and acknowledging Sam's essence. This might help Sam generate the energy to recall early memories of how his habitual patterns of acting and feeling developed and persisted. With some direction, coaching, and compassionate support, he can discover how to experience a sense of connectedness that has the potential to interject new life into their relationship.

Similarly, by exploring Mary Beth's experience of Sam's apparent freedom, I also acknowledge her pain and affirm that what she did was the best she could at the time. This affirmation of her efforts is a starting for point for helping Mary Beth to begin to connect with her own essence and energy. As with her husband, affirming her essence helps Mary Beth to recognize the contrast between past experience and present experience. With some direction and coaching, there is potential for a new beginning.

With each new beginning we celebrate new-found freedom. Sam and Mary Beth may discover a renewed relationship or they may discover they want to go in different directions. Each will be more solidly based in their own essence.

CONCLUSION

My fictional case shows how I might use the four Tibetan Buddhist themes to enrich the therapeutic process. The four contemplations helped Sam and Mary Beth connect to actual life realities. This generated the motivation for developing new, effective life strategies. Awareness helped the couple open the door to the possibility of self-directed change and enhanced the flow of compassion between them. By releasing attachment, the partners freed energy previously bound up in past-life strategies. This in turn created space for connecting with essence, so that Mary Beth and Sam could experience the free flow of life energies within themselves and the environment, extending beyond their transitory wants and wishes. All four of these elements are necessary ingredients for a realized life.

To sum up, I have found that the simple principles embedded in Tibetan wisdom teachings resonate with my Christian heritage, my psychotherapy training, and my experience of what actually works in the therapeutic setting. I have found these teachings provide a comprehensive framework to help my clients go beyond their present level of development.

I continue to practice the discipline of a daily period of meditation. This is my time to let go, to allow new awareness to arise, and to reconnect with essence. It is time that I set aside to gain new perspectives. I consider this practice to be a significant element in my psychotherapeutic encounter, and all the therapeutic techniques I have learned are connected to this central element. An analogy would be a mirror's reflection. A clear mirror, or central element, reflects a clear image. If the mirror is cloudy, the image is cloudy, and the technique may be compromised.

ACKNOWLEDGMENTS

I want to acknowledge my family and friends for assistance in feedback and typing, as well as Jo-Anna Lutz Jones for her professional writing skills in editing the final draft.

NOTES

1. Vajrayana Foundation, *Three Roots Daily Practice* (Watsonville, CA: Bero Jey-dren Publications, 2002) 37, 39.
2. Victor Frankel, *Man's Search for Meaning* (Boston: Beacon Press, 1959).
3. Robert L. Goulding and Mary McClure Goulding, *The Power is in the Patient* (Trans Publications, 1978).
4. See anything by Longchen Rabjam (written in the 14th century), and, in particular, *The Precious Treasury of the Basic Space of Phenomena* (Junction City, CA: Padma Publishing, 2003).

CHAPTER 11

RESEARCH AS
A PATH OF MINDFULNESS

Paul Ritvo, Scientist

When I took refuge vows and became a Buddhist in 1974, my prevailing view was that immersion in the scientific process might make one a soulless machine. Mindfulness meditation changed that view and resolved my implicit anxiety about science. My life course led me to study clinical psychology, and mindfulness became increasingly relevant in understanding psychotherapy and other human attempts at mutual help.

What mindfulness offered and still offers is the integration of practices that support unbiased precision with practices that cultivate compassion.

Inner Peace—Global Impact: Tibetan Buddhism, Leadership, and Work, pp. 151–153
Copyright © 2012 by Information Age Publishing

While practitioners might see these links as self-evident, these experiences are often fragmented in everyday life. If one is precise and unbiased, it seems to conventionally prefigure situations where compassion is difficult or impossible. Perhaps the key to overcoming such fragmentation is the exploration, through mindfulness, of transitions from distortion to clarity. During mindfulness one becomes increasingly sensitized to the burdens of personal distortions and to the palpable relief when there is liberation from such burdens through increased clarity and precision. Compassion for one's self naturally evolves from precision and an absence of bias.

When first practicing as a clinical psychologist, I became more accepting and respectful of science, but had no serious aspirations towards a career in research. But a shift occurred as a direct consequence of meditative insight. It was an insight that may be obvious to many people, but it became personally and viscerally relevant to me. If one could serve individuals, in psychotherapy, through helping them clarify and revise self-distortions, the culture-at-large could be similarly served through the clarity, precision, and creativity of scientific discovery. I therefore saw research as a vehicle for direct service to society.

Now, admittedly, "bitten" by the research "bug," I was prone to the obsessionality that often plagues researchers and to the pride that can motivate and result from scientific success. In addition to mindfulness practice resulting in insights into the scientific work-at-hand, it also was an immediately accessible method for resolving egoistic ruts and resurrecting the pure curiosity that energizes research.

The phrase which, for me, most thematically bridges research and mindfulness practice is "letting go." Researchers must ultimately "let go" of the thoughts and findings that fire imagination and discovery (as apparent findings) one day, but are revealed to be illusions the next. Mindfulness involves "letting go" and level-headedness or "equanimity," while simultaneously opening the practitioner to visions of a wider world. In research terms, the wider-world visions involve a broader array of factors, hypotheses, and explanations.

The next shift in my life, once it was increasingly devoted to research, was identification with the job of *scientist* and an implicit challenge to view this occupation in optimal terms. I was, and remain, challenged to look for a process aspect, a *path*, especially when overwhelmed with the stress and tedium of particular projects. Mindfulness supplies an integrative momentum. While, of course, the discovery *goal* of research can seem opposite to mindfulness practice, such goals are relative, not unlike the goals of meditating a certain number of minutes or hours each day. These goals are just "way stations" along a journey that is ultimately more relevant than residing within any particular conceptual hub.

This brief retrospective review of experience suggests that modern science can be seen as mindfulness-in-action, a process resulting in discoveries and new technologies, but most consistently involving attention to the present moment within an unending search for truth. As simple as this may seem to mindfulness practitioners, it is an important bridge for scientists who can feel continually threatened by specters of not obtaining the next grant or publication. Not only is mindfulness important as a process of attentiveness to each step in a generative path, it reminds one that rejections can occur because of too much novelty in the work (not too little) and because the work is too good (too new) rather than not good enough. The equanimity developed in mindfulness practice fosters resilience in the face of apparent failure and thus enhanced productivity.

Quite in contrast to earlier fears of losing soul to science, I now see science as a discipline by which we find and sustain compassion in current society. I will reference a scene from recent experience. In a past study, my colleagues and I demonstrated that simple text messages, communicated once a week, resulted in the increased adherence of HIV+ Kenyans to antiretroviral medications.[1] Recently we convened about 50 East African colleagues in Nairobi to explore the next step in using cell phone communications and text messaging to quell the AIDS epidemic. There was a wonderful spirit to the gathering. We were, through scientific discipline and inspiration, revising the history of European colonialism within an inter-racial enterprise devoted to saving lives and reducing the adversity of AIDS. We did no formal mindfulness practice during these meetings. But I can attest to an atmosphere of mindfulness, where unbiased precision was wedded with compassion.

NOTE

1.   RT Lester et al, "Effects of Mobile Phone Short-Message Service (SMS) on Antiretroviral Treatment (ART) Adherence in Kenya: A Randomised Trial," *Lancet* 376, no. 9755 (Nov 27 2010):1838-45. Epub 2010 Nov 9.

SECTION III

ORGANIZATIONS:
ORGANIZING FOR THE FUTURE

> *... naturally, when you transform your mind, the whole society is transformed.*[1]
>
> —HH the 14th Dalai Lama

This section addresses the organizational or systemic level of change. It focuses on the entrepreneurial leadership of a few key Tibetan teachers and the rapid growth of what became perhaps the largest global organizations teaching the Tibetan wisdom traditions in the West. As described in the introductory chapter, I was seeking to understand the factors by which Tibetan Buddhism was taking root around the globe, so it mattered that some were able to grow effective global organizations, when previously Tibetan Buddhism had no such organizations. While the process would not be complete or as rich as it is without the participation of all the teachers and lineages, these are those that have perhaps touched the most people. Many highly influential global teachers are not here. This is not a comprehensive presentation of the major teachers; the three chapters and chart are intended to encourage further thought about what may be strategic actions over the next 10, 20, or 100 years.

The Tibetan culture and spirit have been sustained, and these traditions have become accessible to the entire world—something that has no precedent in history. The section shows how rapidly this evolved: how a

Inner Peace—Global Impact: Tibetan Buddhism, Leadership, and Work, pp. 155–161
Copyright © 2012 by Information Age Publishing

culture that had almost no use of modern technology adopted it. Teachers who spent up to 20 years in silent, solo retreat now fly globally to teach, while electronic technology increasingly connects centers, with live streaming of teachings from one continent to another becoming increasingly prevalent.

In order to show the pace and actions involved, since there is almost no data on this topic, I worked with the people from the various organizations, in addition to using data from the web, to develop a table that shows the life of His Holiness the 14th Dalai Lama juxtaposed alongside the development of the organizations. Two of the Tibetan Buddhist teachers who first taught extensively in the West are the focus of the following chapters. They are seen through their own words and through the eyes of two people who were deeply involved at that time.

Nick Ribush tells the story of the Foundation for the Preservation of the Mahayana Tradition—the FPMT. He is uniquely qualified for this task, as he is a former ordained monk and was one of the key Western contributors to the development of the FPMT. He discusses the nature of the organization, the way it sustains relatedness, interdependence, and independent functioning of its centers around the world, and the way it develops leaders and community, grounded in the words of its original leader, Lama Yeshe.

The next chapter addresses the uniqueness of Chogyam Trungpa and his analysis of how to reach Westerners. **Susan Skjei** is a 30-year student of Tibetan Buddhism and is the Founder/Director of Naropa University's Program in Authentic Leadership. A former corporate executive, she knows both Buddhism and the corporate world intimately. She describes what Chögyam Trungpa brought to the West, the work of the ALIA Institute, and the program she directs to train leaders in authenticity. She also discusses the Shambala tradition, which was Trungpa's vision for creating enlightened society. Note that she describes what is known as the *Shambhala Prophecy*, which is also mentioned by **Bronwen Rees** in her action research study, in the next section of this volume.

The section on organizations and organizing closes appropriately with reflections by **Sogyal Rinpoche**, a widely-respected contemporary global teacher of Tibetan Buddhism who has built a far-reaching organization, named Rigpa International, that uses technology very skillfully for teaching. In addition, **Philip Philippou**, who is member of Rigpa International's Executive Board, describes what it has been like being a Buddhist practitioner for over 25 years and involved in developing a growing global Buddhist organization.

Sogyal Rinpoche shares his perspectives on the current state of Buddhism in the West and briefly describes one of his major innovations in teaching: the way he adapted a very traditional way of teaching in Tibet, the Three Year Retreat, for use in the West. Long regarded as essential for serious students, a lengthy retreat enables the student to contemplate on the full meaning of the foundational teachings and make them his or her own—to embody them, rather than simply learn about them in a cognitive manner. As Rinpoche describes, his organization held such a traditional retreat, but also included almost 10 times as many students studying around the world, from their homes, in a *home study intensive retreat*. They studied the same texts as the Three Year retreatants, but over a longer time period, and received the teachings streamed by video into teaching centers on three continents. I have personally experienced the skillful way that Rinpoche and Rigpa have increasingly integrated video as a way of experiencing a person directly, when they are far away. While I was at a course in Ireland during the of 2009 summer, a noted elderly teacher from Tibet was to visit the main center in France. Sogyal Rinpoche greeted him remotely, by video, in Tibetan. The Tibetan teacher was greeted personally on his arrival in the traditional manner, yet from a great distance. Recently, Rigpa has begun to stream teachings live from one center to others throughout the world, so that students can participate wherever they may live in the same teaching at the same time. Such creativity with technology helps Sogyal Rinpoche and his organization become increasingly able to span the globe.

NOTE

1. His Holiness the 14th Dalai Lama, foreword to Robert Thurman, *Inner Revolution: Life, Liberty, and the Pursuit of Real Happiness* (New York: Riverhead Books, 1998), xiii.

Table 1.   THE SPREAD OF TIBETAN BUDDHISM IN THE WEST,
as seen in the life and activities of the Dalai Lama and the three
organizations discussed in this book (Many other dates are
important for the complete history—these paint an overview)

YEARS	His Holiness the Dalai Lama	Lama Yeshe and the FPMT	Chögyam Trungpa and Shambhala	Sogyal Rinpoche and Rigpa
1930s, 1940s	1935–Born in Amdo, Eastern Tibet.	1935–Lama Yeshe born in Tolung Dechen, Tibet. 1945–Lama Zopa Rinpoche born in Thangme, Nepal.	1939–Born in Kham, Eastern Tibet.	Late 1940s–Born in Kham, Eastern Tibet.
1950s	1959–Left Tibet and arrived in India.	1959–Left Tibet and arrived in India.	1959–Left Tibet and arrived in India.	1955–Left Tibet and arrived in Sikkim.
1960s	1962–Published first book: *My Land and My People*. 1967–First travel outside India, to Japan and Thailand.	Eight years in Buxa Duar refugee camp, West Bengal. Lama Zopa becomes his student. 1967–Lama Yeshe and Lama Zopa meet their first Western student in Darjeeling. 1969–Kopan Monastery established.	1963–67 Studied at Oxford University. Founded first Western meditation center in Scotland. 1966–Published *Born in Tibet*, first of his books.	
1970s	1973–First trip to Europe.	1971–First course for Westerners at Kopan Monastery, Nepal. 1972–Tushita Meditation Centre, Dharamsala, established.	1970–Arrived in North America and established communities in Vermont and Colorado.	1971–Studied Comparative Religion at Cambridge University.

(Table continues on next page)

Table 1. Continued

YEARS	His Holiness the Dalai Lama	Lama Yeshe and the FPMT	Chögyam Trungpa and Shambhala	Sogyal Rinpoche and Rigpa
1970s		1974–First trip to West (U.S., Australia, New Zealand). –First Western center established: Chenrezig Institute, Australia. 1975 onwards: annual teaching tours to the West.	1973– Incorporated *Vajradhatu*, an international association of Buddhist meditation and study centers, now known as Shambhala International. Published *Cutting Through Spiritual Materialism*.	1973–Helped to arrange the Dalai Lama's first visit to Europe, in Rome, Switzerland and the UK. 1974–Began teaching in London. 1975–Founded first center, in London.
		1975–FPMT established and Wisdom Publications founded. 1976–First Wisdom Publications book published: *Wisdom Energy*.	1973–1979 Conducted six 3-month seminars and countless seminars and workshops in North America and Europe. 1974–First brought HH the 16th Karmapa to North America.	1976–Began to teach in Paris. 1979–Taught in the United States for the first time, in Berkeley. Gave the name *Rigpa* to his work.
			1974–Founded The Naropa Institute, a contemplative studies and liberal arts college, now fully accredited as Naropa University.	
			1975–Created Shambhala Training, a series of weekend meditation programs.	

(Table continues on next page)

Table 1.   Continued

YEARS	His Holiness the Dalai Lama	Lama Yeshe and the FPMT	Chögyam Trungpa and Shambhala	Sogyal Rinpoche and Rigpa
1970s			1976–Appointed Thomas Rich (Vajra Regent, Ösel Tendzin) to be his successor. 1976–81–Received and taught the cycle of terma teachings on Shambhala.	
1980s	1981–Visit to Boulder CO, hosted by Chögyam Trungpa.	1980–International Office started. 1982–Lama Yeshe visits Tibet; FPMT organizes European tour of HH the Dalai Lama.	1980-1985 Conducted three 3-month seminaries and Kalapa Assemblies 1987–Chögyam Trungpa's death. Over 60 Teaching centers existed.	1983-Spoke at the *New Dimensions in Care for the Dying* conference in California, along with Elizabeth Kübler-Ross and Kenneth Ring.
	1987–Proposed 5-Point Peace Plan for Tibet; First trip to U.S.; First private Mind & Life gathering on Buddhism and science. 1989–Awarded the Nobel Peace Prize.	1983–FPMT board established. 1984–Lama Yeshe's death. Fifty FPMT centers existed. Lama Zopa Rinpoche takes over as spiritual director of FPMT. 1985–Lama Yeshe's incarnation, Ösel Rinpoche, born. Recognized by HH the Dalai Lama in 1986.		1985–Taught in Australia and Germany for the first time. 1989–Invited the Dalai Lama to give teachings to 5,500 people in San Jose, California–the largest gathering of Buddhist practitioners and teachers in America up to that point.

(Table continues on next page)

Table 1. Continued

YEARS	His Holiness the Dalai Lama	Lama Yeshe and the FPMT	Chögyam Trungpa and Shambhala	Sogyal Rinpoche and Rigpa
1990s	1990–Published 20th book.	1991–Sera Food Fund established to offer 3 vegetarian meals a day to 2,600 monks at Sera-je Monastery, India.	1990–Chögyam Trungpa's dharma heir, Vajra Regent Ösel Tendzin, dies. 1990–Sawang, Ösel Rangdröl Mukpo, Trungpa Rinpoche's oldest son, becomes the leader of Vajradhatu. 1994–Sawang changes name of *Vajradhatu* to *Shambhala*.	1990–Organized major teachings by Dilgo Khyentse Rinpoche for 1,500 people at Prapoutel, France. 1992–Published *The Tibetan Book of Living and Dying*. Over two and a half million copies have been printed in 80 countries and 34 languages.
		1995–*Mandala Magazine*, the journal of the FPMT, begins. 1996–Lama Yeshe Wisdom Archive established in Boston. 1998–First Masters Program begins.	1994–Sawang recognized by Penor Rinpoche as an incarnation of *Mipham the Great* 1995—Sawang enthroned as Sakyong or *Earth Protector* by Penor Rinpoche 1999–Sakyong presents first teachings on Shambhala Buddhism.	Main retreat center, Lerab Ling, opened in southern France. 1993–Founded Spiritual Care Education Program to bring Buddhist teachings to professionals and volunteers in end-of-life care. It has trained over 30,000 people.

(Table continues on next page)

Table 1. Continued

YEARS	His Holiness the Dalai Lama	Lama Yeshe and the FPMT	Chögyam Trungpa and Shambhala	Sogyal Rinpoche and Rigpa
2000s	2003–First public Mind & Life gathering on Buddhism and science (at MIT) 2007–U.S. Congressional Gold Medal 2010–Published 70th book	2006–Maitripa College, first FPMT accredited college, founded in Portland OR. 2010–Mongolia bestows highest civilian award, the Polar Star, on Lama Zopa Rinpoche for services to restore Buddhism there.	2000–2009 Sakyong teaches annual Vajrayana Seminary, Dzogchen retreats and countless workshops and seminars. 2003–Sakyong publishes *Turning the Mind into an Ally* 2005–Sakyong conducts first Rigden Abhisheka for over 1,000 people	2000-The Dalai Lama visited Lerab Ling in France to give 5 days of teachings to 12,000 people. 2002–Started *Practical Wisdom Leaders' Retreats* for Australian CEO's to integrate the principles of wisdom and compassion into the workplace.
	–FPMT standard education programs start to go online.	2005–Sakyong marries Khandro Tseyang. 2005–Sakyong publishes *Ruling Your World.*	2006–Rigpa's Three-Year Retreat began, with 400 people taking part in France, and 3,500 students following a "home retreat" in their own countries.
	2011–30th anniversary of Tushita Delhi's annual Dharma celebration with HH the Dalai Lama. –Number of geshes in FPMT centers reaches 40.	2007–Sakyong introduces the *Way of Shambhala* curriculum, also offered online. 2008–Sakyong introduces Scorpion Seal cycle of teachings based on Shambhala *terma.*	2008–The Dalai Lama inaugurated the traditional Tibetan temple at Lerab Ling in France. 2009–Dechen Shying Spiritual Care Center opened at Dzogchen Beara in West Cork, Ireland.
2011–12	Awarded the Templeton Prize.	FPMT: 160 centers; 40 countries.	Shambhala: 170 centers; 36 countries.	Rigpa: 130 centers; 41 countries.

Note: All data gathered by Kathryn Goldman Schuyler, with the assistance of Nick Ribush, Susan Skjei, and Andy Fraser, as well as others from *Rigpa* International. I am solely responsible for any errors and thank them for taking the time and care to help me compile the data for this overview.

Nicholas Ribush
(Photo by Jeb Byrne)

Lama Yeshe
(Photo by Carol Royce-Wilder)

CHAPTER 12

BAMBOO THROUGH CONCRETE.... GROWING TIBETAN BUDDHISM IN THE WEST

(The Story of the Foundation for the Preservation of the Mahayana Tradition—the FPMT)

Nicholas Ribush

Inner Peace—Global Impact: Tibetan Buddhism, Leadership, and Work, pp. 163–182
Copyright © 2012 by Information Age Publishing
All rights of reproduction in any form reserved.

NOTE: As you read, you will note that this chapter has two styles of text. This was done in order to make clear the distinction between the portions written by the author and those selected from talks by the teacher whose work was the initial inspiration for the organization, Lama Yeshe. The author, Dr. Nicholas Ribush, has been a key figure in the development of the FPMT (one of the larger Tibetan Buddhist organizations in the world) since its start. As one of the early participants and someone who has devoted much of his life to archiving the talks given by its original main teacher, Lama Yeshe, he was in a rare position to write about the organization. He suggested locating selections from Lama Yeshe's talks so today's readers could have the "original source material"—the actual ideas about the process of organizing as they were expressed to the organization over time. Probably no one else could have written such an article. It is rare to have access into the views on organizing of a key leader.

I was standing on the steps of the Kopan Monastery[1] with Lama Yeshe when he gazed into the distance, as if surveying with his mind's eye his already wide-ranging Dharma works, and said, "We need an organization to keep this together."

It was November 1975 and we—Lama Yeshe, Lama Zopa Rinpoche and I—had just returned from a 9-month international tour that had taken us around the world from Nepal to Darjeeling and Dharamsala in India, to Thailand, Australia, New Zealand, America, England, Switzerland, Italy and back to India and Nepal again. This was the most extensive tour the Lamas were ever to undertake and one that resulted in the formation of four new *Dharma* centers. What Lama Yeshe wanted to "keep together" was a mushrooming collection of 12 centers and related activities, the external manifestation of his total dedication to spreading the Buddha's teachings for the benefit of all beings.

Accordingly, Lama Yeshe summoned together nine of his senior students who were present at the time to discuss the coordination of this rapidly growing Dharma network. He called this group the Council for the Preservation of the Mahayana Tradition (CPMT)—a mouthful that Lama (as everybody always called Lama Yeshe) insisted was necessary to spell out exactly what his (and our) purpose was, a kind of succinct mission statement. Later this name was extended to denote the body that comprises the directors of the centers and other divisions of Lama's worldwide organization, which itself became known as the Foundation for the Preservation of the Mahayana Tradition (FPMT).[2] We wanted to call it the Yeshe Foundation but of course, Lama would have none of that.

Lama Yeshe was always less than complimentary about Dharma students who eschewed organization and management. "Some hippies reject organization," he said.

> They can't even organize their own lives let alone organize to benefit so many others. We have not landed on the moon; we are living on earth in the twentieth century. Everybody lives in a certain environment with a certain structure. We should too; otherwise we'll get confused. Therefore I have put forward guidelines to show how our centers should be. In a place where hundreds of people are involved, we're responsible for using their lives in a worthwhile way instead of wasting their time. So we have to organize.

Since those embryonic days, the FPMT has grown exponentially, without a business plan, an articulated vision, or any kind of serious funding. It has developed organically, day-to-day, month-to-month, year-to-year, pretty much as Lama would have wanted it to. In other words, as Lama Yeshe and Lama Zopa Rinpoche traveled the world (and Rinpoche alone after Lama passed away), more and more centers and related activities were seeded. As the FPMT has grown, the nature of the central organizing body has developed accordingly.

Of course, Lama Yeshe never took any credit for all this. He always put the worldwide spread of Tibetan Buddhism down to the power of the Dharma, not the charisma of the lama. But there's no doubt that up until his death he was, after His Holiness the Dalai Lama, the most influential Tibetan Buddhist monk in the world. (And after Lama's passing away, Lama Zopa Rinpoche has assumed that mantle.) For one thing, Lama Yeshe was totally fearless (one of the ten powers of a buddha). Despite his "breaking English," as he called it, he would expound upon the most profound aspects of Buddhist philosophy to audiences of any size directly in English without the safety net of an interpreter anywhere in sight. He was able to get away with this because he communicated not only through language but also by facial expression, gesture, laughter, often raucous, and silence. In many ways, his teachings were more performance than lecture.

He was unconventional in many other ways as well. He rarely wore the traditional monks' maroon robes completely correctly. Often they were not even maroon but closer to cerise or pink. And he did not mind wearing lay clothes if the situation demanded it. He always taught in robes but when traveling or relaxing he might be in trousers, swimming trunks, or even a caftan. This, coupled with the fact that he spent most of his time with Westerners, made him the object of criticism among the conservative Tibetan community. Many doubted the purity of his motivation. They thought he was in it for the money. In fact, he owned almost nothing, and whatever funds did come to him he put into supporting the young Tibetan monks at Kopan Monastery. "My children," he called them.

He was criticized for not completing his formal education by sitting for his *geshe* degree, the title monks get after 20 or 30 years of study in the great monasteries, which continued in India after the 1959 Chinese invasion of Tibet. He completed and excelled in his studies and was a renowned debater, but he knew that if he did his exams and became a geshe he would be obliged to stay at the monastery to teach successive generations of monks, which is what you were supposed to do. Instead, he became a "Tibetan hippie," as he put it. "I dropped out," he would always laugh.

Nevertheless, he fulfilled his monastic obligations in other ways. He raised money for the monastery himself and, as more and more FPMT centers came into being, sent geshes to the West as resident teachers, where they themselves were able to find sponsors for their students back in the monastery and raise funds to build more facilities for the increasing numbers of Tibetan monks fleeing Chinese oppression to continue their studies in India.

Despite Lama's superficial unconventionality, he remained a pure monk with perfectly untarnished vows and, unlike some other prominent and influential Tibetan teachers in the West who had disrobed and were now laymen, attracted not the slightest breath of scandal because there was not the slightest cause for it.

Lama Yeshe was born in Tibet in 1935 and educated at the great Sera Monastic University in Lhasa. With the Chinese occupation, he escaped to India, where he spent the next 8 years at the Buxaduar refugee camp in West Bengal. It was there he met Lama Zopa Rinpoche, who was born in Nepal in 1945, went to Tibet in 1956, and also escaped to India in 1959. In 1967 the Lamas met their first Western disciple, Zina Rachevsky, in Darjeeling and accompanied her to Nepal in 1968. Soon after their arrival they purchased a hilltop property about 40 minutes' walk from the great stupa of Boudhanath, where they established what was then called Ogmin Jangchub Choeling or the Nepalese Mahayana Centre Gompa, but is now simply known as Kopan Monastery.

At Zina's insistence Lama Yeshe and Lama Zopa Rinpoche began teaching Westerners at Kopan around 1970 and gave the first of their now world famous annual meditation courses in 1971. There were about 20 people at each of the first two courses. The third, which was the first I attended, was held in the fall of 1972 and attracted more than 50 students. The fourth took place in the spring of 1973; 120 people showed up. The fifth course, in the fall of 1973, saw 200. At the sixth, in the spring of 1974, there were over 250 people, more than the small monastery could handle and some 70 people left before the end. Most of these people found out about Kopan by word of mouth; there was essentially no advertising. The course has now been taught 44 times, and since 1975 an average of 200 students have been in attendance each time.

Kopan is the heart of the FPMT. It is where most of the early students met the Lamas, received teachings, and became Buddhist. Many of these students returned to the West and, fired up by what they had heard, wanted to share it with their family and friends. So they started inviting Lama Yeshe and Lama Zopa Rinpoche to the West, and in the summer of 1974 the Lamas made their first overseas trip, which took them to the United States, Australia, and New Zealand. During that time, two centers were created, one in Indiana, which closed a year later, and one in Australia—Chenrezig Institute for Wisdom Culture. Each center came into being because the local students asked Lama Yeshe if they could start a center and he said yes.

That is how the four centers (in New Zealand, the United States, England, and Italy) were established during the tour of 1975. And so it went. Every year the Lamas would travel to the West and new centers would be founded. When Lama Yeshe passed away in 1984 at the age of 49, Lama Zopa Rinpoche took over the spiritual leadership of the FPMT and, under his guidance, the work that Lama Yeshe started has continued without a break. At this time the FPMT consists of about 160 centers, projects, and services in some 40 countries worldwide.

Over the years, Lama Yeshe gave many pep talks to his directors, each containing a wealth of good advice and fresh perspectives on the purpose of the FPMT and encouraging us to share the FPMT's reality with others in a "clean, clear, dynamic way." Perhaps the best way to present Lama's views about organizing is to offer what Lama Yeshe himself said about the organization's objectives, structure, and function in his final address to his center directors in 1983,[3] at which time there were about 45 FPMT entities.

THE PURPOSE OF THE FPMT

Why have we established the FPMT? Why are we establishing these facilities all over the world? I think we are clean clear as to our aim—we want to lead all sentient beings to higher education. We are an organization that gives people the chance to receive higher education. We offer people what we have—the combined knowledge of Buddha's teachings and the modern way of life. Our purpose is to share our experience of this.

We know that people are dissatisfied with worldly life, with the education system, and everything else. It is in the nature of the dualistic mind to be dissatisfied. So what we are trying to do is to help people discover their own totality and thus discover perfect satisfaction.

Now, the way we have evolved is not through you or me having said we want to do these things but through a natural process of development. Our organization has grown naturally, organically. It is not "Lama Yeshe wanted to do it." I've never said that I want centers all over the world. Rather, I came into contact with students who then wanted to do something, who expressed the wish to share their experience with others, and put together groups in various countries to share and grow with others.

Personally, I think that's fine. We should work for that. We are human beings; Buddhism helps us grow; therefore it is logical that we should work together to facilitate this kind of education. And it is not only we Lamas who are working for this. The centers' resident geshes and the students are working too. Actually, it is you students who are instrumental in creating the facilities for Dharma to exist in the Western world. True. Of course, teachers help, but the most important thing is for the students to be well educated. That is why we exist.

When we started establishing centers there was no overall plan—they just popped up randomly all over the world like mushrooms, because of the evolutionary process I've just mentioned and the cooperative conditions. Now that all these centers do exist, we have to facilitate their development in a constructive, clean, clear way; otherwise everything will just get confused. We have to develop properly both internally and in accordance with our twentieth century environment. That's why I've already put forward guidelines for how our centers should be—residential, country communities, city centers, monasteries, and so forth.

The foundation for a center's existence is the five precepts—no killing, stealing, sexual misconduct, telling lies, or intoxicants. We base our other activities—education, administration, accounting, kitchen, housekeeping, grounds and so forth—on those. All this unified energy also depends on the kindness of our benefactors, the devoted people who give us donations. Thus we are responsible to utilize their donations in the wisest possible way, the way that brings maximum benefit to others. For this reason, in a place where hundreds of people are involved, we have to organize—to ensure that we use their energy in the most worthwhile way and not waste their time. Therefore, each of our centers and activities needs a general director—to direct and manage all the human and material resources at our disposal.

THE CENTER DIRECTOR

Lama Yeshe always placed great emphasis on the position of center director. Even now, FPMT center directors are appointed directly or indirectly by the organization's spiritual director, Lama Zopa Rinpoche. Lama Yeshe talks about the role:

What does it mean to be a director? Take, for example, the job of director of one of our country centers. He or she is responsible for everything that happens in the center: education, legal matters, finance, business, community, kitchen, and so forth. Computer-like, the directors have to watch everything to make sure that it's all going in the right direction. And if they see something wrong, it is their responsibility to correct it.

Of course, one person, the director, cannot do everything alone, but under his or her umbrella all center activities function. To control these, we need a good

Figure 12.1. Lama Yeshe and Nick Ribush on the path to Namche Bazaar, Nepal, May 1973. (Photo Lama Zopa Rinpoche, courtesy Lama Yeshe Wisdom Archive)

management committee and a good place for the committee to meet and discuss things. The director alone should not decide how things should be done. In committee meetings we decide upon projects for the forthcoming year and give various responsibilities to different people. It is then the director's job to make sure that these people follow the committee's instructions exactly. If they don't, the director has the power and authority to correct them. He can even ask people who are disrupting the center's harmony and proper functioning to leave.

Thus a center director takes incredible responsibility—for the center's educational success, for its financial success. He has to think like a computer. The directorship is one of the most important aspects of the center. This doesn't mean that other people do not have responsibility; that's not true. They are responsible for the areas they have been given; they have their individual responsibilities. And it is not only the people who have been given jobs who have responsibility. Even students who come to a ten-day course, for example, have a certain degree of responsibility. They are working; they are expending energy for the Dharma; they are giving—to some extent they do have responsibility. As their hearts are touched they slowly, slowly take on more and more. We can see how we too have evolved in the same way.

Figure 12.2.   Lama Yeshe and Lama Zopa Rinpoche with Rinpoche's mother, ten newly ordained Westerners and other students at the Japanese Temple, Bodh-gaya, India, January 1974. (Photo courtesy Lama Yeshe Wisdom Archive)

GETTING ORGANIZED

At first the FPMT was quite small. Lama Yeshe was relatively accessible, and many of the administrative decisions went through him. But as the organization grew, this became unworkable, so Lama established an administrative office to handle center business. It was first run by Peter Kedge, who traveled with the Lamas from 1976 through 1979, and basically, wherever he was, that's where the office was. In 1980, Jacie Keeley took over, and the office was first at Kopan and then Istituto Lama Tzong Khapa, Italy.

> Now, the way to bring the Dharma to the Western world is to bring the nuclear, essential aspect of the Dharma. Of course, you cannot separate the essence from the Eastern cultural trappings immediately: "This is culture; that isn't." However, what you should do is take the practical points of Dharma and shape them according to your own culture. In my opinion, you should be making a new kind of Dharma dependent on each different place and its social customs. Since we are Mahayanists, we have a broad view and don't mind if Dharma takes different shapes. To bring Dharma to the West we should have a broad view.

Because we have so many centers, I can no longer direct them. Of course, at the beginning I had to direct the centers because the students were always asking, "Lama, what to do?" and we were small enough for me to always be in direct communication with them. But eventually we reached the point where I had to ask myself the question, "Am I a businessman, a Dharma teacher, or what?" Hundreds of letters were coming in from all over the world. I had to say, "What is this? Should I spend my life answering letters and running centers?" I thought it was wrong for me to spend my life in business because this was not the best way to serve my students. I thought that the most realistic thing to do to benefit them and make my life worthwhile was to go the middle way instead.

So I began to cut down on administrative work. I even wrote to all the centers telling them that they were responsible to make certain decisions, that I could not decide everything, and that it is too complicated and far too slow to have all the correspondence coming through Nepal. Therefore, I said we should have a central office as the center's business point. Of course, I could still be consulted on important matters and could still make decisions on anything. I'm part of the Central Office; I can give my opinion. But it was not necessary to rely on me for everything. That's why I established the Central Office [now called the FPMT International Office].[4]

However, to some extent, I am still responsible for whatever happens in our centers. I have not let go of all responsibility; I'm not saying, "Let whatever happens happen." Therefore, I have to know something of what's going on in the centers: what problems have arisen, how serious they are, what benefits the centers are offering and so forth. The point is that I am not going to let the centers go completely so that they become totally nonsensical, nonbeneficial to others and just some kind of ego trip. I don't believe that should happen. So I don't want to close myself off. I like to look at and reflect upon what's happening, but at the same time

Figure 12.3.   Chenrezig Institute meditation hall, at FPMTs first Western center in Australia. (Photo courtesy of Chenrezig Institute)

Figure 12.4.   The Garden of Enlightenment, the stupa complex at Chenrezig Institute. (Photo courtesy Chenrezig Institute)

I don't want to spend my whole life writing letters. Thus, taking the middle way meant setting up the Central Office, which has reduced my administrative workload and given me more time to spend teaching Dharma. I haven't done this because I'm lazy ... well perhaps I am lazy, but at least I have to pretend that I'm not!

Quite apart from the fact that I do not have time to do all this administrative work, there are many things to do with running a center that you can do far better than I. You can communicate with people from your own cultural background much better than can a simple Himalayan monk. All the legal and financial work—I can't do that either. Also, there are many positions to be filled in a center; the right people have to be selected for the right job. You students should do these things yourselves.

So, because all this administrative work was taking up so much of my time, I passed many things on to the Central Office. There is a huge amount of this kind of work to do, that's why the Central Office is important. It facilitates communication both between the centers and me and among the centers themselves. You see, we do have the human tendency to shut off from each other: "I don't want you looking at me; I can see my own point of view, I don't want to share it with you." Each center has its own egocentric orientation: "We're good enough; we don't need to take the best of other cultures." This is wrong. We have reached our present state of existence through a process of evolution. Some older centers have had good experiences and have learned how to do things well. Doing things well is not simply an intellectual exercise but something that comes from acting every day and learning how to do things until you can do them automatically. Thus it is good that the Central Office has a pool of collective experience so that all our centers can share in it and help reinforce each other.

We have to be able to focus and integrate our energy and store information in a clean, clear way so that it can be readily accessed. We should make a structure so that we all know what information is there and how to get it. Without a proper structure, we'll go bananas! Even a couple living together needs to be organized so that their house is clean, there is the food they need and so on. In the centers, we are involved in hundreds of people's lives; for some reason Dharma has brought all these people together. We are responsible to ensure that we do not waste people's energy; therefore we have to get ourselves together. This is why organization is very important.

WISDOM CULTURE: WORKING FOR OTHERS

Lama Yeshe included "for Wisdom Culture" in the names of several of his early centers—Chenrezig Institute for Wisdom Culture, Publications for Wisdom Culture (now Wisdom Publications),[5] Vajrapani Institute for Wis-

Figure 12.5. Lama Yeshe and Lama Zopa Rinpoche on the steps of the Kopan meditation hall, December 1980. (Photo Robin Bath, courtesy Lama Yeshe Wisdom Archive)

Figure 12.6.   Lama Yeshe and Lama Zopa Rinpoche with students from the November meditation course, 1983, at Kopan Monastery, Nepal. Lama Yeshe passed away three months later. (Photo courtesy Lama Yeshe Wisdom Archive)

dom Culture and so forth. This was to emphasize the fact that we were supposed to be different from—in fact the opposite of—worldly, mundane or, as Lama put it, samsaric culture. We were to operate from a foundation of wisdom and compassion, not ignorance and selfishness. From the Mahayana point of view, that meant dedicating our body, speech, and mind entirely to the welfare and happiness of others, as Lama himself had. And not just for the present generation but far into the future, for countless generations to come.

> Let's say, for example, that one of the older students and I have started a center. We're impermanent; we're going to die. What happens when we're dead? We established the center; it has never been properly organized; should it die too? No, of course not. Even though our very bones have disappeared, the center should continue to function. But for people to be able to carry on the center's work, there should be clean, clear directions as to why it was established. If things are set up right, religious philosophies can carry on for generations and generations. We know this to be an historical fact.
>
> If you think about it, from the point of view of culture, Buddhism is completely culture oriented; it is a complete culture, or way of life, from birth to death. Therefore we are dealing with a very serious thing; we are giving people something that

they should take very seriously in their lives. It is not just a one-week or one-month trip. We are offering something that utilizes Buddha's method and wisdom in the achievement of everlasting satisfaction. That everlasting peace and happiness is what we are working for.

So we have a very important job; it is not just one person's thing. For that reason I have to say openly to all our center directors that they should not feel they are working for Lama Yeshe—that's too small. I am just a simple monk; you are working for me? One atom? No—you are working for something much bigger than just one man. You are working for all mother sentient beings. That is important. You should think, "Even if I die, I am doing all of these things for the sake and benefit of all other mother sentient beings." That is why it is so important to us to have a clean, clear structure and direction.

For me, this is very important. I don't believe that I am the principal worker and I do everything. No. I believe what Lama Je Tsongkhapa[6] says in his *lam-rim*:[7] "All your success comes from other sentient beings." Thus, other sentient beings are capable of continuing our work, and what will enable them to do so will be having a clean, clear direction—not a temporary, Mickey Mouse direction, but a clean, clear one. Our aim then is to have a perfectly delineated structure so that even when we are all dead, still, as we wished, our Dharma centers will be able to carry on their work. I believe that human beings are very special. They are intelligent. If we write an intelligent constitution, record an intelligent system of direction, other human beings will be able to keep it going. That is why we have to have a structure.

Now, as far as our structure is concerned, it is simple and natural; a structure that could have been thought out by primitive people, not sophisticated twentieth century ones. I am not sophisticated; I have never been educated in organizational structure or learned about it. I am very simple. Our thing has grown naturally. Because we have been giving teachings continuously, the number of students has grown. Those interested students have then returned from Nepal to their homes all over the world and started centers in various places. Some of those have become directors and given different job responsibilities to others interested in helping them.

THE CENTRAL OFFICE

How is the Central Office constituted? Each of our centers is a part of the foundation of the main office; the office manifests from that base. Do you see the evolution? We give teachings; all the original directors manifest from there; from the directors, energy for new centers builds up; more and more new centers come. Like that, there has been a logical evolution, development from an existing foundation. The directors have built up the entity of the foundation and the Central Office, we communicate, and this is the way the structure develops. To my mind, it is not a sophisticated, egotistical structure but one that has occurred and grown naturally. Now all these directors—administrative, spiritual, business—are the principal nuclear resource, and they make up the Central Office, they are the directorate. They meet and put forward ideas. But who keeps the Central Office going? These twenty or more directors cannot remain in the one location, meeting and working together all the time, all their lives. They have to go back to their own places. They have their own business to attend to. So who does all these things? The Director of the Central Office.

Say that a CPMT meeting has decided that all centers should undertake a certain project because of its obvious benefit to the centers, the FPMT, or whatever. It is then the Central Office's responsibility to ensure that all the centers have all the information and everything else they need to carry out the project. On the other hand, some good idea may not be practical. If I have to go to each center to explain why something should not be done it's an incredible hassle. I can save time, life, and energy by simply telling the Central Office my ideas, which can then be circulated to all the relevant places. This is simple and useful, and it's the Central Office director's job to see that all this gets done. We need a clean, clear system with which everybody is comfortable.

Therefore when you, the FMPT directors, come to a final decision that is solid, to be implemented, or actualized, in our centers, the Central Office has the authority to make sure it happens. The Office director cannot direct a center to do something that was not generally agreed, "Because I say so." "I say so" is not authority enough. The thing is, we get an idea, a meeting of the FMPT directors (CPMT) agrees, and the Central Office ensures that it can be and is implemented. I think that this is the correct way to go about things.

BUILDING COMMUNITIES

One day in the mid-70s I was having lunch with Lama Yeshe in the restaurant of the Hotel Crystal in Kathmandu. At one point Lama grabbed a paper napkin and a pen and drew his ideal Dharma community. He drew a perimeter, the boundaries of the property. In the middle he placed the *gompa*, or meditation hall; its upper floor would house the resident teacher (a Tibetan geshe) and his interpreter. Nearby were scattered huts for monks and nuns. Around the edge were houses for lay families. At the gate was a shop. Lama also said that there should be a workshop somewhere so that a moneymaking business could be set up to help support the center. It was a totally integrated community, drawn almost as a *mandala*. (The word mandala has different meanings but in this sense it means an idealized vision of the world or universe. In tantric practice the meditational deity is at the center with other beings and buildings around. Here at the center of Lama's FPMT center mandala, the meditation hall and the teachers were central with other students and buildings spreading out from that.) I wish I'd kept that napkin.

Anyway, our aim is clear; it is to educate people. Each center should have strong emphasis on education. The education system and program are essential for us to be successful. Why are we building communities? Because we have no home? No! We are not refugees; we have not started centers to house refugees. Thus it is important for each center to have a strong educational program and a spiritual director [now termed spiritual program coordinator] to conduct it. This is an essential part of our structure and must be there.

But I am not going to keep telling you things that you know already. Still, it is important that I clarify the reason for our existence and what we are doing. It is important work; we are not joking. We are real. Also, we are confident. I have great confidence in my involvement with Western people; I believe in them. I think that there are things that we can understand in common. We understand each other; therefore we can work together.

Also, it is important for directors to have a great vision; they should not neglect their center's growth. They should have a very broad view in order to be open to people. In many of our centers we find that already the facilities are too small. Of course, to build adequate facilities takes time and energy; but we should have a broad open view: "We would like to have things this way, without limitations...." Having a broad view is not forcing any issue but simply saying that if we have the opportunity to do various things, we'll do them. You never know when somebody might come up to you and say, "I'd like to do something beneficial with my money." At that time you can reply, "Well we have this project ready to develop," and show that person your plans. If, however, you feel suffocated with what you already have and don't have any vision of how to expand, you can't show potential benefactors anything. Therefore you should plan ahead with great vision and have everything ready to show people how you want to expand and improve your facilities.

For example, we have always said that our centers should be living communities. But through experience we have discovered that we cannot yet be self-sufficient. To be a self-sufficient community in the Western sense requires an immense input of energy. Let's say that the twenty of us here are a community. Can you imagine what we need in order to live according to this society's standards? We have to live in reasonable comfort. That means we have to have cars, a certain amount of regular income for living expenses and so forth. So how do we do it? From the realistic point of view, it is an incredible job to make each center into a self-sufficient community. You know how much energy you have to take from the outside world.

My observation is that our centers are not really run professionally as self-sufficient communities. Even though we call ourselves communities, from the Western standard of living point of view, other communities are much more comfortable than our Buddhist ones. One of the problems that we are beginning to experience is that of overcrowding. This is not right—we must create the right conditions for people who live in or visit our centers, be they monks or nuns, single laypeople or parents and their children. We are in trouble because we are not doing things according to the Western way of life. Therefore we should take a look at where we are and where we should go from here.

Community life should be normal. Parents and children should be accommodated in our centers so that they can live as normally as possible. Our experience is that they are not; we should learn from that. Of course, our students have big hearts and try their best. It is all a part of our evolution, not something that we have done wrong. But now we have reached a certain point and learned something. Our Dharma family has grown and we need to improve the living conditions at our centers to accommodate everybody. There should be a section where families can live normal family lives; there should be part of the center where strict retreat-type courses can be conducted; there should be monastic conditions for the monks and nuns. Everybody should be normal and comfortable in his or her own way of life and everybody should have something constructive to do.

So, not only do we need a clear structure for our international organization; there should be one within each center too. As I said before, each center needs a director and a management committee. The committee consists of heads of the important sections of the center: the resident geshe, the spiritual program director, the business manager etc. and, of course, the director. Thus the committee is not elected but made up of those who hold positions of responsibility in the center. These people meet regularly and discuss how things should be done on a day-to-day basis. When they have agreed, they call the residents together and inform them of what they have decided. If the residents agree, well and good, but the committee does have to check with them. Thus all the center's members are consulted and have a say in decisions that affect them.

In general, this is the way we do it, but sometimes it might be hard for everyone to understand which way the director is going. If they don't understand, perhaps he can just let go. But most of the time this is the way we work: there is a committee, it makes decisions, we see how the residents feel about them, and if they don't like the decisions, we can change them. If they agree, then whatever it is, it can be done. In this case, it is the director's responsibility to see that it happens; he has to make sure that the committee's decisions are implemented in much the same way that the Central Office director has to see that the CPMT's decisions are carried out.

However, with respect to major decisions within a center, even the director and committee cannot decide alone. For example, say all the center's buildings have to be torn down and rebuilt. I don't think they should make a decision of that magnitude without consulting the other FMPT directors. It is too risky to have just a few people deciding whether or not to demolish an entire center. Similarly, say a center receives a donation of a million dollars. We should definitely call a meeting of all the other directors to decide on how that money should be spent. The director and the committee alone cannot make their own immediate decision, even though they know the local situation much better than all the other directors. The director of that center should put forward her proposals for the others to comment on.

In the same way, there is a limit to the decisions that the Central Office director can make. Above a certain level the other directors should be consulted. Then the Central Office makes sure that what has been agreed to gets done. Also, the Central Office helps me to get information about the centers and passes my messages through to the centers. My mail comes through the Central Office, too. The Central Office is a tool that helps me implement ideas I might have for ways to improve the centers. In this way and the ways already mentioned, the centers benefit from the Central Office. Thus it is important for them to support the Central Office through annual contributions.

Because we are doing constructive things with long-term plans, we should not expect to be able to judge the benefits of the contributions made to the Central Office on any short-term effects: "This year we gave x dollars to the Central Office but received only y amount of benefit." The benefit you receive may not necessarily become apparent in this material life. We are planting seeds and it takes time for them to grow. Therefore, as long as you can understand why your center puts money into the Central Office, you can analyze what is going on in the present situation and what the short- and long-term benefits for the entire FPMT mandala are, and check all that against the needs of our growing organization. Only then can you judge whether or not your contribution has been worthwhile. Remember—to bring Dharma to the West we have to have a broad view.

THE FPMT AFTER LAMA YESHE

When Lama Yeshe passed away in 1984 there were about 50 centers, projects and services around the world, and the Central Office was located at Istituto Lama Tzong Khapa in Italy with a staff of two. About a year before his death, Lama Yeshe had created a board of directors, whose purpose was, he said, "To look after the administrative aspects of the FPMT when I die so that Lama Zopa Rinpoche can just focus on teaching." There were twelve members; I was one of them. The first meeting the FPMT board actually had was at Lama Yeshe's cremation in California in March 1984, where the main order of business was to request Lama Zopa Rinpoche to take over. He suggested we ask some of his other teachers, such as HH Song Rinpoche, Geshe Sopa, and Geshe Rabten, but unsurprisingly they were not interested and said Rinpoche should do it, so he eventually accepted our request.

As mentioned above, since that time Rinpoche has not only continued teaching extensively but has also totally immersed himself in the administration of the organization. The board, whose composition has often changed, has continued to meet from one to four times a year, and CPMT meetings are held irregularly, averaging one every 3 years.

Much of the recent development of the FPMT has been in the area of social service. Rinpoche has established projects such as an eye clinic in Amdo, Tibet; a teachers' fund to support senior Tibetan teachers who hold and transmit the Gelug lineage; an education and scholarship fund; a food fund to support the 2,600 refugee monks at Sera-je Monastic University in south India, which has offered more than 15 million vegetarian meals over the years; an animal liberation project; and many more general Dharma projects such as prayer wheel and stupa funds, a text translation fund, various puja funds and so forth.

Publishing is also a large part of the FPMT. In 1975 I cofounded Wisdom Publications with Lama Yeshe at Kopan Monastery in Nepal. In 1978 Wisdom moved to England and in 1989 to Boston, where it is now the largest and most highly respected general Buddhist publisher in the world, having published more than 300 titles from all Buddhist traditions. Over the years several non-English-language FPMT publishers have also come into being, such as Ediciones Dharma, Spain; Chiara Luce Edizioni,

Italy; Editions Vajra Yogini, France; Diamant Verlag, Germany; Maitreya Publishing, Holland; and Bodhicitta Publishing, Taiwan.

In 1996 I left Wisdom Publications to establish the Lama Yeshe Wisdom Archive (LYWA), to focus on the teachings of Lama Yeshe and Lama Zopa Rinpoche. Since that time we have digitized over 10,000 hours of audiocassette recordings and, since the digital age began, added several thousand more hours of Rinpoche's teachings to this collection. Much of this material has been transcribed and thousands of pages published on the LYWA website, where it and hundreds of hours of audio are freely available. The Archive has also published some 600,000 copies of books for free distribution.

For more than 15 years the FPMT has published *Mandala Magazine,*[8] which is now distributed worldwide quarterly through subscription and the organization's network of centers. Six recent issued serialized in detail the history and development of the FPMT, which would greatly amplify to interested readers what I have written here.

Another significant development has been the creation of FPMT Education Services, which has become a major publisher in its own right, putting out the hundreds of prayers, practices and related materials required by centers and students, both FPMT and other. Education Services have also created 10 different study programs, both in-center and home study, covering all stages of student development, from introductory to advanced, the latter being a remarkable 7-year master's program.

In 2006 the FPMT established Maitripa College[9] in Portland, Oregon. Maitripa recently received state accreditation and is well on the way to becoming a fully functioning accredited university.

The FPMT also strongly encourages and tries to support Western monastic communities. Many Western Buddhist organizations tend to downplay the importance of practitioners' ordination as monks and nuns but the FPMT considers the ordained Sangha as the lifeblood of the tradition. The main monastic center is Nalanda Monastery in France, which was established by Lama Yeshe in 1981, but there are several smaller monastic communities around the world. FPMT monastics belong to the International Mahayana Institute, the Sangha organization Lama Yeshe created in 1973.

Lama Zopa Rinpoche also stresses the importance of holy objects such as statues and stupas, the main activity in this arena being the spectacular 500 foot Maitreya Buddha state, which is to be built in Kushinagar, India, the site of the Buddha's death, and the Great Stupa of Universal Compassion in Bendigo, Australia, which will be a replica of the famous Gyantse Kumbum in Tibet.

All in all, I think the FPMT is probably the largest Tibetan Buddhist organization in the world, with about 160 centers, projects and services in some 40 countries around the world. Its main focus is preserving the tradition of the great fourteenth century Tibetan master Lama Je Tsong-khapa, founder of the Gelug tradition, the Dalai Lama's branch of Tibetan Buddhism. From the beginning, Lama Yeshe and Lama Zopa Rinpoche have carried out their Dharma work in close consultation with His Holiness the Dalai Lama. His Holiness has often praised Rinpoche's vast activities in public. In 2010, the president of Mongolia also honored Rinpoche when he awarded Rinpoche that country's highest civilian honor, the Polar Star, which is rarely given to foreigners, for his efforts in restoring Buddhism in Mongolia.

Since the focus of this article has been the early development of the FPMT, I have written more about Lama Yeshe than Lama Zopa Rinpoche, but it would probably be fair to say that over the decades Rinpoche's influence has been even greater than that of Lama.

CONCLUSION

As I said at the beginning, the FPMT has developed in these various ways without an articulated plan. It has grown organically out of the pure motivation of its founders—Lama Yeshe and Lama Zopa Rinpoche—and the needs of seekers around the world. As I look back on these 4 decades of Dharma activity I cannot help but wonder in some amazement how this could have happened.

Actually, it all comes down to the leadership of our teachers. The way they have led is not only by words but also through example. Personally, I experienced such great benefit from my first meditation course and derived such great inspiration from Lama Yeshe and Lama Zopa Rinpoche that I wanted to be like them and benefit others in the way that they had benefited me. I think most of us who have been actively involved in the organization over all this time have done what we've done for the same reasons.

The lamas studied, meditated, and taught. They were monks. In the early days, many of us also got ordained, studied, meditated, and taught. The lamas traveled the world establishing centers. Many of us went to those centers to further the lamas' work. They led; we followed.

There was a good deal of faith involved, too. Not blind faith but faith based on experience and reason. In my own case, after the 1972 Kopan meditation course had finished, I remember saying to Anila Ann McNeil, the nun who was assisting Lama Zopa Rinpoche, "I really want to do Dharma but how will I support myself? I don't have that much money." She looked at me as if I was a bit simple and replied, "Oh, if you give yourself to the Dharma, the Dharma will always looks after you." I thought, "Oh, OK," and the course of my life was set. So far, so good.

POSTSCRIPT

In April of 2011 Rinpoche suffered a stroke while teaching in Australia and underwent intensive physical and speech therapy. His rehabilitation continues and seems to be going well. Rinpoche has resumed teaching and traveling, albeit much less than before, but we are hopeful for a full recovery and his continued guidance for a long time to come.

NOTES

1. Just outside of Boudhanath, Kathmandu, Nepal. www.kopan-monastery.com
2. The FPMT is now headquartered in Portland, Oregon, United States. www.fpmt.org
3. At Istituto Lama Tzong Khapa, Pomaia, Italy, January 1983.
4. Lama pronounced it "senchal" office, which sometimes made us think, "Is he saying central or essential?"
5. Wisdom Publishing is now located in Boston, Massachusetts. www.wisdompubs.org
6. Lama Je Tsongkhapa (1357-1419) founded the Gelug tradition, the most recent of the four main lineages of Tibetan Buddhism.
7. The lam-rim (stages of the path) is a presentation of all the teachings of the Buddha in a step-by-step arrangement that makes it easy to understand and practice the entire path to enlightenment. The first lam-rim text was written by Atisha (980-1052), the great Indian scholar who reestablished pure Buddhism in Tibet in the 11th century after a period of decline.
8. www.mandalamagazine.org. *Mandala eZine* is also published quarterly as an online addition to the print edition.
9. For more details on Maitripa College, see www.maitripa.org

CHAPTER 13

LEADING WITH AUTHENTICITY AND PRESENCE

The Legacy of Chögyam Trungpa Rinpoche

Susan Skjei

Inner Peace—Global Impact: Tibetan Buddhism, Leadership, and Work, pp. 183–200
Copyright © 2012 by Information Age Publishing

Figure 13.1.   Chögyam Trungpa Rinpoche, courtesy of Shambhala Archives. (Photo by George Holmes)

When you meet a person who has inner authentic presence, you find he has an overwhelming genuineness, which might be somewhat frightening because it is so true and honest and real. You experience a sense of command radiating from the person of inner authentic presence. Although that person might be a garbage collector or a taxi driver, still he or she has an uplifted quality, which magnetizes you and commands your attention. [1]

These words from Chögyam Trungpa paint a powerful and intriguing picture of an essential quality of leadership that often goes unacknowledged but is desperately needed during this time of social, economic, and environmental turbulence. This chapter provides a brief history of Chögyam Trungpa's life, describes some of the organizations and institutions he created, discusses his teachings on enlightened society, known as *Shambhala*, and shows how his teachings on leadership are currently influencing the development of leaders in the West.

Born in a small village in Tibet, Chögyam Trungpa (1939-1987) was a pioneer in bringing Buddhism to the West and became one of the most dynamic and provocative teachers of his time. He was renowned as a scholar, meditation master, poet, artist, and leader. Throughout his life he offered the deepest teachings from his tradition to his western students and showed them how to live their lives with confidence and compassion. Out of the destruction of his own homeland and culture, he created new institutions, rituals, and practices that integrated the directness and profundity of his own tradition with the artistry and practicality of many other cultures including the Japanese, Chinese, British, and North American cultures. His teachings on authenticity, presence, and confidence are particularly relevant for leaders in today's fast-paced complex world and have influenced the direction of current leadership theory and practice. [2]

Trungpa made a powerful contribution to the popularity and relevance of Buddhism in the West and helped to open the door for the current generation of Tibetan teachers and practitioners. Although his teaching methods were often unconventional, he was widely respected among his peers. Dzongsar Khyentse, prominent contemporary Tibetan teacher, described his influence this way:

> Western disciples might appreciate that what Chögyam Trungpa Rinpoche has done takes great talent. However, as a person from a similar background, I cannot even begin to fathom the amazing courage that he had—this may be more difficult for others to understand.
>
> One of the main challenges in the world today is the inability to understand others' points of view, cultures and traditions, and therefore being unable to communicate effectively. Rinpoche not only managed to understand the culture and thinking of the West, but was then able to interpret Buddhist wisdom, coming up with everything from terms to symbolism and disciplines. He created and communicated all of this incredibly effectively, from the smallest terms to a whole new culture and kingdom, while never diluting the fundamental Buddhist view.
>
> To this day, I think many of us are struggling to teach Buddhism beyond Tibet, beyond the East. We owe him a lot for opening that world.[3]

A CATALYST FOR CHANGE

Chögyam Trungpa came to the United States in 1970, during a time of tremendous upheaval and social change and became a catalyst for those seeking to find a genuine path in the midst of the "spiritual supermarket" that was taking place at the time. He had just completed a long retreat in Padmasambhava's famous cave at Taktsang, Bhutan, during which he realized that the biggest obstacle to enlightenment in both the East and the West arose not only from a lack of authentic teachers or spiritual practices, but from a materialistic mindset that funneled everything—even the spiritual path—into the service of ego. His popular book, *Cutting Through Spiritual Materialism*, was based on a series of lectures he gave to his students in Boulder, Colorado. The book became a modern spiritual classic because of its accessible language and relevance to students' everyday lives. In it, Trungpa described a common trap that practitioners of any spiritual tradition can fall into—using spiritual practice for self-improvement and aggrandizement of ego, rather than for unmasking self-deception. Rather than seeking blissful experiences, Trungpa advised students to recognize moments of disappointment and despair as the true gateways to the spiritual path. For some, this approach was threatening, but for many, it provided a powerful, new, and refreshing perspective on spiritual practice.

Known by many as a "crazy wisdom" master, Trungpa's methods were often unconventional and at times shocking and could be challenging to Buddhists and non-Buddhists alike. For example, he openly smoked, drank alcohol, and had sexual relationships with his female students—behavior which did not fit most people's expectations of a spiritual teacher. *Crazy wisdom* refers to a type of selfless or compassionate action on the part of a spiritual teacher that is beyond conventional reference points and can sometimes appear "insane" to those more comfortable with the status quo. It can be very direct and immediate and expresses itself in accordance with the situation, rather than with societal norms of politeness or propriety. In both India and Tibet, meditation masters (known as *siddhas*) often demonstrated this quality in their interactions with students. At times they provoked criticism, attack, and even ostracism from people who misunderstood their intentions and methods. According to Tibetan scholar Keith Dowman:

> The siddha has no choice but to respond selflessly to the stimulus provided by the highest function of interaction with his disciples, the function of release from human limitations. Thus he acts to liberate the people he encounters from the confines of their emotional and mental prisons. Since the siddha's personal karma has no place in determining the nature of his actions, and because his action is a reflex of beings seeking their own salvation, it is styled "no-action," a concept that the Taoist expresses as *wu wei*.[4]

Early Indian and Tibetan siddhas, including Padmasambhava, Tilopa, Marpa, Milarepa and Naropa, were all known for their rigorous and sometimes surprising teaching methods. These methods were intended to wake students up to their own potential and often required them to stretch beyond their personal limits. For example, Milarepa had to repeatedly build and then tear down a series of towers for his teacher Marpa. Marpa himself was required by his teacher Naropa to make the difficult trip from India to Tibet again and again, to bring the esoteric teachings to the unschooled Tibetans, while Naropa risked his scholarly reputation in order to study with his teacher, the fishmonger Tilopa. Reggie Ray, a student and senior teacher in Trungpa's tradition commented:

> Trungpa Rinpoche was and remained a siddha whose crazy wisdom was unrelenting—assuming now one, now another manifestation, depending on the needs of the situation. He was I think, a siddha of the highest order and, as such, taught a dharma that cut through all kinds of self-serving spiritual materialism, especially that found within Buddhism itself, and even through the outrageousness expected of crazy wisdom itself.[5]

These very qualities of outrageousness and passionate engagement that Trungpa demonstrated, magnetized students from all walks of life, and allowed him to make a deep connection to the western psyche that was unique among the Buddhist teachers of his day. Some of his students have written about their interactions with Trungpa and the surprising and sometimes disorienting effect of these encounters. Often these stories involve a situation in which the student's preconceptions and psychological momentum are interrupted by something that Trungpa says or does (or doesn't say or do) that creates a "gap" in the student's perception of the world. What happens in this gap is revealing. Is the student able to stay with her or his actual experience, or does s/he immediately fill it in with further thoughts, storylines, justifications, criticisms, conclusions, and the like? Without this gap—which can be surprising, painful, disorienting, confusing, or embarrassing—a genuine spiritual path cannot take place. As Trungpa himself pointed out, Buddhism too can be co-opted by ego's game of familiarity, control, and comfort, and he was not afraid to use humor or surprise to challenge religious beliefs that might be getting in the way of experience.[6] In his biography of Chögyam Trungpa, Fabrice Midal recounts an incident in which, over dinner, an extremely elegant lady asked him:

> "Rinpoche, my guru has taught me the practice of White Tara, but he hasn't explained what it is. What is White Tara?" Chögyam Trungpa replied: "It's cottage cheese." Then, after a few moments of silence, he pointed at another dish in front of him and added: "And Green Tara is spinach."[7]

A skillful teacher can redirect the student's attention from anxiety and self-consciousness to authenticity and presence, using humor or familiarity to disarm his or her defenses. One such incident is described by Dr. Jeremy Hayward, senior teacher and former director of Tail of the Tiger retreat center.

> When I arrived at Rinpoche's house, he saw me and beckoned for me to come in. I sat down opposite him at the round table by the window. It was a lovely summer afternoon, and I was completely stiff. Here was my chance; I was sitting right opposite Rinpoche, just him and me. I sat looking down at the table, unable to think of a thing to say. He offered me a cup of tea.
> Finally, I said to him, "Rinpoche, how do you think Tail of the Tiger is doing?" What I really had in mind was the dirt and the garbage and so on, and I was hoping he would say, "Well I think maybe it needs a little more discipline, and a little bit more cleanliness"—something about tightening up and making it more like what I thought a contemplative center should be. But instead of that he just smiled and said, "I think it's doing just fine." While that was very helpful in turning my mind from the judgmental dissatisfaction toward something more positive, still I just sat there at the table,

not knowing what else to say, still caught in the discomfort of intense self-consciousness.

After a while, he said, "Is that a lawn mower?" I opened up my ears and listened, and far away in the distance I heard the sound of a summer lawn mower, a very familiar sound which I used to love when I was a child. I loved the feeling of the outdoors, and of people doing gentle gardening things on a summer afternoon. I listened, and then replied, "Yes, I think it is." Somehow that opened up the whole space between us. It was as if I were here at last, or the space was here at last. It was also a direct teaching on the freshness of panoramic awareness. I stayed just a while longer, and there seemed to be more lightness between us.[8]

BORN INTO LEADERSHIP

Figure 13.2.   Chögyam Trungpa Rinpoche as a young monk, courtesy of Shambhala Archives.

Born in eastern Tibet in 1939 to a poor nomadic family, Chögyam Trungpa was recognized by the 16th Karmapa, head of the Kagyu school of Tibetan Buddhism, as a descendent in the Trungpa *lineage*—important teachers in the Kagyu tradition and historical advisors to the Chinese emperor. When he was 18 months old, he left the tent village, where he lived with his family, and moved into a large monastery teeming with thousands of monks. He underwent the rigorous monastic training befitting a *tulku* or incarnated lama,[9] studying and practicing long hours every day, until he was 18 years old. In addition to his training in two of the traditional schools of Tibetan Buddhism, he was also an active adherent of the *rimé* or "non-sectarian" movement.

Notably, he was one of the last in his generation to receive the complete cycle of Buddhist teachings available in Tibet at that time.

When his training was complete, he became the head of the Surmong Monasteries in Eastern Tibet. However, his tenure was abruptly interrupted by the Chinese invasion in 1959. He was forced to escape, leading a group of refugees over the Himalayas to safety in Northern India when he was just 20 years old. This harrowing and spiritually challenging journey, which lasted for over 10 months, is described in his book *Born in Tibet*.[10] Chögyam Trungpa went on to attend Oxford University where he studied comparative religion, philosophy, and fine arts on a Spaulding Fellowship. He also studied and practiced Japanese flower arranging and developed a keen appreciation for the arts. After graduation, he moved to Scotland and through a series of sharp encounters with reality (including a car accident that left him paralyzed on his left side) he decided to give up his monastic vows. It was during this time that he wrote *Meditation in Action*, the first of the 14 books that he would publish during his lifetime.[11]

Figure 13.3.   Chögyam Trungpa at Dharma Art Installation, courtesy Shambhala Archives.

The following year he married Diana Pybus and moved to the United States where he established his first meditation center in Barnet Vermont called Tail of the Tiger (now Karme Choling). Throughout the next decade Trungpa traveled continuously, published six books, and established a contemplative university (Naropa University) in Boulder, Colorado. He also conducted six 3-month residential seminaries, presented a vast array of Buddhist teachings, and established Vajradhatu, a network of over 100 meditation centers and retreat centers in North America and Europe. It was then that he began to develop a reputation for his unconventional teaching methods and his ability to penetrate the Western mind with sharp humor and deep insight. His fresh approach attracted a number of notable students, among whom were Pema Chödrön, Allen Ginsberg, Anne Waldman, Diane di Prima, Ken Wilber, Francisco Varela, José Arguelles, and Joni Mitchell, who portrayed Trungpa in the song "Refuge of the Roads" on her 1976 album *Hejira*.[12]

Chögyam Trungpa aspired to share this wealth of teachings throughout his life with the broadest audience possible and developed a series of weekend programs called Shambhala Training that provided a secular introduction to meditation. These programs attracted thousands of students and emphasized the importance of cultivating gentleness and fearlessness in daily interactions. In addition to meditation, he also encouraged his students to practice traditional arts such as archery, dance, theater, tea ceremony, film making, and flower arranging and to integrate the profundity and practicality of these teachings into their lives as teachers, therapists, business people, politicians, and leaders. Trungpa's wife, Diana, explained his approach.

> Rinpoche also understood that Western society is fundamentally a secular society and that the transmission of dharma would have to take place in a secular context. In the West, we will never have a monastic culture like the one in Tibet. The Buddhist teachings, he felt, should relate to our everyday lives in the West, so that we can have a living religion, a living spirituality. The teachings must apply to ordinary life: what we do when we get up in the morning, what we do at work, how we relate to our families, even what we do in our spare time.[13]

Chögyam Trungpa died in Nova Scotia in 1987 after having taught over 13 seminaries and countless seminars, established Naropa University as the first accredited Buddhist-inspired University in North America, founded Gampo Abby in Nova Scotia, created the Nalanda Translation Group, established professional associations such as the Amara Health Care Group for health professionals and the Ratna Society for business professionals, created the Dorje Kasung service organization, and developed Shambhala Training. His life and work touched tens of thousands of students worldwide who have continued to incorporate what they have learned into their lives and work.

The Shambhala teachings, combined with his deep roots in Buddhism, became the legacy that he left to his eldest son Sakyong Mipham, Rinpoche. Under Sakyong Mipham's leadership, the organization, now called Shambhala, continues to carry out the spiritual and societal vision that Trungpa brought with him when he first came to North America.[14]

In 1990, Sakyong Mipham (then known as the Sawang Ösel Rangdröl Mukpo) who had been trained from childhood to take on this role, returned from a period of study and practice in Nepal to lead the community. He consolidated the many projects and activities of his father's students under the umbrella of Shambhala International, and integrated spiritual training, community and cultural activities into the mandate of each local Shambhala Center. In May 1995, he was officially installed as the Sakyong, leader of both the spiritual and secular aspects of Shambhala and was recognized by Penor Rinpoche—then supreme head of the Nyingma lineage—as the reincarnation of Ju Mipham, a revered nineteenth-century Tibetan meditation master and scholar.[15] Shambhala International continues to thrive under the direction of Sakyong Mipham and the organization provides the basis for the transmission of the teachings that Chögyam Trungpa brought into the world as well as teachings that Sakyong Mipham is now introducing. In addition to centers and groups on five continents and a robust online network, the Shambhala mandala includes a range of other programs and institutions, reaching out into education, health care, social work, organizational change and innovation, publishing, and a broad spectrum of the arts.[16]

ENLIGHTENED SOCIETY

Although ChögyamTrungpa was thoroughly trained in the deep medita-tion traditions of Tibetan Buddhism and transmitted them in their entirety to his senior students, his most unique contribution was the body of teachings on Shambhala that he presented in the last 10 years of his life. These teachings relate directly to the challenges that modern leaders are facing and offer specific guidelines and methods for practice.

According to Tibetan lore, Shambhala was a mythical kingdom that existed somewhere in central Asia and represented the best of human society. It is said that the Buddha offered a special teaching to the King of Shambhala to help him recognize his own enlightened qualities as a mon-arch.[17] Shambhala's inhabitants lived together in peace, harmony, and great prosperity, and the kingdom has been a source of inspiration for culture, art, politics, and military strategy for many cultures in Asia. While some say Shambhala is just a myth, others contend that it continues to exist somewhere in the collective psyche and can be summoned when the world is in trouble. Thrangu Rinpoche, a highly respected Tibetan Bud-dhist teacher said, "The Buddha said that when *Buddhadharma* degener-ates in the world, the Shambhala tradition will revitalize it."[18]

Joanna Macy, Buddhist activist and scholar, was told about the proph-ecy of Shambhala by Choegyal Rinpoche, during her travels in Tibet. She describes this in her book *World as Lover, World as Self.*[19]

> There comes a time when all life on Earth is in danger. In this era, great barbarian powers have arisen. One is in the western hemisphere and one in the center of the Eurasian land mass. Although these two powers have spent their wealth in preparations to annihilate each other, they have much in common; weapons of unfathomable destructive power, and technologies that lay waste our world. In this era, when the whole future of sentient life seems to hang by the frailest of threads, the kingdom of Shambhala begins to emerge.

The prophecy goes on to say that tremendous courage will be needed by the warriors of Shambhala. These warriors do not use conventional weapons. Because they understand that conventional weapons are created by the human mind, they can be undone by human wisdom using the weapons of compassion and insight. The warriors will penetrate into the depths of societal power in order to disarm these conventional weapons and bring about a new golden age.

WARRIORSHIP

Chögyam Trungpa had a particular connection with the legend of Shambhala. He was a direct descendent of Gesar of Ling, the most famous of the legendary Shambhala warriors of the past, and was committed to bringing this vision of an enlightened society to the West. He learned about Shambhala in his youth, and later became a *terton*, or receiver of wisdom texts in the Shambhala tradition. At that point, he shifted his focus from purely Buddhist teachings to the Shambhala teachings on basic goodness and enlightened society.[20]

> The Shambhala teachings are founded on the premise that there is basic human wisdom that can help to solve the world's problems. This wisdom does not belong to any one culture or religion, nor does it come only from the West or the East. Rather, it is a tradition of human warriorship that has existed in many cultures at many times throughout history.[21]

The term *warriorship* describes someone who is courageous and brave and is willing to fight the battle with habitual patterns (at both a personal and societal level) that keep humanity tied to self-serving and destructive actions. In order to cultivate the strength necessary to overcome these negative influences, Shambhala warriors train in the view that human experience is wholesome and basically good, and that aggression and negativity are reactions to a misunderstanding of the nature of reality. There is no fundamental problem that cannot be overcome with compassion and insight. However, human beings do not always have access to this viewpoint, so various practices are necessary to inspire confidence and to access this place of resilience and courage. However, as Trungpa writes, this experience is actually very ordinary.

> Discovering real goodness comes from appreciating very simple experiences. We are not talking about how good it feels to make a million dollars or finally graduate from college or buy a new house, but we are speaking here of the basic goodness of being alive—which does not depend on our accomplishments or fulfilling our desires."[22]

The primary practice Chögyam Trungpa taught for discovering basic goodness was meditation. However, he considered all of life's challenges to be opportunities to practice and incorporated the various elements of everyday life into rituals for waking up. He emphasized the importance of decorum in everyday life, including how one eats, wears one's clothes, and speaks to others. All of these practices were intended to invoke the openness, fearlessness, and tenderness that is the hallmark of the Shambhala warrior. The path of warriorship provides an inspiring and uplifting journey toward greater wholeness and authenticity.

DISCOVERING AUTHENTICITY

The definition of authenticity within the Shambhala tradition refers to a state of awakened presence in which the individual has access to the profundity of basic goodness as well as appreciation of his or her own uniqueness. The Tibetan term for this awakened presence is *wangthang*, translated as "authentic presence" or "field of power." Although authentic presence is inherent, discipline and rigor are needed in order to access it. According to Trunpga, "The cause of authentic presence is the merit you accumulate and the effect is the authentic presence itself."[23]

Merit or virtue comes from emptying out and letting go—the ability to empathize and exchange oneself with the suffering and aspirations of others. It is a result of gradual development as well as instantaneously letting go of the habitual mind.

Although these qualities of authenticity are familiar to us, Trungpa said, most people only experience them in glimpses. In order to sustain the glimpse, there is a need for discipline. This can be accomplished through the practice of meditation. There are two meditation methods that can assist with the journey toward authenticity. The first is called *shamatha*, which in Sanskrit means "development of peace." First the practitioner must be able to simplify external stimuli, and thorough a simple technique, such as following the breath as it goes in and out of the body, bring his or her awareness into the present moment. The goal is not to try to think happy or pleasant thoughts or to think about peacefulness, per se, but through the process of acknowledging that one is thinking, and letting go of specific thoughts, peace can naturally arise. According to Trungpa, "It doesn't really matter what thoughts you have in the practice of meditation, whether you have monstrous thoughts, or benevolent thoughts, all of them are regarded purely as thinking. They are neither virtuous nor sinful."[24]

The second meditation discipline is called *vipassana* or clear seeing. It is not enough to have stability of mind. One must also cultivate clarity and the ability to see the interaction of cause and effect that can result in insight. The meditation technique involves opening up to the environment or "space" and noticing what happens when the practitioner attempts to rest his or her mind in this. Trungpa also emphasized the value of meditation for learning to synchronize one's body and mind.

This method of synchronizing your mind and body is training you to be very simple and to feel that you are not special, but ordinary, extra-ordinary. You sit simply, as a warrior, and out of that, a sense of individual dignity arises. You are sitting on the earth and you realize that this earth deserves you and you deserve this earth. You are there—fully, personally, genuinely. So meditation practice in the Shambhala tradition is designed to educate people to be honest and genuine, true to themselves.[25]

Jack Kornfield, senior teacher in the Theravadan tradition, who studied with Trungpa at Naropa University, wrote

According to how Trungpa Rinpoche taught the dharma, the way of practice wasn't to see that the things that make up our personality are a problem, but rather to see that they're part of the fabric and pattern of being, and that they become workable and in fact usable as we become wiser. Part of the playfulness of Trungpa Rinpoche was that he saw not only the difficulties but also the potential in all of the aspects of practice.[26]

ROUSING UNCONDITIONAL CONFIDENCE

There are many aspects to the Shambhala teachings, but perhaps the one that is most important for leadership development has to do with how to rouse unconditional confidence, regardless of external circumstances. This is called raising *lungta* or "windhorse." It involves tuning in to one's body, emotions, and mental state, fully acknowledging and synchronizing them, and then letting go. In this way, a leader can learn to access the energy (or wind) of a situation and engage with it powerfully, as if riding a horse. By practicing this in a variety of ways, in both formal and informal settings, it is possible for the leader to develop strength and presence, or "merit" as it is known in this tradition. There are clear stages in the development of authentic presence. These stages are known as the four dignities. Trungpa's son, Sakyong Mipham, described the four dignities in his book, *Ruling Your World*.[27] The first dignity, known as "meek" is symbolized by the tiger. The tiger has his feet on the ground and moves deliberately with mindfulness and awareness. He is discerning and deliberate and has developed contentment in the midst of life's unfolding challenges. For leaders, this represents an acknowledgement of who they are, as genuine human beings, and what the situation includes. When their sense perceptions are awake and their hearts and minds are open, leaders can make good decisions based on knowing *what is*, rather than what they wish were happening. A modern leader whose work exemplifies this dignity is Mother Theresa. She did not minimize the difficult social problems that were rampant in Calcutta, India, but, with full awareness and tireless action, engaged the poverty, illness, and social injustice she encountered and transformed them for the better.

The next stage, known as "perky," is represented by the snow lion. The snow lion leaps and plays in the highland meadows and is able to engage fully with situations with joy and resourcefulness. For leaders, this represents having a vision and engaging others along the way. It means relating with the emotional ups and downs of life with a sense of humor and resilience. A modern leader who exemplifies this dignity is Martin Luther King. He was able to communicate a powerful vision for society while continuing to experience the very conditions of racial inequality that he was fighting against.

The third stage, called "outrageous," is represented by a mythical bird called the *garuda*. The garuda soars in the sky without any need to measure his accomplishments or compare himself to others. For a leader, this means having perspective, and not being afraid to initiate change, especially if it challenges the status quo. This is the realm of unconditional confidence, while still staying open and connected with the situation at hand. Mahatma Gandhi's courageous use of nonviolent resistance or *satyagraha*, in the Indian independence movement is an example of this dignity.

The last step is called "inscrutable" and is represented by the dragon. The dragon soars into heaven and down into the earth, joining the two with perfect timing as the seasons unfold. For the leader, this means having the wisdom and skill to know what action is appropriate in which situation and to allow the natural cycles of life and death to take their course. Nelson Mandela's ability to patiently withstand the hardships of decades of incarceration, and yet lead his country with determination and compassion when he became president of South Africa is an example of this dignity in action.

LEADERSHIP PRESENCE

The importance of courage and leadership presence in the midst of difficult situations has been well documented in the leadership literature. Warren Bennis and Robert Thomas have said that good leadership is about making sound judgments when confronted with *crucible moments*.[28] Bill George, former CEO of Medtronic, expanded on this idea and emphasized the importance of *moments of truth* for authentic leaders.[29] Similarly, Joseph Badaracco described *moments of courage* or *defining moments*.[30] All of these refer to the turning points at which a leader faces a challenge and then responds with the sum total of whoever he or she is at the time with whatever level of training and experience he or she has at that moment.

Many leadership experts have sought to analyze and evaluate the actions leaders take in these critical moments in order to recommend additional training to help them respond more appropriately in the future.[31] This is certainly useful, but it does not address the inner experience of the leader and how awareness impacts not only what the leader sees, but how he or she responds to the situation. As Bill O'Reilly, CEO of Hanover Insurance said, "The success of an intervention is determined by the internal condition of the intervener."[32] When a leader faces an emerging, complex challenge that is different from anything that has happened before, he or she must innovate on the spot. These moments require the leader to access a deeper level of authenticity, coherence, resourcefulness, and presence to respond appropriately (or at all). It might be said that authentic moments are those when we are most at home with ourselves or at one with ourselves. However, leaders cannot take these moments for granted. In order to understand authentic moments more fully, a deeper exploration of leaders' lived experience is needed. This is what Chögyam Trungpa offered the world through his teachings on authentic presence—both an understanding of authenticity and a pathway for cultivating it.

WORKING WITH FEAR

According to Trungpa, the biggest obstacle to authentic presence is fear. Leaders cannot eliminate fear, but must get to know their fear intimately in order to know how to work with it. Bravery is not the absence of fear but the ability to take wise action in spite of the fear. Pema Chödrön, a Western student of Trungpa's who became a monastic, wrote,

> To the degree you face yourself and face your fear, you know what it triggers in you and all of the ways you try to run away from it, and trust the potential that you and all other beings have to open up, be wakeful and be kind, you don't right away discover courage, but you discover tender vulnerability.[33]

The antidote to fear is not a brittle confidence born of certainty, but the vulnerability of an open heart. Thus the Shambhala path emphasizes the importance of gentleness and vulnerability as well as fearlessness and confidence. The authentic leader balances these two qualities with discernment and intelligence.

DEVELOPING LEADERS FOR TOMORROW

The immediacy and power of Chögyam Trungpa and his teachings have influenced many of the key organizational theorists and practitioners of our time. The writings of Ken Wilber, contemporary philosopher and developer of Integral Theory, have been strongly impacted by Tibetan Buddhism and by Trungpa in particular.[34] Otto Scharmer and Peter Senge, both from MIT, have participated in programs led by Chögyam Trungpa's students, and Scharmer has incorporated Shambhala-inspired mindfulness and embodiment practices into his work with leaders and change agents.[35] Margaret Wheatley has included Chögyam Trungpa's teachings on fear and fearlessness in her writings, workshops, and consulting with social entrepreneurs and women leaders.[36]

In 2001, a group of Trungpa's senior students founded a leadership institute in Canada based on the principles and practices of enlightened society.[37] We named it the Shambhala Institute for Authentic Leadership and for many years we have convened over 250 international leaders, consultants, and educators annually in Halifax, Nova Scotia for a week of intensive training in contemplative practice, creative process, and organizational methods.

At the beginning, we reached out to other thought leaders who were developing innovative approaches to leadership, organizational development, and social change, whose approaches were based on living systems theory, complexity science, and organizational learning and were deeply aligned with the vision of Shambhala. Our early partners included Juanita Brown, Art Kleiner, Marianne Knuth, Toke Moeller, Peter Senge, and Margaret Wheatley, who all played key roles and continue to offer their support and creativity as the institute unfolds.

In 2009 the institute began to expand, and we changed the name to Authentic Leadership in Action (ALIA) Institute. ALIA sessions were convened in Ontario, Canada, as well as in the Netherlands. In addition, ALIA became involved in several rural initiatives in Nova Scotia that were designed to increase leadership capacity. Margaret Wheatley, author and social activist, said of ALIA, "Increasingly I am seeing established leaders not being able to handle the challenges they face. Leadership renewal is very much needed, and the ALIA Institute is able to provide that renewal."[38] We also provided consulting and coaching, based on the synthesis of mindfulness, creative process, dialogue, and skillful organizational methods to a variety of leaders and their organizations, primarily in Canada. In 2011, we convened the institute for the first time in the United States, in Columbus, Ohio. According to ALIA's Executive Director Susan Szpakowski,

The leadership practices that converge at the ALIA Institute each play a part in revealing, amplifying, and harnessing this authentic nature, this hidden potential. Those of us who have been involved in organizing and convening the Institute have been building a body of tacit understanding about how these practices work together and how they can be applied in various professional fields.[39]

Collaborations are currently taking place among faculty from the ALIA Institute, Naropa University, the Presencing Institute, Berkana, the Human Systems Dynamics Institute, The Society for Organizational Learning, as well as many other partners and colleagues. As Peter Senge has said about ALIA, "Few other leadership programs create such a dynamic, living laboratory of personal and collective learning."[40] These circles of collaboration have continued to grow, and ALIA's faculty, advisors, and program alumni, from diverse backgrounds and perspectives, continue to shape ALIA's direction.[41]

Another program inspired by Chögyam Trungpa's teachings on leadership and enlightened society is a 16-week Authentic Leadership certificate program at Naropa University that I developed in 2001 and have offered annually ever since.[42] The faculty has included dancer and performance artist Arawana Hayashi: master coach, Julio Olalla; international mediator, Mark Gerzon; storyteller Laura Simms; Sounds True CEO, Tami Simon, and many others. The program, which includes online learning, coaching, and two 5-day workshops, provides in-depth training for leaders in self-awareness, skillful communication, and leading change. Over 450 alumni have graduated from the program and have applied new skills to specific projects in their lives and work. The curriculum emphasizes many of the themes and practices from the Shambhala teachings in language that is accessible to leaders from business, government, and non-profit organizations. Participants also practice mindfulness and other contemplative disciplines that help them access intuitive, emotional, and somatic intelligence on their journey to becoming authentic leaders.

In addition to programs offered at the ALIA Institute and Naropa University, other leadership initiatives are being developed by Shambhala International that will provide further opportunities to study and practice these teachings.

Beyond the Buddhist tradition that he inherited, Chögyam Trungpa's life and teachings demonstrate how leaders can discover the sacredness inherent in their own culture and begin to transform it into an enlightened society. By embodying authentic presence and living fully in the challenge of everyday reality, leaders can inspire people to go beyond conventional answers and create organizations and communities that value human wisdom and compassion and generate new responses to the most difficult societal questions. As Chögyam Trungpa wrote about the warrior/leader,

> He constantly challenges his students to step beyond themselves, to step out into the vast and brilliant world of reality in which he abides. The challenge that provides is not so much that he is always setting hurdles for his students or egging them on. Rather his authentic presence is a constant challenge to be genuine and true.[43]

NOTES

1. Chögyam Trungpa, *Shambhala: The Sacred Path of the Warrior* (Boston: Shambhala, 1988) 160. Hereafter referred to as Chögyam Trungpa, *Shambhala*.

2. Fabrice Midal, *Chögyam Trungpa: His Life and Vision* (Boston: Shambhala, 2005). Hereafter referred to as Midal, *Chögyam Trungpa*.

3. Dzongsar Khyentse, Letter (downloaded on 4-15-11) http://www.chronicleproject.com/tributes/5.html

4. Keith Dowman, *Masters of Mahamudra: Songs and Histories of the Eighty-Four Buddhist Siddhas* (Albany: State University of New York Press, 1984), 22.

5. Reginald Ray, "Chögyam Trungpa as a Siddha," in *Recalling Chögyam Trungpa*, ed. Fabrice Midal, (Boston: Shambhala, 2005), 197-219 .

6. Chögyam Trungpa, *Cutting Through Spiritual Materialism*, (Boston: Shambhala, 1973) 249.

7. Midal, *Chögyam Trungpa*, 25.

8. Jeremy Hayward, *Warrior-King of Shambhala: Remembering Chögyam Trungpa* (Sommerville, MA: Wisdom Publications, 2008).

9. Tulkus are considered to be incarnations of awakened energy and are reborn in specific times and places to benefit beings.

10. Chögyam Trungpa, *Born in Tibet* (New York: Penguin Books, 1966).

11. Chögyam Trungpa, Meditation in Action (Boston, Shambhala, 2010); Trungpa. *Cutting Through Spiritual Materialism*.

12. Stephen Butterfield, *The Double Mirror: A Skeptical Journey into Buddhist Tantra* (North Atlantic Books, 1994) 239.

13. Diana J. Mukpo, "Forward" in *Recalling Chögyam Trungpa*, ed. Fabrice Midal, (Boston: Shambhala Publications, 2005), xi-xiii.

14. For more information on Sakyong Mipham Rinpoche please see www.shambhala.org

15. Adapted from www.shambhala.org downloaded on 12-29-11.

16. Ibid.

17. The Kalachakra teachings were given to Dawa Sangpo by the Buddha

18. Thrangu Rinpoche in *Vajradhatu Sun*, June/July 1980. p.4. quoted in Fabrice Midal, *Chögyam Trungpa His Life and Vision* (Boston: Shambhala, 2005), 204.
19. Joanna Macy, *World as Lover, World as Self,* (Berkley, CA: Parallax Press, 1991), 179.
20. Midal, *Chögyam Trungpa*, 216.
21. Chögyam Trungpa, *Shambhala*.
22. Ibid., 30.
23. Ibid., 159.
24. Ibid., 40.
25. Ibid., 41.
26. Jack Kornfield, "Holding the Banner of the Dharma," in *Recalling Chögyam Trungpa*, ed. Fabrice Midal, (Boston: Shambhala, 2005), 25.
27. Sakyong Mipham, *Ruling Your World: Ancient Strategies for Modern Life* (New York, NY: Morgan Road Books, 2005).
28. Warren Bennis and Robert Thomas, "Crucibles of Leadership," *Harvard Business Review,* September, 2002.
29. Bill George, *True North: Discover Your Authentic Leadership* (San Francisco, CA: Jossey-Bass, 2007).
30. Joseph Badaracco, *Defining Moments: When Managers Must Choose between Right and Right* (Boston: Harvard Business Review Press,1997).
31. Michael Useem, *The Leadership Moment: Nine True Stories of Triumph and Disaster and Their Lessons for Us Al,* (New York: Random House, 1998).
32. Quoted in Otto Scharmer, *Theory U: Leading From the Future as it Emerges* (Cambridge: Society for Organizational Learning, 2007), 7.
33. Pema Chödrön U-Tube video from "Crazy Wisdom" film preview (downloaded on 4-15-11), http://www.viddler.com/explore/wideeyecreative/videos/2/
34. Ken Wilber, *A Brief History of Everything* (Boston: Shambhala, 2000), 225.
35. Otto Scharmer, "Advanced Presencing Lab" workshop at the Presencing Institute, Cambridge, MA. May 10-14, 2011.
36. Meg Wheatley, "Leader as Shambhala Warrior" workshop at the ALIA Institute in Halifax, Nova Scotia, June 6-11, 2011.
37. The founding group was led by Michael Chender and included Ken Friedman, David Sable, Susan Szpakowski, Bob Zigler and me.
38. Susan Szpakowski, *Little Book of Practice for Authentic Leadership in Action* (Halifax, Nova Scotia: ALIA, 2010) 7.
39. Ibid, p. 6.
40. From ALIA website (downloaded on 4-1-11) www.alia.org
41. Ibid.
42. Fred Kofman, Barbara Lawton and Mark Wilding assisted me with the curriculum and also taught in the program.
43. Chögyam Trungpa, *Shambhala*, 179.

Sogyal Rinpoche
(Courtesy Tertön Sogyal Trust)

Philip Philippou (Courtesy
Tertön Sogyal Trust)

CHAPTER 14

TIBETAN BUDDHISM IN MODERN WESTERN CULTURE

Sogyal Rinpoche, with additional essay by Philip Philippou

In October 2010, Sogyal Rinpoche gave a keynote speech at an International Conference on Tibetan Buddhism held in the United States at Emory University, Atlanta. His Holiness the Dalai Lama, along with many eminent Buddhist teachers, scholars, and translators, took part in this important conference, which was designed to explore the current state of Tibetan Buddhism in the world. It embraced topics ranging from science to social engagement, Western culture, translation, the arts, and academic study. Sogyal Rinpoche's keynote speech focused on how these teachings can

Reprinted with permission from *View*, July 2011. Copyright © 2011 by The Tertön Sogyal Trust.

Inner Peace—Global Impact: Tibetan Buddhism, Leadership, and Work, pp. 201–212
Copyright © 2012 by Information Age Publishing

be applied most effectively in the modern world. This is the text of that speech, slightly modified for inclusion here. The International Conference on Tibetan Buddhism was cosponsored by the Office of Tibet, New York, and Emory University, with support from the Conservancy for Tibetan Art and Culture in Washington, DC, and Drepung Loseling Monastery in Atlanta.

The second essay describes what it is like to have been involved in developing Rigpa International over the years, as experienced by one of the members of the Executive Board of the organization.

I would like to share with you a few words about Tibetan Buddhism and Western culture. I will speak from my own experience—for example of having traveled in the West with some of the great masters. In 1973, I had the privilege of accompanying His Holiness the Dalai Lama on his first ever visit to the West, and then for a number of years I traveled with Kyabjé Dudjom Rinpoche as his translator. I will also speak from my experience of teaching in different places around the world and of working with many groups and individuals seeking to practice Tibetan Buddhism in the midst of modern Western culture.

Let me begin by saying how moved I am by the lamas and teachers of today and the way they care so deeply about the Dharma and its future. I would like to start by paying homage to them and to the great work that they and their students have done.

Countless people in the modern world have discovered, through their own personal experience, how profoundly helpful and relevant Buddhism, and Tibetan Buddhism, can be. At the same time, many Western students, especially when first meeting Tibetan Buddhism, can find the intellectual information overwhelming, leaving their emotional side untransformed. If everything is taught at a cognitive level, it can bypass the student. Their heads and hearts begin to separate.

This is why a number of lamas teaching in the West see the need for a simpler kind of study and practice curriculum: one that draws out of the Tibetan Buddhist teachings an essential, authentic curriculum that is transformative in itself, and relates to the needs, mentality, and emotions of people today. A curriculum like this would then also serve as the launching pad for a complete study and practice of the whole Buddhist path.

In 2008, when His Holiness the Dalai Lama came to Lerab Ling, our retreat centre in France, to inaugurate the new temple, he spoke about the future of Tibetan Buddhism. He said he was very encouraged by centers of learning and practice in the West such as Lerab Ling, because they gave him great hope for the future. Then he gave this advice: "We are not thinking about just our own generation, but the generations to come.

This is why the proper training of teachers is crucial—training not only in knowledge, but also in a real feeling, real involvement, real compassion, and a real sense of *bodhichitta*. This is highly important."

He also added that what is vital is that more and more practitioners should be able to embody the teachings and become *authentic holders of the Dharma*. For we all know how life-changing it can be to meet a great practitioner of the Dharma. Individuals who embody the teachings and who carry the Dharma in their very being, in their heart, naturally radiate a profound simplicity and warmth, in a deeply human way.

More than being given a detailed road-map to enlightenment, people are much more inspired and moved by seeing such "live" examples of the teachings and by glimpsing the compassion in their hearts. But for this to happen, it is crucial that those who are following the teachings are helped to find the right inner and outer environment in which fully to practice them, to follow them through, and to come to realize and truly embody them. This is a challenge amidst the many distractions of the modern world.

THE THREE YEAR RETREAT

It was in order to see what really works, and to integrate the teachings in Western culture, that we shaped the Three Year Retreat that we held for 400 long-term students between 2006 and 2009 at Lerab Ling. It was based on my own experience of teaching in the West and on serious discussions with many, many lamas.

The whole retreat was like a great experiment, or research, you could say. We did not collect scientific data, but, even without it, we could see quite visibly the transformation and changes in those who took part. The results were actually quite remarkable. We are gathering our experience and what we have learned, so that we can offer it to others, for the benefit of Buddhism as a whole. It is in this spirit that I would like to share a few main points with you.

For this Three Year Retreat, we set out to convey the teachings in a way that was relevant, accessible, and at the same time authentic and complete. During the retreat we made a special focus on study. For 6 months each year, nearly every day, I guided the students experientially through teachings, practice and integration, along with emotional work, and working in groups. The fact that we invested time in going through the teachings and studying them in depth—especially Shantideva's *Bodhich-aryavatara*—rather than simply sitting and reciting mantras, met with His Holiness the Dalai Lama's whole-hearted approval. During the other 6 months of the year, the students put these teachings into practice, in the context of strict retreat.

At specific points during the retreat, we invited lamas from different traditions who are known for the depth of their understanding and their gift for explaining the teachings. They were very inspired to see long-term practitioners who were practicing the Dharma so genuinely and so enthusiastically. A number of lamas said, "This is a place where the Dharma will remain." They also said, "If we do not teach these people, then who do we teach?" So they gave a wealth of instructions, including even some of the highest *Dzogchen* instructions.

Many of those taking part in the retreat had a lot of experience working in the world in various fields. Some had been my students for about 30 years, and my whole idea was to train them so that they would go back into the world to enact compassion in a genuine way, as *servants of peace*. As Buddhists, being of service to others and relieving their suffering must be at the heart of whatever we do.

Following the tradition of teaching according to the capacity of the student, we developed three levels of study. Every student had a *carer*, who was like a counselor and looked after their emotional and practical needs. We had some very experienced therapists who were also very good Dharma practitioners. Whenever students needed, the carers were on hand to help them, and through this experience they gained new insights. What I hope will emerge from this is a new kind of therapy—one that combines Western experience with deep Dharmic understanding.

We discovered that some students had a history of childhood trauma, panic attacks, pain, or depression. What was gratifying was that during the retreat they were actually able to transform their sufferings in a deep and enduring way. Many said that it was the most precious thing they could have done in their entire lives. Comparing themselves with how they were when they began the retreat, some said it felt now "like a new life." A doctor, who worked for 10 years in the fight against AIDS in South Africa, said the teachings equipped her better for her job than any of the professional trainings she had received. Many people shared very moving stories of how the retreat helped them to face themselves, and to overcome deep anxiety, trauma, fear, and low self-esteem.

Fundamentally, their basic being changed, and they became more loving and compassionate. Year by year, the lamas said, their faces changed and they could see in their eyes that fear had gone and was replaced by a confidence in their true nature. Above all, what the retreat has brought them is a personal faith and trust in both the teachings and their own nature. In a sense, you could say that their being and the Dharma merged into one.

RELATING BUDDHISM TO TODAY'S WORLD

The impact of this retreat has been far-reaching. People have found that now—after the retreat—when they face problems, their whole attitude and how they relate to misfortune and difficulties has changed. Often, when a difficulty arises, they find they can actually evoke the practice and the view of the nature of mind, and amazingly the difficulty will dissolve, enabling them to find a more stable ground in themselves.

Though the Three Year Retreat has finished, we are continuing. We keep a close personal connection with those who took part through a website and by using the Internet to link them every month. We have developed a support system to hold them individually, and every year they come back to Lerab Ling for an extended period of time to continue the deeper teachings and integration. Many of them have returned to their countries to contribute in different ways, in our teaching centers or with other kinds of work in society.

We also developed a way of sharing the Three Year Retreat teachings with over 3,500 dedicated students around the world. We call it the *Home Retreat*. They follow the same training but at a more gradual pace, practicing for 3 to 4 hours a day, while still balancing their commitments to work and family. This, of course, is both a challenge for them and at the same time an immensely rewarding experience—real ongoing integration of their practice into life.

I think one major point about Buddhism in Western culture is that it must be taught, practiced, and experienced at a deeper level, so as to relate to today's world. The *Three Year Retreat* and *Home Retreat* have been an effort towards this. All in all, we realized many things; for example, how important it is to "keep it simple": to practice experientially and hold the crucial point, so as not to get lost in the details. When practitioners are given the crucial point (the *mengak*, in Tibetan), then all the teachings they receive fall into place, make much more sense, and relate to them personally. As a result, they have greater faith. Another of the most important factors is loving care: both the care within the sangha, with therapy and emotional work, and the teacher's personal attention and care for students on an individual level. These are crucial for maintaining a real, meaningful *samaya* connection between teacher and student.

So, what began as a Three Year Retreat has become much bigger. It is a much more long-term endeavor—to care for people not only in life, but also up to the moment of death, when we give them emotional and spiritual support, offer their names to the great lamas to pray for them, and ensure all the important practices are done both by our sangha and the monasteries of these great lamas. They feel really deeply cared for.

WORKING TOGETHER

For some time now, I have been having discussions with a number of great Tibetan teachers, all thoroughly trained in the tradition yet not confined by it, and with considerable experience of teaching in the West. It is so helpful to hear what has worked and what has not worked for them. It seems that so many lamas are searching, asking questions, and developing their own ways of transmitting the teachings. It is extremely inspiring that we all seem to be moving in the same direction. But all the while, it is crucial for us to work together, because I do not think we have a habit of doing so. If we can start working together, then I feel a new *Rimé* spirit, a new way of Dharma, will emerge.

We are at a very important juncture, and one where we all have a tremendous opportunity to contribute to the future of the Dharma as a whole. That's why this conference is significant, as long as we do not leave it here, but continue, with vision, action, and a long-term plan.

I feel that we should discuss and look into these questions further, in an in-depth dialogue that brings together lamas of all schools, and particularly those of the younger generation. I would like to make a call for this to happen. Otherwise, I feel we are missing a great opportunity by not making full use of the genius and discoveries of these lamas. It is vital, of course, that this include Western teachers, students, and practitioners, because the wisdom and creativity they have is incredible.

We have to prepare the ground for the future, as His Holiness the Dalai Lama is continuously urging us to do—both for the benefit of beings and in gratitude to the Buddha and the masters of the past who have done so much. If we can bring together the ancient wisdom and experience with modern methods, then I think the results will be tremendous, just as when the great Indian *panditas* [Sanskrit: *learned masters or scholars*] came together with the Tibetan *lotsawas* [Tibetan: *translators*, from the Sanskrit term meaning "eyes of the world"] many centuries ago in Tibet. We all need to see this as our task, a collective responsibility.

While we have some of the great masters like His Holiness still alive, under their guidance, and with the dynamism of many of the brilliant, authentic younger generation of masters, we can work together to create a brighter future for the Dharma and for the modern world.

Developing Rigpa as a Spiritual Organization

Philip Philippou

Sogyal Rinpoche gave the name *Rigpa* to the organization that developed as a vehicle for his work. Rigpa is a Tibetan word that in a general sense means "intelligence" or "awareness." According to the highest teachings in the Buddhist tradition of Tibet (Dzogchen), *rigpa* has a deeper connotation, "the innermost nature of the mind." Guiding people towards an understanding of the innermost nature of their mind has been Sogyal Rinpoche's lifelong mission, and this one word elegantly captures the entire purpose of his work.

The Rigpa organization has grown rapidly over the thirty plus years that Sogyal Rinpoche has been teaching in the West. Our emphasis has been on embodying and living up to the spiritual principles of our Buddhist path, and becoming an organization guided by authentic spiritual values, rather than an organization that is successful or efficient in a merely conventional sense. Over the years, a steady stream of organizational consultants have shared with us their sophisticated management theories and supposed secrets of success. They invariably failed to impress Rinpoche, however, because of the lack of any spiritual dimension to their approach. Sogyal Rinpoche's main focus is how we integrate our spiritual understanding and practice in our working life and interactions with each other, above questions of organizational structure or process. This is the heart of our work and what Rigpa is truly about.

In the course of Rigpa's development, Sogyal Rinpoche has worked very closely with the main students who assume positions of responsibility within the organization. Rinpoche would continuously remind us that we were engaged in spiritual work and as such, how we were, our state of mind, the quality of our being, our motivation and self-awareness, were of paramount importance. Questions of organizational structure and process were always secondary. Rinpoche's overriding concern has always been for us to find a way to embody and extend our spiritual view and practice into our work. At the same time, I think Rinpoche firmly believes that if we are able to achieve this in an authentic way, then we will also be successful in all our endeavors.

Figure 14.1. Dzogchen Beara: A Rigpa center on the coast of Ireland. (Courtesy Tertön Sogyal Trust)

In Buddhism, when setting out on the spiritual path, a great deal of emphasis is placed on one's motivation. For Sogyal Rinpoche, this was a natural starting place for his training of all those working for Rigpa. We follow the *Mahayana* (Greater Vehicle) tradition of Buddhism, in which the noble path of the bodhisattva is a central principle.[1] Within the Mahayana, we also follow the *Vajrayana* path, the tradition that reached unparalleled heights of development in Tibet, within which purity of perception is of paramount importance in one's spiritual training. These principles—of *bodhichitta* (the compassionate wish to attain enlightenment for the benefit of all beings) and purity of perception, were to form the cornerstone of our work.

Sogyal Rinpoche would urge us to recall the greater vision of our work and to make prayers of aspiration each morning, before we set about our tasks. For Rinpoche, like many other Tibetan teachers, it was more important that the student demonstrated a good heart, a genuine wish to serve others, and possessed an open, nonjudgmental mind, than being a "high-achiever" or especially talented in a particular field of work. Spiritual integrity was valued above worldly talent. We came to discover that the process of resetting our motivation and reminding ourselves of our spiritual goals each day helped not only to safeguard the authenticity of our work, but also to enlarge our capacity and elevate us out of our self-centred concerns. Through this, we have been capable of ever greater accomplishments.

The practice of meditation and cultivation of awareness features prominently in our Buddhist training, and it is here that Sogyal Rinpoche has had perhaps his greatest impact in shaping the Rigpa organization. For Rinpoche, the practice of meditation is not confined to the limited time we might sit motionless on our chair or cushion, but is extended throughout all aspects of our life, touching everything that we do. Rinpoche is always pointing out to us how we can bring the mindfulness and awareness that we cultivate in our meditation practice into all spheres of our life—our work, relationships, and interaction with others. The spaciousness, presence of mind and attentiveness we develop through meditation can enhance our ability to plan, communicate, and generally be more in tune with life, to far greater effect than when we are in our normal state of mind, which is usually dull, preoccupied, or distracted. Many Tibetan masters have taught the principle of "meditation in action," and this is one of Rinpoche's great fortes.

Sogyal Rinpoche's predecessor, the great nineteenth century mystic and teacher, Lerab Lingpa, revealed and taught a special meditation practice for bringing about harmony when disruption occurs internally (in our minds) and externally (in outer circumstances), based on a profound understanding of the Buddhist teachings of *dependent arising*. In his training, Sogyal Rinpoche always teaches us how to be aware of interdependency in an entirely pragmatic way, related to real-life events and happenings. For Rinpoche, theoretical knowledge should never be divorced from its practical application.

The ability to visualize all the factors that are involved in one's actions, to preempt outcomes, and to know how to bring everything together in a harmonious and successful result, is given a special flavor by meditation practice, especially the cultivation of awareness. So often, our efforts go

Figure 14.2.   Aerial view of Sogyal Rinpoche's main retreat center, Lerab Ling, in the south of France. (Photo Jan Pieters. Courtesy Tertön Sogyal Trust)

Figure 14.3.   The path to the temple at Lerab Ling. (Courtesy Tertön Sogyal Trust)

awry and we make mistakes when we are not aware or in tune with our field of experience. We make assumptions, are prone to blind spots, and simply don't think deeply enough before we act. As Rinpoche often quotes, "Fools rush in where angels fear to tread!" Rinpoche's training in awareness has been hugely influential in Rigpa's development, in our ability to organize major events, develop worldwide educational programmes for our students, and create Dharma centres.

Sogyal Rinpoche is a communicator par excellence, as testified by his teachings, writings, and trainings. Another hallmark of Rinpoche, which pervades his organization, is his quality of care. This care expresses itself in a profound and unrelenting wish for students to understand the teachings in a way that brings about deep-rooted and enduring transformation.

Both these qualities feature prominently in Rinpoche's training as a leader. When we communicate, we often do so more or less for the satisfaction of "saying our piece," airing our own point of view or objective, without much regard for the other person. Rinpoche trains us to listen openly, to empathize deeply, and to genuinely meet the other person, so that we are able to communicate to them in a way that they will relate to and understand. Communication is only effective when the other person has truly heard and understood your message. There is no need to spell out just how vitally important this ability to communicate is, in all aspects of our work.

Similarly, when it comes to taking care of other people, Rinpoche coaches us in how to listen and be attentive to the other person, so that we can truly know what their needs are and what kind of help might be an effective support to them, rather than imposing our own preconceived ideas. In the course of Rinpoche's teachings to his students worldwide, we are witness to a continuous stream of examples of how such communication works. These interactions are magical moments and often have a profoundly transformative effect on the student as a genuine meeting of minds unfolds.

Rinpoche's passion to communicate the Buddhist teachings and engender a true understanding in his students has led him to embrace new technologies that enhance his already prodigious capacity and reach. Thus, the live streaming of teachings worldwide, interactive video conferencing to small groups of students or individuals, and digital transmission of recorded messages for students who are at distance or seriously ill are all regular happenings in our organization now.

There are other characteristics of Sogyal Rinpoche that carry through into his role as a leader. One such quality is his sense of humor, the importance of which should not be understated! Rinpoche has a playful spirit and is always able to draw out the humor in a situation, in an infectious and liberating way. There is something tremendously loosening about humor—it prevents us from taking ourselves and our outer circumstances too seriously, and helps us to let go. This is no trivial matter—the tight grip with which we hold onto our identity, concepts and false assumptions is the very source of our suffering. Rinpoche's injection of humor into his teachings and his work is always an opening experience, as well as an obvious source of joy.

Another quality is Rinpoche's fearlessness to address core issues that may be uncomfortable for us to look at and that we would rather hide and avoid. How often is our work hampered by the presence of sticky, no-go areas that everyone skirts around but no one musters the courage to face up to? Rinpoche will lay open such blockages with delicate precision and deep insight, rather like a master surgeon, but also in an utterly compassionate and open-minded way. Though at times this might be painful for us if we are resistant to self-examination and humility, these moments are always tremendously liberating.

In our work, we too have found ways to create an atmosphere of openness and trust to look into deeper blockages that might arise, whether interpersonal or created through our own habits. This has benefitted us enormously, in helping to defuse problems before they become major impediments.

Finally, it would be appropriate to conclude by speaking of the emphasis Sogyal Rinpoche places on a process that is called *the dedication of merit*, a distinctly Buddhist practice. At the end of each day, or at special times—such as when in the presence of sacred shrines or upon completion of a retreat, project or material object of work—Rinpoche reminds us to dedicate the merits of our accomplishment for the enlightenment and happiness of all living beings. This act recalls the greater purpose of our work and instills in us the inspiration to continue our efforts ever further. According to the law of karma (cause and effect), through this intention of mind we create the positive impetus for our aspirations to be realized in the future. Rinpoche encourages us to be precise and expansive in our aspirations for the Dharma and to focus always on serving the lineage of enlightened masters and all living beings.

NOTE

1. For those unfamiliar with them, most of the Buddhist or Tibetan terms used throughout this essay can be found in the glossary.

SECTION IV

RESEARCH: TIBETAN BUDDHISM IN WESTERN SITUATIONS

Some people find much greater benefit through the analytical approach of a scholar through which doubts and lack of understanding can be gradually cleared away.... The style of a scholar is to study numerous details and carefully reflect upon them, refining one's understanding....

—Chokyi Nyima Rinpoche[1]

This section contains research studies about ways that practices grounded in Tibetan Buddhism may have broader impact within Western society.

In the first chapter, **John Eric Baugher** presents his study of the unique approach to caring for dying persons that was developed by Rigpa's Spiritual Care Program. He enables readers to grasp the overall cultural significance of Rigpa's influence on care for dying persons in the West by discussing the secularization and professionalization of hospice and palliative care in the context of the founding ideals of the hospice movement. His case studies and interviews bring information on a process that has developed worldwide over many years, yet with little research carried out about its methods or effectiveness. With the coming silver tsunami of the aging baby boom generation, the importance of understanding the needs of dying persons and their caregivers continues to grow.

Inner Peace—Global Impact: Tibetan Buddhism, Leadership, and Work, pp. 213–214

Bronwen Rees presents her work in developing a *Crucible Research* project at the Centre for Communication and Ethics in International Business of the Ashcroft International Business School at Anglia Ruskin University. How she contextualizes her focus on individual and group reflection in relation to Foucault's views on the evolution of corporate power in the West offers a perspective on the importance of Buddhism that is not typically seen. Note that she refers to the *Shambhala Prophecy*, which is also discussed by **Susan Skjei** in her chapter on the legacy of Chögyam Trungpa.

The **final chapter** of this section is an exploratory study that I conducted of entrepreneurial leaders who had seriously practiced Tibetan Buddhism and their experience of its impact on them and their organizations. Doing this study helped me develop the themes that led to this book: the first portion and conclusion contain my earlier thinking on the potential importance of Tibetan Buddhism for Western culture, including a discussion of the role of *tacit knowledge* to confirm the need for practice, rather than just study.

The report on this research may help the reader think about how Tibetan practices impact managers in the workplace and how they are useful for management development. Particularly interesting is how the participants report being influenced in their day-to-day actions by their intent to live what they study and practice. For them, there is no gap between practicing meditation and working with others. As one participant said, "my work is my practice." And as I wrote, "It appears that they create workplaces where people like to be." This clearly has implications for leadership and work!

NOTE

1.   Chokyi Nyima Rinpoche, Foreword to Tulku Urgyen Rinpoche, trans. Erik Pema Kunzang, *Repeating the Words of the Buddha* (Hong Kong: Rangjung Yeshe Publications, 2006), 9.

CHAPTER 15

THE "QUIET REVOLUTION" IN CARE FOR THE DYING

John Eric Baugher[1]

Don't let their appearance or their suffering ever make you forget who they truly are. In the essence of their being, no matter how they appear, each person is perfect, whole, and complete.

—Christine Longaker[2]

I would encourage you, from the bottom of my heart, to follow with complete sincerity the path that inspires you most.

—Sogyal Rinpoche[3]

When Sogyal Rinpoche and Daniel Goleman met for the first time in 1977, Rinpoche proposed that the two of them write a book together. "On what topic?" asked Goleman. Rinpoche had already been giving teachings in the West on death and dying, and when he suggested the topic, Goleman assured him that no one would be interested in reading such a book. In a recent public talk Goleman delighted in how he had underestimated the reception Sogyal Rinpoche's work would have.[4] Since the publication of *The Tibetan Book of Living and Dying* (1992), Sogyal Rinpoche has become the most influential leader to bring Tibetan wisdom principles and practices to the care of the dying in the West. This influence has resulted largely from this book, which has been printed in 31 languages and sold over 2 million copies worldwide. An equally important aspect of his work has been the International Spiritual Care Education Program, hereafter referred to as *The Spiritual Care Program*, which Rinpoche and

Inner Peace—Global Impact: Tibetan Buddhism, Leadership, and Workt, pp. 215–242
Copyright © 2012 by Information Age Publishing
215

his close student Christine Longaker founded in 1993 with the vision "to inspire a quiet revolution in how we look at death and care for the dying, and how we look at life and care of the living."[5] The Spiritual Care Program has since provided seminars and training sessions for tens of thousands of individuals working in hospice and other health care organizations throughout the West. Instructors in the Spiritual Care Program come from a variety of professional backgrounds and are all members of *Rigpa,* a nonprofit Buddhist organization founded by Sogyal Rinpoche which currently has 130 practice centers in 41 countries, including Australia, France, Germany, Great Britain, Holland, Ireland, and the United States. At the same time, most of the participants in the Spiritual Care trainings are not Buddhists, and one of strengths of the Spiritual Care program is that it is nondenominational and open to all persons regardless of religious or cultural background.

To understand the profound importance of the Spiritual Care Program offered by Rigpa consider the observation made in 2001 by the Reverend Mark Cobb, an ordained minister in the Anglican Church and experienced chaplain specializing in palliative care, that "there are generally no structured opportunities for disciplines other than chaplains to develop spiritual care practices."[6] Nearly a decade later Cobb's observation still accurately describes the international hospice and palliative care scene, with the exception of the Spiritual Care Program founded on Sogyal Rinpoche's teachings and two other small Buddhist-based programs.[7] In recent years governmental agencies such as the National Health Services in Scotland and the National Institute for Clinical Excellence in Great Britain have begun to recommend "guidelines and standards" for the delivery of spiritual care, yet the important question remains of how hospice and palliative care workers are to meet such recommendations in the absence of adequate training and support in their work.[8]

Despite the critically important work of Sogyal Rinpoche and his students, very little research has been conducted on the Spiritual Care Program. Two studies have been published that attempt to evaluate the potential benefits of specific trainings offered through the Spiritual Care Program. A survey of participants in a course held in Munich, Germany in 2002 indicated that the course deepened the capacity of health care workers to compassionately care for dying persons and themselves in several respects, although many of the benefits showed declines in a 6 month follow up.[9] These findings are quite understandable, since the capacity to sit with one's own fears regarding embodiment and death, which is so essential to caring for the dying, cannot be acquired through a one-time training, but instead requires an ongoing process of cultivating mindfulness in the face of human suffering.[10] Another study based on focus groups with 17 individuals who completed a mixed on-line and residential course offered through Naropa University in Colorado found several general outcomes, including a deepened ability to communicate empathetically and greater confidence in being authentically present with the dying.[11] These exploratory studies offer a good starting point for understanding the benefits of the Spiritual Care Program, and in this chapter I investigate more deeply the broader significance Sogyal Rinpoche's work has for end-of-life care in the West.

This chapter is outlined in four steps. I begin by presenting a framework for interpreting the cultural significance of Rigpa's influence on care for the dying in the West in light of the threat that secularization and professionalization of hospice and palliative care pose to the founding ideals of the hospice movement. I then outline the basic philosophy, guiding principles, and essential practices of the Spiritual Care Program and illustrate how many of the original ideals and aims of the hospice movement outlined by Cicely Saunders, the founder of the modern hospice movement, are mirrored in the critically important work of Rigpa. In contrast to the view that the Christian foundation of hospice has been "hijacked" by Buddhism,[12] I interpret the work of Rigpa as keeping alive some of the most important founding ideals of the movement, ideals which have become even more important in the contemporary age of anxiety, materialism, and frivolous optimism.[13]

Next, I present findings from my research to illustrate how specific practices from the wisdom tradition of Tibet have benefitted participants in spiritually caring for others at the end of life. Research for this chapter included interviews with Spiritual Care Program educators and students of Sogyal Rinpoche from Australia, France, Germany, Great Britain, Ireland, and the United States; interviews with participants of Rigpa workshops from the United States, Ireland, France, and Belgium; participant observation during an 8-day site visit in March 2010 to Dzogchen Beara, the main training center located on the southwestern coast of Ireland; participation in a 2-day Rigpa workshop on the care of the dying held in New York City in May 2010 and a 4-day workshop held in Berne, NY in October 2010; attendance at Sogyal Rinpoche's inaugural teachings at the Tenzin Gyatso Institute in Berne, New York in June 2010; and contemplative study throughout the project of the primary texts that form the foundation of the Spiritual Care Program, particularly Sogyal Rinpoche's *The Tibetan Book of Living and Dying* and Christine Longaker's *Facing Death and Finding Hope: A Guide to the Emotional and Spiritual Care of the Dying*.

My goal here is not to present an exhaustive survey of the many benefits the trainings have had for workers in a variety of care giving capacities, but instead to focus on a particular context where caregivers face tremendous challenges attuning to the spiritual needs of others and themselves: caring for a loved one with dementia. My intention in taking this approach is twofold. First, the teachings of Sogyal Rinpoche are quite subtle, and I seek to offer a corrective to ethnocentric interpretations of Buddhist practices that have been made by Western social scientists. A case in point is the mistaken claim that meditation taught in Rigpa trainings helps caregivers of the dying "to gain a sense of control in a situation of powerlessness."[14] This view articulates a broader misunderstanding current among Western social scientists that reduces meditation to a form of emotion "management" or a "passive" strategy for "coping" with unpleasant emotions.[15] In contrast, I present the narratives of two participants of the Spiritual Care Program—a nurse in Ireland and a Catholic nun in New York City—which illustrate that Rinpoche's teachings have nothing to do with gaining a sense of control, suppressing feelings, or in any way distracting oneself from the emotions one experiences as a caregiver. Instead, embodying confidence and compassion in caring for others involves being present to all that is, a direct way of being in the world beyond the anxiety and fear produced by attempts to manage or manipulate one's experience. Second, scholars have critiqued constructions of the "good death" in the hospice movement for being premised upon cancer as the model disease and thereby excluding those who are unable to talk with others about their experiences or otherwise face their death "consciously."[16] Sociologist Clive Seale argues, moreover, that the suffering associated with certain forms of dying, such as those involving dementia, simply cannot be overcome even by the best human care.[17] Of course, the validity of such a view is premised upon what is meant by "overcoming" suffering and how one understands "the best" care we can offer each other. The data I present below offers the view that abiding in compassionate presence with others is unbound by limited cultural constructions of good or bad conditions of dying.

Finally, I consider the importance of the Spiritual Care Program in the future of spiritual care for the living and dying by highlighting how the main insights of this chapter reflect the nondualistic vision and practice of Sogyal Rinpoche's "quiet revolution." I conclude by discussing the opening of Dechen Shying, the first of many respite and spiritual practice centers for terminally ill individuals and their caregivers located in Southwest Ireland, in light of existing hospice services, contrasting models of grief, and Sogyal Rinpoche's own experience of losing his first master when he was around 12 years old.

INTERPRETING THE TURN TOWARD THE EAST IN CARE OF THE DYING

Dame Cicely Saunders, the visionary founder of the modern hospice movement, revived a Christian tradition of medical care by integrating medical science with an ethic of Christian compassion in caring for the dying. Saunders believed that such care would be ineffective at alleviating many of the pains and symptoms of chronic diseases without the most up-to-date medical knowledge. More important, without compassion, medical care would be reduced to the application of technique, leaving the deepest needs of the patient unmet.[18] As Saunders explained at a talk given in 1965, just 2 years before St. Christopher's Hospice was founded, "the most important foundation stone" for St. Christopher's is Christ's command to his disciples to "watch with me" as he struggled in prayer and grief in the garden of Gethsemane on the eve of his betrayal and subsequent crucifixion.[19] Writing 2½ decades later Saunders described "spiritual pain" as resulting from feeling that neither our own life nor the universe has purpose and from being disconnected from any truth greater than ourselves to which we can commit.[20] Here Saunders highlights the anxiety and ontological insecurity that by the late 1980s had come to characterize late modern Western societies where truth is increasingly reduced to fragile self-referential narratives that are vulnerable to radical doubt, particularly at times of crisis such as those faced by dying persons.[21] She continued that "the command 'Watch with me' did not mean 'Take this crisis away,'" rather, the essence of spiritual care involves caregivers "trusting in a Presence that can more easily reach the patient and his family if they themselves concentrate on using all their competence with compassion and say little to interrupt."[22] In the process caregivers will learn that "the real work is not ours at all," since it is God's presence and "oneness with all sufferers" that is "redemptive."[23]

Spiritual care, the guiding ethos of Saunder's vision, has largely been lost in modern hospice and palliative care. There is a general agreement among scholars that the increasing routinization and professionalization of hospice care has led to the "dilution of the original ideals" of the hospice movement and has compromised the focus on spiritual care of the dying.[24] In the words of David Clark, Professor of Sociology at Glasgow University and expert in the history of hospice and palliative care, "the specialty of palliative medicine is so focused on a narrow medical agenda and really just does not know how to tackle the bigger story that was of such interest to Cicely."[25] Spiritual care is not completely absent from contemporary hospice and palliative care, but a focus on the spiritual needs of patients has increasingly become distanced from religion and Christianity in particular. Scholars have offered two main interpretations of this movement, both of which are relevant to the current investigation.

One position (exemplified by Ann Bradshaw of the *National Institute for Nursing* in Oxford) is that the redefinition of spirituality as an "existential search for human integrity" distinct from religion results not from the needs and desires of patients, but from the ideological and professional strivings of social scientists and health care workers.[26] Bradshaw mourns the loss of the Christian foundation of the hospice movement on several grounds, but largely because it implies the ascendency of the values of the "expert" which repress the needs of the soul in an attempt to manage and audit the dying process as efficiently and effectively as possible. As she writes, "The relationship of genuine 'real care' gives way to the application of 'palliative care' techniques," such that "death is no longer a truth to be confronted but a process to be managed."[27]

Bradshaw's thesis is consistent with my earlier research on how the therapeutic management of "grief work" in the hospice worker-patient dyad has led to the transposition of "listening" as a spiritual gift *of* the dying into "facilitating," a therapeutic technique practiced by the hospice worker *on* the dying.[28] This process of emptying out the meaning of spiritual care in mainstream hospice discourse is linked with the broader behaviorist turn in social work and humanistic nursing that reifies "presence" as a "therapeutic tool" that can be applied to encounters with dying persons.[29]

A second interpretation (offered by religious scholar Kathleen Garces-Foley pertaining specifically to the United States) is that over the last 2½ decades Buddhism has become "a predominant voice in the 'good death' or 'conscious dying' movement, the central vehicle for which is the hospice movement."[30] She suggests that a major factor contributing to the influence of Buddhism in care for the dying in the U.S. has been the success of prominent Buddhist organizations that have sought to revolutionize Western death practices, including Rigpa International founded by Sogyal Rinpoche. Garces-Foley accurately points out that these organizations offer practical approaches for compassionately caring for dying persons in a nonsectarian language of spirituality that appeal to many hospice workers in the United States, an interpretation consistent with Charles Prebish's argument regarding the growing prominence of Buddhism in American popular culture.[31] Yet Garces-Foley ultimately reduces hospice workers' use of Buddhist teachings on death and dying to the ability of "Euro-American" authors and their savvy book publishers "to appeal to the American always shopping for new, exotic but not too exotic, solutions to perennial problems."[32] For starters, we could note that Sogyal Rinpoche is Tibetan, not "Euro-American," and logic would suggest that the international appeal of *The Tibetan Book of Living and Dying* cannot be reduced to a desire among Americans to consume a simulacrum of the exotic.

The problems of interpretation in Garces-Foley's analysis result from her meta-methodological decision to situate the influence of Buddhism on hospice discourse and practice in relation to the history of Buddhism in America rather than the history of the hospice movement. A focus on

the latter history indicates that the problems contemporary hospice workers face in caring for the spiritual needs of the dying are not "perennial,"
but are of recent origin. As outlined above, the substantive meaning of the
original ethos of the hospice movement that focused on the spiritual care
of the dying has been all but eliminated by the increasing routinization
and professionalization of hospice care.[33] Hospice and palliative care
workers are attracted to Buddhist practices for caring for the dying, not
out of a desire to consume the exotic, but in an attempt to recover meaning lost in the institutionalization of hospice under the managerial professional model. Earlier proponents of the hospice movement saw their work
as offering an "alternative" to bureaucratic and medicalized forms of
dying, although in many ways hospice and palliative care appear more as
areas for professional specialization rather than an alternative mode for
being with dying.[34] In other words, the turn toward the East in the care of
the dying coincides with a 180 degree turn back into the same Western
biomedical model that the hospice movement originally sought to critique.[35] The deeper importance of Rigpa's Spiritual Care Program created by Sogyal Rinpoche and his students has less to do with their skill in
"marketing their product"[36] than with the broader context of care within
which those teachings are received, namely where the values of therapeutic managerialism threaten to eclipse "religious explorations of illness,
suffering and death."[37]

THE FOUNDING, PRINCIPLES AND
PRACTICES OF THE SPIRITUAL CARE PROGRAM

In *Facing Death and Finding Hope*, Christine Longaker, Education Director
of the Spiritual Care Program and student of Sogyal Rinpoche since 1980,
describes how she became involved in hospice work following her experience of caring for her husband Lyttle who died of acute Leukemia in 1977
at the age of 24.[38] During Lyttle's illness she read an article about hospice
care and thought that this was exactly what she and her family needed. At
the time, however, there were only four hospices in the United States, and
none were available to them in Los Angeles. After her husband died she
moved with her son to Santa Cruz to help establish a hospice program
where she worked for 7 years. She taught courses on spiritual care of the
dying for many years independently and then in 1993, following the publication of *The Tibetan Book of Living and Dying*, she worked closely with
Sogyal Rinpoche to develop the Spiritual Care Program. From the beginning, the intention of the program has been to bring together the wisdom
of the Buddhist tradition (as expressed in Rinpoche's teachings) with the
knowledge, skills, and best practices of hospice and palliative care, in

order to provide healthcare workers with the tools, insights, and skillful methods for healing and nurturing themselves and deepening their capacity to remain present with another's suffering without taking on their burdens. Longaker recounts how the Program's focus on compassionate care for caregivers was borne out of her own experience of grief in the first couple of years after her husband's death as she was trying to "untangle this accumulated frustration or anger" resulting from the less than ideal way in which she and her husband had been cared for during his illness.

> I started out after my husband died feeling a bit angry and expecting a lot of the healthcare workers that they were more humane and were more present and loving, and the more I understood all that they had to hold, the more compassion I felt in wishing that the caregivers themselves could be very, very well cared for and very well nurtured.[39]

Longaker's experience of ongoing healing and growth through her work as a hospice worker and educator resonates with the basic view of the program that spiritual care is a mutually-beneficial relationship of service between two persons with the same basic nature. She writes, "We should view our relationship with the dying as one of mutual healing, one of giving and receiving. In a sense, we are both facing death together and have something important to learn from each other."[40] The focus on mutual healing expresses a quintessentially Buddhist approach to hospice care,[41] although this view also resonates closely with Cicely Saunders' understanding of "listening" as simultaneously a way of attending to the needs of dying persons and also a spiritual gift of the dying to their caregivers in the form of lessons in how "to be gentle and to approach others with true attention and respect."[42] In this way, Buddhist and Christian approaches to caring for the dying contrast sharply with the hegemonic professional therapeutic model that reifies listening as a set of techniques to be performed by the hospice worker to shape the experience of the patient.[43]

In Sogyal Rinpoche's teachings spiritual care involves relating to dying persons and ourselves with "compassion" and "wisdom" or "confidence," understood as inseparable aspects of a way of being in the world. What dying persons most desire is for others "to relate to them as people who are *living*, compassionately accepting their vulnerability and suffering while still seeing them as whole."[44] Spiritual care involves communicating with another not as an expert, but as an equal, as a fellow human being who shares the same basic goodness.[45] Saunders likewise understood spiritual care as involving "not only skill but compassion" and was explicit that compassion had nothing to do with "pity and indulgence." As she wrote, dying persons are "not going through a strange, dramatic or just unlucky experience, to be written up as such with sentimentality or sensationalism, but an all-too-common experience such as ordinary people have always faced and somehow managed to come through."[46] In the same tradition, the Reverend Mark Cobb defines spiritual care as moving "beyond the conventional approach dependent upon expertise and into an encounter between two vulnerable human beings alert to the creative possibilities of transcendence despite being grounded in life's fragility."[47] Buddhist and Christian perspectives on spiritual care are not reducible to one another, yet the common ground between these traditions is deeply important in light of the ascendency of the "expert" in hospice and palliative care outlined above. That historical shift mirrors a wider trend in Anglo-American societies of a therapeutic "inward turn" that, despite promises of liberating individuals, actually cultivates a sense of inadequacy and increases dependency on professional experts.[48] In light of these societal tendencies, the view expressed by the Spiritual Care Program is very much needed in contemporary Western societies.

Compassion, for Buddhists, is an expression of wisdom, understood as seeing the nature of reality as it truly is beyond the dichotomies that routinely imprison our perception, such as self/other, pleasant/unpleasant, birth/death, and heart/mind. Whereas in dualistic Western thinking wisdom is often thought of as pertaining to the mind and compassion to the heart, in Buddhism both are seen as inseparable aspects of the same way of being in the world as expressed in the Sanskrit term *Bodhichitta*, which can be translated as "awakened heart" or "the mind of enlightenment."[49] In the work of Sogyal Rinpoche and his students, wisdom is also referred to as embodying confidence. Relating to dying persons with confidence has nothing to do with a feeling of arrogance or esteeming oneself, thinking we have all the answers. Instead, we embody confidence, seen as "the most valuable asset we can offer to others facing death, loss, or bereavement," as we gain insight into *Rigpa*, "the innermost nature of mind." Buddhists believe that our basic nature (our "Buddha nature") is a "primordial, pure, pristine awareness that is at once intelligent, cognizant, radiant, and always awake," although much human life is spent in *sem*, the discursive, dualistic mind which Rinpoche defines as the mind that

> creates and indulges in waves of negative emotions and thoughts, that has to go on and on asserting, validating, and confirming its "existence" by fragmenting, conceptualizing, and solidifying experience. The ordinary mind is the ceaselessly shifting and shiftless prey of external influences, habitual tendencies, and conditioning: The masters liken *sem* to a candle flame in an open doorway, vulnerable to all the winds of circumstance.

Freedom for Buddhists, what is often called "enlightenment," is the "unexpectedly ordinary" process of slowly peeling away the delusions of ordinary mind and resting in the confidence of our innermost nature.[50]

The goal of the Spiritual Care Program is to support healthcare professionals in attuning to their own spiritual needs through finding meaning in their lives, healing their relationships with others and with themselves, learning how to understand and transform their suffering, and preparing spiritually for their own death. As Christine Longaker writes, it is through working with these "four tasks of living and dying" *in their own life* that allows individuals to compassionately care for the spiritual needs of others with confidence and equanimity.[51] The Program's focus on caring for one's own spiritual needs as a necessary precondition for effectively caring for others now reflects a wider consensus expressed in the field of palliative care.[52]

One of the unique contributions of the Rigpa Program is the extraordinarily practical and skillful means offered to caregivers for attuning to the spiritual needs of themselves and others, including *shamatha* or "calm abiding" meditation, *tonglen*, the loving kindness meditation, the unfinished business exercise, the exchanging self for other practice, the forgiveness practice, the heart practice, and the essential *Phowa* practice. It is beyond the scope of this chapter to discuss all of these in any depth, and I refer the reader to Rinpoche's *The Tibetan Book of Living and Dying* and Longakers's *Facing Death and Finding Hope* for detailed descriptions of these practices. What is critical here is that these practices are presented in Rigpa trainings, not as a grab bag of tricks one can use in the course of one's work, but as opportunities for integrating spiritual practice into one's work grounded in Buddhist teachings on the nature of mind, suffering, and compassion. At the same time, teachings are presented in a manner that resonates with individuals of diverse religious faiths,[53] and no attempt is made in the Spiritual Care Program to convert participants to Buddhism.

EMBODYING COMPASSION AND CONFIDENCE IN THE PRESENCE OF SUFFERING

Caring for a loved one suffering from dementia can push caregivers to the limits of their being. As the disease progresses, caregivers often experience anger, resentment, guilt, and feelings of ambivalence as they adjust their life in an attempt to meet the many and changing needs of the patient.[54] These conflicting emotions leave many family caregivers with a "continuous and profound sense of loss and subsequent grief," particularly as they experience the loss of the "person" they once knew even though they are still physically alive.[55] Providing spiritual care in such a context requires particularly skillful means. Below I present the experiences of two caregivers who have completed extensive training in the

Spiritual Care Program, which highlight how shamatha meditation, the loving kindness meditation, and the heart practice have inspired in them the compassion and confidence to lovingly attune to the spiritual needs of an elderly parent suffering from dementia. These narratives illustrate the powerfully quiet way in which the teachings of Sogyal Rinpoche are transforming human suffering and the practice of spiritual care in the threshold between this life and that which is beyond.[56]

Finding Refuge

Donal had been working as a nurse in Ireland for many years when a copy of *The Tibetan Book of Living and Dying* came into his hands. He explained how he had regularly witnessed tremendous suffering in his work as a nurse that simply could not be addressed through medical means and he was "trying to find answers" regarding other ways of being with or relating to his patients. He recounted how what began as a search for answers in his professional work had led to a fundamental turn around in how he relates to suffering in all areas of his life as a nurse, therapist, friend, father, and son.

After reading Rinpoche's book in the early 1990s Donal began taking meditation instruction at the a Rigpa center in Ireland where he learned about the Spiritual Care Program being offered at Dzogchen Beara, a Rigpa retreat center situated on the breathtakingly beautiful Beara peninsula in Southwest Ireland. He indicated that he has since participated in at least one weekend training and one 8-day course per year over the last 10 years. Donal expressed deep gratitude to Sogyal Rinpoche and the instructors of the Spiritual Care Program for introducing him to teachings and practices that have been "transformative" in his life. He indicated that all of the practices he had been introduced to through the Spiritual Care Program have been "deeply meaningful" for him and he related them to a pith instruction he received from Christine Longaker during a training on "Wisdom and Compassion" in 2002: "We need not let a person die empty handed."

Two practices that have had particular resonance with Donal and that he describes as being central to his own healing are the "loving kindness meditation" and the "heart practice." What both of these visualization practices have in common is that they can help individuals reconnect with the source of love within themselves in situations where "our own heart is wounded or walled up" or when "we believe that we don't have enough love in us" to meet others in their suffering.[57] These practices can be particularly helpful to caregivers who are overwhelmed with anxiety or fear in the course of their work or when feelings of burnout begin to discon-

nect caregivers from the compassionate motivation that originally led
them to care for others. In the words of a nursing home administrator
who completed the Naropa contemplative end-of-life care course: "I
gained from this course a re-emergence of my passion towards caring for
the elders. The teachings, especially the meditations, have rekindled my
compassion and what I consider to be my purpose in this life: to serve the
elders and assist people as they prepare for death."

The *loving kindness practice* involves remembering someone who has
loved you deeply and visualizing them now in your presence pouring
their love upon you. The visualization involves first feeling the love flowing towards you, breaking down the wounds or barriers around your
heart, and then allowing your love and gratitude to naturally and uncon-
ditionally go back out to the person who has evoked it. This giving and
receiving of love can then be visualized to embrace all beings, beginning
with those one feels most closest to and then gradually extending to those
who seem to be your enemies. During the visualizing, loving kindness can
be extended to self and others through phrases such as "may I be free
from danger," "may I be at ease," "may I be happy," and the like.[58] Similarly, the *heart practice* involves invoking before oneself whomever is for
that person a source of divine inspiration (e.g., God, Jesus, Mother Mary,
the Buddha) or simply a figure of light, calling out to that being for help
with all the pain and suffering one feels, and imagining that his or her
love, compassion, and wisdom enters one's heart and transforms that suffering into bliss. This practice can be done either for oneself or for others,
including those who have died.[59]

Donal describes how drawing on these and other practices taught in
the Spiritual Care trainings have become for him "a way of life." He
spoke, for example, of being a father of adult children and how he used to
worry about them when they were teenagers and old enough to drive a
car and socialize in the city. He indicated that these practices became for
him "a real antidote to fear" in those early hours of the morning as he
found comfort in the phrases "may they be happy," "may they be well,"
"may they be safe." He explained how he "weaves" shamatha meditation
and compassion practices, such as the loving kindness meditation and the
heart practice, into his professional work as well although without necessarily naming them as Buddhist. As a guided meditation, he describes the
heart practice as a "really practical and skillful means" for supporting
others going through a difficult time "to *find* their refuge and then supporting them to *use* their refuge." He explains that what he has learned
from the Spiritual Care Program and from his own experience is that "We
are much more than our suffering, although when we are in a crisis we
often lose sight of this and need someone to remind us to come back to

our refuge, our safe place, and doing so often requires the presence and confidence and knowing of the other person to guide us."

Donal indicated that many clients have found great benefit from the heart practice, although perhaps the most profound way he has supported others with this guided meditation is in spiritually caring for his mother who is in her 90s, living in a nursing home, and suffering from Alzheimer's. Donal explained how he had been receiving phone calls from the nurse caring for his mother indicating that she was distressed and wanted to speak with him. He expressed how his heart went out to her in those difficult times when he heard the distress in her voice and knew that she was feeling frightened and lost. He explained that "Sometimes just hearing my voice was all the reassurance she needed, but on other occasions nothing I said or comforted her with brought her ease." It was at this point that he spoke with nurse about supporting his mother in the heart practice, explaining that she should:

> Begin by sitting with my mother and reminding her of all the people who are holding her in their prayers especially her family, friends, the Catholic Nuns and my friends at Dzogchen Beara. Then bless her with Holy Water and place her rosary beads in her hand and remind her that the Blessed Mother Mary is near and has not forgotten her, calling out and praying to her to dissolve my mother's suffering.

The next time Donal visited his mother in the nursing home she expressed to him in so many words the comfort she received from the practice, exclaiming "that nurse is an angel!" Donal shared with me his own relief and gratitude and indicated that this way of supporting his mother with the heart practice has been a turning point in her care. Now every visit with his mother ends with him blessing her with Holy Water and both of them saying the "Angel of Guardian Prayer." He indicates that since then his mother has become much more settled and the distressing phone conversations have faded out.

Donal described other ways he cares for his mother when she becomes terrified. One very simple means involves guiding her in shamatha (or calm abiding) meditation using whatever object of meditation presents itself at the time. At one point it was quite difficult for him and his mother when she was receiving oxygen, and he described how "she was frightened and restless and did not want the oxygen, and I was also developing an aversion to the sound of the nebulizer because it seemed to be more of a hindrance than a help." He continued that in the midst of this anxious scene "it just came to me that all sounds are mantra" and he explained how he began using the sound of his mother's oxygen machine as the object of meditation. He described how he now simply sits with his mother and helps her to stay with the mantra.[60] Donal's confidence in spiritually caring for his mother is not solely a result of the simplicity and practicality of the practices, but also of how those practices are grounded in the broader "view" expressed in the teachings of Sogyal Rinpoche. Notice how the Buddhist understanding of *shunyata*, the emptiness of all phenomena, is critical to his own spiritual well-being and his capacity to compassionately care for his mother in the most difficult circumstances:

> The other thing with Alzheimer's is that she'll say unusual things and it's not really your mother that's saying these things and that can be really distressing. And so just going with the teachings, this is all empty, not a reflection of her essence, it's just all empty what she's saying and so not to get too into the content and get distressed about that and just try to hold my presence and see her sanity through it all that she is much more than she is saying.... When we have a trust and a refuge we can just relax and let go and not be so attached, let go of attachment.

Here he expresses how embodying wisdom, compassion, and confidence are inseparable in the practice of spiritually caring for others and our self.

Seeing More Than Diminishment

Sister Catherine completed the 15-week "contemplative end-of-life care" course offered by Rigpa through Naropa University in Colorado about 2½ years prior to our interview. The course was comprised of 2 weeks in residence at the Shambhala Mountain Center in Colorado with the remaining weeks of the course completed online. She described how the course had been beneficial for her in many capacities of her work including orienting new volunteers and serving as a "spiritual guide" for elderly sisters. She expressed in rich detail how the course and the teachings of Sogyal Rinpoche were immensely helpful for her in caring for her mother who had been placed on hospice care just 3 weeks prior to our interview. Let me begin by explaining how she came to participate in the Spiritual Care Program and by outlining what it might mean for a Catholic nun to describe her involvement with Rigpa as "life altering."

Sister Catherine was given a copy of *The Tibetan Book of Living and Dying* by a family member of a man she was "journeying with" as a hospice volunteer. She had not heard of Sogyal Rinpoche's work prior to this encounter, although she indicated that for many years she had been drawn toward Eastern Mysticism, and Tibetan Buddhism in particular. As a devout Roman Catholic, she indicated that her "natural bent is to having more of a contemplative form of prayer" and expressed how the focus of the Rigpa course on "being mindful" has "really become such a part of me in terms of the way I pray." Her greatest inspirations in the Catholic faith are Thomas Merton, Anthony de Mello, and Henri Nouwen, and she found it "very exciting" that she was exposed more deeply to the work of these "spiritual giants" through the Naropa course. She expressed quite clearly that her involvement with Rigpa was not a form of "spiritual tourism," but instead has led her more deeply into the contemplative practices of her own faith and has deepened her commitment to serving humanity:[61]

> Not that you're trying to water down anything or broaden it so far that it no longer has its essence ... I mean when I was up at Shambhala doing the Rigpa program we had centering prayer ... I bought my book on "Awakening" from de Mello up at Shambhala Mountain Center, so you know, it's that kind of thing that I find very exciting because I think unity and harmony and oneness, you know, instead of seeing what separates us, what are the things that really hold us, you know, really together.[62]

She continued by saying that the "weaving" of traditions comes naturally to her because of her ecumenical upbringing:

> I came from an ecumenical family: my father was Protestant, my mother Roman Catholic and we're Irish, so you can just imagine what this is like, and they're both from Ireland so, I think it's human things that keep things separate instead of like the oneness there, and I've just come over life to see more things that unite and harmonize and when I see that unification and harmony I find God there more solidly.[63]

She indicated that she would have been open to doing a training course on spiritual care at the end of life in her own tradition had she been aware of one being offered, but it would have had to have been "much more of an Eastern way, like the de Mello, Merton, the more contemplative stance." She distinguished the Rigpa course from other trainings she had done on caring at the end of life, stating that they were "somewhat academic as opposed to that deep, deep amount of spirituality and practicing together" that she experienced in the Naropa course. For her, the course was "life altering" due to "the intensity of it, and then being with it long enough for it to become something," but also because it came "at a part of my life when I was very ready for it." She had worked for many years with children with developmental disabilities and she took the Naropa course in response to a "call" to work in geriatric care.

Sister Catherine spoke of receiving many gifts from specific aspects of the Rigpa course, but above all what she took away from the course was a deep sense of gratitude for the confidence and "the sense of spaciousness" she experienced through the guided meditations and the practice of shamatha. She described herself as living "a crazy life in New York

City" traveling regularly from place to place on public transportation and indicated that "the quietness and the sitting" had become an integral part of her daily practice, in part with the help of her iPod which she keeps loaded with her favorite devotions (e.g., The Chaplet of Divine Mercy) and guided meditations by Sogyal Rinpoche, Sharon Salzberg, Christine Longaker, and others. The guided meditation that resonated most deeply with Sister Catherine was the heart practice, which she experienced as "the most perfect Sacred Heart spirituality." Paralleling Donal's experience, this practice of supporting another in finding refuge has deeply inspired Sister Catherine as she too is now spiritually caring for her mother at the end of life.

> I had an experience 3 weeks ago, my mother's very, very, dedicated to Mary, Jesus' mother and she loves the rosary. This is actually when I saw the journey starting another way. She was in great distress and so I kind of got in bed with her so that she could lean against me and she would be a little more elevated and I tried to synchronize my breathing with hers, and I just found her relaxing. And before I got in I put the close circuit television on [to a Catholic station] and the rosary started and there was some reflective music in the back and all of the sudden I saw these tears running down my mother's face, and they weren't the distressed tears from the breathing, the agitation. This was a peaceful, a real deep experience was going on, and how incredible is to be able to sit and be with that in such closeness, and then she started trying to say Mary all the time as the Hail Mary was being said, that Mantra over and over again, and the tears and a great sense of bodily peace.

Sister Catherine described her mother as having been a "great storyteller" all her life, and told how that evening her mother blessed her with "her last story":

> And then I went home, I was exhausted, I felt like more grief, also, and I fell into a very deep sleep that evening, really, really deep. And I had a dream that I was in the same exact position with my mother with her there [on my chest] and we were watching the television, darkened, and then a door appeared. Here comes her story: the door was opened with a blue essence which I really believe was Mary, and my mother was standing in the light.

For Sister Catherine spiritual care involves "allowing the spirit to really enter and help you journey with that person," a process she described with many metaphors, including "finding the keys to people," "hearing what's not being said," and "allowing the spaciousness for other people to teach you." What all of these metaphors point to is the capacity to *behold* the fullness of life precisely in the presence of tremendous suffering, a capacity that is easily lost under the modern approach to medicalized dying. As Sister Catherine explains, we are "not just looking at the suffering or those other aspects which someone that came from a medical model could get very into instead of really looking at that whole other part of the journey and reverencing that."[64] In addition to the dementia, her mother had experienced a series of strokes that left her bedridden, with difficulty swallowing, and unable to communicate verbally. Sister Catherine felt deeply saddened and grieved about her mother's suffering, yet also felt "a sense of validation" that she was able to attune to her mother's deepest unspoken needs.

> Even if a person has dementia so much is going on ... I mean I'm really trusting it, I trust this, this is as sure as the air we breathe for me.... And it's really hard I feel in a way, I feel a little bit of sadness for some of my other family members who don't see it, you know what I mean, they only see diminishment.... And it's a very privileged moment, it's very incredibly privileged. And I think it's a gift of my own religious inheritance, but very much Rigpa as well, very much so. And I'm very grateful.

The Rigpa training helped Sister Catherine deepen both her capacity to see contemplatively and her confidence to compassionately respond to her mother from that stillness. And she explained how in the process her mother revealed to her her own "key," which was there "in the quiet, in the sitting." In this way her experience illustrates the mutuality of spiritual care outlined in the writings of Sogyal Rinpoche, Christine Longaker, and Cicely Saunders.

THE QUIET REVOLUTION:
TRANSFORMING THE DELUSIONS OF WESTERN RATIONALITY

This chapter began by outlining how the spread of a professional managerial ethos in hospice and palliative care threatens the vision of spiritual care that so deeply inspired the work of Cicely Saunders, the founder of the modern hospice movement. Commenting on that historic shift, the Reverend Mark Cobb suggests that "In contrast to the broader developments in hospice and palliative care it would appear that the spiritual dimension has remained at an early developmental stage."[65] From one perspective, Cobb's assessment seems quite accurate. Consider, for example, the experience of French and Belgian palliative care workers attending a week-long workshop at Dzogchen Beara, the Rigpa retreat center in Southwest Ireland, in March 2010. Several participants impressed upon me the tremendous barriers they faced in trying to address the spiritual needs of those in their care, including a therapist working at a private hospital in Brussels whose boss recently chided her that "Most patients do not think about spirituality all their lives so you cannot talk about spirituality with them when they are dying." She explained that in her hospital the patient is basically compartmentalized and seen as a body, and that hospital workers such as herself are, likewise, treated "not as subjects, but objects." Similarly, a young palliative care doctor indicated that in France there is such a strong separation between church and state that one simply cannot speak about religion or spirituality in any way in his or her capacity as a doctor, teacher or other public service professional. Even on the palliative care unit he directs, there is no space for him to speak with patients about their spiritual needs or with colleagues about his own needs as a caregiver for dying persons. This condition leaves him carrying a tremendous burden in the face of the great suffering he witnesses every day at work, which, he indicated, is why the Rigpa workshop he was attending was so deeply important to him. The instructor of the workshop indicated that the situation for healthcare workers in France and Belgium has changed somewhat over the last decade and a half, although she indicated that "we still have to be very careful when we speak about spirituality."

The situation these workers describe sounds reminiscent of the "conspiracy of silence" that so moved visionaries such as Cicely Saunders and Elizabeth Kübler-Ross to found the modern hospice movement.[66] Yet there is at least one crucial difference: today doctors and other healthcare professionals in the United States, Australia, Ireland, Great Britain, Germany, France, and numerous other European countries can turn to the Spiritual Care Program for support in their work, and tens of thousands already have since the program was founded in 1993. The routinization of hospice care has diluted the original ideals of the hospice movement, yet the ascendency of the values of the expert discussed in the first part of this chapter has been far from total. To the contrary, the investigation of the work of Sogyal Rinpoche and his students presented in this chapter suggests that the resources for a deep spiritual renewal in end of life care are readily available for even the most trying conditions of care. So what does the future hold for end of life care in the West?

At the beginning of the last century, German sociologist Max Weber envisioned a bleak future for humanity locked in the "iron cage" of bureaucracy. Despite the promise of the Western Enlightenment of a brighter future of human progress, Weber concluded that "not summer's bloom lies ahead of us, but rather a polar night of icy darkness and hardness."[67] Weber's wholly pessimistic outlook was premised upon the view that the modern world was fundamentally inhospitable to a committed life of deep spiritual practice, and that the formal rationality of the market and bureaucratic organization would inevitably empty out all that is sacred of meaning leaving only the values of efficiency, competition, and compulsive acquisitiveness. What Weber essentially argued, expressed in terms of a Buddhist understanding of the causes of suffering, is that once "the three poisons" of greed, ill will, and delusion have become institutionalized in the structures of society they create an irresistible logic that crushes all other modes of being in the world.[68] Weber's analysis of modern bureaucracy is helpful in understanding how the therapeutic managerial ethos in hospice and palliative care has come to dominate Saunders' deep ethic of spiritual care, yet whenever a theorist interprets social processes as "irreversible" or "inevitable" we can be sure they have missed an important element of the story.

In Western social science, efforts to bring about social change have typically been seen as one group struggling to have its ideals realized in conflict with the vision of others, with "revolutionary" change involving an attempt to overthrow an existing order and replace it with another. In contrast, the Spiritual Care Program focuses on transforming *capacities for being in the world* rather than seeking to create a specific type of organizational structure or champion any particular policy initiative. As one senior educator in the Spiritual Care Program expressed, the "quiet revolution" means that it's "very organic" and "grassroots," responding to needs rather than pushing an agenda:

> We're not trying to move into health care policies saying, "You need to change and do it this way." But it's more this organic growth, and this is what people are asking for from health care professionals to people who are ill and dying, they want this kind of care and training. That's what they're asking us for in a certain way and so the need is already well established.

Another instructor spoke more metaphorically that "a noisy revolution makes people defensive, but a quiet revolution is very nonthreatening" such that people want to listen to what you have to offer.

The heart of the Buddhist path involves realizing and actualizing nonduality. This fundamental principle is illustrated in view of the Spiritual Care Program that supporting others in facing their mortality requires a willingness in caregivers to do same. The broader significance of this approach is expressed in David Loy's *The Great Awakening: A Buddhist Social Theory*, which interprets the failed attempts in the West to solve social problems through the nondualistic lens of the Buddha's teachings. Loy writes:

> The first implication of Buddhist social praxis is the obvious need to work on ourselves as well as the social system.... If we have not begun to transform our own greed, ill will, and delusion, our efforts to address their institutionalized forms are likely to be useless, or worse. We may have some success in challenging the socio-political order, but that will not lead to an awakened society. Recent history provides us with many examples of revolutionary

leaders, often well intentioned, who eventually reproduced the evils they fought against. In the end, one gang of thugs has been replaced by another.[69]

It is no coincidence that Sogyal Rinpoche's teachings on spiritual care revolve around relating to dying persons and ourselves with *compassion* and *wisdom* since they, along with *generosity,* are seen by Buddhists as the respective antidotes to the three poisons, ill will, delusion, and greed. It is beyond the scope of this chapter to discuss the many ways these three poisons have become institutionalized in contemporary healthcare systems in the West. Instead, I simply ask the reader to consider how the narratives discussed above on "finding refuge" and "seeing more than diminishment" point to a transformation of the delusion that some forms of suffering are beyond the reach of our care. The deepest intent of the Spiritual Care Program is to offer skillful and practical instruction for dissolving the fundamental delusions that imprison the heart's wisdom, most notably that there are two categories of persons—the living and the dying. As Christine Longaker expressed in a recent public talk, "not only the person with the life threatening illness, but we ourselves are on the same journey towards death, and the truth is that we don't know who's going to die first."[70] She continued that the spiritual resources offered in the Spiritual Care Program are not "tools that we put in our pocket to *fix* the patient in front of us," but instead are "the doorways we ourselves must open and go through in order to realize or own wholeness or holiness. When we train in compassion and deepen our confidence in this fundamental goodness of our being then we can attune ourselves well to those who are suffering."

"HEAVEN OF GREAT BLISS": THE FUTURE OF SPIRITUAL CARE

This chapter has sought to offer an initial interpretation of the deeper significance of Sogyal Rinpoche's influence on the care of the dying in the West. Given space limitations it was not possible to systematically evaluate the broader extent to which the teachings of Rinpoche have helped transform how healthcare workers in a variety of contexts and professions seek to meet the spiritual needs of those in their care. Such will be a focus of my ongoing research. But for now let me suggest that instead of Weber's imagined polar night of darkness and hardness, what could lie ahead is a "heaven of great bliss" or *Dechen Shying*, the name of the new spiritual care center that was recently launched at Dzogchen Beara after more than a decade and a half of planning. Dechen Shying is the first of many such centers that will be built in the coming years in Europe and the United

States (the next is scheduled to open in 2013 in Bad Saarow, Germany, a small town about 70 kilometers southeast of Berlin), and the intention is for these centers to serve both as a place of respite for terminally ill persons, their caregivers, and the bereaved as well as training grounds where professional and lay caregivers can come to receive spiritual care training and directly observe Sogyal Rinpoche's teachings on spiritual care being put into practice. Dechen Shying will provide holistic end-of-life care, although the center is different from a hospice in several important ways. Most important among those differences is that Dechen Shying is designed as a contemplative practice center where terminally ill and dying persons as well as their caregivers have the space to reconnect with their own spiritual resources and find meaning in life and hope in death.

The scope of after death care will also be much broader than that provided by hospice organizations. Hospices typically offer bereavement services to survivors during the first year of their loss, sometimes in the form of one-on-one grief counseling with hospice social workers, but most typically through bereavement groups that seek to normalize and valorize the experiences of the bereaved. Such bereavement services are typically premised upon a medicalized understanding of grief as a syndrome requiring proper resolution in a timely fashion (particularly during the first year) so that the grief does not become chronic. In contrast, bereavement services at Dechen Shying will be life-long trainings and spiritual retreats offered to bereaved persons at various points following their loss (e.g., within the first year, 5 years later, 20 years later) in the view that grief is an ongoing opportunity for profound reflection and spiritual practice rather than a problem that must be "resolved." The understanding of bereavement that informs the Spiritual Care Program is consistent with new models of grief which focus on "continuing bonds" between the living and the dead, rather than seeking resolution through detachment from the loss.[71] And just as the guiding principles of the Spiritual Care Program are grounded in Christine Longaker's own healing through loss, so too is the vision for Dechen Shying reflective of Sogyal Rinpoche's own experience of losing his first master, Jamyang Khyentse, who supervised his training and raised him as his son. Rinpoche was about 12 years old when Jamyang Khyentse died, and he explains how he still mourns this "incalculable loss" for Tibet and the world so many years later even as Jamyang Khyentse continues to inspire his work and provide inner direction as "the foundation and basis of the spirit behind everything I do."[72]

In this chapter I have interpreted the cultural significance of Rigpa's influence on care for the dying in the West in light of the founding ideals and practices of hospice care and the potential threats to those ideals posed by the secularization and professionalization of the field. I then presented the narratives of two caregivers to illustrate how Sogyal Rinpoche's teachings have been of profound benefit to individuals offering spiritual care at the end of life. These narratives were consistent with two prior studies evaluating the positive effects of specific Rigpa trainings on course participants.[73] At the same time, the significance of the Rigpa International Spiritual Care Education Program is much greater than what any individual participant takes away from a given course, a point stressed to me by Dr. Tony O'Brien, Consultant Physician in Palliative Medicine at Marymount Hospice and Cork University Hospital in Cork, Ireland. Dr. O'Brien served as a consultant throughout the planning stages of Dechen Shying and over the last decade and a half has witnessed the "quite substantial" benefits to local palliative care workers and general practitioners who have participated in Rigpa trainings even among those who, like himself, come from a very different faith tradition. Even more important than such individual changes has been the cultural shift that is taking place as the "culture, ethos, and philosophy of care" at Dechen Shying radiates out into more mainstream medical settings in the surrounding area.

One indicator of that cultural shift is that "grand rounds" on spiritual care have been held at Cork University Hospital as a direct result of the 1st International Conference on Spiritual Care hosted by the Rigpa Spiritual Care Education Program in Killarney, Ireland, in April 2009. As Dr. O'Brien explained,

> The pinnacle of the academic week is "grand rounds" which normally invite a doctor to speak on a major piece of research but on some minutia of concern. Up to that time there would have been no question of such a subject matter [spiritual care] having been a topic for grand rounds.... The fact that it was accepted in the core of academia says a huge amount.[74]

As an academic myself I appreciate the significance of this development which bodes well for the future of spiritual care for the dying *and* for the living. The focus of this chapter has been on the influence of Rigpa on end of life care in the West, although the most recent curriculum of the Spiritual Care Program introduced in the U.S. and some parts of Europe in the fall of 2010 has been geared towards a broader audience of caregivers. In my own field of higher education, a growing number of teachers and administrators are developing and offering curricula in "contemplative pedagogy," and many of us draw inspiration from Sogyal Rinpoche and other Tibetan Buddhist teachers.[75] In this way, the quiet revolution in care for the dying is interconnected with efforts to further inner peace and global vision in other spheres of society.

NOTES

1. I thank my family, members of the International Spiritual Care Team, and participants in the Spiritual Care Program for their generosity and support in making this research possible. I thank Jörn Ahrens, Andrea Mortello, Patrick Gaffney, Trent Schroyer, Kathryn Goldman Schuyler, and members of the International Spiritual Care Team for helpful feedback on earlier drafts of this chapter. I dedicate any merit that comes from this writing to the benefit of all guests, educators, staff, and volunteers at Dechen Shying and all subsequent spiritual care centers now and in the future.

2. Christine Longaker, *Facing Death and Finding Hope: A Guide to the Emotional and Spiritual Care of the Dying* (New York: Doubleday, 1997), 233. (Hereafter referred to as *Facing Death*.)

3. Sogyal Rinpoche, *The Tibetan Book of Living and Dying* (New York: Harper-Collins, 2002), 135.

4. Daniel Goleman recounted this story in his public comments made at the One-Day Inaugural Celebration, "Ancient Wisdom for the Modern World: Celebrating Tibet's Culture of Compassion," at the Tenzin Gyatso Institute in Berne, New York on June 19, 2010.

5. Sogyal Rinpoche, *Tibetan Book of Living and Dying*, 362.

6. Mark Cobb, *The Dying Soul: Spiritual Care at the End of Life* (Buckingham: Open University Press, 2001), 116. (Hereafter referred to as *The Dying Soul*.)

7. Two other notable programs in the United States are the Upaya Institute's "Being with Dying" program founded and directed by Roshi Joan Halifax (http://www.upaya.org/bwd/), and the Metta Institute's "End-of-Life Care Practitioner Program founded and directed by Frank Ostaseski (http://www.mettainstitute.org/EOLprogram.html).

8. Professor David Clark of Glasgow University, personal communication with the author, 7/1/2010; S. J. Yardley, C. E. Walshe, and A. Parr, "Improving Training in Spiritual care: A Qualitative Study Exploring Patient Perceptions of Professional Educational Requirements," *Palliative Medicine* 23 (2009): 601-607; see also Christina Puchalski *et al.*, "Improving the Quality of Spiritual Care as a Dimension of Palliative Care: The Report of the Consensus Conference," *Journal of Palliative Medicine* 12, no.10 (2009): 885-904, 899.

9. Maria Wasner, Christine Longaker, and Gian Domenico Borasio, "Effects of Spiritual Care Training for Palliative Care Professionals," *Palliative Medicine* 19 (2005): 99-104.

10. John Eric Baugher, "Facing Death: Buddhist and Western Hospice Approaches," *Symbolic Interaction* 31, no. 3 (2008): 259-284.

11. Anne Bruce, "Evaluation of an Innovative Contemplative End-of-Life Care Course," *Spirituality and Health International* (2007): www.interscience.wiley.com. Bruce also used the same quantitative measures as Wasner et al. (2005), although I was unable to interpret her findings given how the data is presented in her report.

12.   Art Moore, "Hospice Care Hijacked?," *Christianity Today* (March 2, 1998): 38-41.

13.   On anxiety as a central experience in contemporary Anglo-American societies, see Furedi, *Therapy Culture*; Gergen, *The Saturated Self*; Giddens, *Modernity and Self-Identity;* Micki McGee, *Self-Help, Inc.: Makeover Culture in American Life* (New York: Oxford University Press, 2005); On the materialistic and frivolous views regarding death in the modern world see Sogyal Rinpoche, *The Tibetan Book of Living and Dying*, 7-10.

14.   Kathleen Garces-Foley, "Buddhism, Hospice, and the American Way of Dying," *Review of Religious Research*, 44, no. 4 (2003): 341-353, 351.

15.   On meditation as a form of "emotion management" see Peggy Thoits, "Emotional Deviance: Research Agendas," in *Research Agendas in the Sociology of Emotions*, ed. T. D. Kemper (Albany: State University of New York Press, 1990), 180-203; On meditation as a "passive coping strategy," Leonard I. Pearlin and Carmi Schooler, "The Structure of Coping" *Journal of Health and Social Behavior* 19 (1978): 2-21.

16.   As my earlier research shows, hospice workers socialized under the professional therapeutic model who view their role as helping dying persons "open up" and "process" their feelings of grief and loss may very well pull away from those suffering from dementia who threaten their sense of efficacy in fulfilling their role. Baugher, "Facing Death: Buddhist and Western Hospice Approaches," and "Facilitating 'Grief Work': The Behaviorist Turn in Hospice Care," in *The Many Ways We Talk about Death in Contemporary Society: Interdisciplinary Studies in Portrayal and Classification*, ed. M. Souza and C. Stoudt, (Edwin Mellen Press. Lewiston, NY, 2009), 331-345.

17.   Clive Seale, *Constructing Death: The Sociology of Dying and Bereavement* (Cambridge: Cambridge University Press, 1998), 190-191.

18.   Ann Bradshaw, "The Spiritual Dimension of Hospice: The Secularization of an Ideal," *Social Science Medicine* 43, no.3 (1996): 409-419.

19.   Dame Cicely Saunders, *Watch with Me: Inspiration for a Life in Hospice Care*, (Sheffield: Mortal Press, 2003), 1. The passage from the Bible that Saunders draws upon is Matthew 26: 36-44.

20.   Cicely Saunders and Mary Baines, *Living with Dying: The Management of Terminal Disease*, 2nd. *Ed.* (New York: Oxford University Press, 1989), 52-53.

21.   Anthony Giddens, *Modernity and Self-Identity* (Palo Alto, CA: Stanford University Press,1991); Kenneth J. Gergen, *The Saturated Self* (Ney York, NY: Basic Books, 1991); Zygmunt Bauman, *Liquid Modernity* (Malden, MA: Polity Press, 2000).

22.   Saunders and Baines, *Living with Dying: The Management of Terminal Disease*, 54.

23.   Saunders, *Watch with Me*, 5-6.

24.   Emily Abel, "The Hospice Movement: Institutionalizing Innovation," *International Journal of Health Services*, 16, no. 1 (1986): 71-85.

25.   Personal communication with author, 7/1/2010.

26.   Bradshaw, "The Spiritual Dimension of Hospice" 416.

27.   Ibid., 418.

28.   Baugher, "Facilitating 'Grief Work.'"

29. Anne Bruce and Betty Davies, "Mindfulness in Hospice Care: Practicing Meditation-in-Action," *Qualitative Health Research*, 15, no. 10 (2005): 1329-1344; for a critique of contemporary "therapy culture" more broadly see Frank Furedi, *Therapy Culture*.

30. Garces-Foley, "Buddhism, Hospice, and the American Way of Dying."

31. Garces-Foley, "Buddhism, Hospice, and the American Way of Dying"; Prebish, *Luminous Passage: The Practice of Buddhism in America* (Berkeley, CA: University of California Press, 1999).

32. Garces-Foley, "Buddhism, Hospice, and the American Way of Dying," 352.

33. Bradshaw, "The Spiritual Dimension of Hospice"; Nicky James, and David Field, "The Routinization of Hospice: Charisma and Bureaucratization," *Social Science and Medicine* 34, no. 12 (1992): 1363-1375.

34. On hospice as an "alternative" form of care, see Anne Munley, *The Hospice Alternative: A New Context for Death and Dying*, (New York: Basic Books, 1983).

35. See Baugher, "Facilitating 'Grief Work.'"

36. Garces-Foley, "Buddhism, Hospice, and the American Way of Dying," 347.

37. Cobb, *The Dying Soul,* 121.

38. Longaker, *Facing Death and Finding Hope*, xiii-xiv.

39. Jurgen, Gude (Director), "Spiritual Care," DVD, Buddhist Broadcasting Foundation (2006), http://www.buddhistmedia.com/uitzending .aspx?lIntEntityId=159&lIntType=0&lIntYear=2006

40. Longaker, *Facing Death and Finding Hope*, 141.

41. See Baugher, "Facing Death: Buddhist and Western Hospice Approaches."

42. Quoted in Sandol Stoddard, *The Hospice Movement: A Better Way of Caring for the Dying* (New York: Vintage Books, 1978), 14.

43. Baugher, "Facilitating 'Grief Work.'"; see also Bradshaw, "The Spiritual Dimension," 414-415.

44. Longaker, *Facing Death and Finding Hope*, xv.

45. Sogyal Rinpoche, *The Tibetan Book of Living and Dying*, 179-181.

46. Saunders, *Watch with Me*, 3.

47. Cobb, *The Dying Soul*, 125-126.

48. Frank Furedi, *Therapy Culture*.

49. Pema Chödrön, *The Places that Scare You: A Guide to Fearlessness in Difficult Times* (Boston: Shambhala, 2001), 1; Patrul Rinpoche, *The Words of My Perfect Teacher* (Boston: Shambhala, 1998), 7.

50. Sogyal Rinpoche, *The Tibetan Book of Living and Dying*, 47-48, 54. For further discussion of the distinction between *rigpa* and *sem* in the Dzogchen teachings see John Powers, *Introduction to Tibetan Buddhism, 2nd ed.* (Ithaca, NY: Snow Lion Publications, 2007), 388-390.

51. Longaker, *Facing Death and Finding Hope*, 42.

52. See, e.g., Christina Puchalski *et al.*, "Improving the Quality of Spiritual care as a Dimension of Palliative Care."

53. In Wasner et al.'s study 77% of participants found the Rigpa training helpful in coping with difficult aspects of their work in palliative care, although only 10% of the participants were Buddhist, 71% were Christian, and the

remaining 19% had no religious affiliation. Wasner et al., "Effects of Spiritual Care Training for Palliative Care Professionals."

54.   Lynda A. Markut and Anatole Crane, *Dementia Caregivers Share Their Stories: A Support Group in a Book* (Nashville: Vanderbilt University Press, 2005); Deborah Sherman, "The Reciprocal Suffering of Caregivers," in *Caregiving and Loss: Family Needs, Professional Responses*, ed. K J. Doka and J.D. Davidson, (Washington, DC: Hospice Foundation of America, 2001), 247-264.

55.   Kenneth J. Doka, "Grief and Dementia," in *Living with Grief: Alzheimer Disease* (Washington, D.C.: Hospice Foundation of America, 2004), 139-153.

56.   Names and some demographic details have been changed to protect the anonymity of respondents.

57.   Longaker, *Facing Death and Finding Hope*, 69; Sogyal Rinpoche, *The Tibetan Book of Living and Dying*, 199.

58.   For a fuller description of the loving kindness meditation, see Sharon Salzberg, *Loving kindness: The Revolutionary Art of Happiness* (Boston: Shambhala Publications, 2004); Christine Longaker, *Facing Death and Finding Hope*, 69-71; Sogyal Rinpoche, *The Tibetan Book of Living and Dying*, 199-206.

59.   For a fuller description of the heart practice see Sogyal Rinpoche, *The Tibetan Book of Living and Dying*, 317-320.

60.   Mantra can be defined as "that which protects the mind." A mantra is a sound, syllable, word or phrase that is recited as a form of meditation. What is essential in mantra recitation is the quality of one's mind, not the external verbal act of recitation. Even the sound of an oxygen nebulizer can protect one from harmful states of mind if that sound is used to turn oneself towards something positive, such as inspiring faith or compassion. See Sogyal Rinpoche, *The Tibetan Book of Living and Dying*, 71; The Dalai Lama, *Mind in Comfort and Ease: The Vision of Enlightenment in the Great Perfection* (Boston: Wisdom Publications, 2007), 11-12.

61.   The term "spiritual tourism" comes from the Reverend Mark Cobb who writes that "The diverse cultures of humankind are diminished in attempting neat synthesis, and distinct spiritual orientations are disrespected if they are classed as essentially similar. However, within limits, we can find common ground and ways of approaching spiritual traditions that are sensitive to different experiences, practices, and philosophies." Cobb, *The Dying Soul*, 127. Cobb's critique of "spiritual tourism" in favor of deep interreligious dialogue resonates with the perspective outlined by Sogyal Rinpoche in *The Future of Buddhism* (London: Rider, Random House, 2002), 4-5. See also his discussion of the "shopping mentality" and "how to follow the path" in *The Tibetan Book of Living and Dying*, 135.

62.   "Centering prayer" is a form of Christian meditation made popular by Father Thomas Keating. One of Father Keating's students is invited each year to teach this practice at the contemplative end-of-life care course Rigpa offers through Naropa University. More information on centering prayer can be found at the Contemplative Outreach website: http://www.centeringprayer.com/.

63. Sister Catherine's openness to integrate Tibetan Buddhist imagery and practices in her devotional life has generational roots as well. As she explained: "I'm one of the [baby] boomers. I'm finding that people that were trained in my years were always the people that stretched in religious life." Her experience is consistent with Courtney Bender and Wendy Cadge's observation that the Vatican II reforms (1962-1965) that required all Catholic orders to scrutinize their habits and practices and invited them to look outside their own order for practices that would deepen their sense of community purpose promoted the conditions in which some Catholic nuns sought out Buddhism. Several of the Catholic nuns Bender and Cadge interviewed felt that the Vatican II reforms "woke their orders up to the 'emptiness' of their devotional practices, dress codes, daily habits and community life patterns" and in the words of one nun made them realize that "we were without a base and what we were missing was the deeply contemplative piece of our lives." Courtney Bender and Wendy Cadge, "Constructing Buddhism(s): Interreligious Dialogue and Religious Hybridity," *Sociology of Religion* 67, no.3 (2006): 229-247, 233.

64. For an insightful exploration of the relation between contemplative seeing and a reverential "attitude of mortality," see Christopher A. Dustin and Joanna E. Ziegler, *Practicing Mortality: Art, Philosophy, and Contemplative Seeing* (New York: Palgrave Macmillan, 2007).

65. Cobb, *The Dying Soul*, 135.

66. See, for example, Elizabeth Kübler-Ross, *On Death and Dying: What the Dying Have to Teach Doctors, Nurses, Clergy, and Their Own Families* (NY: Touchstone, Simon & Schuster, 1969); Barney G. Glaser, and Anselm L. Strauss, "The Ritual Drama of Mutual Pretense," in *Death: Current Perspectives,* ed. E. S. Shneidman, (Palo Alto, CA: Mayfield Publishing Company, 1984), 161-171.

67. Max Weber, "Politics as a Vocation," in *From Max Weber: Essays in Sociology,* ed. H. Gerth and C.W. Mills, (NY: Oxford University Press, 1946), 77-128.

68. On the fundamentally delusional nature of Western rationality, for example, Weber writes "Specialists without spirit, sensualists without heart; this nullity imagines that it has attained a level of civilization never before achieved," *The Protestant Ethic and the Spirit of Capitalism* (NY: Charles Scribner's Sons, 1958), 182.

69. David Loy, *The Great Awakening: A Buddhist Social Theory* (Boston: Wisdom Publications, 2003), 35. Here Loy speaks directly to Weber's bleak view that social movements may change whose vision dominates the social order for a period of time, but it is impossible to exit the cycle of domination. The fundamental flaw of Weber's dualistic outlook is the assumption that efforts to change the social order could never involve a transformation of being, but instead are simply zero-sum struggles over who will dominate whom in the immediate future.

70. Talk titled "Spiritual Care for the Living and Dying" given on the opening day of *Compassion and Presence: Spiritual Care for the Living and Dying,* the First International Conference on Spiritual Care hosted by the Rigpa Spiritual Care Education Program, Killarney, Ireland, April 27 and 28, 2009.

71. For a critique of the medicalization of grief and a discussion of "continuing bonds" see chapters 10 and 11 of Glennys Howarth, *Death and Dying: A Sociological Introduction* (Malden, MA: Polity Press 2007).

72. Sogyal Rinpoche, *Tibetan Book of Living and Dying*, 276-277.

73. Wasner et al., "Effects of Spiritual Care Training for Palliative Care Professionals"; Bruce, "Evaluations of an Innovative Contemplative End-of-Life Care Course."

74. Telephone interview with the author, August 10, 2010.

75. See, e.g., Line Goegen-Hughes, "A Higher Education: A Survey of Colleges and Universities Offering Contemplative Alternatives to Conventional Education," *Shambhala Sun* 19, no. 6 (2011): 59; John Eric Baugher, "Contemplating Uncomfortable Emotions: Creating Transformative Spaces for Learning in Higher Education," Forthcoming in O. Gunnlaugson, H. Bai, E. Sarath, and C. Scott (eds.),*Contemplative Approaches to Learning & Inquiry Across Disciplines* (New York: SUNY Press).

CHAPTER 16

EAST MEETS WEST

The Development and
Methods of Crucible Research

Bronwen Rees

The institutions and structures of economic markets are in crisis, and along with this has arisen a call for innovative approaches to business education, business, and leadership. Even conventional, influential world bodies are calling for radical change, and recognizing that this needs to take place in the actual mindsets of managers and business leaders. For example, the

Inner Peace—Global Impact: Tibetan Buddhism, Leadership, and Workt, pp. 243–268
Copyright © 2012 by Information Age Publishing
243

World Economic Forum 2009 Report raised the following call for action: "It is time to rethink the old systems and have a fundamental rebooting of the educational process."[1] Gary Hamel, in a seminal *Harvard Business Review* article, called for a "retraining of managerial minds."[2] Some radical institutionalist and Buddhist economists argue that these problems can only be solved through the transformation of the deeper structural relationship of institutions and culture. According to Joel Magnuson, this can only happen when a deeper, evolutionary transformation of human consciousness takes place.[3] Along with other wisdom traditions, Tibetan Buddhism has predicted this state of affairs through what has become known as the *Shambhala* prophecy:

> There comes a time when all life on earth is in danger. Great barbarian powers have arisen. Although these powers spend their wealth in preparations to annihilate one another, they have much in common: weapons of unfathomable destructive power and technologies that lay waste our world.... Now is the time when great courage—moral and physical courage—is required of the Shambhala warriors, for they must go into the very heart of the barbarian power. To dismantle the weapons, in every sense of the term they must go into the corridors of power where the decisions are made. The Shambhala warriors have the courage to do this because they know that these weapons are ... mind-made. Made by the human mind they can be unmade by the human mind.[4]

The Shambhala warriors train in the use of two weapons: *compassion* (the recognition of our pain for the world) and *wisdom* (the experience of our radical inter-connectedness with all life.) Within this prophecy lies a possible approach for meeting the economic and institutional crisis: the powerful transformative potential that is at the heart of Buddhist practice. It was this understanding, along with the fear that seemed to rule much organizational life in the United Kingdom and which has since accelerated, that led me to create the Crucible Research team in 2002 to explore the possibilities of introducing secular forms of Buddhist meditation into organizations. I created this team as part of a research project at the Centre for Communication and Ethics in International Business (now the Centre for Transformational Management Practice) at Lord Ashcroft International Business School, Anglia Ruskin University.

In this chapter, I discuss the inspiration and theoretical framework behind the project and set out the basic principles, as well as the empirical findings and problems that we encountered in carrying out the work. The underpinning methodology was that of action research, and in keeping with its methods, I also describe the ongoing projects and initiatives that have since flowered as a result of the initial project.

ORGANIZATION AND POWER

Organization can be said to be the set of institutions and practices of collectively engaging in the sourcing, manufacturing, and exchanging of goods and services that enable human beings to survive as a collective. This process has become globalized through new technology and consumer capitalism. One of the outcomes of new technology throughout the globe is that there is less and less need to relate face to face; relationships at work are increasingly mediated through technology and monitored through managerial systems such as performance management which bear little relationship to the tasks and the consequences of the tasks that are carried out. Within these systems, accountability is not registered through the effects of one's actions on others, but by reference as to whether one has met the abstract criteria of, for example, a competence-based system, where one's actions are reduced to a limited number of "excellent behaviors."

This condition is reflected in the way in which offices and daily work life are spatially organized. People can be linked up world-wide with China, Hungary, or America, for example, yet fail to keep in contact with those people with whom they are physically sitting. Because technological tools remove the sense of physical contact, the sense of working together physically as human beings, as a community or embodied collective is also decreasing. This encourages an alienation from bodily and sensory experience and overreliance on one's intellectual concepts about how the world is. While we toil in front of a computer screen, we may lose physical contact with, or even conceptualization of, the product that we are manufacturing or exchanging. The products of our efforts become less tangible; they are merely recorded on the virtual world of the computer and beamed across the world through e-mail. Actual things become figures on a screen. Achievement is reached through manipulation of these figures. As these figures lose connection with the material world they become meaningless; an extra "0" on the spreadsheet or a bit of fudging on the management accounts does not seem very important. This can lead to loss of an ethical accountability for the effects of our actions. Viewed in this context, ethics may become merely a question of how the organization presents itself to the outside world and how its members can avoid blame for their actions.[5] This danger was pointed to quite clearly several decades ago by the philosopher Habermas, who showed how the "systems world" could take over from the "lifeworld."[6] My team members and I developed *Crucible Research* to see how we might impact this situation.

The Workings of Power

We inferred that this state of affairs must have something to do with the workings of power. But this was not power relations as traditionally understood in the form of overt economic or social exploitation. These relations of power seemed invisible. There was no place to voice any resistance to demands communicated from senior management. A body of management theorists in the United Kingdom and Europe have shown how power relations are maintained through the way that people internalize systems of knowledge so that they are no longer able to question what is happening.[7] These studies draw in particular on the writings of the French philosopher Foucault, who showed, through his notion of disciplinary practices, how power relations are maintained by documenting and then measuring human behavior in specific spheres of activity. From this perspective, power works through the ways in which knowledge is classified, codified, recorded, and inscribed.

For Foucault, power exists everywhere and comes from everywhere and acts as a type of relation between people, a complex form of strategy, with the ability to secretly shape another's behavior. Foucault did not see the effects of power as negatives that exclude, repress, censor, mask, and conceal, but rather, as a producer of reality. Power, for Foucault, was both constraining and enabling. Foucault was most well known for his use of the metaphor of the *Panopticon* to describe the workings of power. This was an architectural design put forth by Jeremy Bentham in the mid-nineteenth century for prisons, insane asylums, schools, hospitals, and factories. This was to replace the dungeons that were used to control individuals under a monarchial state. The Panopticon offered a powerful and sophisticated internalized coercion through the constant observation of prisoners, each separated from the other and allowed no interaction. From this structure, guards could continually see inside each cell from their vantage point in a high central tower, unseen.

My earlier study of eight organizations considered the human resource practice of *competence-based appraisal systems*.[8] It showed quite clearly how the micro politics of power spread throughout organizations through these systems such that employees were "divided" and partitioned into isolated cells. Those with access to the documentation were those with power in the organization, so that filling in a person's appraisal became a vehicle of this power. And further, employees' behavior became governed by the criteria by which they were judged in these appraisals. Thus the appraisal form came to have significance not merely as a document of measurement, but it actually defined the conduct and behavior expected of employees. As the language in which this was expressed was generally that of encouragement, there was little room for expressing resistance, so individuals suffered from an internal dysfunction of feeling powerless, yet ostensibly being "empowered." These human resource systems are the products of a universalized managerialism that, at the time the study was carried out (1996), was just beginning to be taken up in both the private and public sector, championed by the growing number of management consultants who could sell such systems to an entire organization. The method has since proliferated throughout many more organizations— from private to public—even down·to primary schools.

Since these systems offer recognition and reward based on prescribed behavior, then employees tend to internalize the behaviors and take them for granted as a normal part of reality. Those employees not behaving in this manner become emotionally or even physically excluded from the organization. Under these conditions, it is not possible to express resistance and therefore take responsibility for the consequences of one's actions, since the power relations are not seen or experienced. Thus, employees are placed in the situation of being told that one thing is happening, while often something else is taking place. This is the classic double bind of the wounded infant with an inconsistent mother. In order to make sense of the organizational stories, employees have to deny the reality of what is happening, so that they can feel that they are contributing to the organization. It is this dysfunction between what is said and what actually happens that leads to increasing levels of fear and depression in the workplace. It is in this denial that isolation and madness abound. It is perhaps this spawning of such systems that is reflected in the statistics in the U.K. that one in six workers suffers from depression.[9]

A Buddhist Understanding of Power

Buddhism does not historically offer a social critique since its main objective is the relief of individual suffering through enlightenment. In this sense, all the world is considered to be conditioned, and suffering arises from our ignorance of the true nature of reality. Human beings exist in a continual state of *samsara* which can only be relieved when they can see through into the true nature of suffering. One of the causes of this suffering is the illusion of a separate self, which is driven by the three poisons of greed, hate, and delusion. It was on his night of enlightenment that the Buddha saw through into the conditioned interdependence of all things. He released himself from a fixed sense of a self that constantly grasps to meet its individual needs and does not understand the interconnected nature of existence.

Several commentators have noted how the Western postmodern mindset is constructed within an economic system that has growth and profit as the prime goal. As Loy pointed out: "A modern corporation tends to function as a socially constructed vehicle of *institutionalized greed*."[10] These corporations are co-constructed within the context of managerial ideologies that serve to break down resistance, so that employees learn to serve the needs and desires of an invisible elite. By their divisive and hidden nature, such managerial ideologies lead to an isolated sense of individualism with an emphasis, above all, on personal achievements of wealth and status. By their nature, they encourage behaviors that Buddhism (and indeed other religions) would say point to greater suffering. It is precisely this emphasis on individual greed that creates an environment of fear, rather than one that enables wise action.

Buddhist practices have evolved to break down this overemphasis on the attachment to the self. Buddhism can be conceived of as a set of practices, a methodology, through which one can gain a greater sense of interconnectedness and "transcend" an isolated sense of self. It offers an invitation to experience oneself in greater and greater depth and to experience how that sense of self is a mere construction. Throughout its long history, Buddhism has developed a subtle system of meditation practices that vary across the different Buddhist traditions. At its heart, however, is the intent to inquire into the conditioned nature of the human mind and transform the three poisons of greed, hate, and delusion that are said to cause suffering. In all Buddhist traditions, meditation is part of the three-fold spiral path of meditation, ethics, and insight. By spending time in meditation, one develops insight into the way things are, leading to more ethical behavior since one understands the interconnectedness of all things. Ethics in Buddhism is considered to be related to the quality of the mental states with which one acts. If one acts in anger or anxiety, then one is likely to cause harm to oneself or to the other. More ethical behavior leads to deeper insights into the nature of reality. This is an ever-unfolding and deepening path, leading ultimately to full enlightenment.

Through meditation, individuals learn to loosen their connection to the self by recognizing that things are interdependent. With this realization, individuals can let go of grasping and act from a place of love, rather than from one of self-interested power over others. Furthermore, since Buddhism maintains that the world is socially constructed, it implies that when an individual succeeds in transforming him or herself, the world is also transformed. This would equally be the logical endpoint of a Foucaultian analysis, except that Foucault does not offer solutions or methods of collective practice, although in his later work, he focused more on theories of the self. It was on this theoretical basis, supported by our own meditation practice, that the Crucible team felt that Buddhism potentially contained both a philosophical and practice-based possibility for resistance to and emancipation from the managerial ideologies that function through the imposition of power, as described above.

Buddhist Meditative Practice and Its Potential for Emancipation

Simple awareness practices form the basis for meditation. Awareness practices support the individual in recognizing how the mind is, at any moment. This leads to the meditative state known as *mindfulness* which is a natural mental state that is available to all. It is not a trance-like state, as some may believe. Mindfulness is most simply and profoundly understood as an awareness of how the mind is—not as an abstracted experience, outside of the physical, social or historical context in which it occurs. This involves recognizing how the mind is *in the actual context that the mind finds itself*. It is grounded in that situation. If one understands mindfulness as being grounded in this way, it becomes clear that the ground is of great importance to the effectiveness of the practice or inquiry.

In such a model, the individual is challenged to acknowledge that his or her behavior always contributes to all conditions that make up the situation as it is. It means taking a step towards taking fuller responsibility for the situation, in that the individual is located in an interpenetrating and interdependent field of human activity. This practice takes effort, and is often met with resistance, as the practice breaks down the "ego" or the conditioned self. This resistance may manifest as either of the twin poles of restlessness or drowsiness, as the mind seeks to stay in its state of ignorance.

As an outcome of meditative practice, an opening takes place that enables the individual to look more deeply into the conditions in which he or she finds herself. It is, of course, one thing to experience this on the meditation cushion, but another to be able to apply it in an organizational context where one is subjected to the strong collective conditioning forces explored earlier. However, if meditative practice can lead to greater awareness of the conditions in which one finds oneself, it holds the possibility for breaking through the conditioned channels of power described above when applied in the workplace. The challenge for the Crucible team was to see how we could find a way of translating Buddhist meditational practices into a language and form that could help individuals surface their internalized patterns of power and to "see through" the conditions of power in which individuals found themselves. If this were possible, we felt that it could empower employees to become fully grounded and take responsibility for their own choices.

THE FOUNDATION AND METHODS OF
THE CRUCIBLE RESEARCH TEAM

The History of the Crucible Team

The origins of Crucible Research go back to 1999 when I collaborated with Patrick Dunlop, then Chairman of the Cambridge Buddhist Centre, who was an experienced meditation teacher of some 20 years. The Cambridge Buddhist Centre is part of the Friends of the Western Buddhist Order (now the Trinatna Buddhist Order), which is one of the largest Buddhist organizations in the United Kingdom, with many smaller centers throughout the world. At the time, I was Director of the Centre for Communication and Ethics in International Business at Lord Ashcroft International Business School, Anglia Ruskin University, Cambridge, U.K. (now the Centre for Transformational Management Practice). Patrick and I carried out a number of different projects with schools in the Cambridge area. During this time we began to meet with Richard Huson, who became the third member of the Crucible team. Richard is also a very experienced meditator and meditation teacher. In addition, he had been a practicing psychotherapist for over 10 years. The three of us met periodically over a period of 18 months to discuss the application of meditation to educational and other organizations, resulting in the production of a joint conference paper titled "Unity in Diversity and Diversity in Unity: Consciousness and Myth in Organizational Life."[11] At this time John Wilson joined the team to take up a PhD scholarship at the Lord Ashcroft International Business School in Anglia Ruskin University. He had recently returned from San Francisco where he had spent 8 years establishing a Buddhist center in the Mission district of the city.

By the autumn of 2002, the four team members had come together, dedicated to seeing whether and how they could develop a shared language and methodology that could be taken into the business context. In March 2003, the team received funding from Anglia Ruskin University, Cambridge, to see whether these practices could cross cultures, and from this arose a further collaboration with the East/West Research Institute of the Buddhist college in Budapest (now the Budapest Buddhist University, the only state-funded Buddhist university in Europe).

Through our dialogue and practice, the idea of *alchemy* emerged—interestingly two of us came up with this idea spontaneously and separately. This idea had three benefits: it could relate to Western understandings and origins; it carried with it the notion of transformation; and the process of alchemy itself was mirrored in the *action research* methodology that the team had adopted. The process of alchemy, though traditionally associated with the West, is equally part of many wisdom traditions and is an innate part of esoteric Tibetan Buddhist practices. Here was an intricate set of interconnections that carried a symbology transcending both time and space and East and West.

Method: Action Research

The traditional "scientific" modes of inquiry were not appropriate for the types of inquiry implied by the Crucible intent. Action research was ideal, in that its methods bridge the gap between theory and practice by emphasizing the experiential basis of knowledge and practical application of understanding. In action research, the intent is to study human situations in order to enhance the quality of action within them. The approach is flexible and takes account of the process of research as it unfolds. The theoretical connections between action research and Buddhism have been explored by Richard Winter, who acted as adviser throughout some of the project.[12]

Action research engages with an on-going situation in order to improve the understanding of those in that situation and, if possible, bring about change through collaborative action. The aim of the method is to describe what is learned from the process of change as it occurs. It is a method of encouraging positive change in the way a group of people work together. As much as possible, it places the power within the collective of the group. The group actively participates in all aspects of the research; defining the problem; setting aims; designing the intervention; assessing the results; setting modified aims. That is why the crucible was such a suitable metaphor to use for our team, since what happens in the alchemical crucible is an on-going process of transformation.

Just like in a crucible (where the alchemist also changes), the researchers are equally participants in action research. This means that the facilitation within the Crucible team is also subject to action research and therefore is self-evaluative and questioning. As Buddhist meditation traditionally is a personal and individual affair, combining it with an action research method meant that this provided a vehicle for a collective reflective process.

It was this type of conscious embodied reflection that we felt was lacking from organizational life and decision making. By setting up a model of collective reflection, we support one another both in reflecting on and changing our actions, even when we are unsure of the outcome. Action research provides an excellent model for this reflection at a collective level, combined with the individual practices of mindfulness and awareness that underpinned Crucible's methodology. In their common cycles of reflection (action research at a collective level and Buddhism at a personal level), there is opportunity for tackling both the subjective and objective conditions of the power condition, as described by Foucault. We felt that this could be ideal in organizational contexts, in that a process could be set up that might be self-sustaining. This would mean that the community would have the opportunity to constantly develop and inquire into its own functioning. Often, change programs do not sustain themselves when individuals who have undergone such training find it impossible to maintain that change after returning to their own setting.

Research Design and Context

Our project aimed to develop and pilot a collective method of working that could be used to help organizations to surface and meet the hidden dimensions of power. One of our hopes was to enter organizations as consultants, but this proved difficult in the initial stages, so instead we ran a series of trials and workshops in various contexts from which, in action research manner, a collection of concepts and practices emerged as a Crucible method. Further projects and initiatives emerged both during the project and after that were directly informed by the people and practices involved in the original project. Table 16.1 indicates the initiatives that were set up as part of the original project, along with those that emerged afterwards. Much of our work addressed the idea of building community, whether this was in a business, spiritual, or educational context. All the original workshops had a planning day, the workshop, debriefing, reflection, and sometimes questionnaires distributed either among the team members and/or with the participants.

The Emergent Crucible Method: Ethical Inquiry

During the initial two years of discussion, we developed a Crucible process based our understanding of Buddhist meditation. This process underpinned nearly all of the workshops that we carried out in the different contexts. While the process appears simple, it is based on a subtle understanding of human consciousness and many years of collective sustained practice. We called the process "ethical inquiry," following from our understanding of the threefold path. The underlying conceptual and working principles can be summarized as follows:

1. Establishing the Reflective Ground

The reflective ground refers to the physical as well as the emotional space in which the inquiry takes place. Participants are helped to be aware of the space. The space is recognized as being significant in terms of it being the space where a sense of awareness and kindness will be evoked. The space—and in particular the ground—brings and holds those there in relationship to one another. This may be achieved in different ways, one of which is a walking meditation. This has the effect of slowing down mental, physical, and emotional processes, so that people can become aware of their feelings in relationship to themselves, to others, and to the context in which they find themselves.

2. Establishing the Crucible Through Encouraging a Sense of Embodiment

In this stage, an awareness practice is used to encourage the individuals to be as present as they are able to be. The term "crucible" is used to delineate the space or ground in which fundamental change may occur, just as the crucible was the container for transformation used by the alchemists. The crucible or ground of transformation is created through attentiveness to how things really are, which is also the underlying method of Buddhist meditation.

This crucible is established through a strategic positioning of the team members, so that they sit in the four corners of the space, in order that they can evoke and then hold the energies of transformation that the process initiates. In terms of field dynamics, this meant that participants would not look to one person as leader but instead were encouraged to draw upon their own personal processes and reflection and to meet different parts of themselves that might be held back under normal organizational group processes. This is an important element in the Crucible process, as it prevents the usual authority projections from taking place, so the individuals can begin to surface emotions in a safe context.

3. Reflection

Reflection is a process in which participants are encouraged to reflect upon some aspect of themselves in relationship to their workplace and work. For example, in a business school the team has asked questions such as "What brought you into education?" A fairly simple question in itself, but when asked in the context of the reflective ground, then a person's deepest values may emerge. This can then be offered to the rest of the group through a process of dialogue.

4. Dialogue

This may take place in one large group or small groups, once the reflective ground has been established. The inquiry takes place in the actual situation, by which we mean taking into conscious account the on-going dynamics of the emotional/ethical situation as it is, and using this as

Table 16.1. Birth, Development, and Unfolding of Crucible Research Work

1994 -7	Bronwen Rees carries out research on power and gender relations in eight large U.K. organizations			
1999–2002	Bronwen Rees, Patrick Dunlop, and Richard Winter set up meditation for schools project in Cambridgeshire, U.K.			
2002	Creation of Crucible Research			
2002–6	*Workshop activities funded by grant*			
	Business	**Spiritual**	**Therapeutic**	**Cross-cultural**
	Action research projects Cornwall Business College (6 month intervention) Lord Ashcroft International Business School Workshops for staff. Workshops for students. Right livelihood Project Cambridge Buddhist Centre.	*Building community* Cambridge Buddhist Centre (x3 weekend). North London Buddhist Centre (x3 weekend). Western Buddhist Order National Convention (x5 short workshops)	*Inquiry* into the Underworld (x3 weekend)	*Hungarian* *Crucible team formed* 3 workshops in Hungarian Buddhist University. One weekend workshop in Nagykovácsi, near Budapest, Hungary.

Later unfoldings

2006 onwards

Business programs
Contributions to Buddhist Economics conferences and programs. Teaching Buddhist Economics at Ubon Ratachani University Thailand. Keynote speech on Crucible Method at Second Buddhist Economics Conference in Thailand. Centre for Transformational Management Practice created from Centre for Communication and Ethics in International Business. Creation of journal *Interconnections*

East West Sanctuary
Center for Evolutionary Inquiry set up in Hungary called East West Sanctuary. Series of meditation workshops. Development of foundation training in Buddhist psychotherapy. Workshop on creation of European Buddhist University. International seminars at EWS on sustainable business published in *Interconnections*. Setting up of "ethical inquiry" programs for young people working on community projects. Development of "holonomics" program. Creation of "eastwestinterconnect" webpage

Research
PhD thesis "The Ontology of Inquiry" by John Wilson.[13] Development of holonomics at EWS Development of "engaged Buddhism" programs at EWS. International expert community writers developed through *Interconnections*.

Hungarian business consultancy set up. Coworking between East West Sanctuary and Buddhist University

255

much as a ground for inquiry, as trying to change it. Thus, if emotions such as fear or anger were present, the dialogue surfaced this, to see how it is affecting the more "objective" or "rational" elements of the situation. These are considered to be as important to the dialogue as is the actual intellectual content. It should not be thought that a perfect, reflective ground has to be established before the inquiry can progress.

CRUCIBLE IN ACTION: THREE PHENOMENOLOGICAL ACCOUNTS

The Crucible team carried out its work in business, educational, and spiritual contexts, each of which had slightly different aims. While the exercises changed from one context to another, the process outlined earlier underpinned our work throughout. What follows are three descriptions of our work: one in a business school, the other in a cross-cultural context, and finally some of my own reflections on the Crucible journey.

Account 1: Cornwall Business School

We carried out an intervention in Cornwall Business School that culminated in a 2-day workshop with the senior managers and new dean. We had been invited by the new dean to establish new ways of working with the senior management team as the Business School was expanding. I spent 3 days over a period of 6 months interviewing all the senior managers about their roles and their perceptions of how the Business School should be grown. We decided to set up a 2-day program in order to improve communication and build a supportive team for the new dean. This program took place over the summer holiday. It was quite a high risk for the new dean to take, especially as the methods we were using were highly unusual at that time for this type of environment.

Twelve managers were present. We began sitting in a circle, and then set up the reflective ground through a walking meditation. People were invited to begin walking swiftly throughout the room, in any direction. Gradually participants were asked to slow down, and begin bringing awareness to their breath, to their environment, and to note the movement of their feet on the floor. They were asked to reflect on the nature of the foot, to note the contact with the ground, and to place each foot with a feeling of compassion and gratitude for how much, and how long, it had sustained the individual. This process took about 40 minutes, until there was a general settling of energies. The workshop was taking place in one of the offices of the business school, and there was some embarrassment at first, especially from one of the male managers, who appeared to be walking in a very rigid way.

This was followed by the reading of a poem. One of the members of the Crucible Team then opened a dialogue and reflection on what we felt we were doing at this particular place and this particular time—and how we had gotten here. Each participant was asked to reflect on a moment in his or her life when he or she had felt most excited and inspired. This was shared within the group, and some very moving personal accounts emerged. For example, one woman shared that she came from Spain, and how her parents had fled from the Spanish Civil War, bringing her as a baby with them. The rest of the group, even though many had worked in the college for decades, were very surprised to hear this and other stories. Despite working together for such a long time, they had not shared this type of personal information, and they considered that it deepened and enriched their understanding and communication. It was very moving to hear what had brought this set of people into an educational environment and to learn about their inspiration to teach. The day came to a close with a meditation on the body, bringing people further into contact with their embodied sense of themselves sitting in a particular moment in time and space.

The second day again began with a walking meditation. Participants reflected on how they felt and on what their expectations were for that day. Unlike Day 1 which had focused on personal histories, Day 2 focused on the conditions and obstacles found in the workplace. This was more discursive, using flipcharts. Participants were asked to reflect in small groups on what they perceived as obstacles to meeting the aspirations that we had explored the day before. A member of the Crucible Team sat with each of the groups. At this stage, the energies in the room became more heated. This grew in intensity as we joined together into a plenary group, sitting once again in a circle. Real grievances about communication and expectations emerged at this point, some in relationship to the new dean. As a member of the Crucible team, I was grateful to feel the presence of the other members of the team who were able to encourage and sustain this level of disclosure. As the discussion unfolded, it became clear that much of this was about misunderstandings of the real obstacles faced at different levels of the school's hierarchy.

In the afternoon, the discussion focused on distinguishing between those issues that could be dealt with within the school itself and those that were outside of the collective control of the group. This enabled the team to work together as a whole and to surface both new and long-standing resentments that had affected communications.

In following up, we learned that as a result of this program, the Business School was embarking on a series of communication exercises, as the managers felt they had benefited from the two-day program. This was encouraging news.

Account 2: The Cross-Cultural Challenge

From 2004-8, the Crucible team expanded its activities to the international arena and formed a collaboration with the Budapest Buddhist University who were interested in the Crucible methods and in developing their own methods for business. The Budapest Buddhist University is the only state-funded university in Europe. It was set up in 1989/90 by Dr Mireisz Laszlo and others in a window of opportunity when the Berlin Wall had fallen. At this stage, any religious and spiritual institutions were given the chance to register. Since that time it has expanded and now has about 200 people registering per year for a degree in Buddhist studies. It has developed its own MA, and an MA that will be offered in English. There are about 25 teachers, some full or part-time, and among its studies it also teaches four Eastern languages.

Initially, the U.K. team ran a workshop for people interested in our methods, translated by Dr Tamas Agocs, head of the East West Research Institute at the Buddhist University. The following is an account of the first workshop. There were eleven participants from different backgrounds: Some participants were students at the Buddhist University; others were business consultants interested in how the practices could be used; and yet others were psychologists seeking new methods.

We followed the usual Crucible method of a walking meditation as described earlier and then carried out a communication exercise where participants were asked to sit opposite one another in silence and experience the other person energetically. This was followed by a talk exploring the use of the Buddhist symbol *The Wheel of Life,* where participants were invited to compare the different realms with their own work environment. The six realms of the Wheel of the Life are said to represent different states of mind, and they can be loosely compared with organizational cultures.

After the workshop, we received a variety of diverse comments below are some of the written comments from the participants. They were selected to reflect the range of responses to the possibility of using such methods in their own work.

> Crucible is a good term because it is a melting pot for the values of different cultures. I think the method works.
>
> I liked the Crucible workshop; it came to mind very often during summer. I was fascinated by the communication exercise. All lecturers were very interesting personalities. All methods seemed very helpful ... I would like to

participate in developing such workshops for use at school, for both children and adults.

It helped me see how to apply Buddhist practices in daily life; this is what I was wanting. The wheel of life is a good image to use, the teachings are universal, they should be made more accessible to people.

The above comments showed to us that the method we had developed had possibilities for use in cross-cultural contexts. We were pleased with the understanding that participants demonstrated after only a day, although some people were already familiar with meditation, so it was an easier process than in the business school context.

A further set of comments raised many other issues, highlighting the challenges of working in a cross-cultural arena:

This was not what I expected. I think this is about popularizing and selling out the Buddhist teaching. I think Buddhism is much more valuable than that, it should not be turned into a customer's product. It is better if it remains accessible just to a favored few.

I would be cautious about implementing such methods in schools and at companies. This should not be conceived as Buddhist missionary activity. All such practices should be done on a voluntary basis.

I think the method has a lot of potential, but there are some conditions that must be met. Team cohesion is very important. An external observer should be asked to report back on joint procedures, in order to ensure safety.... An oriental authority should be consulted. We should not advertise ourselves as Buddhists, as it would arouse suspicion.... Participants must be solicited on a voluntary basis. We must expect assaults from the professional community, so we should justify ourselves by doing scientific research. Some famous professionals should be included in the project.

These comments raise important issues of the translation of Buddhist practices into different contexts and their effectiveness in addressing issues of power. In a few countries in Europe, Buddhist practice has become a respected intellectual and experiential ground of knowledge and practice. There are several Buddhist monasteries in the United Kingdom and many different Buddhist traditions. The call for "famous professionals" perhaps shows Hungary's youth in this area, as well as a continuing Hungarian hope that Western Europe would bring riches. The comment about the need for acclaimed psychologists for professional backing-up/validation of our practices, with the simultaneous call for an "Eastern authority," indicates again a difference in educational histories. Hungary had been for many years subject to Soviet educational systems, and people were perhaps accustomed to holding the teacher in great authority without challenging him or her. The Crucible method of shared leadership could be seen as confrontational in this context. In summary, the workshops in Hungary raised as many questions as solutions. However, after the initial three work-shops, a Hungarian team was created, and a later consultancy created that worked indirectly with notions of awareness and mindfulness in business. So, we could so say that an indirect and later flowering of the project unfolded through integration into a different country and context.

Account 3: My Own Journey

Much of my own work in organizations had been concerned with issues of power, particularly in relationship to gender, which had been the focus of my doctoral research. This work emerged from a theoretical back-ground of critical theory and Foucault's understandings of power. While these theories formed some valuable insights into the nature of power at work, I had become increasingly frustrated by their abstract and often very obscure nature. It was this that led me into creating the Crucible team. This provided my own ground for transformation, since I was engaged in introducing new and challenging methods into organizations to see if this could tackle issues of power, and also in bringing together a team of people who had no knowledge or experience in the business envi-ronment. Not only that, but all of us in the Crucible team had different experiences and had developed different meditative and therapeutic approaches. The setting up of Crucible was a slow and sometimes difficult process. Every time that the team met or carried out a workshop, part of our practice was to reflect as individuals and as a team. The work itself was creative, but also challenging to all of our ego structures.

As a woman academic in a business school, I have experienced much of the work as a struggle: a struggle to overcome my own personal condi-tioning in stepping forward; a struggle at times to lead the Crucible team; a struggle to introduce countercultural practices into a business school that largely makes its money from a curriculum based on managerial ide-ologies, as described earlier in this chapter. Every time I came up against my own resistance I learned to reflect more deeply on my own internal conditioning. One of the most difficult experiences was conducting the workshop within my own business school. There were roughly 70 partici-pants in a long, narrow, echoing room. I was frightened that my col-leagues would think I was some type of "woolly and pink" woman. A couple of my colleagues did actually walk out. However, when reflecting in small groups, most reported back on their love of education, combined with their feelings of frustration at being unable to share this with others.

On the other hand, much of the process has felt deeply meaningful. For example, I led a 2-year series of action research workshops with my team of researchers. This was largely discussion, but was always preceded by a meditation sometimes led by me, sometimes by John. I vividly remember one occasion when I was sitting in my office with three other researchers at the business school. I led a short meditation. Voices echoed outside, as students and staff moved up and down the corridors. For some reason, after the meditation, instead of dialoguing, we all fell, quite naturally and spontaneously, into a long, shared silence. I felt the tears welling up from my colleagues as the collective weight of our practice jostled with the activity and noises outside. The practice had opened us to one another in a way that contrasted starkly with the realities of the workplace. It was as though something missing and unfelt had entered as a presence between us and had enabled us intuitively to relate to one another in a different manner. There was no need for words.

Carrying out this work has transformed me and the work that I do. Since the time when I was developing the Crucible Method and Team, I have been invited to Thailand to teach Buddhism and Buddhist economics at a university. Here again, the principles of Crucible are evoked, as I am a woman and not a born Buddhist.

The work further precipitated me to set up the East West Sanctuary in the center of Europe—a physical manifestation of the principles of Crucible. Just as the research itself addresses issues of internalized power, so my work actively engages me in looking deeply into and changing the conditioned habits that would otherwise keep me repeating the same actions. Throughout this process, I repeatedly meet my own terror as I plunge more deeply into contexts with which I am unfamiliar. In accord with the hermetic statement "As above, so below," my external activities are equally reflected in the internal process. An important practice in the Tibetan Buddhist tradition is for practitioners to go to cremation grounds and meet their fear of death. The transformation required for me to reconcile these different worlds internally has at times necessitated such an experience, albeit in a different context. Despite this, I am still employed at the business school and find my place within it, even as I challenge its structures. The process has left me more open, more in contact with my colleagues, less fearful, and freer to be creative within different conditions. I would like to think that the process has helped some of my colleagues feel freer and more able to challenge their own particular conditioning.

THEORETICAL AND METHODOLOGICAL CONCLUSIONS

Our project set out to develop a method of working that could break through the micropolitics of power as described by Foucault. We had felt that Buddhist practices, since their nature was to explore and break down conditioning, might help to shift this cycle. Our project, which lasted for several years, has many interesting theoretical and methodological implications, some of which are summarized below.

Method: Embodiment

In the first 2 years, we created a method that we used in all the different contexts. While there were differences in our approach and participants had different expectations and levels of experience with some of the methods (i.e., in spiritual contexts some people were used to meditation), our aim in all of these was to encourage a collective sense of responsibility and awareness of how each person was being in the group. In other words, meditation and communication exercises were used to invite people to explore their embodied sense of who they were in different contexts. I had noted earlier that the lack of physical context with the environment and one another had, in my judgment, allowed the entry of those abstract systems of knowledge that Foucault had observed to be part of the processes of power. This was particularly evident in the groups that were already preexisting, such as the Cornwall Business School and the North London Buddhist Community. By opening a relationship with how things were really being experienced and allowing them to be voiced, the method was strong enough to sustain and improve these situations. By becoming personally embodied—present to the situation in all its conditions including one's own emotional states—it was possible for transformation to take place.

Resistance and Transformation

One of the aspects of power as described by Foucault is its diffuseness. It is not visible, and therefore there is no possibility of resistance, except through surfacing its tentacles. Crucible's ideas had been to provide a container where such processes could be unearthed, surfaced, articulated, and from that point, hopefully transformed. It was a point from which resistance could be made visible. For example, in the Cornwall Business School, resistance emerged on the second day. The deepening of the meditative process allowed this to happen. Meditation can be considered to be a process where the light of awareness is brought into areas of resistance. At this point a transformation occurs. By collectively bringing into the light areas of concern in the different communities we worked in, transformation was effected.

Unfortunately, we did not have the possibility of working for a sustained period with these processes to see the kind of long-term transformation that would be part of a future research agenda. To do so, would have been to have worked more explicitly with the notion of the three-fold path, as mentioned previously. Over time, the workshops would have given rise, we believe, to more ethical behavior, and this would have increased insight. What our workshops highlighted (in both of the business and educational contexts) was the entrenched nature of current managerial practices. As one of our team noted in the workshop at Anglia Ruskin University:

> How is it that there is so much powerlessness in the face of the passion for education? How is it that all members of staff retire to the sanctuary of their own classrooms without feeling confident to discuss this issue with their colleagues? How is it that we are all educators here, yet all feel unable collectively to carry out this task?

To us, this seemed to exemplify the way in which power divides and excludes at an unconscious level, according to Foucault. Despite this, the workshops and my own personal journey showed that when there is an opportunity for insiders to look more deeply into what is happening, there is a chance for something new to emerge—even if this is initially not long-lasting. The meditation with the research group, for example, definitely enabled some changes to be made later. One of the researchers later went on to make substantive changes in his own practice and within his own workplace, which was a large corporation. Indeed, he succeeded in developing a center for innovation and sustainability, which he attributes in part to some of these workshops—at least as a starting point. Working consciously with structures of power gives individuals opportunities to make individual and conscious choices, even if they challenge the status quo.

Cross-Cultural Context

The cross-cultural aspect of our work highlighted some very important distinctions and similarities. Despite the differing comments that we received, the initial projects showed that meditative practices have the capacity for crossing cultures and inviting real dialogue. We would like to have spent more time on these projects, as the method could be translated into the context of international education where difficulties of cross-cultural issues are becoming more urgent. As these practices cut through the purely discursive or conditioned nature of our perceptions, I believe they hold an important key in a globalizing world.

Collective Leadership

One of the principles of our method is that of collective leadership. This was by no means an easy task. What is needed is an approach which allows each individual's creativity to enhance rather than distract from the creativity of the others on the team, as well as the overall performance of the team. As Patrick wrote in 2004 on a Crucible questionnaire:

> My understanding of the basic principles at work in Crucible are to foster awareness and its application in organizational settings. In a way this is awareness as the quality of an individual being seen as part of a group or collective. That individual's awareness is at the same time something which arises in dependence upon a group or collective. So there is a tension and an interplay between these two elements which we could in a creative sense term the mutuality of diversity and unity.

For many people, the shared leadership was experienced as an exciting part of the workshops. In one of the spiritual settings, in a workshop of some 35 people, one person commented that it was like having "four very different archetypes" in the room. Personally, there were several occasions where I was very grateful for the support, when I felt that the tensions of our work were growing. This was particularly important for me in the workshop held at my own university! It was not always necessary to have all four of the team members present, but there was clearly a different resonance when this occurred. Collective leadership was not easy, but it contained possibilities for personal and hence group transformation.

Ongoing Unfolding: The East West Sanctuary

While the initial program was to find ways of interpreting Buddhist ideas to improve the quality of organizational life, the project later unfolded in unexpected ways, and in Tibetan and action research fashion, the seeds that have been laid are now taking root in different contexts. One of the understandings in Tibetan Buddhism is that teachings themselves may be hidden and only emerge when the time is ripe. This may be several centuries later. So, while we employed the scientific method for the purposes of Western research, our understanding reached deeper and further into the recesses of human wisdom, and thus we ask the reader that the flowering of our work can be interpreted in different ways!

In keeping with the principles both of Buddhism and the underlying action research method, the work has taken another unexpected twist: the creation of the East West Sanctuary, Centre for Contemplative Inquiry, based in Budapest, Hungary—a symbolic and concrete manifestation of the potential of the East and West coming together not only in terms of the East and West (Buddhist ideas and practices and Western philosophy and psychology), but also in term of East and West Europe. Hungary lies at the heart of central Europe, but has had a history of occupation, beginning with the Turks in the fifteenth century, then the Austrian Empire, followed by the Russians. Nevertheless, it has preserved a rich tradition of culture and wisdom, and draws its strength from its ability to look both East and West.

The vision behind the East West Sanctuary is to bring together Buddhist practitioners and researchers from Eastern and Western Europe dedicated to finding ways of translating Buddhist ideas into contemporary culture and society. This takes the form of international dialogue seminars using some of the methods of Crucible Research, which are often published in the journal *Interconnections*, published by Anglia Ruskin University. It works closely with the Budapest Buddhist University and is now engaged in joint research and teaching programs.

REFLECTION AND A WAY FORWARD

The work undertaken by Crucible Research in both the United Kingdom and Hungary was complex. At one level, it began as the simple application of meditation procedures in order to develop community in different contexts, but at another level, it represented an attempt to bring together different ontological and practical ways of working together. The work raised real issues: how can individuals bring together different methods (Buddhist meditation and modern Western psychology); how can we preserve the integrity of work without being drawn into the imperatives of globalized organizations? Can this effect long-term transformation? What are the ethical implications of introducing potentially transformative practices into organization?

On reflection, it is not surprising that we met with limited success in the business organizational context, as what we were doing went against the prevailing tendencies within business practice. Crucible did not offer solutions to problems, but rather attempted to encourage deep questioning of people's values and goals. What we were trying to offer has the potential to challenge the culture of organizations, just as spiritual practice—the background that all the team shared—is orientated towards a thorough revision of fundamental values. We now feel that we had a degree of naïveté in anticipating that such an approach would be welcomed by organizations. What we offered at the time was potentially disruptive. With hindsight, it is not surprising that we were unable to find commercial organizations willing to work with us, despite our efforts.

However, in the current climate, organizations are beginning to notice what they need is radical change, and thus the methods that have been developed may well be more welcomed now. Indeed there are several well-documented examples of the use of mindful practices or contemplation in organizations.[14]

The approaches used by Crucible, although based on mindfulness and awareness, drew on Tibetan Buddhism and alchemical processes of transformation. This is a more radical approach than many mindfulness practices and is at once the strength and weakness of the work. The collective, participative approach of mindfulness combined with ritual added a depth to our work that has greater potential for transformation, but also is more difficult to implement. Tibetan Buddhism has a subtle understanding of the mind that moves beyond cultures and time.

The work has now flowered into different contexts (see Table 16.1), and, in particular, is being developed as "evolutionary inquiry" at the East West Sanctuary. The ideas are beginning to spread in ways that we could not have envisaged at the start of the project, which bears witness to the strength of the nonrational process itself. The work has unfolded and moved into different directions. To us, this shows us the power of the nonrational when it is allowed to come into consciousness and flow freely. This experience takes us back to the original Shambhala prophecy and to a deeper resonance with the forces of change that surround us currently. The ancient earth of Hungary provides the bedrock for this emergence. Hungary, geographically and historically, offers a bridge between the traditions of the East and the traditions of the West.[15]

Its potential strength lies in the possibility of finding ways of relating that go deeper than that of language, since the awareness practices work at emotional, bodily, and intellectual levels, and therefore of finding ways of communicating that undermine the common Western drive towards a task-based outcome. Relationship is privileged over outcome. Diversity is welcomed in an open approach that encourages a mutual exploration of experience. Transcendence is seen as a transcendence of self and a heightened and ever-growing understanding of the interpenetration and connection of our lives. Hopefully, this can penetrate deeper than the rhetoric of globalized consumerism and foster a united sense of community.

ACKNOWLEDGMENTS

Acknowledgments for this chapter go to Anglia Ruskin University for the Capability Funding to carry this work out. To the other members of the Crucible Team: Patrick Dunlop, Richard Huson and John Wilson. To the Hungarian Buddhist University for hosting and organizing the Hungarian Crucible Team. Thanks are due in particular to John Wilson for helping to theorize and develop the methods of Crucible Research represented here.

NOTES

1. World Economic Forum, *Educating the Next Wave of Entrepreneurs* Global *Education Initiative Report of the World Economic Forum Report* (World Economic Forum, 2009). Retrieved from, https://members.weforum.org/pdf/GEI/2009/Entrepreneurship_Education_Report.pdf

2. Gary Hamel, "Moon Shots for Management," *Harvard Business Review* 87, no. 2 February (2009): 91-98.

3. Joel Magnuson, "Making Small Beautiful," *Interconnections* 5 (2009). Joel Magnuson, economics scholar from Portland, Oregon is the author of the influential *Mindful Economics,* which provides a radical systemic critique of the pathology of the capitalist system (New York: Seven Stories Press, 2008).

4. Joanna Macy and Molly Young Brown, *Coming Back to Life: Practices to Reconnect Our Lives, Our World* (Gabriola Island, Canada: New Society Publishers, 1998), 60-61.

5. Bronwen Rees "Crossing the Theory Practice Divide: The Emergence of a New Worldview and its Implications for Business Education," *Interconnections* 1 (2008): 9-16.

6. Jurgen Habermas, *Knowledge and Human Interest* (Boston, US: Beacon, 1972).

7. Michel Foucault, *Discipline and Punish: The Birth of the Prison* (London: Penguin, 1977). Other critical writers from this school include: Paul Du Gay, Graham Salaman, and Bronwen Rees "The Conduct of Management and the Management of Conduct: Contemporary Managerial Discourse and the Constitution of the 'Competent Manager'," *Journal of Management Studies* 33, no. 3 (1996); Barbara Townley, "Foucault, Power/Knowledge and its Relevance for Human Resource Management," *Academy of Management Review* 18, no. 3, (1993): 518–545; M. Alvesson and S. Deetz, *Doing Critical Management Research* (London: Sage, 2000).

8. Bronwen Rees, *The Construction of Management: Competence, Gender and Identity at Work* (London: Elgar, 2004).

9. R. Layard et al, "The Depression Report: A New Deal for Depression and Anxiety" Centre for Economic Performance, London School of Economics, June 2006.

10. David Loy, *The Great Awakening: A Buddhist Social Theory* (Boston, MA: Wisdom, 2003), 99.

11. Bronwen Rees, Patrick Dunlop, and Richard Huson, "Unity in diversity and Diversity in Unity: Consciousness and Myth in Organizational Life" Workshop on A New Agenda for Organization Theory in the 21st Century,

Brussels, Belgium, February 7-8, 2002 and "Its a Relational World" Warwick, March 13-15 2002.

12. See, for example: John Heron, *Co-operative Inquiry: Research into the Human Condition* (London: Sage, 1996); Richard Winter and Carol Munn-Giddings, *A Handbook for Action Research in Health and Social Care*, (London & New York: Routledge, 2001). Professor Richard Winter has acted intermittently throughout as mentor and adviser, and has himself written on the theoretical and methodological connections of Buddhism and action research. See, for example, "Buddhism and action research: towards an appropriate model of inquiry for the caring professions in *Educational Action Research 11*, no. 1 (2003).

13. "The Ontology of Inquiry" Unpublished PhD thesis, (Cambridge: UK Anglia Ruskin University, 2010).

14. There is a growing body of practices of mindfulness in organizations, especially in the health sector. See, for example the Centre for Mindfulness Research and Practice based in Bangor, Wales, U.K. http://www.bangor.ac.uk/mindfulness/ . Much of this work is based around the groundbreaking work of Jon Kabat Zinn.

15. Katalin Illes and Bronwen Rees, "Unlocking History: The Shadow of Hungarian History," *Journal of Eastern and Central European Management*, 2001. For further development of these ideas: look at eastwestsanctuary.com and eastwestinterconnect.co.uk

CHAPTER 17

BEING A
BODHISATTVA AT WORK

Perspectives on the Influence of Buddhist
Practices in Entrepreneurial Organizations[1]

Kathryn Goldman Schuyler

Reprinted with permission from the *Journal of Human Values*, 2007: *13*(1), 41-58.
Copyright © 2007 by Sage Publishing

To me, going to work is like a bunch of guys making a rocket-ship, and it's really hard, and nobody wants to talk about anything else, it's about the rocket-ship. In that context, people aren't first, the rocket-ship is first. Buddhism is saying "you have to put how you are with people" first. If you just think about the rocket, you go nuts. So for me, the challenge is to go back and forth. The whole world of Buddhism is like a cooling antidote to the overheated "working on the rocket-ship until you die."

(Interviewee)

Often in work situations people feel that since they paid you they've bought the right to mistreat you or treat you like a machine.

(Interviewee)

Although having the mind that wishes to shun suffering, they rush headlong into suffering itself. Although wishing for happiness, out of naïveté they destroy their happiness as if it were a foe.

(Shantideva, 8th century: p. 11)

INTRODUCTION

I explored the fit between the lived reality in entrepreneurial organizations and the centuries-old Buddhist concept of the *bodhisattva* in order to see whether the juxtaposition of these two very different realities might shed light on the impact of spiritual values in the workplace. It is critically important for entrepreneurial organizations to be learning organizations. Moving from nothing to something—from no organization, simply an idea or dream, into functioning as a concrete, productive organization—requires tremendous learning and innovation on the part of all involved. Entrepreneurs must be able to create not only new products, but also new organizational roles and forms, and then to move through iterations of change in these roles and forms as the organization grows. This process of ongoing development and change seemed to hold intriguing parallels with Tibetan Buddhist practices for developing wisdom.

Since Buddhist concepts are unfamiliar to many behavioral scientists, in this chapter I initially clarify what it means to be a bodhisattva (very roughly: a person committed to helping all sentient beings become enlightened and thereby free from suffering), then share the results of my pilot study, and afterwards discuss the theoretical and practical implications. The main concepts to be presented are the bodhisattva notion itself, *bodhicitta* (the altruistic wish to relieve others' suffering), *emptiness* and *impermanence* (the nature of objects and mind), *dependent origination* (a Tibetan Buddhist term for what we regard as systems thinking), and the impact of *self-cherishing* (preoccupation with one's own well-being, rather than that of others).

I conducted exploratory interviews with an array of entrepreneurs who had been practicing Buddhists for over 3 years. I sought to discover whether these entrepreneurs were using core elements of Buddhist practice in their daily work and, if so, how they experienced the value and impact of these notions within the workplace. I asked the same simple series of questions of all participants without mentioning the notion of the bodhisattva ideal, in order to see whether it would turn out to be a core construct in their approach to everyday work and leadership.

The interviews showed that this notion and its constituent elements were very much a part of the participants' daily work lives and seemed to be a force in creating a happier, more nourishing work environment. All participants brought up the notion unasked and provided stories describing how it influenced their relationships with people at work.

THE SOURCES OF MY INTEREST IN THIS TOPIC

I grew up in the 1960s and came of age in a generation which felt we must step up to the largest challenges, if we wished others to. I and many people whom I knew felt that the world might be dying at the hands of our human brethren and that we must take whatever risks were necessary to reinvigorate ourselves and one another so that humanity could face and deal with these challenges. Many of us believed that incredible imagination and creativity would be needed, as well as the re-shaping of existing organizations in order to transition to a world less involved with mutual destruction. As I experienced the message of our generation, it was very similar to the Tibetan Buddhist ideal of the bodhisattva, yet without any contextual framework, training, or support from traditions and culture.

It was several decades ago that I first heard this term used to describe beings who exist in order to help all other beings become enlightened. I was drawn to the notion, but assumed it was a fictional ideal from the past. In 2002, I was astonished to learn that a course about how to live like a bodhisattva was being taught nearby by a Tibetan *geshe* (which I learned was equivalent in their educational system to a PhD). I immediately began to attend the course.

I am interested in both entrepreneurs and bodhisattvas, because both can help humanity evolve sufficiently so as not to destroy itself and our planet. The past century's acceleration in the development of technology, including the technologies of both warfare and communication, means that human beings are in a position to create great enterprises. Such endeavors can function to serve individual greed, continue old feuds—or serve the evolution of humanity. Our generation seems to have this choice, yet few of us ever feel that our actions have such a major impact. Effective entrepreneurs are those among us who have the potential to effect such changes.

The term *entrepreneur* comes from the French word "entreprendre"—to undertake. According to a recent dissertation, scholars have offered a wide range of definitions of entrepreneur and have found it difficult to reach agreement.[2] A typical definition is "somebody who sets up and finances new commercial enterprises to make a profit."[3] I see this as too limited, for there are entrepreneurs in many arenas. The most famous are those who become rich, but not all do. When I speak of *entrepreneurs*, I am referring to people who have the know-how to create enterprises out of nothing. From my standpoint, the more they put this skill and power to work for the good of all beings, the better.

I believe that the world hungers for such people—people who have the skill to create vital, viable enterprises and the values and commitment to serve the evolution of humanity. A bodhisattva is a being who is enlightened, who sees the suffering of all beings (not only humans, but all beings) and who uses his or her wisdom and skills to help evolve the whole planet, the billions of beings thronging our globe, the people of all nations, religions, ethnicities, races, genders, ages—all the divided groups that seem to be clamoring for recognition of their individual types of needs. The bodhisattva does "feel our pain," as people say lightly, but feels our pain so deeply and is so aware of the value of life of all beings, that all of such a being's entrepreneurial skills go towards developing enterprises that will help others become enlightened. We might say that a bodhisattva is an *enlightenment entrepreneur,* in contrast to the bulk of today's entrepreneurs, who are business entrepreneurs.

I have wondered for some time whether Buddhist practices can be fully transferred from the high frozen slopes and tundra of Tibet to the crowded, bustling, Internet-interconnected urban areas of our Western "communication society." Can these values and practices take root in our culture, when they were nourished for centuries by a culture that was isolated from most others, with a lifestyle where there were no roads, no cars, no telephones, travel took place by walking, and so on? The gulf between the cultures is huge, and the contrast in assumptions and *weltanschaungen* (world-view) is equally large. A research-based exploration of the lived experience of entrepreneurs in applying these concepts as leaders of contemporary organizations seemed like one way to begin to answer this question.

My question comes from a series of intertwined interests. As a child, I used to look out the window at the starry night sky and wonder why people fought wars and hurt each other so much. As an adult and applied social scientist, I ask the same questions and seek practices that may make some inroads on this situation.

As a social scientist, I am fascinated by the experiences of an ancient culture struggling to survive after being thrown out of its homeland. Its members find themselves living in societies that have dramatically different ways of life, values, and practices from those with which they grew up. The potential implications of the Tibetan response to having their country taken from them presents an alternative to terrorism and other forms of extremism—something critically important for today's world. I am also drawn to the Tibetan version of Buddhist teachings as a systems thinker concerned with the survival of humanity and the planet, because they address patterns of change on a global level, with implications that there are influences and levels of being beyond what we know to exist. As an organizational consultant, I am on the lookout for practices that people can use to develop organizations that help the planet thrive, enable people to serve worthwhile purposes, and also provide nourishing places to work.

Nor am I alone in this. Although Tibetan Buddhism was little known when the Chinese invaded and took over Tibet in 1959, it now has a global presence.[4] However, its impact in organizations has scarcely been studied, so this research is a pilot study.[5]

THE BODHISATTVA CONCEPT AND ITS CONTEXT

The bodhisattva ideal is strangely practical and enduring. It is not a story of megalomania and outer power (as many entrepreneurial stories are), but of inner development. It is a story that is intrinsically cross- or multicultural, as it has traveled to the United States from India via Tibet. And it is a tale that has lasted for at least 1,200 years, for one of the best books about it was written in the first half of the eighth century C.E.[6] It is not about gods, nor is it a fairy tale—it is a story about human beings like us who want to be and do something more than be born, do a lot of things, and then die. It lives even within the world of business for those who don't believe the current credo that "he who dies with the most toys wins."

What is this story and how is it relevant to entrepreneurs and to the survival of our increasingly small planet? It is said that there are people who, through contemplating life and the world, develop a very special kind of mind—a mind of great compassion. The Sanskrit word is *bodhicitta*: *bodhi* or wisdom/enlightenment and *citta* or heart/mind. One definition of bodhicitta is "the altruistic intention, or determination, to reach enlightenment for the sole purpose of enlightening all sentient beings."[7] A mind of bodhicitta wishes enlightenment for all beings, so that none will suffer. This awareness and this wish for others' enlightenment takes primacy over all other aims. Wanting this to be so is said to be the foundation for all genuine Tibetan Buddhist practice, whereas living in a way that this is really so makes one a bodhisattva—a being of wisdom, one who is enlightened, but chooses to forego peace, ease, and delight in his or her own life to aid others on their path. Rather than meditating and practicing in order to leave one's own suffering behind, a bodhisattva chooses to remain in the middle of the difficulties of ordinary life, simultaneously "practicing" and providing service to others, until the time that not one unenlightened being remains on the planet.[8]

The path to living as a bodhisattva involves recognizing and developing what are often referred to as the *six paramitas* or *six perfections*: generosity, ethical discipline, patience, joyful perseverance, mental stability, and wisdom (discriminating awareness). These are taught in numerous places among the Buddhist teachings and provide the structure for the guidelines to living as a bodhisattva. This means that to be a bodhisattva is not a matter only of meditation or contemplation, but requires transforming the way one lives and interacts with others on a daily basis. Core practices involve cultivating love (taking on responsibility for helping all find happiness, including those who have harmed us) and compassion (through contemplating others' suffering and imagining oneself in their situation) and training the mind through specific mental practices to exchange oneself with others.[9]

The fundamental component in aiding others is not material generosity, but instead involves enabling people to realize their own nature and the nature of reality. Only those who grasp what is real and what is not can help others to do so. Such help may include material generosity, as it can be useful, but material generosity that is not rooted in wisdom generally does not help others live well or wisely. By recognizing what might be described as the fundamental *emptiness* or *suchness* of all seemingly concrete things, the bodhisattva teaches others to avoid cherishing themselves and holding onto things that inevitably will not last. Having the wisdom to realize such underlying truths allows one to contact the richness and re-creating that is at the heart of life. An assumption is that by enabling others to realize the source of mental and emotional well-being, one helps them more permanently than if one provides only material assistance. This approach to life places considerable demands upon one and gives a clear path and set of guidelines. The Buddha taught that neither he nor anyone can transmit wisdom to other people directly; all have to discover for themselves how to live wisely. At the start, a student develops *aspiring bodhicitta*: the desire to be enlightened and aid others. Full bodhicitta, whereby a person is *actually* aiding others and is already enlightened, is understood to be extremely rare.[10]

In order to develop such a mind, one must come to realize that all things are empty and impermanent—that things have no innate capacity to endure independently and only exist in interdependence with all other things. To grasp at material things and attempt to hold onto them is pointless; this would be grasping at that which cannot last. Such emptiness is the essential nature of mind and is considered to be the foundation for all spiritual practice.

> The underlying premise of all *Vajrayana* thought and practice [the highest and most subtle part of Tibetan Buddhism] is that the essential nature of each being's mind is pure and clear and that the main task along the spiritual path is to discover and identify with this essential purity, or *Buddha-nature.*[11]

In order to relieve human suffering, the aspiring bodhisattva recognizes the importance of lessening attachment to people, things, and states of being—all of which are transitory. A person can become both happier and more free by reversing "deluded habits of thought that come from misunderstanding reality."[12]

> In our ordinary perception of the world, we tend to perceive things as enjoying some kind of absolute status, as having concrete, objective reality. If we subject them to deeper analysis, however, we find that things do not exist in the way that they appear to us. All things and events lack inherent nature, and this absence of inherent nature is their ultimate reality, or emptiness.

> … when you subject all phenomena to reductive analysis and search for their true essence, you will arrive at a point where you cannot find a solid, concrete reality. However, our own personal experience affirms the reality of things, because we experience their effects. Some things cause us pain, others cause us happiness, so they must exist in some way. At the same time, however, these things and events do not possess the inherent, independent existence that we tend to project onto them.[13]

Note that this is not a claim that objects have no concreteness: simply that we *construct* our realities, as contemporary social scientists increasingly affirm.[14] There is a distinct parallel between the Tibetan Buddhist view of the use of the mind in generating a "concrete, objective reality" and the perspectives that come from constructivism. A belief that things that are concrete may be constructed into alternate realities fits well with the entrepreneurial enterprise of generating new products, new companies, new markets. Entrepreneurs not only construct their own realities:

they construct ours as well! Tibetan Buddhist teachings recognize that this construction of realities happens with all objects and forces in interdependence with everything else, which is referred to as *dependent origination*. Dependent origination is very similar to what modern social scientists describe through systems theory: that "all entities are in a state of mutual simultaneous shaping."[15]

Existing behavioral science studies of spirituality tend to contrast Western scientific thought with what is referred to as "New Age" thought.[16] In the realm of spirituality, behavioral scientists expect to see notions that are "soft and fuzzy" and that substitute "feelings and emotions for conventional methods of science."[17] These do not. Like Western philosophy, Tibetan Buddhism has extensive scholarly traditions, with schools of thought that have debated the meaning of concepts (like those described here) for centuries.[18] Buddhist scholarly procedure is "that any system of thought that is subject to fewer critical objections is more acceptable than one that contains more contradiction and inconsistency."[19] Definitions and discussions of emptiness, dependent origination and all other Tibetan Buddhist concepts have been extensive and thorough. They have developed over many centuries within a context of sophisticated, rational, scholarly debates. This chapter presents an overview, but Western scientists should be aware that there are long scholarly traditions behind my brief descriptions.

RESEARCH RESULTS

In order to gather data on the lived experience of entrepreneurs for whom these concepts are important, I conducted exploratory interviews with a snowball sample of entrepreneurs active in business and Buddhist organizations. They met my qualifications if they had founded, led, or worked extensively in an entrepreneurial organization and had maintained a Buddhist practice for at least 3 years. When a Buddhist refers to his or her "practice," it means activities, such as meditation, prayer, or visualizations, that are carried out regularly, usually daily, in combination with ongoing study. I identified potential participants by asking the initial ones for suggestions, and concluded the series of interviews when I began to perceive repeating patterns in the responses—there seemed to be conceptual saturation.

This process led to conducting seven semistructured interviews—a format that allowed participants to explore the questions in depth. One commented that his experience of the interview was "like one of those dates where the man spends the evening talking about himself and then says he had a great evening, because he talked the whole time." He was surprised that there were little or no interruptions, and that he was given encouragement to develop and explore his thoughts completely.

I asked the same five basic questions of all participants, but they responded differently with regard to how easily they gave concrete examples from their lives, as compared with discussing their thoughts and concepts. Initially, I asked each to briefly describe their current and recent roles in entrepreneurial organizations, as well as the duration and nature of their practice of Tibetan Buddhism. I then asked whether and how their practice influenced the way that they interacted with people at work, and how they experienced and handled stress at work. Next, I asked whether they had thought about connections between entrepreneurship and their practice before this interview, and if so, what implications they saw. I closed by asking whether they had other comments or thoughts that they had like to share, and also asked for suggestions as to other appropriate people to interview.

The participants include a founder of a small business (a gelato parlor), the founder and current manager of a major Tibetan Buddhist retreat center, an organizational leadership coach, a media artist with a world-wide reputation who makes interactive work that use a person's body to interact with projected light, a successful marketing executive, a manager who has worked in nothing but high-tech start-up companies, and a woman who was a Tibetan Buddhist nun while working as an engineer. All have been in close contact with the first generation of Tibetan lamas (teachers) who matured in Tibet and left to teach in the West. They are board members of some of the major Tibetan Buddhist organizations in the United States and are also successful entrepreneurs. Most have experienced difficult challenges, both personally and organizationally. All went out of their way to accommodate my request to participate on short notice, shared their time generously, and seemed to enjoy reflecting on my questions. Most are serial entrepreneurs. Several had thought about entrepreneurship in depth and were delighted that someone was finally asking, while others found my juxtaposition of entrepreneurship and Tibetan Buddhism to be surprising.

THEMES

The Importance of Their Practice

Many said things like practice "colors everything I do," "practice is an essential piece in my work," and "my work is my practice." They described meditation as being useless if it only took place when one was "sitting on a cushion," emphasizing its role in "taming" their minds and transforming the way they related to people.[20]

> The point is that when I get off of my cushion, that there is not that dramatic departure but to try to carry over the awareness into all my activities – sort of awareness in action, … That's the whole point—if you just meditate for 60 minutes or two hours and that's just an isolated component and it doesn't carry over into your daily activities, it's sort of a waste of time.

Many said something similar to "the message I got was our work can be our practice." However, this did not eliminate the need for specific spiritual practices as well. All meditated and did other practices daily, following through on what is known as the *bodhisattva vow*. "Having a meditation practice where one is training the mind, it's possible then to look at the issues that arise that may be uncomfortable, to see them for what they are, which is a ripening of one's own personal karma, with no basis out there." This theme of focusing on training their own minds rather than on trying to "fix things out there" is an important one. "There is no pressure to fix things. Instead, I need to change my mind."

Centrality of the Bodhisattva Ideal in Their Practice and Contribution of Other Key Concepts

All interviewees brought up the bodhisattva concept on their own, without prompting, as a core part of their practice and a source of energy in their daily work. Other concepts that all mentioned were emptiness, compassion, bodhicitta, and impermanence. They did not simply mention them as concepts, but instead spoke of them in the context of their experiences. All attempted to live and work in such a way that they were using their work to help others be happy and enlightened. This took varied forms: art, interaction, teaching, preparing food, bringing young people into a business and helping them develop their own values and approach to life. All felt that their goals were different from most people they met, but that often people seemed to change through working in their organization, with them, or with others whom they felt exemplified the bodhisattva ideal.

As mentioned previously, a core element in this was compassion—cherishing others more than themselves. Although they agreed that most of their life was influenced by studying the bodhisattva way of life, "it takes a long time to really understand." They saw that aspiring to live with an attitude of bodhicitta (or exchanging themselves with others) helped in concrete ways, such as making them better listeners. I heard the word "intention" often: the intention to live with compassion, to be kind, to be altruistic, to remember that all is impermanent.

The understanding of impermanence and emptiness were perceived as "what distinguishes Buddhism" from other ways of living. For example, the artist noted that

> People are always trying to add more permanence to the pieces. I really resist that. I explain to people that the impermanence of the pieces is very important. Like there's a piece that records your shadow. After the last one's recorded, it starts to override the earlier ones. Some people get really disturbed by that and want to know if I can save the images. And then I tell them that the piece is really about that impermanence and about pushing you to more action in the present, rather than trying to record or re-live what you did in the past. If you watch how people interact with those works, you see that born out. People really do get so caught up in the moment because they know it's just projected light—it's so empty in its essence. It's not even really there in the first place, you know even more so than the way we think about our bodies—it's light. It has no material essence—I think that people start to intuitively absorb that idea of impermanence.

Managing People

Most had a lot to say about the impact of their Tibetan Buddhist practice on the way they related to or managed people. The word "kindness" came up again and again. This seemed to be the core of their practice, which is not surprising, since according to the bodhisattva teachings, ordinary people are more precious than the greatest teacher. They agreed that the process of learning was slow and did not easily fit into Western expectations. "It's very hard for Westerners—we're used to instant gratification, we're smart, and we can "get it" and want the highest teachings. It takes a long time to really understand." Although they said that emptiness was what they thought distinguished Buddhism from all other religions, the most concrete stories had to do with kindness and patience—patience towards themselves and patience when others did something wrong or got angry.

It appears that they create workplaces where people like to be. As one said, "I've only had to fire two people out of over a hundred. People stay here. They say it's much nicer to be working here." The gelato parlor is staffed partially by monks who work in Western clothes and otherwise by university students. "You can never get them to say anything negative about anybody."

> Monks work in the business and make the ice cream. The young employees notice their kindness and calmness. The kids are very interested in the monks' special qualities. They dress in Western clothes—the kids see how they treat people ... and how kind they are.... Having them around—it's great—I'm always remembering how to be.

Several said they tried to get people not to speak ill of others at work, which was something they found people tended to do otherwise. "We try very hard not to do that—to speak of a third person." Another said "my employees are so dedicated, and I really don't pay much either. I don't expect that kind of dedication. They've been staying and really not wanting to leave. When they've had to leave, they've said, 'this is the best job I ever had.'"

One focused on acknowledging the contribution of people to his projects. He said that he aimed to say "thank you" strongly, letting his staff know that he would not have been able to pull of the project without them and to make it clear he was very grateful for their contribution. As he said, "Paying them is only a small token for their efforts, since they have choices of many other things to do, and choose to spend their time with me."

Handling Stress

As one said, "The whole world of Buddhism is like a cooling antidote to the overheated 'working on the rocket ship until you die.'" Another commented that his employees were helping him relieve stress by applying his concepts with him, even though they are not practicing Buddhists themselves. Yet another described how it helped after being laid off from a job after 14 years. "Losing your job after fourteen years is pretty stressful. The biggest help was meditation practice and having studied the dharma [the Buddha's teachings] for so long. It provides a way to handle our own minds: what I'm thinking, why. It gives me a more objective and removed way to focus my mind and that helps a lot with stress." Impermanence was a key theme in managing stress. "I meditate on death every day. I don't have illusions that my body will last all that long. It helps me have lightness."

Transforming Anger Through Patience

Most brought up the topic of anger and their desire not to allow it to impact them. As one described it, "It's supported my own struggle to help me live the way I want to live and be." Another commented,

The classic thing—you go to work and get pissed off over stupid things. The Buddhist path is just torment—you can no longer do that thinking that the other guy is the asshole and you're just an innocent person.... I know now that it's not that simple. The whole philosophy of emptiness tells us that our experiences are an expression of how we are to others. So when we meet others, it robs us of our innocence. I have to ask how have I been like that? And it's torture. It's much more fun to be blithely innocent and be surrounded by idiots. But that pleasure is horrible, because you become a resentful person.

Another emphasized the impact of his work with anger on his relationships with his employees when they did something wrong and they were actually at fault. He viewed this as the best opportunity to practice patience, show a lot of kindness, make it really clear that it's ok, and talk about it immediately.

It's time for me to try to be really kind and patient and show them the alternatives—really focus on solutions, rather than getting angry or frustrated. I've found it really is the opportunity that it's hard to see it as. The relationships get so strong with my employees, like their dedication, and the emotional connections really get strengthened after those times. Once they realize that I'm not going to get angry or be punishing them, they realize that it's created a chance for us all to grow together and make the company better. It's created a huge amount of loyalty, dedication, and teamwork that I never realized before on other jobs, because I didn't have the same tool as from studying Shantideva [*Guidelines to the Bodhisattva's Way of Life*].

The same interviewee described how this happened in cross-cultural settings, since he works internationally.

In other countries and other cultures, they have really different ways of communicating, so it's a lot more normal to get angry. I've found that being patient in those situations really pays off. With the angriest people, it usually takes three attempts. They'll get super angry and I'll deflect it.... After three times, that person totally changes. All of a sudden my relationship with that person really changes and we become kind of friends or allies to solve the problem together.... I can't tell you how many times I've seen this happen!

Connection Between Buddhism and Entrepreneurship

Here we had varied views, depending upon where the person worked. Only the interviewee who was isolated from the Buddhist community, working in a technology company, saw a conflict between the two: "To me it seems like somewhat of a contradiction to put spirituality first and be an intensely devoted creative entrepreneur.... For them, it's completely about the game, the play, the company—and I'm not. If you really take spiritual development seriously, it's in opposition." Most saw entrepreneurship and entrepreneurial settings as a good fit for practice.

The artist commented that the ideas he had always been interested in "turned out to be core Buddhist ideas." Engaged in developing his art and his business, he not only saw no conflict, but described how his Buddhist practice enhanced both his art and his way of managing the business side of his work.

> It certainly made me clarify the way that I talk about my artwork and the type of work that I make, so it became much more clearly about emptiness, interdependence, and compassion—especially with my goal of connecting people with each other, making strangers communicate with each other, creating a sense of joy and energy. Trying to create spaces where people enter a kind of mindful space where the experience is so engaging and so social that they stop regretting the past and they stop anticipating the future for a few minutes and really connect with other people.

Perhaps the core notion for the interviewees was the idea that all practice involves changing one's own state of mind, while focusing on cherishing others rather than oneself. When asked about the relationship between Buddhism and entrepreneurship, I heard their thoughts on leadership, compassion, and intention towards service for all beings. Several mentioned the importance of their teacher or lama in setting an example for them and for leadership. One of the more intriguing examples of such entrepreneurial leadership is the worldwide organization of Gelugpa teaching centers: two monks who had no previous organizing experience generated a large and well-organized international entrepreneurial web of teaching centers.[21] Many of the participants had been profoundly impacted by their experience of these two lamas, as well as by the entrepreneurial leadership of the Dalai Lama. I was speaking with entrepreneurs, but they tended not to speak about entrepreneurship itself, but rather about the concrete details of their everyday experiences, which happened to be in entrepreneurial settings. This meant that one emphasized patience, another kindness, another leadership—because these were their foci. Since they were "aspiring" rather than "fully-realized bodhisattvas," it is natural that they would emphasize different things.

CONCLUSIONS AND IMPLICATIONS

It was not easy to go behind the stories to the underlying way that they constructed realities. Some spoke very concretely about what had happened in their lives. Others tended to expound Buddhist teachings. Still others used the opportunity to reflect on the deeper issues brought up by the nature of entrepreneurship when looked at alongside of Buddhist practices. What is crucial, from the perspective of this study, is that all emphasized the importance of the bodhisattva concept in their work lives and said that practice was essential both for understanding it and for manifesting it in action.

Fit With Previous Studies of Spirituality in Organizations

In auditing the current state of spirituality in American corporations, Mitroff and Denton described five possible models.[22] Their research led to the following list of organizational types: (1) "religion-based organizations" that tend to be at an early stage of religious development in which people are taking the religion and its rules very literally, (2) "evolutionary" organizations that are transforming from a religious base to ecumenical values, (3) "recovering" organizations that adhere to the 12-step process for recovering from addictions and use this process as a model for most interpersonal interaction, (4) "socially responsible" organizations that are dedicated to the betterment of society as a whole, and (5) "values-based" organizations that have leaders who are guided by a set of clear values or philosophical principles. The Tibetan Buddhist practitioners interviewed for my study offer perspectives that do not fit easily into this typology.

Except for the Buddhist meditation center directors, the participants didn't want their organizations to become entirely Buddhist, nor did they want others to adhere to their own values. All aimed for the betterment of society as a whole, but the means were not necessarily through social change, but individual transformation. To me, it seems that this approach reflects a different set of underlying assumptions about the nature of religion and the social world than those from which Mitroff and Denton wrote. This distinction between the Tibetan Buddhist "view" and other "religions" may be important. As described by one of the eminent Tibetan teachers who received both a traditional Buddhist education and an Oxford degree, Buddhists use the term "view" rather than "philosophy" or "religion" to describe their overall perspective on life precisely because neither of the other terms describe its nature accurately.[23] It is not obvious that Tibetan Buddhism fits the definition of what we have come to call "religion." It cuts across fields that Western notions about knowledge regard as separate and distinct.[24]

Practice and Tacit Knowledge

While some Western philosophical traditions assume that study and reading are sufficient for learning, this is not so in the Tibetan Buddhist traditions. The element of practice is treated as a core element in learning, so it is assumed that one cannot come to comprehend the view through reading and study alone. Understanding requires a combination of experience with the development of specific skills, developing something, which has recently been dubbed *tacit knowledge* in the field of knowledge management.[25] In Western traditions of trade apprenticeships, students need teachers who are skilled in particular crafts, so they will absorb both what can be written and also the teachers' tacit knowledge. Such tacit knowledge is highly personal and context specific. In contrast to formal knowledge, which "derives from the separation of the subject and the object of perception," tacit knowledge comes through the understanding of patterns as meaningful wholes, which comes from what Polanyi calls "indwelling"—an embodied type of knowledge.[26] From the perspective of knowledge management, all knowledge can be divided into explicit (objective) knowledge and tacit knowledge. The latter "breaks the traditional dichotomies between mind and body, reason and emotion, subject and object, and knower and known."[27] This notion is close to the importance in Tibetan Buddhist practice of going beyond subject-object perceptions and thinking.

Although I have not seen Tibetan Buddhist authors use the concept of tacit knowledge (most likely because it belongs to Western behavioral science), I believe that the reason they insist on the importance of a teacher for those who wish to master the "higher" practices is that these practices involve considerable tacit knowledge. Until the last 20 years, the Tibetan texts were not available publicly, because it was assumed that one could not master them without a teacher. Looked at in terms of the necessity of embodying tacit knowledge, this is quite reasonable. The following comments need to be read in this context.

Visualization—Its Importance in Tibetan Buddhist Practice and Entrepreneurship

A core element in the subtlest portions of Tibetan Buddhist practice is the visualization of what are referred to as "deities."[28] A deity in Tibetan Buddhism is not an object of worship. Instead, the term refers to beings that exist in a different way from that of physical beings. They are mind-created and, in that sense, can exist forever, because they are not born and do not die. There are a great many such deities who represent different aspects of being and forces that support enlightenment, such as compassion for others or wisdom to see things as they are. One visualizes oneself as these deities in order to remember the parts of oneself that are beyond living and dying and that partake of the huge complex system that is life in our universe. Each deity "functions as an archetype, evoking responses at a very subtle level of our being and thereby aiding in the delicate work of inner transformation."[29]

There are very precise practices that develop the mind's capacity to function in this way. I have not seen research specifically on this topic, but I believe that such practice trains the mind to combine what we sometimes refer to as left and right brain thinking, because of the complex process of picturing, turning things into symbols, and the detail involved. Western neuroscientists have recently begun studies that measure the brain function of highly trained Buddhist meditative adepts using fMRI, and EEG neuroimaging techniques and other psychological, neurological, and immunological measures.[30] In one such study, EEG measures of brain changes in an experienced practitioner of specific types of Tibetan Buddhist meditation showed that "the very act of concern for others" well-being ... creates a state of well-being within oneself."[31] The research is suggestive of a possibility that some have long suspected: that such persons have a powerful effect on those around them.[32] Rather than the typical pattern that we observe in organizations, whereby those who are anxious or upset in turn disturb many others, this offers the potential for leaders who are more aware and awake to transform those close to them by the qualities of compassion and awareness that they bring.

The practices that train the mind in visualization seem to involve the following stages, from my experience. One learns—

1. to visualize increasingly complex deities and scenes.
2. to make the deities appear out of symbolic Tibetan letters.
3. to make them disappear into light.

With permission (through contact with a genuine teacher), one visualizes oneself becoming the particular deity and then having the deity disappear into light, so one becomes oneself again. Practices may involve visualizing oneself as different beings, with different supercharacteristics, such as lovingness, wisdom, or purity. All of this trains one in uses of the mind that are very different from that of typical analytic thinking, which most university-educated Westerners generally regard as the *sine qua non* of mind activity. Unless one is particularly open-minded or has had unique experiences, it is hard to conceptualize how differently the mind can learn to function, with appropriate training.

Entrepreneurial leaders inevitably use the imagining and imaging capacity of their minds. Training leaders in such practices, combined with living in accordance with the bodhisattva concept, could yield leaders who would be less likely to contribute to the cascading debacle of "Enrons" and "Parmalats" that we have seen over the past few years. Moreover, such leaders might be far less likely to become ill from handling toxicity.[33] One of the research subjects is engaged in such work through his consulting firm.

Similar Underlying Forces

All Tibetan Buddhist teachings aim to assist humans to value human life as being the only opportunity to understand the nature of reality. Because it is so precious, human life is to be used to enable all beings to become enlightened. To be enlightened is to understand what causes suffering (which is attachment, or holding onto things and people out of a feeling that they are permanent, without recognizing their transitory nature) and to live in contact with what is real, while helping others to do the same. This is not necessarily a fit with leading an entrepreneurial learning organization, where the focus is not transcendence but effectiveness in producing the right product at the right time, with the right distribution channels. However, there are intriguing underlying similarities.

As I studied these phenomena, I began to suspect that under the layers of actions and material manifestations, both entrepreneurship and Tibetan Buddhist practices might be conceptualized as different expressions of a fundamental level of agency, as it manifests in two radically different cultures. I am using the definition of *agency* as "the capacity, condition, or state of acting or of exerting power."[34] Looking at agency as the underlying thrust towards undertaking or acting upon something, one might see this creative, energized "acting upon" in the U.S. context turning outward, focusing upon changing the world around itself, undertaking activities with things and building enterprises. In contrast, in the traditional Tibetan culture, creative agency was directed inward towards "taming" one's own mind in order to impact the surrounding world. Such a culture used the human force of agency to generate enlightened beings and took seriously the notion of the bodhisattva—beings that exist to generate more enlightened beings.

From this perspective, *agency* might be viewed as the ground of all action. Because of the power of the bodhisattva ideal and related training, agency in Tibet became a force for individual enlightenment, to the great-

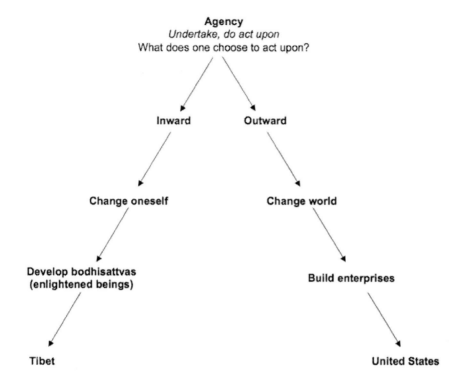

Figure 17.1.   Contrasting uses of Agency in Tibet and the United States.

est extent possible, whereas in the West, similar forces were channeled into social and economic development. What we see in these Buddhist entrepreneurs is a fusion of these two traditions, whereby both influenced the participants' thoughts and actions. They have been striving to develop thriving businesses or organizations in order to further the enlightenment of all sentient beings.

In addition to the overarching thrust that I sense, in terms of the different focus of agency, one participant pointed out another strong source of similarity.

> Entrepreneurs do not take things on authority. People in insurance or law take authority incredibly seriously. Entrepreneurs look at the world and use mind or intuition. The whole world is open. It doesn't matter if something hasn't been done. This is similar to Buddhism—there is a willingness. "Don't take my words at face value—test them as you would gold, to see if it's real gold," said the Buddha. One whole strand in Buddhism is "don't base your life on received authority, base it on your own experience."

This strong trust in one's own experience is a deep underlying theme that bridges the very different phenomena we see in Tibetan Buddhist life and entrepreneurial organizations. It is as though two underground streams were flowing that fed both sets of appearances. A raw force of agency flowed, in one part of the world exerting power in the world of the mind and in the other, in the world of things. Throughout both worlds, there is an orientation towards questioning everything and not accepting things on authority. The willingness to risk all for what one finds most important connects these diverse sets of people.

Implications: Globalization

But can these teachings travel from the closed, spiritual society of Tibet to the open, materialistic society of the United States, Europe, and other portions of what we call "the West" and retain their integrity? Today's world is one of increasing globalization. One way of looking at globalization is through the writings and thinking of sociologist George Ritzer. He has described globalization as the propagation of *nothing*—by which he means "a social form that is generally centrally conceived, controlled and comparatively devoid of distinctive substantive content."[35] An example that he gives for this kind of globalization is a shopping mall that has basically similar content no matter where it is located in the world. He labels this as *nothing* in contrast to the highly particularized *somethings* constituted by locally-developed, very individualized things that were prevalent in the past. A contemporary example would be a gourmet meal that uses local ingredients: a thing that cannot travel without being substantively changed. From Ritzer's perspective, this kind of "nothing" is being spread primarily by Western corporations and is becoming common world-wide. Local, unique "somethings" are disappearing.

Ritzer intends that neither "nothing" nor "something" be considered inherently good or bad, but he does point to the importance of the loss of these "somethings." This loss is structural in society and is not necessarily felt by those experiencing the current global transition. While Ritzer acknowledges that this is not all that globalization does, his intention was to explore and characterize this one aspect of it in a way that makes a distinctive contribution to the scholarly literature on trends in today's world.

Tibetan Buddhism is a prime example of what Ritzer means as a "something." It was a unique form of spiritual practice and scholarship that developed in a portion of the world that was closed to outsiders for centuries. In other words, it was a locally-developed and very unique culture. The practices, while fully grounded in the Buddhist teachings and practice that came out of India, changed over time in Tibet. Moreover, the very notion of *emptiness* itself could be juxtaposed with Ritzer's term "nothing," because to the uninformed Western mind they seem similar. If something is empty, we in the West are likely to say that there is nothing there. However, as mentioned previously, within Tibetan Buddhism this notion of emptiness is the very foundation of wisdom. All teachings of the Buddha were "aimed either directly or indirectly at the attainment of this wisdom."[36]

It is paradoxical, as well as unfortunate, that the continued existence of the Tibetan teachings now depends on their ability to survive outside of their native environment. A form of thought and learning that developed and thrived in a closed culture is now taught more outside of its traditional home than within it—and the home no longer retains the characteristics that enabled it to thrive. Lhasa, the capital, known for its towering Potala Palace and huge, ancient monasteries, is now dominated by modern concrete high-rises. The central government of China has encouraged such a large migration of Han Chinese into Tibet that Tibetans risk becoming a minority population in their own country. Since the Chinese conquest, many of the most learned Tibetans have been killed or imprisoned and tortured. Many of the Tibetan-educated teachers have already died of old age and others will in the near future.

What happens when such teachings are exported to a radically different culture? Can such a radically different perspective on life thrive within a culture with opposing values? Here history suggests an intriguing possibility. Although Tibet became a nourishing home for Buddhism over the course of about 10 centuries, when these practices initially arrived there, it was a fierce and in many ways implausible site for them. When the earliest teachers began to teach Buddhist practices, Tibet was ruled by warlords and had a thriving religion (*Bon*). If we read the texts of the teacher who is regarded by many as the main progenitor of Buddhism in Tibet, during the eighth century he commented to his main student "Ah—you are the only one who practices—no one practices."[37] In their own way, the Tibetans valued material things, prestige, and power, although this took different external forms than it does in contemporary society.

Perhaps Western societies will prove to be as conducive an environment for the further evolution of Buddhist teachings as was eighth century Tibet. New practices developed in what was at that time the "new environment" provided by Tibet: perhaps something analogous will happen here over the next few centuries. As Tibet's unique form of aliveness was infused into Buddhism without changing the core constructs or values, perhaps what is alive about Western culture (such as entrepreneurialism) will nourish analogous new forms—also without altering the core of the teachings. It is an intriguing possibility in the realm of the sociology of knowledge and religion, but one that only time will reveal.

NOTES

1. An earlier version of this chapter was presented at the Academy of Management annual conference, 2006, and was published as Kathryn Goldman Schuyler, "Being a *Bodhisattva* at Work: Perspectives on the Influence of Buddhist Practices in Entrepreneurial Organizations," *Journal of Human Values* 13, no.1 (2007): 41-58.

2. Frauke Schorr, "Becoming a Successful Entrepreneur—A Phenomenological Study," PhD Dissertation, Alliant International University, San Francisco, 2008.

3. Merriam Webster's Collegiate Dictionary (2006). Encyclopedia Britannica, DVD version.

4. Many people worldwide have demonstrated interest in such practices, as can be seen from the vast increase in numbers of books published about Tibetan Buddhism, the movies produced on this theme, and the large number of study centers distributed around the globe. A search for "Tibet" on Amazon.com brings up over 1,900 books, 34 DVDs, and 248 CDs. A number of popular movies have been made in the last fifteen years, some of them by major directors, including Bernardo Bertolucci's *Little Buddha* (1994), *Seven Years in Tibet* (1997), *Martin Scorsese's Kundun* (1997), *Tibet, Cry of the Snow Lion* (2002) and other films, including a re-make of the Somerset Maugham's The Razor's Edge in 1984. There are two major publishing houses devoted to Tibet and Tibetan Buddhist titles in the United States and many smaller ones. Books about applications of Buddhism at work are increasingly popular, such as Michael Carroll's *Awake at Work* (Boston: Shambala, 2006). Most large cities across the world have from one to ten Tibetan Buddhist centers. The Dalai Lama draws such huge crowds that he has taught one major teaching known as the Kalachakra Initiation twenty-eight times to a total of roughly 1,350,000 people.

5. What happens when such teachings are exported to a radically different culture? This study is part of a larger project in which I am exploring this question. I am investigating how such a radically different perspective on life and values can thrive within a culture with opposing values. This includes additional interviews on other questions and narrative analysis of autobiographies written by leading Tibetan teachers.

6. Shantideva, *Engaging in bodhisattva behavior*. Translated from the Tibetan, as clarified by the Sanskrit, by Alexander Berzin. (Printed from www.berzinarchives.com, 2005) (Several other excellent translations of this 8th century text exist, both from the Sanskrit and from the Tibetan).

7. Tenzin Gyatso, (His Holiness the Fourteenth Dalai Lama of Tibet), *Illuminating the Path to Enlightenment,* ed. R. Novick, Thubten Jinpa, N. Ribush; trans. Geshe Thuben Jinpa (Long Beach: Thubten Dhargye Ling Publications, 2002).

8. Geshe Sonam Rinchen, *The Bodhisattva Vow*, trans. R. Sonam. (Ithaca: Snow Lion Publications, 2000).

9. Ibid.

10. Shantideva, *Engaging In Bodhisattva Behavior.*

11. Jon Landaw and Andrew Weber, *Images of Enlightenment: Tibetan Art in Practice* (Ithaca, NY: Snow Lion Press, 1993): 8.

12. Gyatso, *Illuminating the Path to Enlightenment*, 9.

13. Ibid., 142, 152-3.

14. Peter L. Berger and Thomas Luckman, *The Social Construction of Reality: A Treatise in the Sociology of Knowledge* (New York: Doubleday, 1966); D. McGuinness, K. Pribram, and M. Pirnazar, "Upstaging the stage model" in *Higher Stages Of Human Development*, ed., C. Alexander and Ellen Langer (New York: Oxford University Press, 1990); J. G. Berger, "Living Postmodernism: The Complex Balance of Worldview and Developmental Capacity", *Revision* 77, no. 4 (2005): 20-27.

15. Yvonna Lincoln and Egon G. Guba, *Naturalistic Inquiry* (London: Sage, 1985).

16. Ian Mitroff and Elizabeth A. Denton, *A Spiritual Audit of Corporate America: A Hard Look at Spirituality, Religion, and Values in the Workplace* (San Francisco: Jossey-Bass Publishers, 1999).

17. Ibid., 18

18. Kenneth Liberman, *Dialectical Practice in Tibetan Philosophical Culture: An Ethnomethodological Inquiry into Formal Reasoning* (New York: Rowan and Littlefield, 2004).

19. Gyatso, *Illuminating the Path to Enlightenment*, 145.

20. This refers to the fact that most people sit on a cushion when they meditate.

21. Tibetan Buddhism includes four lineages of teaching. In each one, the wisdom teachings have been passed on directly from the teacher to the student for many centuries. Until recently, no one could learn a set of practices unless taught directly by an authorized teacher. The Gelugpa is the school that emerged latest (in the fourteenth century) and includes the Dalai Lama.

22. Mitroff and Denton, *A Spiritual Audit of Corporate America*.

23. Sogyal Rinpoche (November, 2004), Lecture at Clear Lake, CA.

24. Most Western scholarship makes a sharp distinction between religion and science, but the Buddhist "view" (as it is called by the Buddhist practitioners, rather than referring to it as philosophy or religion) incorporates elements of both. In my role as a sociologist of knowledge, this is one of the more intriguing aspects of Tibetan Buddhism.

25. Michael Polanyi, *The Tacit Dimension*, (Garden City, NY: Anchor Books, 1966).

26. Ikujiro Nonaka, and Hirotaka Takeuchi, *The Knowledge-Creating Company: How Japanese Companies Create the Dynamics of Innovation* (New York: Oxford University Press, 1995), 59-61.

27. Ibid., 60.

28. Reginald A. Ray, *Secrets of the Vajra World: The Tantric Buddhism of Tibet* (Boston: Shambala, 2001); Landaw and Weber, *Images of Enlightenment*; Judith Simmer-Brown, *Dakini's Warm Breath: The Feminine Principle in Tibetan Buddhism* (Boston & London: Shambala, 2001); Lama Thubten Yeshe, *Introduction to Tantra: The Transformation of Desire* (Boston: Wisdom Publications, 2001).

29.   Landaw and Weber, *Images of Enlightenment*, 6.
30.   Zara Houshmand, Anne Harrington, Cliff Saron, and Richard J. Davidson, "Training the Mind: First Steps in a Cross-Cultural Collaboration in Neuroscientific Research," in Zara Houshmand, R.B. Livingston, and B. Allen Wallace, (eds.) *Science and Compassion: Dialogues between Tibetan Buddhism and Biobehavioral Science*, (Ithaca, New York: Snow Lion Press, 1999).
31.   Daniel Goleman, *Destructive Emotions* (NY: Bantam Books, 2003), 12.
32.   Daniel Goleman, Richard Boyatzis, and Annie McKee, *Primal Leadership: Realizing the Power of Emotional Intelligence*, (Boston: Harvard Business School Press, 2002).
33.   Peter Frost and Sandra Robinson, "The Toxic Handler", *Harvard Business Review* 77, no.4, (1999): 96-107.
34.   Merriam Webster's Collegiate Dictionary (2006). Encyclopedia Britannica, DVD version.
35.   George Ritzer, *The Globalization of Nothing* (Thousand Oaks: Pine Forge Press, 2004), 3.
36.   Gyatso, *Illuminating the Path to Enlightenment*, 141.
37.   Padmasambhava, *Advice from the Lotus-Born: A Collection of Padmasambhava's Advice to the Dakini Yeshe Tsogyal and Other Close Disciples*, ed. Marcia Binder Schmidt and Erik Pema Kunsang, (Boudhanath: Rangjung Yeshe Publications, 1994).

SECTION V

REFLECTIONS:
THOUGHTS FROM EAST AND WEST

In the past, families and small communities could exist more or less independently of one another.... Such is no longer the case. Today's reality is so complex and, on the material level at least, so clearly interconnected that a different outlook is needed.... In view of this, I am convinced that it is essential that we cultivate a sense of what I call universal responsibility ... [which entails] a reorientation of our heart and mind away from self and toward others.[1]

—HH the 14th Dalai Lama

The closing section begins with reflections from a Tibetan master—**Lama Tharchin Rinpoche**. He inspired the founding of an important teaching center that offers Western students the opportunity to learn and participate in ancient Tibetan ritual and dance, and shares what it has been like for him to come to teach the Dharma in the West. Tibetans do not commonly speak about themselves or their personal experience; it is not part of their culture. Therefore, this chapter offers a precious opportunity to get a glimpse of ourselves as students from the "other side of the mirror," so to speak. This perspective enhances and deepens what "outsiders" to the higher practices of Tibetan Buddhism can appreciate about what has allowed it to provide such meaningful teachings for centuries within Tibet

Inner Peace—Global Impact: The Influence of Tibetan Buddhism on Leadership and Work in the West, pp. 293–296
Copyright © 2012 by Information Age Publishing

and what is needed for it to do so in the Western context. It is not a given that merely because a teaching or book is labeled *Vajrayana Buddhism* or even *Dzogchen* that it retains the living essence that generated a transformational process within Tibetan culture. This particular chapter may be challenging to read for those completely unfamiliar with the traditions of Tibetan Buddhism. I have included it because Lama Tharchin shares his experience of the difficulties of teaching such wisdom traditions to those unconnected with the culture in which they originated—something not often found in print.

As discussed in earlier chapters, Tibetan Buddhism often uses a *mandala* to convey progressive levels of depth as an organizing principle. From this perspective, the visible presence of His Holiness the 14th Dalai Lama and the growing activity of major global organizations such as the FPMT, Shambhala, and Rigpa could be seen as the outer sources of the impact of Tibetan Buddhism in the West. The increasing amount of practice by Westerners might be the inner source, where one brings oneself into the field of action. The teaching and presence of people like Lama Tharchin and others may be regarded as expressing what is meant by the secret level, and the presence of translated texts from great masters like Padmasambhava, Longchenpa, and Jigme Lingpa could be seen as an even more secret level.[2] Remember that the term *secret* does not mean that something is hidden gratuitously, but rather that it is only useful for people once they develop a certain level of understanding. *Wisdom teachers and teachings* bring something into today's world that otherwise most of us would have no access to—the tacit knowledge of other cultures, from other times and places on our planet—lived realities that are grounded in a different version of what is "obviously so," as sociologists of knowledge might describe it.[3]

From the perspective of social psychology and management studies, the challenges of introducing Westerners to Vajrayana Buddhism can be seen as an example of the difficulty of sharing such *tacit knowledge*: knowledge that can only be passed on directly from one person who knows how to do something, whether it is meditation, cooking, or painting. Anything that involves a combination of knowing and doing at a high level of subtlety tends to involve such tacit knowledge. Rather than seeing the term "secret" as implying a desire to keep such wisdom teachings private, I invite you to reflect on the importance of having a tradition of such secret or tacit knowledge as a way of passing down important learnings for centuries without diluting them. If diluted or changed, new learners would not have access to what was originally known!

In closing, three eminent Western social scientists who have advanced the teaching and practice of leadership development reflect on the importance of meditation and Tibetan Buddhism for leadership development, social science, and change. All are based on interviews I conducted with these scholar-practitioners, each of whom has been contributing in significant ways to understanding Tibetan Buddhism's implications for the West and all of whom have been meditating for many years, giving them a unique fusion of Western and contemplative knowing.

Bill George is the former CEO of a major U.S. corporation, Medtronic, who became a professor of management practice at Harvard.[4] Known for his books on executive development, he has meditated for 30 years in the Christian tradition and collaborated with Yongey Mingyur Rinpoche, a prominent young Tibetan teacher, to create a leadership workshop during the summer of 2010. His contribution focuses on the way that Buddhist practices further the development of compassion and suggests ways they could be incorporated into executive education.

Peter Senge's writings on open systems and individual development in the early 1990s generated considerable interest among both scholars and executives in what could be done to create more open cultures where individuals took responsibility for ongoing growth and development.[5] With 30-plus years of Buddhist practice, Dr. Senge spoke to me in depth about Buddhist culture and what it has the potential to contribute to education, focusing on the importance of its theory of human development—and how this is lacking in western education. He contributed a trenchant critique of business schools, grounded in their lack of focus on both practice and human development. A great many concrete actions could be developed based on his insights about Buddhism and management education.

The book closes with **Margaret Wheatley's** critique of Western culture, grounded very much in her own experiences as an international organizational consultant.[6] She describes why she became a Buddhist many years ago, how her awareness practice has become increasingly important to sustain her ongoing work in organizational and community development, and discusses in some depth a concept that will perhaps be new to many social scientists—that of lineage, or being part of an ongoing tradition, rather than valuing individual thought and novelty above all. Her contribution adds another way of looking at Western education and its current focus on developing *cultures of evidence*, by suggesting that evidence may be fine, but that we in the West are leaving out much of what is most important about human beings in what we are willing to regard as *evidence*.

I chose to close with her contribution because of the way that she so personally conveys the combination of compassion and wisdom that is embodied in Tibetan culture and its contrast with her experience of the culture of the social sciences today. I wanted to leave you, as reader, either energized by her vision or outraged by her bold conclusions, in the hope that you will continue to explore questions that I hope this book raises, such as:

- What can the role of wisdom teachings become in the practice of leadership development?
- What can social scientists learn from these wisdom teachings about human nature, and how might this shift our theories and ways of doing research?

Finally, I hope that you have enjoyed this banquet of offerings about this intriguing meeting of traditional Tibetan culture and the twenty-first century's electronic, consumer-oriented, and fast-paced societies and that it will lead to continuing research and study, as well as increasing personal awareness practice.

NOTES

1. *Ethics for the New Millennium* (New York: Riverhead Books, 1999), 161-162.
2. For a book that conveys visually the quality of the contemporary Tibetan masters, see Don Farber, *Portraits of Tibetan Buddhist Masters* (Berkeley: University of CA Press, 2005) which includes photos and brief biographies of many, including Lama Tharchin Rinpoche. Another beautiful photography book that conveys the quality of people being discussed here is Sandra Scales' *Sacred Voices of the Nyingma Masters* (Junction City, CA: Padma Publishing, 2004).
3. As described in the Introduction, and based primarily on the work of Peter L. Berger and Thomas Luckmann, *The Social Construction of Reality: A Treatise in the Sociology of Knowledge* (New York: Anchor Books, 1966).
4. See books by Bill (William W.) George: *Authentic Leadership: Rediscover the Secrets to Creating Lasting Value* (San Francisco: Jossey-Bass, 2003); *True North* (San Francisco: Jossey-Bass, 2007); *Finding Your True North: A Personal Guide* (San Francisco: Jossey-Bass, 2008); *Seven Lessons for Leading in Crisis* (San Francisco: Jossey-Bass, 2009).
5. As mentioned in the Introduction, see Peter Senge, *The Fifth Discipline: The Art and Practice of the Learning Organization* (New York: Doubleday, 1990/ 1994); *The Necessary Revolution* (New York: Doubleday, 2008); Peter Senge, C. Otto Scharmer, Joseph Jaworkski, and Betty Sue Flowers, *Presence: Human Purpose and the Field of the Future* (Cambridge, MA.: Society for Organizational Learning, 2004).
6. See Margaret Wheatley, *Leadership and the New Science: Discovering Order in a Chaotic World* (San Francisco: Berrett-Koehler Publishers, 1999/2006); Margaret Wheatley and Myron Kellner-Rogers, *A Simpler Way* (San Francisco: Berrett-Koehler Publishers, 1998); Margaret Wheatley, *Finding Our Way: Leadership for an Uncertain Time* (San Francisco: Berrett-Koehler Publishers, 2007); and Margaret Wheatley, *Turning to One Another: Simple Conversations to Restore Hope to the Future* (San Francisco: Berrett-Koehler Publishers, 2009).

CHAPTER 18

TEACHING WISDOM CULTURE IN THE WEST

An Interview With Lama Tharchin Rinpoche
Pema Ösel Ling, July 28, 2009

Kathryn Goldman Schuyler

Inner Peace—Global Impact: Tibetan Buddhism, Leadership, and Work, pp. 297–308
Copyright © 2012 by Information Age Publishing

Kathryn Goldman Schuyler: What would you say, if anything, has changed in the way you teach since coming to California in order to communicate with the people that grew up here in the West?

Lama Tharchin Rinpoche: We don't have to change anything. All that is needed to teach the Dharma already exists in the nine *yanas [KGS: the traditional Buddhist path]*. The Dharma is so vast. Buddha Shakyamuni taught 84,000 different levels of teaching, and the Dzogchen teacher Garab Dorje taught 6,400,000 Dzogchen tantras, and the result is exactly the same—the path of Dharma.

For example, if we want to go someplace, that's the goal. Let's say we're planning to go to San Francisco. There are many ways to get there. There is only one place, San Francisco, but people may travel by many different vehicles: one person wants to go to San Francisco by airplane, another by train, by car, by bus, by bike, and some people, some Tibetans—yes we may walk there! I have friends who walked all across the country because that is what they wanted to do! The single goal of the Dharma path is to reach fully enlightened Buddhahood. The same as with traveling to San Francisco, there are many ways to get to that same state. That is the purpose of the 84,000 teachings of the Buddha.

In Buddhism, everybody doesn't have to do the same thing. Buddha's point is that every single sentient being's mental capacity and physical structure of nerves, channels, and energy is different. In relation to this physical structure, mind-energy becomes inseparable from whatever kind of nerve and energy structures we have. Everyone is different with regard to mental capacity and to belief systems as well. The Dharma has to be suitable for you! Today, most people like fast airplanes, but some may say, "I want to have fun and go by foot; I've never done that before." That's their choice.

Buddhism has nine yanas *[KGS: paths]* which include all of the 84,000 different teachings.[1] All of these teachings are synthesized into three yanas, and people have different mental capacities as well. So there are different paths for different levels of ability, just like when you go to school you have to be in the level that is suitable for you. All three yanas include the understanding that sentient beings engage with the three poisons: anger, desire, and ignorance. These are poisons from the perspective of all three yanas, because they act as obstacles for us in life and become obstacles for fully attaining enlightenment. In the *Hinayana* approach to the path, the approach is to "fix" things, because the training is at a physical level and uses the physical body and speech, or the material aspects of training. It is gradual training, and our attention is on our behavior and speech. Then the next level, or *Mahayana*, is suitable for more broad-minded people. I'm not comparing people and saying that some are better than others, but people are different. Those for whom the

Mahayana is suitable find that not only physical training is helpful, but training their mind is even more helpful. The mind is like a king while the body and speech are like servants. Whatever the king commands, they do. So direct training for the mind is faster; the technique is more profound. Training in *bodhicitta* (or compassion, the mind of awakening) is a direct path for our mind. Then, beyond the ways of mind that are based on dualism [considering things to exist in a subject-object relationship], one finds *Vajrayana* training. Here the student engages with the essence level of mind, which is called "awareness," fully enlightened mind, or the nature of mind. This needs to be introduced by a teacher who has experienced it, because although we have it, we don't recognize it without this introduction. Although it is not complicated, we don't recognize it. Vajrayana introduces us to this essence level of mind. Where the Hinayana path takes three eons of time to attain full enlightenment, in Vajrayana and especially the Great Perfection, it can be attained in one lifetime.

Ultimately Western people have very capable minds. Their minds are in some ways like a knife that they sharpen all their lives. They are educated and use their minds in ways that are very sharp and clear. They have good capacity, and, like all people, are not all the same. Among them, some say they "like" Vajrayana and Great Perfection teachings. They feel that they love this path, but they love it with a kind of material clinging. They say, "Oh, that's the highest path—I love it!" But when they practice, their behavior isn't always what a teacher wants to see.

For example, years ago *Tricycle Magazine* published an article about American Buddhism that brought out my disappointment with certain aspects of some Western practitioners. They published a highly critical interview with my own teacher, Dungse Thinley Norbu Rinpoche, who is a true embodiment of wisdom mind, and also printed articles and letters to the editor basically saying, "We don't need the lama tradition and lineage in the West. We can attain enlightenment by ourselves." However, the biggest obstacle in the Dharma is the sense that we have nothing to learn from our teacher. To say "We can do it by ourselves" means that we only understand *material* phenomena. We can train our good heart—that we can do—but nobody has even a small clue of how to go beyond the mind that you already know to the nature of mind, unless they are introduced to this nature of mind by a teacher who has fully realized wisdom nature.

Why don't we have a clue? Because we don't have lineage. This is not just somebody's idea. Lineage comes to us from the *dharmakaya*.... *[KGS: Lineage carries the teachings from one wisdom mind to another, across centuries, starting with an emanation from the dharmakaya—the basic and all-pervasive nature of all phenomena.]* "Buddha" doesn't refer to a person: Buddha actually means the three *kayas* or bodies of enlightenment (*dharmakaya*, *sambhogakaya*, and *nirmanakaya*). We talk about attaining full enlightenment. That means manifesting these three kayas, which exist naturally, but are hidden. Nobody has the key to open this up for oneself by oneself. Nobody knows how to look at the inner luminosity and clarity that is expressed by what is called the sambhogakaya buddha phenomena, originating from the dharmakaya. Sentient beings have no ability to manifest these two kayas on their own (sambhogakaya and dharmakaya). They are always present but they are covered by the defilements of dualistic mind.

Buddhas can take material form so that for humans, they appear as a human; for animals, they appear as an animal; and so on, appearing in whatever way is suitable for beings. In that way they can make a connection. Without this connection, Buddha remains Buddha, and sentient beings remain sentient beings. There is no connection and no way to get beyond being a sentient being—beyond one's materialistic, dualistic mind. But that nirmanakaya form *[KGS: The aspect of enlightenment that can be perceived by ordinary beings. Rangjung Yeshe Wiki]* will deliver the dharmakaya and sambhogakaya directly to us. As soon as that is introduced to us, our Buddha nature can blossom. That is called practice. Therefore, we do truly have to rely on realized wisdom teachers.

The Western idea of democracy—which relies on collective consensus from partial, worldly knowledge and opinion—is not the same as the wisdom mind of a teacher holding lineage and realization. Looking around, we can see that this worldly approach never leads to unchanging consensus and happiness. Collecting the opinions of confused beings only leads to a larger pile of confusion. We cannot vote to select the Buddha who will follow our agenda! Even if so many people vote for a worldly president, there is no guarantee that it is the best one.

I'm not complaining. Dharma is totally new here, so nobody has any real clue. Western culture is primarily material, so in the beginning it's difficult for the approach to Dharma to not also be a material approach. In the West, immaterial wisdom culture doesn't exist! Then how can this fit your culture? But in the West, we do have democracy phenomena, so people feel they should be able to decide who should be a teacher. Sometimes people even vote about this and the one who gets the most votes wins.

Kathryn Goldman Schuyler: But the people don't know.

Lama Tharchin Rinpoche: Exactly. This immaterial wisdom culture is a totally different culture. There's no connection with the Buddha or the nature of mind unless we rely upon lineage. Ordinary sentient beings do not have the innate capacity to choose enlightened teachers, just like those uneducated about jewels don't have the ability to distinguish between diamonds and glass. However smart we are, it is impossible to use the intellectual dualistic mind to realize nondual wisdom mind. We must rely on a wisdom teacher because, although we have Buddha nature, ultimate wisdom does not exist in our dualistic minds. *Samsaric* ego *[the ego caught up in believing material perceptions to be real, rather than "mere perceptions"]* always tries to protect itself, and will trick us into thinking that we have gone beyond dualistic mind when, in fact, we have not.

Although we intrinsically have Buddha nature, without a teacher, it is like churning water to get butter—it won't manifest. Of course, this teacher can be male or female, Asian or Western, or from any country, because realization is not related to culture. Before judging, we must know the appropriate qualities of a teacher and examine our own motivation as students. It is critical that the teacher hold pure, unbroken lineage, and have realization of wisdom and compassion for all beings impartially.

These types of wisdom teachers often do not fit with our confused culture, so we criticize them. For example, although now we all claim to appreciate a teacher such as Milarépa, if he actually came to the West, we would quickly have him admitted to a mental institution! Even in Tibet, many people did not recognize Milarépa's qualities and wanted to control him. This is still the case with many wisdom teachers when people with worldly habits view them. We often say that from samsara's point of view, Milarépa is crazy, and from Milarépa's point of view, samsara is crazy. If people had been allowed to vote on whether or not Milarépa should be allowed to teach, the answer would probably have been no. It was through karmic connection and developing their own spiritual view that practitioners could recognize the qualities of a teacher such as Milarépa, not through ordinary consensus.

There are many kinds of Dharma teachers and they are beneficial to us in different ways. But the highest teacher is one who is "fully realized," not someone who merely has good intentions. This means that they do not only teach us about the mind, which can be good, bad, or neutral; they teach beyond mind, to nondual wisdom mind. This is possible because they hold pure wisdom lineage which is alive and unbroken. Wherever Buddhism has spread, in Asia or elsewhere, whether Hinayana, Mahayana, or Vajrayana, it was transmitted through unbroken oral and written lineage from teacher to student. Tibetans had to respect and rely upon Indian lineage holders in order for Dharma to take root with Tibetan lineage holders. Today, we still think with appreciation for this lineage, praying and receiving its blessings. Our respect for this lineage is not partial to any country or worldly tradition, and it does not arise from blind faith. Its value is demonstrated again and again by those who hold pure lineage and do pure practice.

But you are asking about my experience. When I first came to America I had a hard time. At first, I didn't speak the language at all. Then I could speak a little of the language, but communication was very ordinary.

There was no way to make a Dharma connection. I said to my friends, "If somebody can give me a plane ticket, I want to go back to Nepal." But then my teacher, His Holiness Dungse Thinley Norbu Rinpoche, told me to stay, and his father, His Holiness Dudjom Rinpoche, also wanted me to stay and teach here. His Holiness Thinley Norbu Rinpoche said,

> I want you to stay in America. There are two reasons: First, I'm planning to stay in America, so I want you to stay too. Second, American people need the Dharma so badly. And lots of teachers get involved in Dharma politics, and then they cause confusion. You can teach pure Dharma. Everywhere sentient beings have suffering, but in the West the suffering is heavier, deeper. In the East suffering is related to being poor materially, but the mental suffering in the West is far deeper. For mental suffering, nothing can help besides Dharma. If you focus your teaching where it is most needed, the merit and benefit is higher.

That's what Rinpoche told me. Then I was so funny—I asked him "Since Western people have no faith in Dharma, how can I teach?" Then he gave me such beautiful wisdom advice. He said, "We are in a season of spring, a beginning. You can continue to teach, and summer will come. They don't know Dharma. If they're pretending to know Dharma, that's fake. You can teach Dharma, so then they will understand Dharma, then they will have faith, and then they will do practice." That's true prophecy. That's a profound prophecy.

Kathryn Goldman Schuyler: That's exactly it—that change.

Lama Tharchin Rinpoche: Exactly.

Kathryn Goldman Schuyler: How do you go from not having faith to being able to have faith or confidence and really do practice? How do you have that happen?

Lama Tharchin Rinpoche: So then I had to stay. I couldn't say "I don't want to," to my teacher. I didn't have much confidence, but I did see that it made sense. Then I stayed, and I learned. My English was still not good of course, but I could begin to communicate. Then I had more friends, and they had questions. So I told stories about the Dharma, and then personal connections developed. Then there were more and more Dharma connections. Now, after almost 30 years of teaching, I have a great many friends. As soon as we connected, the relationship became very stable, and their Dharma practice got deeper and deeper. The more they practiced, the more they wanted to practice, and they could get the genuine taste of Dharma. But not many people have the taste. It's like that everywhere.

Kathryn Goldman Schuyler: In Tibet too?

Lama Tharchin Rinpoche: Everywhere. You know, many people believe in buddhadharma, but they are not necessarily strong practitioners. Now it's getting easier, as they have confidence. Anyone connected with me is getting a deeper connection with practice. Lots of people have done 3-year retreat. Many who have done a 3-year retreat want to do more. Lots of our *sangha* have done 6-year or 9-year retreat. They don't want to stop. As soon as you have that Dharma taste of your wisdom nature, or awareness, the fully-enlightened essence of your mind, when you've got that taste, it's like nectar—nobody wants to spit it out after they have a taste. [laughs]

Kathryn Goldman Schuyler: How did you get started doing 3-year retreats with students?

Lama Tharchin Rinpoche: Some years ago, during the monkey year (1992), which was very special because it was Guru Rinpoche's birth year, I thought, "I'm not young. Nobody knows whether I'm going to be here or not for the next Monkey Year. I want to start something special this year." I came up with three good things to do. I said, "I want to build a Guru Rinpoche statue; I want to start a *drubchen* eight manifestations dance; and I want to start holding 3-year retreats." That year, I started all three. And that was 17 years ago. It's been so satisfying!

Figure 18.1.   20-foot Guru Rinpoche statue in the shrine room of Pema Ösel Ling, designed by Kyabje Thinley Norbu Rinpoche and Lama Tharchin Rinpoche. (Photographer Michael Broderick. Courtesy Vajrayana Foundation)

You asked me for my story. First we started the Vajrayana Foundation with seven people [laughs]—and now there are a lot of people! [Hundreds of people studied at Lama Tharchin Rinpoche's center in California, Pema Ösel Ling, during the summer of 2011.] There has been so much increasing connection that is helpful for them, for the buddhaharma, and for me, and it has been very satisfying for my root teacher His Holiness Thinley Norbu Rinpoche, who is in America. He is so kind to us. He comes every year or so to give a teaching at Pema Ösel Ling, and he is like *teaching yeast*, in a sense. We are getting this wisdom being of light, and then I can be like a tutor and take care of what he has started for us all with his *yeast*. That is what is satisfying. I don't want to chase after more people or become famous—I'm just not interested in that. What gives me satisfaction is helping anyone who is really doing practice. I put all my energy and time into them, and especially the 3-year retreatants, my Dharma friends. Then we have a long Summer Retreat, a Spring Retreat, a Thanksgiving Retreat, a Winter Trekchöd Retreat, and others. I keep adding pieces of wood, trying to keep that warmth of His Holiness Thinley Norbu Rinpoche's wisdom fire alive. I don't let the fire go out. It's been very successful.

In Dharma practice, you are 100% reliant on the kind of teacher that you have. It is important to rely on a good teacher who has the ability to open our own wisdom and compassion. They will lead us on the path beyond dualistic mind, even beyond samsara and nirvana, to full liberation. Although Buddha nature is inherent in all of us, it has not blossomed due to always relying on our own dualistic mind. So we must develop the ability to choose teachers with wisdom and compassion, who are not teaching out of confusion or for their own fame or gain, or to further their Dharma politics.

Good or bad teachers may appear to us, but we can only perceive them at the level of our own mind. If our minds are negative, then it is like someone with jaundice who perceives a pure white snow-covered mountain as yellow. The qualities and faults that we see in another person depend entirely on our own mental capacity. It is never necessary to reject or condemn others, since we may later appreciate them with a different view. Dharma practice actually means to purify one's own mind until all phenomena are perceived as pure. Practice turns our usual focus on others around to focus on ourselves. Usually we take our own faults, which are like the size of a mountain, and try to hide them. Then we find others' faults, which are like the size of a sesame seed, and display them for everyone to see and talk about. Instead, we should try to practice from a Buddhist point of view. Even though one person may have a hundred different faults, still they have at least one good quality. Instead of judging the hundred faults, we should find that one quality and emulate it. Then we will be connected

Figure 18.2.   The Stupa Peace Park at Pema Osel Ling is a mandala of the eight traditional types of stupas, representing the eight miraculous events in the Buddha's life. Details about the Stupa Project are available on the web at http://www.vajrayana.org/stupa-project/stupa-inscription/ (Photographer Michael Broderick. Courtesy Vajrayana Foundation)

only with positive phenomena, not negative, which will lead us to greater purity. This is the Buddhist way. If we practice pure Dharma to purify our own minds, then we will recognize the qualities of pure teachers and not need to reject impure ones. This wisdom was given to me from my root lama His Holiness Thinley Norbu Rinpoche. Please take this heart advice and put it into sincere practice without thought of worldly gain or politics. I am old now, and neither Rinpoche nor I have any need to collect more students or fame. We only wish to give advice that will actually benefit beings and release them from their suffering and confusion.

Kathryn Goldman Schuyler: I'm going to make a jump here, as I know our time is almost up. Is it valuable to teach leaders who already touch so many people through leading a big organization or team, and to help kindle this understanding in them?

Lama Tharchin Rinpoche: Yes. That is really skillful, because power can be negative or power can be positive. Power can become a source of negativity, hurting or destroying many beings. Some people are creating so much suffering for others by using power in such ways. But the same power can be positive. I will tell you this story. Guru Rinpoche taught the whole country of Tibet, establishing the Dharma in Tibet. With his power and through his actions, he made a country of darkness into a country full of sunshine and wisdom.

Kathryn Goldman Schuyler: That's what could be in America ...

Lama Tharchin Rinpoche: Exactly, exactly.

Kathryn Goldman Schuyler: ... it happened and it hadn't always been like that in Tibet....

Lama Tharchin Rinpoche: When it happened in Tibet, it was a country of demons. There are so many stories! For example, there is a story that Guru Rinpoche went to a cannibal island. Who had the power? The king of cannibals, who had nine heads. Each day, he rang a gong for his minister and commanded, "Today I need nine human beings to feed each of my faces! Prepare them!" What Guru Rinpoche did was to liberate his demonic consciousness and Guru Rinpoche's mind entered the king's mind. The next day the king woke up, rang the gong, and said, "Don't harm any other living sentient being." That is some power: the ability to turn demonic power into wisdom power. How important to have that! What would that look like today?

Things keep changing in history. Buddha Shakyamuni was in India, the whole Dharma was in India, with a life of its own. Then it moved to Tibet. Now in India, hardly anything remains of Buddhism. Centuries ago Guru Rinpoche, Shantarakshita, King Trisong Deutsen, Yeshe Tsogyal, and the 25 disciples helped all of Tibet become Buddhist. Scholars brought incredible Dharma into Tibet. Everything was translated into Tibetan, which became like a totally full "treasure house" for the whole world. Then a funny thing happened. As Guru Rinpoche's prophecy said, "In a future time, horses will have wheels and people will fly in the sky in iron birds looking down at the ground. At that time, my teaching in Tibet will become like a handful of beans thrown on the floor. They won't stay there; they'll go in every direction." There's really no way to predict.

The Chinese Communists intended to end Dharma in Tibet, and the result is that instead Vajrayana has expanded to the whole world! You know that means the beans won't stay there—they go in every direction all over the whole world. In the same way, I tell our sangha so many stories about the *mahasiddhas*, who demonstrated their accomplishment by flying in the sky, passing through rocky mountains, and so on. Deities actually appeared to them as solid beings and solid phenomena dissolved. How did they do it? Through serious practice. We are exactly the same. We're not missing any of the blessings, or lineage, or the source of instructions. Without lineage, we can't have such results from practice, but we've got everything here, so now is the time to do practice. I say, "I want to see that Susan attained the rainbow body *[became enlightened]* or George attained the rainbow body." I want to hear Western names as excelling in practice. That's what I'm in for! We have everything here. Nothing is missing. Now that Dharma comes here, Western people have to take responsibility. This never happened by accident; there's a purpose.

I will tell you a story that's very interesting. We had one oracle[2] in Tibet—a very old lady, in her 80s or 90s. When she walked, she couldn't stand without a cane, but when she became the oracle, the wisdom protector in female form called Yudrönma came into her body, and she would drum and jump and fly like a teenager. In Tibet, when I was young, maybe 6 or 7 years old, I went to see her with my Dad, as she did incredible magical things. I was lying on his lap, watching. Suddenly, she came over to us and said to her attendant to bring a *kata* [*a special silk scarf that one offers as a gift, with great respect*], and they brought a kata. Then she said, "This is not enough. This is a very special occasion—I need a special kata." So they brought a very special kata with the eight auspicious symbols on it, and then she said, "Give me a silver comb!" Then they brought combs, with eight auspicious symbols. Then she came over to us and did prostrations. Of course, everybody thought that she was prostrating to my father since he was a famous lama. But instead, she came to me and gave me the kata and said, "Do you remember how together we liberated so many sentient beings in a past lifetime?" At that moment when she said it, I did feel that I remembered, so I said, "Yes, I do remember." Then she said "This is for this life. This is my last meeting with you. I won't see you with this body, but I will see you in the Western direction. I will go wait for you!" She must be here somewhere.

Kathryn Goldman Schuyler: Ah you haven't met her yet.

Lama Tharchin Rinpoche: Who knows? [laughs] The real Dharma is coming to the West. The more it comes, the more it is deepening. Western people are very smart. They understand. I do believe, I do trust, and I have the experience that His Holiness Dungse Thinley Norbu Rinpoche told me that if you can teach Dharma where there is none, there is more merit than teaching it in places it already exists.

Kathryn Goldman Schuyler: But one needs to be able to do it.

Lama Tharchin Rinpoche: You asked how leaders can be taught to use power to transform negative circumstances in ways that benefit beings? It's just like that. It's very important, I do agree.

Kathryn Goldman Schuyler: Then perhaps we need leaders like Guru Rinpoche....

Lama Tharchin Rinpoche: Yes. We have to have Guru Rinpoche blossoming within our individual mind. That's our job! Practitioners have to be genuine, have to be pure, not only saying words, but truly believing. That is what makes manifest your own original Guru Rinpoche, in our heart. That's what our job is.

Kathryn Goldman Schuyler: Thank you.

Lama Tharchin Rinpoche: Thank you so much [smiling].

NOTES

1. For interested readers who are not familiar with Tibetan Buddhism, there are many helpful texts, such as *A Cascading Waterfall of Nectar* (Boston: Shambhala, 2006), *White Sail* (Boston: Shambhala, 2001), and *A Small Golden Key* (Boston: Shambhala, 1993), all by Thinley Norbu Rinpoche. Additionally, it is important to study with a qualified teacher, because not everything can be transmitted through written words in books.

2. Tibet had a number of *oracles*, people who went into a trance-like state and became very different from their normal selves. Each oracle has lighter physical and mental energy than other beings. Then other beings, such as wisdom protectors, can enter their body. Often people can ask questions of the oracle and they are able to make predictions. When that person's ordinary mind comes back, they don't have that same ability to predict the future. They only have it in that moment when the being has entered their body.

CHAPTER 19

REFLECTIONS ON LEADERSHIP, SELF-AWARENESS, AND COMPASSION

An Interview With Bill George

Kathryn Goldman Schuyler

Inner Peace—Global Impact: Tibetan Buddhism, Leadership, and Work, pp. 309–315
Copyright © 2012 by Information Age Publishing

In August 2010 former CEO of Medtronic and Harvard professor Bill George co-led a leadership summit on mindful leadership with Yongey Mingyur Rinpoche, one of the leading young Tibetan teachers, author of two important books **Joyful Wisdom: Embracing Change and Finding Freedom** *and* **The Joy of Living: Unlocking the Secret and Science of Happiness**.[1] *To my knowledge, this was the first time that a Western leader and business school professor and a Tibetan Rinpoche co-led such a workshop. I was invited to attend, based on interviews I had done for this book.*

As Professor George described the session afterwards on his website,

> The Mindful Leadership retreat enabled us to explore … complex subjects such as the impact of mindfulness on leadership, new neurological research on the impact of meditation on the brain, understanding and framing your crucibles, the role of emotional intelligence and self-awareness in leadership effectiveness, gaining self-compassion, shared awareness through small group support, leading others mindfully, and self-actualization to contribute to a better world.
>
> None of these subjects were easy, nor did we reach definitive conclusions. Our dialogue took the issues to a deeper level that engaged the participants and enabled each of us to gain a deeper understanding of ourselves. Mindfulness—the awareness of one's mental processes and how one's mind works—offers leaders a path to address these issues in a nonjudgmental, nonthreatening way. Meditation is the *secular* process that enables us to develop mindfulness and to approach challenging issues in a calm, thoughtful manner.
>
> After working with Rinpoche and the Dalai Lama during the course of the past year, **I have reached a preliminary conclusion that gaining mindfulness through meditation may be the most effective way to gain self-awareness and to develop self-compassion**. Another important aspect is through group support that provides honest feedback, compassionate support, and deeper understanding of oneself. Having practiced meditation and having been part of a support group for 35 years, I have personally experienced the highly beneficial impact that they have had on my leadership effectiveness.

Having observed hundreds of leaders under pressure, I have no doubt that self-awareness and self-compassion are the essential aspects of effective leaders, especially when they are under stress and pressure. Leaders who develop and maintain these qualities are better able to lead others mindfully and to empower people to perform at a very high level.

Kathryn Goldman Schuyler: What led you to develop and put on such a session?

Bill George: I was at a conference with His Holiness the Dalai Lama and met Rinpoche there. One day we were standing and talking, and a crowd formed around us, listening to our conversation. That gave us the idea for this session.

Kathryn Goldman Schuyler: What stands out for you from the retreat?

Bill George: I learned a great deal from Rinpoche about two areas that I'm interested in: self-awareness and self-compassion. Through his meditation practice, he has enormous depth and great insight into these areas. I'm particularly interested in how practices like meditation can help us develop our self-awareness and self-compassion. In addition, there's a parallel emerging field in neuroplasticity about how these practices can reshape the brain in more permanent ways.

Kathryn Goldman Schuyler: Do you find that teaching with Mingyur Rinpoche or being at the conference with the Dalai Lama have changed how you approach any of these topics or your own practice?

Bill George: It certainly has encouraged me to go deeper into them and given me a greater understanding of the role of compassion and how one gains it. During our workshop, Rinpoche led a four-part compassion meditation, moving from compassion for someone you care about to compassion for yourself to compassion for people you don't know to compassion for someone you don't care for or don't like. I thought it was a very deep and enriching approach to this subject, particularly for understanding where people are coming from, their life stories and life experiences, which is the work I've been doing in leadership for the past seven years. I believe now that self-compassion holds the key to being a solid leader. The lack of self-compassion often leads people to stray from their True North and stray from their beliefs and principles.

Kathryn Goldman Schuyler: I see your work and your focus on life story as going much deeper into life story than others. While others have talked about it, your exercises seem to take people deeper into their own individuality and respect for that.

Bill George: Absolutely. It becomes central to how they see themselves. It's been overlooked by academics for the last 40 or 50 years. They have been searching for the key characteristics of successful leaders. Through our research on True North and in-depth interviews of 125 leaders, which resulted in 3,000 pages of transcripts, we learned that there just aren't any common characteristics of leaders and that leaders themselves don't look to developing those characteristics. In a real sense, they are playing out and reframing their life stories. One could argue, as we did in the book, that it may not necessarily be a history of your life, so much as how you see your life or how you frame it. Take the case of Oprah Winfry, who up to the age of 36 saw herself as a bad person because she was sexually abused. It was only after that time that she realized that she wasn't responsible for what had happened to her, so she could reclaim control of her life. Instead of carrying this huge sense of needing to please others, she was able to take control of her life and not feel this burden.

Kathryn Goldman Schuyler: Do you see significant differences between what meditation or mindfulness does and, say, therapy, which I think is what many people turn to in the West. What other approaches would you distinguish it from?

Bill George: I don't believe that these approaches are in any way mutually exclusive. I'm a believer that one needs to engage in introspective, reflective practices, like meditation. There may be others like compassionate prayer or other things that one may do on one's own, possibly even reading, to gain a greater depth and understanding about yourself. In addition, some form of intimate interaction with others can be very impactful, whether it's therapy or a talk with a good mentor or a spouse or loved one. The key is to combine individual work and a peer support group with whom you meet on a regular basis to discuss these things. Through this process you are taking your experience, processing it through meditation and other practices, and then taking it to a group and getting their feedback and insights. Often, in a group of five or six it's even more powerful than with a therapist. The latter often plays back to you what you're saying, whereas a group of five other people may challenge what you're saying. Your support group may give you insights that you hadn't thought about. Through these multiple processes, one gains the greatest depth of insight. I don't see them as mutually exclusive, but rather reinforcing.

Kathryn Goldman Schuyler: That sounds very useful for leaders. I know that for some time there have been groups where CEOs help one another. Do you know of any that have the components that you're talking about?

Bill George: The Young Presidents' Organization (YPO) has created the Forum of small groups of CEO members. Over 85% of YPOers have joined one of these groups and members report that they are invaluable. We interviewed several of them for our new book. However, in my experience with many CEOs of public companies, it is very hard for them to open up with other CEOs. They may help each other on an intellectual plane or a problem-solving plane, but it's rare that two CEOs, both of whom are in the positions today, are going to share deep personal insights with each other. A lot of CEOs don't feel safe in fully revealing themselves and being that vulnerable. There's an article in the *New York Times*, quoting Howard Schultz about the benefits of being vulnerable. It's interesting that the *New York Times'* editor misinterpreted that to mean "being insecure," as though it's a negative characteristic. The quality of being vulnerable is actually a great strength. There's great power in it. By revealing yourself through life stories, through your crucible, you actually gain power, not lose it. Society, and especially the media, seem to have cast this in a negative light. That's really unfortunate because it causes people in positions of power and authority not to open up publicly.

Kathryn Goldman Schuyler: I think it's really insightful, the notion of safety for CEOs, because they actually are in such a vulnerable position as well as such a strong one.

Bill George: I have much more hope for CEOs than I do for politicians in this regard. Politics is still such a power game, and it can be quite nasty. Far fewer politicians are going to open up than CEOs.

Kathryn Goldman Schuyler: Are you incorporating meditation or reflection in more depth into your teaching at Harvard?

Bill George: Not yet. I don't feel that I'm qualified to teach this. I could bring in someone like Dan Goleman or Jon Kabat-Zinn, who are experts in teaching it. I haven't yet gone that route but would like to eventually. But using meditation as an example of how one develops oneself. Actually practicing it would be an important next step.

Kathryn Goldman Schuyler: I'm wondering how you might be building on this wonderful start with Mingyur Rinpoche, since he's going into retreat?

Bill George: That's a good question. We're working with his organization, Tergar International, which is based in Minnesota. We're also working with His Holiness the Dalai Lama when he travels to the United States to expand some of this work. I'm also looking at doing programs with Dan Goleman to take the work on mindful leadership to the next level.

Kathryn Goldman Schuyler: Do you sense any differences between the Tibetan teachers you've met and the other people who practice mindfulness? The practices are a bit different.

Bill George: I don't think it's the practices that are different, but the capacity of the Buddhists to subordinate their self-interest or sense of ego. I certainly can't say that I've lost myself or my sense of ego! Now ego isn't necessarily a bad thing: I think that for leaders it's a necessary quality, although it's certainly not sufficient. I think that only through in-depth processes, like the lengthy retreat that Rinpoche is going into now [Mingyur Rinpoche had announced that he would be entering a three-year retreat within the year], can one gain that level of clarity and depth of insight. I can't say that I have yet.

Kathryn Goldman Schuyler: I've been wondering for some time how to create support for more leaders to do such in-depth work with themselves.

Bill George: One way I'd like to do it is to get them in True North Groups. Maybe give them a vehicle within their communities to get some training in meditation as well, because I think it's very valuable. It's certainly been valuable for me and for my sons, who have incredibly high-pressure jobs running an $8 billion company and working 80-90 hours a week as a physician. They meditate a couple of times a day. Many leaders just haven't had this opportunity. I'd like to see it become more widely available. I was concerned when we put this conference together and started publicizing it that it might be picked up by some of the media as odd or different and regarded as weird. That has not happened. There was an article on the Harvard Business School's *Working Knowledge* afterward. There were over 80 comments there that were incredibly thoughtful. I was impressed by how insightful they were—not the usual kind of polemics that you sometimes see on the web. These were very serious responses that showed me how broad and deep the interest is in this topic. It may be further along among the public than the media would make us think.

Kathryn Goldman Schuyler: Incidentally, there's one aspect of what the Tibetans focus on that is called *mind training* which relates to meditation but is slightly different. Mind training has more of the ethical component. The article that I wrote focused on that. His Holiness often teaches about such mind training.

Bill George: I believe that. Then you've got to go to the neuroscience work that's going on in neuroplasticity with Dr. Richard Davidson and many others now, studying this in a laboratory and seeing what's actually happening inside the brain. Let me take it one step further. If you look at our academic institutions today, it would be fair to say that of the classroom work, 90% of it deals with the IQ and less than 10% with emotional intelligence. In my work I cannot recall ever seeing a leader fail for lack of IQ, but I've seen dozens of leaders fail for lack of emotional intelligence. Typically, a lack of self-awareness leads them to deviating from their values, getting caught up in their ego, being wrapped up in external motivations like money, fame, and power, rather than internal motivations, such as the purpose of their leadership. Age-adjusted IQ doesn't change, but emotional intelligence clearly does. That has implications for asking what we are teaching and why we aren't concentrating more energy on developing emotional intelligence. As business schools focus more on developing leaders, you'll see them concentrating a lot more on EQ.

Kathryn Goldman Schuyler: I think your combined focus on reflection in groups and individually through meditation seems very worthwhile. Do you find receptivity among CEOs and other leaders to this approach?

Bill George: I do find a growing receptivity. On the part of top leaders like CEOs, there's still a bit of a reluctance to share, because of their fear of vulnerability. A lot of leadership deals with bonding and alignment. How do we get people to feel a common sense of purpose and values?

When they feel that, then they can become empowered to do amazing things. It all starts with that sense of common purpose and values.

Kathryn Goldman Schuyler: Anything I haven't touched on that you think is particularly important?

Bill George: This whole notion of groups. The idea of having a safe place where one can go to reveal and discuss things at a very intimate, deep level is critical. We know that leadership is lonely; that's well established. The question is: how do you deal with that loneliness? It can be quite negative, not only the psychological impact, but it can also lead to very bad decisions, particularly under pressure. That's where the small group comes in. It is the vital link between myself and the large organizations that I go into every day. That includes my job, my community organizations—the many, many organizations that we encounter every day. They can be a pretty scary place these days. A lot of people retreat into themselves or put on their armor when they go into those larger worlds. If they had a True North Group, they could feel more secure within themselves and adapt to their large organizations in a more positive way.

NOTE

1. Both published by Three Rivers Press (part of Random House), *Joyful Wisdom* in 2010 and *The Joy of Living* in 2008.

CHAPTER 20

"LEADERS SHOULD BE PEOPLE WHO ARE DEEPLY INVOLVED IN THEIR OWN REALIZATION OF BEING A HUMAN BEING"

An Interview With Peter Senge

Kathryn Goldman Schuyler

Inner Peace—Global Impact: Tibetan Buddhism, Leadership, and Work, pp. 317–327
Copyright © 2012 by Information Age Publishing

Kathryn Goldman Schuyler: What is it about Tibetan Buddhism that you see as important?

Peter Senge: First, I should say that I'm more interested in Buddhism in general than in Tibetan Buddhism in itself. There's a bias in the U.S. because of the diaspora as you mentioned, but Tibetan Buddhism is just one tradition. My background is more Chan (the Chinese term for *zen*). I think Buddhism is a very fluid system of exploration, and that the Dalai Lama is right, that it's incorrect to call it a religion. It's much more like an inner science that blends very well with many other traditions. In Tibet, it obviously blended extensively with the Bon and other spiritual traditions that predated Buddhism in Tibet, just as in China it blended with Taoism and to some degree with Confucianism, which predate Buddhism in China. One of the things that I think makes Buddhism so interesting is this ability to integrate with many other traditions. I think that's very relevant for an age in which we really don't need a new system of beliefs. Religions have been divisive as much as they've been integrative in history for the last few thousand years. I think the most interesting thing about Buddhism is its capacity to integrate and blend and enhance other traditions.

It helps a lot if you look at Buddhism as a discipline of inner exploration, because then its ability to integrate is much more obvious. If you frame it as a belief system or a religion, then it tends to look like a lot of other religions. Another thing that interest me with Buddhism is that because it's been around a long time and grew up in areas that had very strong intellectual and conceptual orientations (by that I mean India, then later China, and to a lesser degree Tibet), Buddhism has become an extraordinary body of theory. I don't know anything quite like it. This has a lot to do with the Indian roots—it is a very intellectually oriented culture—and then continuing and developing in China where you have very strong traditions of Confucianism and Taoism. The index to the canon, which is the complete teachings of the Buddha, is over 300 pages: just the index. It's a massive amount of material. Very few Westerners know that. They encounter the Four Noble Truths and other very simplistic aspects, and not the depth and breadth of Buddhist theory.

In many ways, the arc of Western culture has been an extremely intellectual one, with Western science being kind of a cornerstone, which the Dalai Lama has emphasized for a long time. The teacher I have in China agrees as well that the real future of Buddhism is integration with Western science and vice versa, because Western science has developed tremendous refined capabilities to understand the manifest or external world, whereas Buddhism has very refined capabilities for exploring the inner world, the world of our direct experience. For any kind of sane approach for understanding the universe, the world, society, culture, where we live, how we live, from the most macro to the most local, you need both.

Kathryn Goldman Schuyler: In that context, not focusing necessarily on the Tibetan, what does Buddhism bring to the work that you are doing?

Peter Senge: You can go back to very simple ideas that are now widely recognized, that nobody has "the world in their head." We don't perceive the world in a passive way, like a tape recorder or a camera that just passively takes in data from the external world and produces a representation of it. We interact with the world, and out of that interaction bring forth what we call "reality" and reality is not a thing ... reality is an experience.

At the simplest level, we spend a lot of our time emphasizing listening, because it's quite clear that the ability to listen is quite crucial for leadership. Our mainstream culture says that it's the ability to talk that defines leaders' capabilities need, but that's only for pretty mediocre leaders. People who are really good have a remarkable ability to take in multiple points of view, to really hear, and to listen you must become aware of your own listening. You must become aware of your own internal process. None of us hear what's said, we hear our listening. So the ability to recognize things that are triggering you, to recognize the habits of your own thought, habits of your own emotion, and how they shape what you hear, is the first step in actually being able to listen to another, or to listen to anything. That's always been very central in our work, and while I don't think Buddhism is essential for that, it's a major contributor. Buddhists go into this in a very unique and distinctive way.

A classic text that had a big influence in the history of Chinese Buddhism is called *The Awakening of Faith*. Virtually every monk studies this, and it's very good for Westerners too. Unlike many of the classic texts, which are very hard for Westerners to understand because they're very embedded in their cultural milieu, *The Awakening of Faith* is laid out in very clear terms and is basically an outline: "Here are the key ideas that comprise the Buddhist view of consciousness." It starts off with "one mind." This is the first step, where it's very hard for us. The traditional Buddhist notion of mind is all encompassing. Literally the totality of the universe is in that phrase "one mind"... so mind is not a function of our brain, it's not just our mind as Westerners would use "mind" (as a kind of "inner world that we create"), the Buddhist notion of mind is absolutely comprehensive. Then, there are two aspects of mind, the "manifest" and the "infinite" and they intersect in what's called the *tathagatagarbha*, the matrix for the intersection of the manifest and the phenomenon. The *tathagata*, which is another Sanskrit term, is actually one of the terms used for the Buddha. The Buddha was referred to as the tathagata, the place where this interaction of the infinite and the manifest is continually occurring. From this comes the notion that human beings exist in that interface, which is why enlightenment is possible. The book is called *The*

Awakening of Faith because the whole point is that enlightenment is possible because the human being exists with one foot in the infinite and one foot in the manifest or the phenomenological. There's a whole progression of developmental stages, the lowest of which we would regard as enlightened. The higher stages are impossible for us to even appreciate. There's no "thing" called enlightenment in that simplistic sense, it's a vast territory where we get little tiny glimpses now and then.

That's what I was referring to when I was saying there's really quite a remarkable body of theory in Buddhism, which is way beyond what most people study or understand. Why is it important? You asked that question before. We start off with the assumption that most of the problems in the world, both those that are clearly in our inner world, our anxieties, our uncertainties and so on, and those that are evident in our world at large, like climate change, destruction of species, et cetera, have a common root in our consciousness, our ways of thinking that shape our ways of acting. You start out with that notion that all of this starts in some sense as mental distress or confusion, then it manifests in ways of acting that produce huge problems in the world. From this perspective, change starts when you go upstream. You've got to deal with the lack of understanding and the lack of cultivation that all of us have in this world of how we perceive and what we perceive. Blake, the English poet, said it beautifully when he wrote

> If the doors of perception were cleansed every thing would appear to man as it is, infinite.
>
> For man has closed himself up, till he sees all things thro' narrow chinks of his cavern.[1]

... but we don't perceive the infinite very much, so consequently we're in a state of confusion. Einstein said "it's confusion that keeps us prisoner"—he called it a kind of optical delusion of our consciousness.[2]

Buddhism has a lot to contribute because it's such a rich body of theory and method to help us correct these problems at their source. I'll state this in terms of the kind of work we do: it's very clear that real changes occur when there's a collective shift in the energy of the group and there is a listening that wasn't there before. There gets to be a sense of good will, humor, laughter; I see this again and again. It's hard to describe, but it's such a common phenomenon: people learning how to think together. Our original course focused on dialogue and the meaning of the word dialogue. People really learned how to think together, how to examine their experience collectively, which invariably shifts the basis for their ability to take action together. Everything that we do is about shifting the capability for collective action, which starts with a different quality of conversation, a different collective awareness.

Today we have all kinds of projects going on all around the world. One example is around global food systems. You have people working seriously towards food systems that are really healthy, for the planet, for farming communities, and for those of us who eat food. That's a pretty basic problem we have today. The global food system is a disaster, a perfect example of all these dysfunctions. It's the largest cause of poverty in the world, if you consider the people being driven off of traditional rural livelihoods into slums and shantytowns around the world. It's an ecological disaster: we've lost half the topsoil on the planet in the industrial age. And nobody wants to eat the food that they get at the end. Obviously, more local food is great, but I think it's a bit of a fantasy to think that everything's going to be produced locally. We're not all going to live in Tuscany. We've come a long way down the path of extended food supply chains, and many people in the food producing regions are quite dependent on this income. We now have to create a global food system that is much more conscious. There are quite a few good examples of this in the book *The Necessary Revolution.*[3]

The important point here is if you look at a global food value chain, it's really a network of relationships, and you cannot transform that value chain without transforming the relationships. You have to really see each other, and understand each other, and appreciate each other's situation, and then you can start to think differently together. We see this happening a lot these days. Costco was one of the first big retailers to get involved in all this. The woman who's been leading a lot of the work at Costco for a long time said the shift in thinking that has now taken hold is quite simple: "we used to buy food from wholesalers and we now buy food from farmers." This awareness of buying food from farmers can contribute to a profound shift for the well-being of those farmers and farming communities and the ecologies upon which they all depend.

Kathryn Goldman Schuyler: What other systems are you working with?

Peter Senge: Primarily fisheries and marine ecosystem conservation and education—primary and secondary education. And then business, particularly as it relates to global value chains or supply chains like food. Those are the three primary domains where I think there are real examples of people doing things differently.

Kathryn Goldman Schuyler: To what extent do the kind of skills and orientation that come from Buddhism impact your work and collaboration with others in these areas?

Peter Senge: It all starts with listening, with the way we relate to one another. Look at schools for example: the people who are never listened to are the kids. Very few children in school actually experience it as a respectful environment for them. Teachers are basically telling them what they ought to learn. And then the teachers tell them if they learned. So the perception of the kids is that the whole system is driven by teachers and their job is to please teachers. You'd say "That's not very mindful approach." The idea that school ought to be about cultivation of human beings, students and teachers both, is very far removed from the way schools work today. That would be a start.

How can you have school without a theory of human development? We have it. We have schools based totally on the notions of *cognitive* development, with a little bit of emotional intelligence thrown in for good measure in the last few years. But in fact, school is about the *development of human beings*. How can you have a school without a theory of human consciousness and the mind-body system? In traditional Chinese schools, if you go back 2,000 years, what the kids did was calligraphy, because it was understood that the creative process was the foundation for all of learning. They studied the mind-body system via traditional Chinese medicine, and they studied meditation. And they recited the classics, which, because of the tonal structure of the Chinese language, is a form of chanting. That was the foundation for education. It was understood that the cognitive, analytic capabilities didn't develop until children were 8 or 9 years old, so this foundation had to be in place prior to that. You have to understand the creative process, you have to understand how the mind works and the bases of health and well being, you have to experience your voice as part of a collective; you have to have a bodily understanding of that, which comes from literally vibrating in unison with others. You want to understand the nature of health and where health comes from, and you have to be familiar with meditation. It's well understood that 6 and 7-year olds aren't going to sit and meditate for a long time, but they will definitely sit for a little while at a time. That's the foundation, and it is based on a very rich theory of human development, almost none of which exists in our present education system. I think this is why most kids hate school.

Kathryn Goldman Schuyler: Are they still using this approach in China?

Peter Senge: No, not at all, they haven't used it in 150 years. It was wiped out by the Western colonialists, although it tended to persist in the countryside, and then it was intentionally wiped out by the Cultural Revolution along with everything else in traditional Chinese culture. For the last 30 years, when everybody's trying to catch up with everybody else in the sense of economic performance, it was outlawed in the urban schools in China. It can still be found in pockets in the countryside. I'm a part of an experiment to start a new school based on this outside of Shanghai.

In the West we have a lot of compelling theorists who have tried to take schools in that direction, many of whom we all know: Piaget, Jerome Bruner, and different kinds of private schools like Steiner Schools, Waldorf Schools, Montessori Schools, but none of that ever gets into the mainstream of our system of education because the mainstream isn't based on any theory of human development. It's just based on cognitive development, not based on understanding human beings. There are many Western educators who have been very articulate about this, but they don't get widespread application because we have a society that doesn't understand human development very much. Schools are public institutions that tend to drift toward the mainstream of what society seeks. Hence they're stuck. That would be the area where I would say a real understanding of consciousness and the mind-body system is crucial for transforming the most influential system there is, which is the system of education, because it shapes all young people and it shapes our collective future.

Kathryn Goldman Schuyler: What do you see as the role of business and business leaders in this process?

Peter Senge: Business is the most powerful institution in our society. Schools are the most important, but business is certainly the most powerful. We'll never change education if there isn't a real mandate from the business world, yet we are under-educating people in a chronic way, and it affects the way our whole society functions. I think businesses have to lead by example, but they're very limited in their ability to do that. Big businesses tend to be very much driven by Wall Street and financial returns, though there's a lot of space for smaller businesses. We see a lot of smaller businesses getting started, very much with the intent to manifest a different consciousness today. I think you can see this all around the world. There's no shortage of businesses that are based on trying to understand what we're doing to the environment and to operate very differently, based upon a different notion of what it means to work together, to foster a deep and common purpose, and to nurture real respect in our relationships. You're not going to see this in large businesses because large business is driven by the mainstream forces, but you see it in pockets. Our work has always been with the radicals—the people in pockets of big businesses who are really determined to shift things, and then we work with smaller businesses that have a lot more latitude to create their own path.

A good example would be a New Zealand company named "Icebreaker," which makes a line of natural fiber clothing made from marino wool. If you go to their web site, they say "inspired by nature," using bio mimicry. Their intent is to make their whole value chain completely transparent, so that not only are all the products biodegradable in principle—the materials, the dyes, everything—but they want you to know who grew it, where it came from, so you can take your bar code on the article of clothing, go online, and find the sheep farmer who raised the sheep that led to that piece of clothing. Their aim is to create what people often call *radical transparency* so everybody knows where everything comes from and what's happened to it on its journey of production. Another company we've worked with for years is Seventh Generation, which basically set itself the task of educating American householders about all the toxins inside a house. You really don't want to have the stuff you have in your detergents in your house. Jeffrey Hollander, who founded Seventh Generation, learned 30 years ago that the average air quality inside an American home was much lower than the average air quality outside the home because of all the toxins that are in everyday products. They became very successful selling biodegradable detergents, nonbleached paper products made from recycled paper, and educating people continually on the risks of living in a highly toxic environment of everyday products, and the waste that we generate. You find these examples in the smaller businesses. I think they're very influential because they show a different model. But as these businesses grow, it can be hard to sustain their distinctive commitments as they become more driven by financial goals. Could any of them become giant corporations? I don't know—it'd be hard. No one can say for sure that it's impossible, but that's the split you see now. You see radicals within big established big corporations and you see smaller businesses that are setting down a different path. Again, all the stories are in the book.[4]

What's often missing is a core belief, based on experience, that sustained high performance goes hand-in-hand with well-being. Most people think it's one or the other: either you have well-being OR you have high performance, but that's not accurate. The idea of well-being is not everyone having their feet up and having a good time, which is exactly the image that gets juxtaposed against "we really have to achieve high level performance here." The two actually go hand-in-hand. You can get a lot of performance out of intimidation and fear in the short term, but it tends not to last. One division of HP that we knew well for a decade was very direct; they simply said "We believe all examples of sustained high performance come only as a result of well-being." They were extremely good at reflecting on what well-being meant to them as a business. It had to do with what they called *networks of collaboration* versus *networks of ambition*. They said that too often organizations are dominated by networks of ambition: people say they want high performance, but what they really want is credit for high performance. It's really about ambition and not performance. Performance, they felt, is very collaborative. It arises from people being helping each other, and being willing to help each other in solving all kinds of problems. They used to spend a lot of time tracking how key accomplishments arose from particular networks of collaboration. That was their basic notion, and they reinforced it again and again through continuous study of *how* they accomplished significant accomplishments. For them there was no tradeoff between well being and performance over the long term. Not only were they the most profitable large division in the company, but they had a tremendous track record for basic technical innovation for over a decade.

A lot of the problem with the business community comes from the business schools, where faculty do not have much real experience with being parts of creative, generative businesses. They're experts in particular domains, like operations, and finance, and marketing, and they teach their expertise. They do not teach, nor do most know how to teach, how people need to work together in order to really create a generative, creative environment in business. In other professional schools, this is different. I think it comes from the relative youth of management as a profession. You wouldn't expect to study surgery from someone who'd never performed surgery, or architecture from someone who'd never built anything, or music from someone who wasn't a musician, so in these other professions that are much older than management, they have developed a rich tradition of connecting education and practice. You see this as well in research. In medicine, for example, you have lab research and clinical research. Clinical research is testing something in practice. But you don't have that in management. You have academic research—rarely are studies done through any effort to intervene in a real setting and see the consequences.

Fortunately, this fragmentation of education and practice is not universal. In Finland, there's a school called Team Academy where students learn to manage by creating companies. In their first week or so of being a student, they create a company, and they have mentors who mentor them on the business plan, marketing plan, whatever issues they develop in their company. Their understanding of business comes from that sort of education. The graduates of Team Academy actually know how to manage businesses. The fundamental problem in business school is that it's too disconnected from practice, and the source of that problem is primarily the faculty, most of whom have very little real experience in growing and managing successful businesses. It's very unusual for someone who's been a very successful manager to get hired as a professor. At MIT they're called executives in residence. But, there's no larger innovation in pedagogy. These people are forced to just give lectures like everybody else [laughs]. So the paradigm of giving lectures prevails! You know there's no real practical experience of growing a business and getting mentored, which is what you really need. You need a process of education as mentorship, not as professorship.

Kathryn Goldman Schuyler: Is there anything that we haven't discussed with regard to the underlying question about the contribution of Buddhist thinking and practice to this process of change in the West?

Peter Senge: There is an old tradition that you see in many parts of the world that if you're going to be in a position of authority, you should be a *cultivator*. Leaders should be people who are deeply involved in their own realization of becoming a human being. I've seen a lot of experiments where people who are Buddhist meditation teachers will open a meditation practice for executives. But usually it's for stress management, not for cultivating wisdom, and it rarely become a foundation for how the person manages. I think that's not trivial, in terms of developing one's capacity to be a leader. In the Confucian tradition it's very clear: in traditional Chinese culture it's well understood that to be in a position of authority you must be a very advanced cultivator. The old saying was that the Emperor should be the wisest person in the land, and if not then the Emperor's advisor should be. While that's an ideal that was not always reached, it symbolized an important connection between cultivation and leadership authority.

In the West, you have the "philosopher king" of Plato. But by and large, to us positions of power are all about power: people who are good at building power and using power. On the other hand if you look at the people that we historically admire in positions of authority, they're people who exhibited wisdom. They're the Benjamin Franklins and Abraham Lincolns in the U.S. history. They're the Nelson Mandelas, to give a contemporary example, someone who cultivated a real capacity for compassion and understanding. I think that's the missing piece, and I think that we need to rediscover that piece. If Buddhism and other cultivation traditions can really take root, then I think the idea could develop that to be a CEO, to be in any kind of senior position, you should be a cultivator. And what do you do cultivate? You become more clear about yourself, your own inner psychology, and your needs and drives, so that you're not driven by them. You're also able to see more of what's happening around you.

In the Confucian tradition, "The Great Learning" is organized around seven meditative spaces of leadership cultivation. The first is learning how to stop; the second is stopping. Learning how to stop means learning how to stop your *mind*. Stopping means actually stopping your mind. The third is called awareness. Until you can stop the habitual thought flow of your mind, you cannot see what's around you. If you're going to be in a position of authority, you'd better have a high level of awareness of what's going on. Otherwise all you can do is project your inner dynamics on the outer world. This is an example of a whole theory of leadership based on a theory of cultivation. You look at our world today, and we've got a lot of people in positions of authority who don't know anything except how to project their own world-view on the larger world, so we have lots of problems.

I use Buddhism as an example of the cultivation tradition. It's important that we not get caught up in too much of the details, because it's really that commitment to cultivate your self, your ability to be quiet, your ability to be present, your ability to control your ego and your fear and self-centeredness, your ability to listen, your ability to suspend your own thoughts, to distinguish what's happening from what you're projecting—all of that is foundational for being an effective leader who can actually do some good. Since Buddhism is popular today, it has an opportunity to make that kind of contribution.

But Buddhism is only one of many cultivation traditions. It's just an example of this larger body of inherited knowledge of the world. The key is to be a practitioner, to be a cultivator, not just a reader of books. What is your practice? For me, sitting meditation is fundamental, so I spent 1½-2 hours a day. I now also do more yoga and tai chi when I have the opportunity to be in nature and connect with Earth *qi*. But that is just me. All must find their own path. We are very fortunate today to have so many paths available. The key is to be moving along the path. Do not be a spectator. This is especially important if you seek to contribute as a leader, to be someone who helps real change occur.

NOTES

1. William Blake, *The Marriage of Heaven and Hell* (Oxford: Oxford University Press, 1975/1789), xxii. And see online http://www.levity.com/alchemy/blake_ma.html for the exact wording and context

2. The actual quotation for this citation from Einstein is the following, but the specific source is unknown: "A human being is a part of the whole, called by us Universe, a part limited in time and space. He experiences himself, his thoughts and feelings as something separated from the rest - a kind of optical delusion of his consciousness. This delusion is a kind of prison, restricting us to our personal desires and to affection for a few persons nearest to us. Our task must be to free from this prison by widening our circle of compassion to embrace all living creatures and the whole nature in its beauty." Retrieved May 17, 2011 from, http://linguaspectrum.com/quotations/by_author_english.php?quoteoftheday_author=Albert%20Einstein

3. Peter Senge, *The Necessary Revolution* (New York: Doubleday, 2008).

4. Ibid.

CHAPTER 21

ANCIENT WISDOM, SOCIAL SCIENCE, AND THE VASTNESS OF THE HUMAN SPIRIT

An Interview With Margaret Wheatley

Kathryn Goldman Schuyler

Inner Peace—Global Impact: Tibetan Buddhism, Leadership, and Work, pp. 329–341
329

Margaret Wheatley wrote in 2005, "I became Buddhist so that I could stay in this world and allow my heart to keep breaking. I work in many different places where people are suffering. These people live in third world countries, confronting a future that is no future. Or they live in modern organizations, confronting the loss of self and meaning. [And—after describing the political issues and challenges....] I became Buddhist so I could see this insanity and not go insane.

> *How do I bear witness to the unbearable?*
> *Why are people so deliberately cruel?*
> *How do I not bring more rage into the world?*

This is why I became Buddhist. To be free from these and many other cries." [1]

Kathryn Goldman Schuyler: What led to your interest and connection with Tibetan Buddhism?

Margaret Wheatley: I have a lovely position in the world. I get to meet thousands of people a year, and many of them are in deep distress. My capacity to be available to them and to offer them something is what causes me to strengthen my practice. It used to be they were in deep distress because they were poor; now they're in deep distress if they work in any kind of large organization.

I've been an increasingly devoted Tibetan Buddhist practitioner since 1997. I have been good friends with Pema Chödrön since 1998, and there is a very deep heart connection between us. In July 2007 I asked her to formally become my teacher, and she has. In one of our conversations, I was telling Ani Pema how depressed I was over the state of the world, and she said "Well, Meg, we're just in kindergarten this lifetime; we're in the early phases of preparing ourselves to be Shambhala warriors or bodhisattvas, for what's coming," and that really helped me [laughs]. Instead of trying to resolve the present day experience in any way, I realized that this is just training, so "stop whining." It was a very helpful repositioning.

Kathryn Goldman Schuyler: What is it specifically in Tibetan Buddhism that you see as helpful or important, especially since you also know Zen?

Margaret Wheatley: It's my lineage; I can't say it any other way. One of the things that Dzigar Kongtrul Rinpoche said to his students a few years ago that has really impacted me is that *we* are now the lineage-holders, not only our teachers. We—Western students—are the ones who will continue the lineage. Western Buddhism now is the main place for the continuation of the Tibetan tradition, which I find quite inspiring personally, so I really want to act responsibly...

Kathryn Goldman Schuyler: That's why you're doing intensive study and taking long retreats?

Margaret Wheatley: ... well in part. It felt like an impossible task (preparing for a 100 day retreat), given my schedule and work life, but I've discovered that it's possible, and extremely beneficial to me personally for the work I want to be doing.

Kathryn Goldman Schuyler: What is it about Tibetan Buddhism that is important for the evolution of how we think about leadership and how people lead?

Margaret Wheatley: For many, many years now, I have been introducing a new way of organizing, based on living systems and how life organizes, and it's a mode of organizing that relies upon people's creativity and their internal motivation and their generosity of spirit.[2] All of those qualities disappear when we're in a command and control leadership structure.

Over the years I've realized that the keystone is whether leaders actually believe in other people's basic human goodness: whether they believe that other people have creativity and entrepreneurial spirit, whether they believe that other people beyond themselves are capable of being dedicated and creative. It really came down to "what does this leader, or what does this leadership theory posit about human nature generally?" That has become more and more clear to me as I've matured in this field of work.

Right now I'm working a lot on how to engage community and how to bring groups together with minimal facilitation, and I keep bumping up against people's basic distrust of other people. Nobody believes that if you put a group of people in a circle with a good question that they'll actually be able to have a meaningful conversation without much facilitation. We're really at the end of a very destructive leadership paradigm, but it's stronger than ever because it's at the end, more vicious and mean-spirited than ever. It's all about fear of the other and not being willing to think that the person I'm trying to motivate is another human being.

I often try to startle people into paying attention by stating that we've forgotten that we're human beings. The rediscovery of human nature and the human spirit—what people are capable of—is where I find an even deeper grounding for that position in Buddhism, and especially Tibetan Buddhism, and especially Shambhala Buddhism. I think of the famous phrase by Thich Nhat Hanh that "you are perfect just as you are, and you could use a little work." That's the essence of it: how do we reclaim, rediscover, re-see the people who are working with us or for us?

I'll tell you a corporate story that's at the far end of corporate blindness. A woman told me she left working for a large pharmaceutical company (she was a midlevel manager), and she left when she realized that she was now described as an "income generating unit." And that, for me, in the extreme, is very telling of what's gone on. Leaders have a great need *not* to notice that people have emotions, that people have spirits, because that gets too complex; and then when they discard that, then they also throw out the fact that people can be internally motivated and generous, not avaricious. One of the things that I loved watching, especially in 2008-2009 when people were trying to hold onto their jobs and companies were trying to survive with the economic crisis, is there were constant reports of food banks—local food banks, neighbor-to-neighbor programs springing up, and a lot of coverage of a very common behavior in organizations, which is that people got together and sacrificed personally so their colleagues could keep their jobs. They'd go on a 4-day workweek so everyone could keep their job, or higher level managers would give up part of their pay so that lower level people could maintain their jobs. Those stories were common for a while, and that's what we don't see when we put on this leadership lens, which sees people as motivated by greed, competition, and fear. Unfortunately, this seems to be the dominant leadership choice these days.

Buddhism in general reorients leaders to rediscover their basic nature—and to do that, we're really swimming upstream. The current view of human nature that's contained in Western mind is so negative. It's based on competition, survival of the fittest, social Darwinism, Calvinistic doctrines, angry gods, and a few righteous people. Buddhism re-grounds us in the understanding that human beings and our natures are fundamentally workable and generous, that we can become awake and aware, that we really want to be in relationship with other people and offer things to other people. I had to leave Western culture to discover this, by working in the third world, and then found an even deeper grounding for it in Buddhist theology.

Kathryn Goldman Schuyler: What can you say about either the concepts or the symbols or the stories about them, which might help people see what Tibetan Buddhism adds that's different? What's added by bringing Tibetan Buddhism to the mix?

Margaret Wheatley: Well nothing's added by naming it as Tibetan Buddhism, but everything is added by trusting that people are capable of more than their hatred, are capable of more than their prejudice, can get past their sense of fear and really discover that the stranger is like them. Tibetan Buddhism is my vehicle, but I've worked quite a lot with Catholic nuns, who I think are the strongest women leaders on the planet, and they are deeply grounded in their Christian compassion. I take strength from certain practices, rituals, and forms of study, but that's only to give me confidence when I'm leading people or encouraging people to have a new encounter with the human spirit and with what people are capable of.

I find that same clarity and confidence in people who have deep faith, like the Catholic sisters.

In addition, the recent history of Tibet and His Holiness the Dalai Lama modeling compassion in the face of terror and repression by the Chinese is very, very moving. They're embodying for the world what compassion really looks like in the face of people who want to destroy you. So for me that does give it a unique role. This isn't just talk. America would be really wonderful if Christians started to behave like Christians. Here we have Tibetans really practicing, embodying compassion towards the aggressor, and that for me is very evident.

I've done a lot of work at the level of paradigms, so I speak rather naturally about what happens when world views collide. Whenever people are in their world view and look at behavior from a very different world view, they just select aspects of it that will make sense within their current way of thinking and dismiss all the information that would require them to truly change their minds. So I look at the criticism of the Dalai Lama and the middle way path that he's chosen as people holding on to their old views; they believe that compassion is a nice thing when it works, but you have to get aggressive when it doesn't. That's the old world view. Look at all the criticisms of His Holiness and his approach to the Chinese. The criticism illuminates traditional ways of thinking about power politics and what you have to do. He's out there just walking the talk of what true compassion is like. Other people who have done this extraordinarily well are Nelson Mandela and Archbishop Desmond Tutu. I think that we barely understand what such people are doing because they are truly sourced by different ground.

Generally people revert to "See, I told you it wouldn't work." "You have to fight force with force," which is still the dominant world-view. I'll stop talking about His Holiness for a moment and say this is also what I encounter in the realm of leadership. Leaders don't want to know, in many cases, that there is an alternative to command and control. They choose power over effectiveness, over and over again.

For me personally, the grounding in Buddhism gives me roots. It gives me a lineage, so that when I come up against this modern day western mindset that "control is the only way to make things happen," I have a different level of confidence. There's so much waste going on. There's so much dishonor and disrespect in our current leadership ways that it's horrifying, as well as sorrowing, to see how many people are beaten down and shrink and lose all sense of their own capacity. The notion of basic human goodness is so fundamentally important within the Shambhala tradition, and is something that I now know to be true, and therefore I work on its behalf quite differently in the leadership arena. When we know ourselves as full human beings, this leads to very different behaviors on the part of leaders and on the part of people, and so part of my grounding in leadership development has come from this ancient lineage.

Kathryn Goldman Schuyler: Can you speak a bit about the notion of lineage and how it contributes to our learning and understanding?

Margaret Wheatley: Part of Western culture at this time is that we think things are always getting better and better, that society is a state of constant progress. From this perspective, you naturally value the youth more than the elders. The elders are seen as being "out of date": Things have changed, and they don't know enough (as seen in everyone's joke about their grandchildren teaching them how to use computer or the remote control). In a society that has no sense of tradition and is always looking to the future and to future inventions, the whole idea of lineage is lost because people of the past are no longer relevant. For me and for many cultures, we find ground in ancestors—we come from people and traditions that give us strength. In my own work within the Berkana Institute, we've noticed that people who go back to their traditional ways to bring their ancestral knowledge forward have a very different strength than those who try to "get modern."[3] For me the root system of lineage is an undeniable source of strength.

Kathryn Goldman Schuyler: What can you say for social scientists, who know very little or only superficial things about Tibetan Buddhism and lineage?

Margaret Wheatley: For me personally, there's a sense of being held accountable for something beyond my own self. As a social scientist I've done research, written books, promulgated theories, but every time I've spoken about a new idea, people have said "Well, if you can just give me some case examples—if you just show me some organizations that are doing this successfully, then I will change my ways." When you are in work that is located at the level of paradigm or world view, you realize that when people are questioning you for evidence they don't really want the evidence—they're not going to use the evidence to change their minds. The real work is not to amass evidence as the means of changing people's minds. It's "how do I change this person's world-view?" I still use Thomas Kuhn's seminal work on scientific revolutions quite a lot.[4] He said that when scientists are confronted with data that disconfirms their world view or challenges it, they either select only the few points that make sense within the old world view or they manipulate the data so that it confirms their old world view, or in some cases, they are physically staring at the data, and they don't see it. Now we're in the era of "evidence-based" decision-making, but my experience has been that people interpret "evidence" in very different ways. It can be just garbage, when we look at the evidence and only take what we want from it. It doesn't change our minds unless we're really willing to move into that process of mind-changing.

For me, that's the journey: changing people's minds. Where do I take the strength for that? It's not just from my current research, not from current evidence, it's realizing that I'm standing on very strong shoulders that stretch back eons—of people and communities that have embodied this and demonstrated this for a great many centuries. It's our own culture's desire to look for information only from the five senses that has put us in such a tiny narrow prison of understanding.

For me *lineage*, regardless of what the lineage is, but *lineage* means that we're not the first to come up with this idea, and even if our present way of understanding reality doesn't want to see it, there are generations and millenia of people who have taught us this. Within Tibetan Buddhism, I have problems with some of the spiritual teachers who are out there who have obviously had great awakenings personally, but don't have lineage, and so it becomes more of an ego expression. It's impossible not to get caught by your ego, if you think you've just had an incredible transformative spiritual awakening, and you attempt to teach it to people. When there's no ground whatsoever except your own personal experience, of course your ego's going to come in.

Kathryn Goldman Schuyler: Let's go into this little further. In university accreditation reviews, they're training educators to look for what they refer to as "a culture of evidence" and if we think of "No Child Left Behind" I see that as part of this paradigm. The people who promulgate it seem to really believe they are creating an evidence-based way of helping people move forward. How does this view of evidence differ from what you're speaking of, and how does that link with the contribution of Tibetan Buddhism?

Margaret Wheatley: When we talk about evidence-based decision making, a key question is "What is the evidence we're using? What are the measures?" As a society, we are caught up in this numeric culture where we want very simple measures to describe very complex experiences. The fundamental flaw is the nature of the evidence we're using to make decisions. It would be so different if you asked the teacher how they would know if a child is learning—what they would look for, what changes would indicate that the child is getting curious, that the child is motivated, that the child likes coming to school—versus the current approach which is to tell teachers "here are the measures ... this is what they need to accomplish in reading, this is what they need to accomplish in math, we won't even talk about creativity or the arts, and this is what you have to teach to." We're just not tracking the right evidence. I would want any child to be growing in curiosity, to develop a love of learning, to become more aware of the world around them. Instead, we have continued to turn schools into testing centers, where even some 5 year olds no longer want to go to school because of the pressures they encounter there. So the problem is the nature of the evidence we're using.

When we say "evidence-based" we don't notice that we are screening or filtering or denying; we're screening out what could be really useful evidence, and instead we're narrowing our measures to what's simplest to measure, so we're losing touch with reality by focusing only on smaller units of information. One of the principles from science that I think is helpful is that any time you settle on one piece of information you're blinded to the rest of what's going on; I recall one scientist saying: "Every act of measurement loses more information than it gains." If we look at our five senses, and we think that's the only way we can know reality (and it doesn't even include mind and meditation, awareness and intuition and consciousness,) what kind of reality are we tuning in to? What I learned writing *Leadership and the New Science* is that the real science has shifted and is much more inclusive of things we can't explain through our traditional five senses.

Now I have to say a little bit about neuroscience at this point, because what I see happening with neuroscience is that it's being used in a very traditional scientific way to validate things that science has excluded in the past, but the trap here is that it's actually reifying traditional science. In other words, if you can find the location in the brain—if you can demonstrate its physical reality then it "proves" that it exists. So what about all those things that we can't prove exist through our technology? I'm watching this now with some curiosity and a fair amount of caution because ...

Kathryn Goldman Schuyler: They are using a narrower, more traditional paradigm for science....

Margaret Wheatley: That's right. So it's not questioning the foundations of science as we currently construct it; it's just trying to use it to prove the material existence for things we know to be true in our experience. We're unintentionally continuing to make science the arbiter of our experience, maintaining its hegemony, even deification in modern culture.

Kathryn Goldman Schuyler: Varela was not intending that.... The part that's not getting heard from *Mind & Life* is the emphasis on the first person research.[5]

Margaret Wheatley: That's right. Because you can't do first person research within the existing scientific paradigm. It's not seen as evidence, but as being anecdotal.

Kathryn Goldman Schuyler: If we just step back from this conversation for a moment and pause and just sit and then see what else should we bring in at this point....

Margaret Wheatley: I want to say one thing to close off a lot of what I've said. Social scientists and leaders may not know about what I've been calling "basic human goodness" or people's capacities, but *people* know. I want social scientists to recognize that they're part of the problem; and that when people relate to someone like the Dalai Lama, who radiates joy and self-effacement and compassion, that people see themselves also, that all people are capable of those capacities. I find in my own work that the way I bypass all of the worldview barriers is to just start conversations with people about their own experience. I ask questions like "When have you worked well with other people?" "What did that feel like?" "When have you experienced other people surprising you by their capacity?" "When have *you* become a leader and why?"

I'm trying to help people surface their own experience and use that, instead of getting caught in this or that kind of typology or "you're only capable of this because you're this kind of person" or "you're poor so you're not capable of anything." I want to bypass all of that and help people understand that as they've lived their lives as human beings, they have discovered a lot about themselves and about other people, and I want to emphasize the higher qualities. I really do feel that our whole mindset is embodied in "science is god," with social sciences as the poor cousins of that, and we're distancing ourselves, destroying ourselves by failing to recognize the power of the human spirit. Tibetans model that. Tibetans embody that often. People have a direct experience of "I felt really good in the presence of that monk" or the kind of contagious energy that can come from a meeting with Tibetans. I don't find it in us Western folk; we're often very serious and struggling, and deep into the struggle of being good Buddhists.

I have this experience over and over in Africa—when Westerners are blown away by how joyful people are in the midst of great suffering, of having nothing material. Yet as visitors, we feel truly welcomed by people who are happy to meet us—Tibetans or Bhutanese or in my experience Zimbabweans and South Africans. I just point out to them that this is what it feels like to be (in the case of Tibetans) raised in a culture where you don't have a focus on your own ego and (in the case of South Africa), where you're taught from childhood that you only exist within a community of other people—that this is all about being one. We need more of these direct experiences of getting out of the prison of our social science descriptions of reality.

It's painful for me to watch how startling it is for people to encounter joyful human beings or people who really welcome them instantly as part of the community. We're just not used to that. We are, I think, a truly paralyzed society in terms of relationships, in terms of connecting with each other, and it's only getting worse. I am not working any longer at the abstract level of what's in Tibetan Buddhism. Here is a whole culture that has been able to cultivate people who do not think of themselves first and who therefore radiate a sense of the delight of being with other human beings. As I said, I find this in Africa too: it's how I sum up my experiences in Africa. I learned what it feels like to be welcomed just because you're there, just because you're another person, and to really experience the fullness of human emotions. I'm filled with sadness that our particular culture has made individualism and separation the modus operandi of how we view the world, because I am so aware now in my own body of what we're missing by shifting into this very narrow way of seeing. For me the practice of Buddhism—exploring my own mind and opening my heart/mind, my *citta*, has connected me with the vastness not just of mind, but the vastness of the human spirit.

Kathryn Goldman Schuyler: To me this feels very core to why I'm doing the work that I am, Meg: This paradigm shift toward being in touch with deep experience—becoming aware of how that's different from daily experience, whether it's in science or leadership, and then how the practice connects one with the vastness of the human spirit or of basic goodness. In various ways, by sensing the Tibetans and their culture, by doing the practices, it seems that the shift may not actually require all of that practice, but the practice contributes to this process of change. What I think I'm hearing you say, and it makes sense to me, is that the practice allows us to stabilize and *ground* this perspective that is so very different from the Western one or scientific one....

Margaret Wheatley: I would say exactly that. The practice enables our hearts to soften and open, so that we become more open to what is and to other people's experience, so that we're not trying to fit them into a little box or a typology, we're just trying to be there with them. For me, the greatest capacity that I have developed from practice is not to be afraid to be anywhere with people who are suffering. I now know how to *be there* with them rather than turn away or feel I have to feel guilty or all of the other defenses that we put up. I am really happy just to sit with people who are sorrowing or joyful, but I'm not afraid of being with anybody. And that's definitely a consequence of practice—that real "tenderizing" and opening of the heart.

Kathryn Goldman Schuyler: When you said tenderizing I had this funny image of Buddhist practice as a heart tenderizer like a meat tenderizer—and it does have some of that ferociousness too! I don't know why I've been called to do all of this writing explicitly about Tibetan Buddhism—sometimes it really makes sense, and sometimes I feel so humble. I'm much newer in it than many of the people I know, but I want to shine light on the importance of what you perceive that many people don't: this whole culture that's been transplanted and is somehow living in our midst, while it's here. We or others will be the ones who carry it forward, but it's still there shining.

Margaret Wheatley: It's really the antidote for everything that I could name about Western culture and the boxes and prisons we've put ourselves in, including our sense of values, sense of Christian righteous God, sense of greed and consumerism and materialism. I heard a quote from His Holiness once when he said "America has really perfected samsara."

Kathryn Goldman Schuyler: ... and marketing it.

Margaret Wheatley: Yes, exactly! We've got it down pat. Then along comes this culture that is truly opposite in all the important ways. On all the important dimensions, Tibetan culture and theology present the contrary view. I think that's important for those of us who are walking in both worlds to understand. I hadn't thought of that before—I like that thought....

Kathryn Goldman Schuyler: Where I actually started on this project was the very interesting paradox that for the Tibetan culture to survive, it has to survive within this one, and either change this one or survive within it, but it can't survive outside of it. There is no "outside."

Margaret Wheatley: That's right, and it's not for the Tibetans, it's for us to do that. It's for us. They can lead us in the practice and in really understanding from inside our own beings and minds what the Tibetan worldview is, and then it's up to us to be ... not the translators, but to be walking that narrow line between the two different worldviews that will hopefully lead in the next generation to something that's different. I do think that this is our work. You know one of the prophecies about the Shambhala warriors that Johanna Macy quotes from her teacher is that when the warriors return they are *inside* the halls of power, and they know how they work. This for me is also prophesied in the Incan tradition where they predict that the new shamans will come from the north, not from Peru or the southern countries, and I'm very inspired by this. It's those who know the culture best, who are inside it long enough to see its failings, who have struggled to renounce it, who can see it clearly—we are the ones who are going to bring in these ancient wisdoms. And we're not going to do it as social scientists of old.

Kathryn Goldman Schuyler: You said this was a new insight for you....

Margaret Wheatley: I have a stronger sense of realization that we're the ones who are bringing the antidote into the culture because we understand the culture. We're *inside* it and understand it profoundly well and have renounced it. It's not the Tibetans who are bringing it in, it's us, because of our position within the culture.

Kathryn Goldman Schuyler: I have been thinking increasingly that what's important is the fullness and rigor of the training that's possible through this process—through the various lineages—and I suspect that they give different colorations to how one is trained. The job is so big that simply being of good will is a prerequisite, but it's not sufficient. It's just too tough a job! One really needs a fuller training, and there are few things that provide that.

Margaret Wheatley: Absolutely ... if you really think (if I can continue my imagery here) that we are the warriors inside the halls of power, the kind of grounding and depth this requires is just what I was speaking about earlier. You can't just float here on your own theories—you need to have a very deep grounding practice. That's the only way we can be strong enough for the task that is ours.

Kathryn Goldman Schuyler: That's what I think the Tibetan Buddhism brings, because it's come to us so complete. I suspect that there were or are many other cultures that train people in this, like you mentioned in Africa, but they've been so abused already....

Margaret Wheatley: I really want to keep the distinction of how Buddhism in all its different forms helps you know your mind, because I have not found that in any other culture, and it's critical.

Kathryn Goldman Schuyler: I know that we've run out of time, but please say a bit more how it helps you know your mind?

Margaret Wheatley: If you can see how your mind works and how you react, then you have that doorway into a much greater reality, and you can move beyond your own narrow mind. That for me is the essence of Buddhist practice.

Kathryn Goldman Schuyler: ... and then that lets you meet the "other" and not be afraid...

Margaret Wheatley: ... that's right, and to not get so overwhelmed by the current view of reality, because you know there's more than meets the eye. And then you move back into the social sciences and it's *only* what meets the eye that is considered useful.

Kathryn Goldman Schuyler: ... I think this is very important ... thank you so much.

NOTES

1. Margaret Wheatley, "To Be Free From"/"Four Freedoms" in *Mindful Politics*, ed. Melvin McLeod, 189-200 (Sommerville, MA: Wisdom Publications, 2006).
2. See Margaret Wheatley, *Leadership and the New Science: Discovering Order in a Chaotic World* (San Francisco, CA: Berrett-Koehler Publishers, 1999/2006); Margaret Wheatley and Myron Kellner-Rogers, *A Simpler Way* (San Francisco, CA: Berrett-Koehler Publishers, 1998); Margaret Wheatley, *Finding Our Way: Leadership for an Uncertain Time* (San Francisco, CA: Berrett-Koehler Publishers, 2007); and Margaret Wheatley, *Turning to One Another: Simple Conversations to Restore Hope to the Future* (San Francisco, CA: Berrett-Koehler Publishers, 2009).

3.   http://www.berkana.org
4.   See Thomas Kuhn, *The Structure of Scientific Revolutions*, 3rd ed. (Chicago: The University of Chicago Press, 1996).
5.   See http://www.mindandlife.org

GLOSSARY

Note: *The following definitions are based on those provided online by three knowledgeable Tibetan Buddhist organizations, so as to ensure their accuracy. These are the Rigpa Shedra, a scholarly organization (www.rigpawiki.org), the Rangjung Yeshe Wiki (http://rywiki.tsadra.org), and the Lama Yeshe Wisdom Archives, compiled and edited by Nicholas Ribush (http://www.lamayeshe.com/index.php?sect=static&subsect=glossary).*

bodhichitta. (Sanskrit, also spelled *bodhicitta*). Bodhi means "enlightened essence" and chitta means "heart" or "mind." The altruistic determination to attain enlightenment for the sole purpose of enlightening all beings and freeing them from suffering.

bodhisattva. (Sanskrit). A being committed to freeing all sentient beings from suffering who realizes that the only way to help them meaningfully is by helping them to train their minds and become enlightened, and that the only way to do that is by becoming enlightened oneself.

Bodhisattvacharyavatara (A Guide to the Bodhisattva's Way of Life, also known as the *Bodhicharyavatara)* was written in the 8th century by Shantideva and is widely studied by all lineages of Tibetan Buddhism.

buddha. (Sanskrit, *sangye* in Tibetan). Totally pure (*sang*) and fully developed (*gye*).

compassion. (Sanskrit: *karuna*). The wish for all beings to be free from mental and physical suffering. One of the most important practices in Tibetan Buddhism is the cultivation of compassion through breathing and visualization practices involving taking on others' suffering (*tonglen*).

dakini (Sanskrit; *khandro* in Tibetan). "Sky-goer"—a female embodiment of enlightened energy.

dependent origination. (Also referred to as *dependent arising*.) All phenomena arise together and are mutually interdependent in a web of cause and effect. The Buddhist insight into what today is understood through systems theory.

343

Nothing has a single cause—everything is interdependent and "empty" of separate existence.

dharma. (Sanskrit). The teachings and the methods of the Buddha that provide a path in life.

dharmakaya. (Sanskrit). "The basic and all-pervasive nature of all phenomena." The primordial space out of which all phenomena arise (http:// rywiki.tsadra.org/index.php/dharmakaya).

Dzogchen. Often regarded as the highest teachings of Tibetan Buddhism and translated as "the Great Perfection," its meaning or importance cannot be conveyed through a definition. Dzogchen involves direct realization of one's Buddha nature without intellectualization or fabrication—simply realizing inner radiance and leaving things in their natural simplicity.

emptiness. See *shunyata*.

enlightenment. Awakening. In Tibetan, the word for *Buddha* is *sangye*, which means "awakening" plus "opening." The ultimate accomplishment of spiritual training. A perfect understanding of the nature of mind and of phenomena.

Garab Dorje was the first human teacher in the dzogchen lineage which traces back to the primordial Buddha, in the context of Nyingma teachings. Garab Dorje means "Indestructible Joy."

Gelug. "The Virtuous Order." The most recently-developed lineage of Tibetan Buddhism, founded by Lama Tsongkapa in the early 15th century; it focuses on monasticism and study. Politically powerful since the 17th century, the lineage of the Dalai Lamas are its most prominent members. Somewhat more centralized in organization than the Nyingma, the Gelugpa lineage had monasteries with thousands of monks in Tibet.

Geshe. Title awarded in the Gelugpa tradition to successful scholars. It has a number of levels, of which the highest is comparable to a doctoral degree.

Guru Rinpoche. See Padmasambhava.

Hinayana tradition. Literally, Small, or Lesser, Vehicle. It is one of the two general divisions of Buddhism. Hinayana practitioners' motivation for following the dharma path is principally their intense wish for personal liberation from conditioned existence, or *samsara*.

Kagyü is one of the four main lineages of teaching within Buddhism in Tibet. It is a school of teaching that includes many great yogis who devoted their lives to meditating in solitude. Literally, it means literally means "oral transmission." It is known for devotional practices, silent sitting meditation, teachings passed down from one teacher to a student that are known as "ear-whispered" transmissions, and the particular teachers and texts that they study. Its most well-known early teachers were Tilopa, Naropa, Marpa, Milarepa, and Gampopa.

karma. Comes from a Sanskrit word meaning "action," and refers to the law of cause and effect, whereby negative actions produce suffering and positive actions produce happiness. In Buddhist traditions of all lineages, all that takes places in beings' lives are the result of previous actions, so that future actions will, in turn, be influenced by our current actions. In this context, the way we think is also action.

lama. A spiritual mentor or teacher, "guru" in Sanskrit.

lineage. "Lineage means the teaching that has been brought down from Buddha to his disciples, then to the translators and then from one Guru to the next— the unbroken line of transmission that has been passed from Buddha himself, up to the present Guru." (*His Holiness Sakya Trizin*). It means that the heart-to-heart connection from one teacher to another has been passed on, often for centuries. The notion of *lineage* for Tibetans is what makes this form of Buddhism a living tradition, as it relies on direct, personal connection and teaching that is unbroken.

lojong. A Tibetan word meaning "training the mind" or "transforming the mind." These teachings emphasize the practice of bodhichitta and are intended primarily for students of the highest capacity.

Mahayana **tradition.** (Sanskrit). The great or universal vehicle. The essence of the *Mahayana* is the aspiration to attain buddhahood as the only means to help all beings find liberation from suffering. It is grounded in the *Prajnaparamita* teachings on emptiness.

mandala. Mandala (Sanskrit) can be translated literally as "center and circumference." A visual meditative aid, the mandala is generally depicted as a circle that revolves around a center. On the simplest level, a mandala can be understood to be our own bodies and minds and the phenomenal world around us. The word also describes an integrated structure that is organized around a central unifying principle. It also means:

1. the sacred environment and dwelling place of a Buddha, bodhisattva, or deity.

2. the two dimensional representation of this environment on cloth or paper, or made of heaps of colored sand, or three dimensionally, traditionally made of wood.

Nyingma. The oldest of the schools of Tibetan Buddhism, known sometimes as the "old translation" school, which included teachings brought to Tibet from India and translated mainly from the 8th through the 10th centuries. It was founded by Padmasambhava and Yeshe Tsogyal, who hid many of the teachings that are regarded as *terma* destined for contemporary times. While it also has important monasteries, it is perhaps most known for its lineages of yogis.

Padmasambhava. Also referred to as "Guru Rinpoche," he is regarded and deeply honored as the founder of Tibetan Buddhism. He traveled to Tibet (and Bhutan) in the 8th century, worked closely with the king of Tibet, and is considered to have been foretold by the Buddha Shakyamuni as the "Second Buddha." Many of the most important teachings originated with him.

rigpa. In *Dzogchen* teachings, the essential nature of the mind. Realizing this and being able to sustain this awareness in a stable way is what is meant by enlightenment.

Rimé. A nonsectarian approach to teaching the Dharma that developed in Tibet in the 19th century, by which the teachers helped to preserve a great many of the ancient texts and lines of unbroken teaching. (Sometimes transliterated as *rimay.*)

Sakya. One of the four main schools of Tibetan Buddhism. Originally a family lineage, its name refers to a "grey earth" region of Tibet. It developed in the

11th century and has a special reputation for scholarship and for the "path and fruit" (*lamdre*) teachings. It is currently led by Sakya Trizin, who teaches often in the West.

samaya **connection**. Buddhism, as a formal process, includes many commitments and vows that a practitioner makes in order to learn and develop. One typically makes such a vow to a particular teacher, thereby establishing a connection that is grounded in living up to one's commitments.

samsara. The state of being unenlightened in which the mind, enslaved by the three poisons of desire, anger, and ignorance, evolves uncontrolled from one state to another, passing through an endless stream of psycho-physical experiences all of which are characterized by suffering. (Ranjung Yeshe Wiki) The dharma is regarded as a path out of the suffering.

sangha. (Sanskrit) Refers to the community of practitioners who are following the teachings of the Buddha.

shamatha **or "calm abiding" meditation**. (Sanskrit). *Shama* means "peace"; *tha* means "to dwell" or "stability." A fundamental practice that enables the practitioner to quiet and focus the mind. After this, practitioners can develop "clear seeing" (*vipashyana*). Tibetan Buddhism includes many detailed practices for training one's mind.

shunyata. (Sanskrit). The perception that all things are relational and without any inherent existence in themselves.

terma. A *terma* is a hidden treasure or teaching that was concealed in order to be discovered in a later, more appropriate time. It is said that these treasure teachings were hidden by Padmasambhava and Yeshe Tsogyal.

Tilopa. One of the founders of the Kagyü tradition, a lineage of teaching that includes many great yogis who devoted their lives to meditating in solitude.

three poisons. In Buddhism, this refers to desire or attachment, anger or aggression, and ignorance or bewilderment.

Vajrayana **tradition**. (Sanskrit.) The teaching and practice of the Vajrayana or "Secret Mantra Vehicle" are the core of Tibetan Buddhist traditions in Tibet. Based on the motivation of bodhichitta—the wish to attain, for the sake of others, the state of complete enlightenment—the Vajrayana is a path centered on cultivating pure perception in order to arrive swiftly at a direct realization of Buddha nature and the nature of reality. Through its practices, ordinary perception is transformed into a sacred outlook, where everything is seen and experienced purely in its true nature. The Vajrayana is not separate from the Mahayana tradition, but is considered to involve practices that help practitioners realize the nature of reality more quickly.

wisdom. There are two different words for *wisdom* in both Sanskrit and Tibetan. The Sanskrit word *prajna* (*sherab* in Tibetan) and the Sanskrit word *jñāna* (Tibetan *yeshe*). The distinction between them is very important for practitioners, but not for basic understanding of the role of Tibetan Buddhism in the West. *Wisdom* refers to the ability to discern correctly the fundamental emptiness that is the ground of all things, including people. It can be described in many ways, but is fundamentally beyond intellectual constructs and is original wakefulness or *nondual knowing*: knowing that moves beyond relationships of subject and object.

ABOUT THE CONTRIBUTORS

 **Kathryn Goldman Schuyler,** PhD, has coached over 200 executives, supporting them in asking the tough questions that help them see themselves more clearly and improve their teams' performance. As she realized how hard it is for people to live up to their dreams for themselves, she began to conceive of this book. She studied at the Ecole Pratique des Hautes Etudes (Sorbonne) on a Fulbright Fellowship, earned a doctorate in sociology from Columbia University (New York), and has consulted to organizations for over 25 years. She has studied in depth with some of the foremost Western teachers of awareness, including Moshe Feldenkrais and Jean Houston, investigated methods developed by Western schools of consciousness like the Arica Institute and Landmark Forum, and has studied with His Holiness the Dalai Lama, Sogyal Rinpoche, Lama Tharchin Rinpoche, Tsoknyi Rinpoche, and Lama Yeshe Wangmo. In addition to coaching executives and their teams, Dr. Goldman Schuyler is a professor in the California School of Professional Psychology at Alliant International University in San Francisco, and an internationally certified practitioner of the Feldenkrais Method of Somatic Education. She teaches graduate courses in organizational ethics, social responsibility, and organization development, and has published widely on organizational and personal change.

John Eric Baugher, PhD, is associate professor of Sociology at the University of Southern Maine. His areas of teaching and research include the Sociology of Death and Dying, Social Psychology, Qualitative Research Methods, and Contemplative Pedagogy. He is currently writing a book on how routine encounters with dying persons shape the caring capacities of hospice workers in the United States and Germany, and how individuals integrate such experiences into their ongoing narratives of self. Contemplative pedagogy provides a link between Professor Baugher's research and teaching activities, both of which focus on the experience of liminal emotions in transformative learning.

Dana Browning (pseudonym) has been flying internationally as a flight attendant for 40 years and practicing Buddhist meditation for about as long, starting as a student of Chögyam Trungpa. She is interested in brain peak performance and mental fitness, and is presently developing a curriculum to teach brain fitness to seniors and creativity and improvisation to children.

Bill George is a professor of management practice at Harvard Business School, where he has taught leadership since 2004. He is the author of four best-selling books *True North*, *Finding Your True North*, *Authentic Leadership*, and *Seven Lessons for Leading in Crisis*. His latest book, *True North Groups*, was released in September of 2011. Mr. George is the former chairman and chief executive officer of Medtronic. He joined Medtronic in 1989 as President and Chief Operating Officer, was Chief Executive Officer from 1991-2001, and Chairman of the Board from 1996 to 2002. Mr. George currently serves as a director of ExxonMobil, and Goldman Sachs, and also recently served on the board of Novartis and Target Corporation. He has been named one of "Top 25 Business Leaders of the Past 25 Years" by PBS; "Executive of the Year-2001" by the Academy of Management; and "Director of the Year-2001-02" by the National Association of Corporate Directors.

Thupten Jinpa, PhD, was trained as a monk and received the Geshe Lharam degree from the Shartse College of Ganden Monastic University, which is the highest degree in the Tibetan scholarly tradition, equivalent to a doctorate. Dr. Jinpa also holds BA honors in Philosophy and a PhD in Religious Studies, both from Cambridge University, U.K. Since 1985, he has been the principal English translator to His Holiness the 14th Dalai Lama. He has translated and edited more than a dozen books by the Dalai Lama including the recently published *Beyond Religion: Ethics for a Whole World* (Houghton Mifflin, 2011). Dr. Jinpa's own works include *The Essential Mind Training* (Wisdom, 2011), *Self, Reality and Reason in Tibetan Philosophy* (Routledge, 2002), and two translations of classical Tibetan texts as part of The Library of Tibetan Classics series. Dr Jinpa is President of the Institute of Tibetan Classics in Montreal and Adjunct Professor at the Faculty of Religious Studies, McGill University, as well as an Executive Member of CCARE (Center for Compassion and Altruism Research and Education) at the School of Medicine at Stanford University. He is Chairman of the Board of the Mind and Life Institute.

Lin Lerner holds a PhD in dance ethnology. She lectures on Tibetan dance and culture and gives workshops on movement and meditation at colleges, universities, schools, and museums. She has taught, directed, and helped organize five Tibetan ritual dance groups in the West. Her articles have been included in the *International Encyclopedia of Dance and the Dance Research Annual,* and the *Tibetan Review.* With Chet Wollner, she collected three albums of Ethiopian Ritual Music released on Eth-

nic Folkways; and created a short educational slide film on Ethiopia for Current Affairs Films. Recently, she was invested as a lama under HH Shenphen Dawa Rinpoche in the Nyingmpa Dudjom Tersar lineage. Under his aegis she teaches Tibetan yoga in New York City.

Carl Mangum, EdD, lives with his wife, Joyce in Houma, Louisiana and practices on a semiretired basis. He has been engaged in the human service sector since his graduation with a Bachelor of Arts in Psychology in 1959 from Texas Christian University in Ft. Worth, Texas. He earned his Master's degree in Social Work in 1972 from Our Lady of the Lake University in San Antonia, Texas and his Doctorate in Education in 1975 from Texas A&M. Since 1981, he has been in private practice as a clinical social worker providing psychotherapy. He has studied and practiced Tibetan Buddhism since 1975.

Philip Philippou has been a student of Sogyal Rinpoche for over 25 years, serving the work of the Rigpa organization in several different capacities. Having graduated from the London School of Economics, he met Sogyal Rinpoche soon after and started to work at the Rigpa center in London. He was Sogyal Rinpoche's secretary and assistant for many years, before establishing and directing Rigpa International in 1994. He has overseen several major development projects for Rigpa, including the construction of a traditional Tibetan temple at Lerab  Ling in France, and organized numerous programs with visiting Tibetan teachers. He is a member of Rigpa International's Executive Board and serves as a board member of several other Rigpa organizations.

Bronwen Rees, PhD, is director of the Center for Transformative Management Practice, Lord Ashcroft International Business School, Anglia Ruskin University U.K., and of the East West Sanctuary, Center for Contemplative Inquiry, Budapest Hungary. She is also founder editor of the journal *Interconnections*. She leads a team of researchers investigating new methods of research She has published widely, and regularly leads workshops and retreats in Europe and Thailand. She is developing a method of ethical inquiry that is used in educational, business and spiritual settings.

Nicholas Ribush, MB, BS, is a graduate of Melbourne University Medical School (1964) who has been a student of Lama Yeshe and Lama Zopa Rinpoche since 1972 and was their attendant and teaching assistant in the early years. He was a monk from 1974 to 1986 and a member of the FPMT board of directors from its inception in 1983 until 2002. He established FPMT archiving and publishing activities at Kopan in 1973 and with Lama Yeshe founded Wisdom Publications in 1975. Between 1981 and 1996 he served variously as Wisdom's director, editorial director and director of development. Dr. Ribush has also established and/or directed other FPMT activities, including the International Mahayana Institute, several meditation and study centers, and the Lama Yeshe Wisdom Archive, which he founded in 1996 and continues to direct

Paul Ritvo is a clinical psychologist and research scientist. He is a 35-year Tibetan Buddhist practitioner currently devoted to scientific research on cancer prevention, AIDS and Diabetes treatment, and mindfulness meditation. He is an Associate Professor in the School of Kinesiology and Health Science and in the Department of Psychology at York University, where he focuses on health behavior change via group therapy, telephone, print, and interactive internet programming. Internationally, Dr. Ritvo is an active researcher in Kenya where, with colleagues, he is studying cell phone (text messaging) interventions supporting antiretroviral therapy adherence in HIV+ patients.

Peter Senge, PhD, is a Senior Lecturer at the Sloan School of Management, Massachusetts Institute of Technology, and is Founding Chair of the Society of Organizational Learning (SoL), a global network of people and institutions working together for systemic change. He is the author *of The Fifth Discipline: The Art and Practice of the Learning Organization,* coauthor of the three related fieldbooks, *Presence: An Exploration of Profound Change in People, Society, and Organizations* and most recently, *The Necessary Revolution: How Individuals and Organizations are Working Together to Create a Sustainable World. The Fifth Discipline* was recognized by *Harvard Business*

Review as "one of the seminal management books of the last 75 years" and by the *Financial Times* as one of five "most important" management books. *The Journal of Business Strategy* named him as one of the 24 people who had the greatest influence on business strategy in the twentieth century. Dr. Senge has a Master's and PhD from MIT.

Judith Simmer-Brown, PhD, is professor of Religious Studies at Naropa University, and an Acharya (senior teacher) in the Shambhala Buddhist lineage of Chogyam Trungpa, Rinpoche and his son, Sakyong Mipham, Rinpoche. She lectures and writes on Tibetan Buddhism, women and Buddhism, Buddhist-Christian dialogue, American Buddhism, and contemplative education, and is author of *Dakini's Warm Breath: The Feminine Principle in Tibetan Buddhism* (Shambhala 2001) and *Meditation in the Classroom: Contemplative Pedagogy for Religious Studies* (SUNY 2011). Currently she is the chair of Cauldron, the faculty senate, at Naropa University.

Susan Skjei, MS, MA, PCC, is a consultant and educator specializing in transformative change, coaching, and leadership. Formerly a vice-president and chief learning officer in the high-tech industry, she designs and facilitates participative approaches to strategic planning, innovation, and organizational transformation for business and community organizations. Susan is a teacher in the Shambhala Buddhist lineage of Chogyam Trungpa, Rinpoche and his son Sakyong Mipham, Rinpoche, and has taught leadership workshops in the United States, Canada, and Europe that integrate mindfulness practice, dialogue and organizational effectiveness. Susan currently lives in Colorado and is the founder and director of the Authentic Leadership program at Naropa University and a founding member of the Authentic Leadership in Action (ALIA) Institute in Halifax, Nova Scotia.

Huston Smith, PhD, is Thomas J. Watson Professor of Religion and Distinguished Adjunct Professor of Philosophy, Emeritus, Syracuse University. For 15 years he was Professor of Philosophy at M.I.T. and for a decade before that he taught at Washington University in St. Louis. Most recently he has served as Visiting Professor of Religious Studies, University of California, Berkeley. Holder of twelve honorary degrees, Smith's 14 books include *The World's Religions,* which has sold over 2½ million copies, and *Why Religion Matters,* which won the Wilbur Award for the best book on religion published in 2001. In 1996 Bill Moyers devoted a 5-part PBS Special, *The Wisdom of Faith with Huston Smith,* to his life and work. His film documentaries on Hinduism, Tibetan Buddhism, and Sufism have all won international awards, and *The Journal of Ethnomusicology* lauded his discovery of Tibetan multiphonic chanting, *Music of Tibet,* as "an important landmark in the study of music."

Scott Snibbe is an artist, filmmaker, and researcher. Whether on mobile devices or public spaces, his interactive art spurs people to participate socially, emotionally, and physically. Snibbe's work is in the permanent collections of the Whitney and MoMA; his projects appear in science museums, airports, and olympics; and he has collaborated with musicians and filmmakers including Björk and James Cameron. Snibbe is the founder of Snibbe Interactive and Scott Snibbe Studio. He holds degrees in Computer Science, Fine Art, and  animation from Brown University and RISD. Snibbe cocreated the special effects software Adobe After Effects, and was a researcher in haptics, computer vision, and interactive cinema at Interval Research. Snibbe has published numerous articles and academic papers, and is an inventor on over 20 patents.

Sogyal Rinpoche is one of the best-known Buddhist teachers of our time. Born and brought up in Tibet, he studied with many of the greatest masters of the 20th century, including Jamyang Khyentse Chökyi Lodrö, Kyabjé Dudjom Rinpoche, and Kyabjé Dilgo Khyentse Rinpoche. In 1971, Rinpoche went to England, where he studied Comparative Religion at Cambridge University. He has spent almost 40 years travelling widely in the West, sharing the wisdom of the Buddha's teachings and introducing meditation to many thousands of people. Rinpoche is the founder and spiritual director of Rigpa, an international network of over 130 Buddhist centers and groups in 41 countries around the world. His groundbreaking book, *The Tibetan Book of Living and Dying*, has been acclaimed as a spiritual classic. More than 2.8 million copies have been printed in 34 languages, and the book is available in 80 countries.

Lama Tharchin Rinpoche is a Dzogchen master of Vajrayana Buddhism. He was born in Kongpo, Tibet, in 1936 and is the 10th lineage holder of the Repkong Ngakpas, a family lineage of yogis that was the largest community of nonmonastic practitioners in Tibet. From the age of 8, Rinpoche trained in His Holiness Dudjom Rinpoche's monastery, engaged in 5 years of solitary retreat, and completed 3 year retreat under Dudjom Rinpoche. In addition to Dudjom Rinpoche, his main teachers have been Chatral Rinpoche, Lama  Sherab Dorje Rinpoche, and Dungse Thinley Norbu Rinpoche. Rinpoche left Tibet by foot with his family in 1960. He lived in Orissa, India, and Kathmandu, Nepal before coming to America in 1984. While in America, Dudjom Rinpoche asked Lama Tharchin Rinpoche to turn the third wheel of Dharma, the teachings of Vajrayana Buddhism. Rinpoche has vast knowledge of Tibetan ritual arts, music, and dance, as well as the philosophical basis of the Vajrayana teachings, and deep meditative experience.

 **Margaret Wheatley** is a well-respected writer, speaker, and teacher for how we can accomplish our work, sustain our relationships, and willingly step forward to serve in this troubling time. She has written six books including *Walk Out Walk On* (with Deborah Frieze, 2011), *Perseverance* (2010), and the classic: *Leadership and the New Science.* She is co-\founder and President emerita of The Berkana Institute, which works in partnership with a rich diversity of people and communities around the world, especially in the Global South. These communities find their health and resilience by discovering the wisdom and wealth already present in their people, traditions and environment (www.berkana.org). Her articles appear in both professional and popular journals and may be downloaded free from her website: www.margaretwheatley.com . Wheatley received her doctorate in Organizational Behavior and Change from Harvard University. She's been an organizational consultant since 1973 and has received numerous awards and honorary doctorates.

CPSIA information can be obtained at www.ICGtesting.com
Printed in the USA
LVOW081214150812

294221LV00001B/7/P